Contemporary Organization Theory

A selection of previous *Sociological Review* Monographs

The Cultures of Computing
ed. Susan Leigh Star
Theorizing Museums*
ed. Sharon Macdonald and Gordon Fyfe
Consumption Matters*
eds Stephen Edgell, Kevin Hetherington and Alan Warde
Ideas of Difference*
eds Kevin Hetherington and Rolland Munro
The Laws of the Markets*
ed. Michael Callon
Actor Network Theory and After*
eds John Law and John Hassard
Whose Europe? The turn towards democracy*
eds Dennis Smith and Sue Wright
Renewing Class Analysis*
eds Rosemary Cromptom, Fiona Devine, Mike Savage and John Scott
Reading Bourdieu on Society and Culture*
ed. Bridget Fowler
The Consumption of Mass*
ed. Nick Lee and Rolland Munro
The Age of Anxiety: Conspiracy Theory and the Human Sciences*
eds Jane Parish and Martin Parker
Utopia and Organization*
ed. Martin Parker
Emotions and Sociology*
ed. Jack Barbalet
Masculinity and Men's Lifestyle Magazines*
ed. Bethan Benwell
Nature Performed: Environment, Culture and Perfermance*
eds Bronislaw Szerszynski, Wallace Heim and Claire Waterton
After Habermas: New Perspectives on the Public Sphere*
eds Nick Crossley and John Michael Roberts
Feminism After Bourdieu*
eds Lisa Adkins and Beverley Skeggs

*Available from Marston Book Services, PO Box 270, Abingdon, Oxon OX14 4YW.

The Sociological Review Monographs

Since 1958 *The Sociological Review* has established a tradition of publishing Monographs on issues of general sociological interest. The Monograph is an edited book length collection of research papers which is published and distributed in association with Blackwell Publishing. We are keen to receive innovative collections of work in sociology and related disciplines with a particular emphasis on exploring empirical materials and theoretical frameworks which are currently under-developed. If you wish to discuss ideas for a Monograph then please contact the Monographs Editor, Rolland Munro, at *The Sociological Review*, Keele University, Newcastle-under-Lyme, North Staffordshire, ST5 5BG.

Contemporary Organization Theory

Edited by Campbell Jones and Rolland Munro

Blackwell Publishing/The Sociological Review

BLACKWELL PUBLISHING
350 Main Street, Malden, MA 02148-5020, USA
9600 Garsington Road, Oxford OX4 2DQ, UK
550 Swanston Street, Carlton, Victoria 3053, Australia

First published 2005 by Blackwell Publishing Ltd

Library of Congress Cataloging-in-Publication Data applied for

ISBN-10: 1-4051-3903-X
ISBN-13: 978-1-4051-3903-8

A catalogue record for this title is available from the British Library.

Printed and bound in the United Kingdom by Page Brothers, Norwich

For further information on Blackwell Publishing, visit our website:
http://www.blackwellpublishing.com

Contents

Contents

Acknowledgements

A project like this is very much a collective undertaking, and there are many to thank. We thank all of the contributing authors for their contributions and for their willingness to respond to our many demands. We also thank Chris Land for his part in early conversations about this project. For their reviews of various chapters, we thank Steffen Böhm, Janet Borgerson, Jo Brewis, Steve Brown, Alexander Carnera, Peter Case, Stephen Dunne, David Evans, Peter Fleming, Lloyd Gray, Shayne Grice, Stefano Harney, Eric Hirsch, Roy Jacques, Ruud Kaulingfreks, Martin Kornberger, Nick Lee, Simon Lilley, Christine McLean, Ken McPhail, John Mingers, Damian O'Doherty, Martin Parker, Carl Rhodes, Stevphen Shukaitis, André Spicer, Sverre Spoelstra, Marilyn Strathern, Emma Surman, Mark Tadajewski, Akseli Virtanen and Hugh Willmott. Thanks to Stephen Dunne for preparing the index.

Organization Theory, 1985–2005

Campbell Jones and Rolland Munro

Introduction

Organization indexes considerably more than the structures that lift us out of 'bare life'. Organization is also intimately, and utterly, connected to thought. While many, and by no means just those in the West, think of themselves as 'free' from enslavement by others, and even free from the organization of the state, who can argue that they are also free from the pervasive effects of language, culture and science? These are matters into which we find ourselves 'thrown', long before we wake up to their organizing effects. If, indeed, we ever do wake up. For if the intricate relations between language and thought came to be examined late in the 19th century, questions about the intercession between science and culture began to be asked only with the rise of the sociology of knowledge in the 20th century.

Questions also arise over what all this organization is for. Who benefits when community is eschewed for markets, when institutions are rendered into bureaucracies, and when sociability is altered in favour of friendship? Are we still to enjoy moments of intimacy, occasions in which compassion comes to fruition? Or are our ideas of organization incapable of being emancipated from the impetuous calls of efficiency and subordination? What place is there today for 'ultimate values' like dignity or happiness? Have these all-too-human dreams been made impossible in the disorganization of global capital? When organizations get busy organizing each other, how then are we to think of 'belonging'? And how can we stop tradition from being the Other of modernization? Are there forms of affiliation and belonging that are not based on exclusion, exploitation, precedent and privilege?

The aim of this monograph is one of advancing thought. As editors we want to draw attention to the quality of writing that is going on today in both organization *and* theory. This collection introduces and overviews the work of eighteen key theorists, with an emphasis on clarifying what makes each distinctive as a contemporary resource for other researchers in the field. These theorists have been selected on the basis that they have, over the past twenty years, made a significant and sustained contribution to organization theory. As we discuss, there are a number of ways of setting up what 'organization theory' means, which makes describing our project in these terms difficult. But what should be clear is that we do not want to abandon either the heritage or the term 'organization theory', but rather to subject it to a careful and persistent examination.

Organization and theory

The idea of organization has been spawned, historically and generatively, from separable, but vitally interconnected domains. In thinking of this volume, we wanted to retain some of this breadth and scope. Any discipline, even one as broad and diverse as sociology, typically masks the organizing assumptions it itself brings to the field. The difficulty here is not just that the early 'organizing' concepts, such as society or modernity, begged the question of organization. The more pressing problem is that it is the very idea of theory that is itself organizing – as came spectacularly to the fore in the debate between Kuhn and Popper over 'scientific revolutions'.

Any discipline not only invests heavily in the very 'order' it helps to establish; the form and structure it takes is consummated in its own emergence. The way that we are talking here might sound familiar to those who have followed discussions in organization theory, following Burrell and Morgan's *Sociological Paradigms and Organizational Analysis* (1979), which stressed the different concepts and politics that inform people analysing organizations (see Hancock and Tyler, in this volume). Burrell and Morgan bequeathed a generation with a particular way of thinking about the relation between theories (in the plural) and also a particular way of thinking about theory. This was a crucially important move at a certain point, in order to open organization theory to a set of possibilities in terms of assumptions about society and about social science that were, at that time, forces of imposition. But their way of conceptualizing theory rested on certain assumptions about theory that are no longer tenable, for at least three reasons.

First, theory is not a singular block or mass that produces regularized and ordered statements, consistent with a 'paradigm' – theory is always a creation and a production, and therefore always at least a tremor and a threat to the community it emerges from. Second, there is therefore no need to think in terms of the structural coherence or unity of theories; there are no fixed 'perspectives'. If we see the task of theory as creation of concepts, we can break with the kind of formalism that simply boxes theory into grids or charts. Third, the idea that there is a single and coherent 'author' who takes one position, unchanged and fixed, is an assumption that denies the very thing that theory does – it gives us different concepts that open onto different ways of thinking and acting.

In addressing explicitly the ideas of a single author, each contributor to this volume is clearly acknowledging the importance of the work of those who have gone before. They do not seek, however, merely to repeat the ideas of their predecessors and would likewise reject the notion of their being caught within paradigms. Through the work of commentary and criticism, they are themselves actively engaged in further theoretical work, which is argued from and in relation to the best ideas of the past. So at the same time as taking stock of advances in thinking about organization, each of the eighteen chapters in this collection also articulates a vision of the range and diversity of current theorizing. Our position, though, is not to suggest these scholars are already in a position to make pronouncements about the state or shape of organization as phenomena of sociological interest. Rather it is to recognize the extent to which those interested in the trope of organization appear ready to scrutinize this rebirth of thought over its scope and relevance.

Fixing organization

Any scrutiny of organization theory must also face up to a long-standing tendency for writers on organization to end up looking for organization in the wrong place. The early 'fathers' of sociology, for example, tended to identify society as such with order and organization. Similarly, the idea of modernity as organizing society also gained a 'totalizing' ring to it. Much of the history of organization theory flows from a series of over-reactions to the initial attempts of Marx, Weber and Durkheim to set up organization in a particular way.

Fifty years ago, the wave that was to become 'organization theory' was still a swell waiting to break. 1956 would see the publication of the first issue of the journal *Administrative Science Quarterly*, headlining Talcott Parson's programme for a 'sociological approach to the theory of organizations' (Parsons, 1956a, 1956b), and two years later would see the launch of the *Academy of Management Journal*. The decade that followed would find numerous attempts to talk the idea of a unified 'organization theory' into existence. A major tendency was towards *reification* in much of this work. This is the Western tendency to 'see' matters such as organization as a things-in-themselves and so obviate the frame or perspective that is 'organizing' what is to be seen (see Munro, this volume).

Subsequent attempts to revive the sociology of organization are invariably characterized by attempts to define organization too narrowly. To a contemporary reader it may well seem strange that in the early 1970s Derek Pugh would assert that 'organization theory can be defined as the study of the structure, functioning and performance of organizations and the behaviour of groups and individuals within them' (1971: 9). While some today retain hope in such a project, and many textbooks on organization theory assume this narrowness, this is probably largely a matter of the repeated exclusion of difference and sanctioned ignorance that have been part and parcel of the history of organization theory.

In this respect, the uncritical use of the term organization to denote diverse entities, from corporations and states to the village fair and the tennis club, has bracketed out many key issues and led to a superficial conflation of the idea of organization with the deeper processes of 'institutionalization' within sociology. Critical attention to such issues from Bittner (1970) and other ethnomethodologists (see also Sudnow, 1972) also identified a holism in perspectives, and an unhealthy abstraction in content, that had reached fever pitch with the 'systems theories' of the 1960s (see Czarniawska, in this volume, also Nassehi, in this volume). This holism still has its residue today and, regrettably, efforts at totalization, along with avoidance of what might be seen as the 'other' of organization, continue to be widespread (see Brewis, in this volume).

Things change, and organization theory now is certainly in a different situation from where it was, particularly from twenty years ago, when the academic reputation of organization theory was at its height. But totalizing ideas of organization, such as 'society' and 'modernity', are not the only kind of fallacy to permeate ideas of organization. Various attempts are made to subsume organization under some other concept. Those in business, for example, frequently assert that their most difficult problem lies in the 'organizing' of people, an old conception that had its day in the subject of 'organization behaviour' but is now practiced as 'human resource management'. This mindset has also led to a conventional wisdom of people being inherently 'resistant' to organization. This is a feature that is played out in the ever-present managerial programmes for 'changing culture' that still pervade contemporary organizational life.

An equally tenacious view – one that has saturated understandings about industrial societies – suggests technology is something for us to 'master'. In holding out the idea that materials are somehow easy to organize, this view is of course the corollary of the view that regards 'people' as the problem. The response to these pernicious views has produced some questionable as well as admirable developments in social theory, prominently if notoriously, in debates on postmodernity, in a realization of the place of power in organization (see Fleming and Spicer, in this volume) and in the recent ideas of actor-network theorists (see Harris, in this volume). The horrendous pitfalls as well as the enormous promise held out by such directions perhaps helps explain the fusion of organization and social theory that is the focus of this book.

A further aspect lies in the elision of rich sociological understandings of social institutions by diffuse terms like culture and lifestyle. Recent debate responds to the trend, if somewhat metaphorical, for people to speak as if their 'lives' *as* individuals have to be organized, not just through an organizing of 'the day', but in each also organizing their 'futures'. More and more, it seems that the responsibility for organization – as well as the accountability for its consequences – is being passed to the figure of 'the individual' (Munro, 1996; 2001). This tendency raises further questions as to why the figure of 'the individual' has become such a dominant part of Euro-American thinking. Just what, exactly, one asks, is the figure of 'the individual' organizing? Hence the need today to rethink the assumptions that have been made about that concept of the individual (see Kaulingfreks, in this volume), and about the possible spaces for autonomy today (see Bowring, in this volume).

4

Changing objects and approaches

The issue for many scholars today remains a hope to bring organization theory to completion, or at the very least to redeem it as a social science. Setting themselves either or both tasks, several recent volumes purport to rethink organization and to outline new thinking in the theory of organization.[1] How far have we come from such gestures of completion or redemption, and the promises they offer? Whether by science or by relativistic pluralism, how far are we away from an organization theory that will, one fine day, capture organization and its consequences? The result, disappointingly, has largely been to include in these volumes only those formally working 'inside' a predetermined disciplinary formation called organization theory. This present collection explicitly eschews this kind of privileging, refusing to accept such exclusions *a priori*. The result is to bring very different kinds of advances alongside each other. So as well as describing each in turn, the goal of the collection is not simply to highlight the existing current directions. It is equally to juxtapose these directions as visions of possible futures for both organization *and* theory.

This strategy of extension is by no means new. An enormous expansion of organization theory has been generated, simply by virtue of researchers turning to issues that were typically not discussed in the past. We can think, particularly over the past twenty years, of the publication of volumes and edited collections of writings on the significance for organization of issues as diverse as aesthetics (Linstead and Höpfl, 2000; Strati, 1999), anti-capitalism (Böhm, 2005), autonomism (Harney, forthcoming), the body (Hassard, Holiday and Willmott, 2000), critical realism (Ackroyd and Thompson, 2000); critical theory (Alvesson, 1987; Alvesson and Willmott, 1992, 1996, 2003), discourse (Grant *et al.*, 1998, 2004), events (Sørensen, 2004), fashion (ten Bos, 2000), feminist organizations (Ferree and Martin, 1995), hygiene (ten Bos and Kaulingfreks, 2001), identity (Linstead and Linstead, 2005), identity politics (Thomas, Mills and Mills, 2004), language (Westwood and Linstead, 2001), literature (Czarniawska-Joerges and Guillet de Monthoux, 1994; Knights and Willmott, 1999), literary theory (Czarniawska, 1999; Monin, 2004), mass intellectuality (Harney, 2002), metaphor (Morgan, 1986; Grant and Oswick, 1996), misbehaviour (Ackroyd and Thompson, 1999), narrative (Boje, 2001; Czarniawska-Joerges, 1998), order (Law, 1994), paradox (Clegg, 2002), popular culture (Rhodes and Westwood, forthcoming), potlatch (Rehn, 2001), postcoloniality (Prasad, 2003), representation (Hassard and Holiday, 1998), representation and information (Lilley, Lightfoot and Amaral, 2004), resistance (Jermier, Knights and Nord, 1994), science fiction (Smith *et al.*, 2001), sex (Brewis and Linstead, 2000), sexuality (Hearn *et al.*, 1989), social movements (Davis *et al.*, 2005), speed (Case, Lilley and Owens, forthcoming), storytelling (Gabriel, 2000), technology (Grint and Woolgar, 1997; Scarborough and Corbett, 1992), textuality (Linstead, 2005); time (Whipp *et al.*, 2002), theatre (Mangham and Overington, 1987) utopia (Parker, 2002b) and violence (Hearn and Parkin, 2001). One could add Gibson Burrell's *Pandemonium* (1997), which offers a veritable cornucopia of issues that were not discussed some years ago, from sexuality and the peasantry to pain and disease.[2]

Again over the past twenty years, there has also been much debate in organization theory journals about postmodernism (see Burrell, 1988, 1994; Calás and Smircich, 1997, 1999; Cooper and Burrell, 1988; Cooper, 1989; Hancock and Tyler, 2001; Hassard and Parker, 1993; Kilduff and Mehra, 1997; Linstead, 2004; Parker, 1992). Much of this reflected the long-running debate in sociology as to whether society is postmodern, late modern, or even whether it had ever been modern at all (Latour, 1993). Certainly Durkheim anticipated something akin to the last view, when he identified the gaps that would open up for the moral order of a society as it sought to organize itself around the ramifications unwinding from the division of labour. At this level of abstraction, debate within sociology has mostly come down to a division between those who continued to see society as still highly 'organized' and those who wanted to abandon the idea that it was organized at all.

Postmodernists, if such a group ever actually existed, proclaimed the vehicle that held an industrial society together – modernity – as dead (and society with it). Unfortunately, with analysis revolving around the idea of 'structure', there was a regrettable conflation in terms between postmodernism and the movement of 'poststructuralism'.[3] If postmodernism was an easy answer for many, this was not so with poststructuralism. The sense was that there was a theoretical sophistication in other disciplines (and in new disciplines such as cultural studies) which could be brought into organization theory. Poststructuralism, in particular, promised to challenge the reductive and deterministic accounts of organization that were in currency at that time, and would hence reinvigorate organization theory by giving more nuanced accounts of organizational life.

While many continue to reject poststructuralism outright, others have set out to rework what might be drawn from poststructuralism. Departing from the first wave of the work of writers such as Derrida, Foucault and Lyotard, we have stressed the importance of poststructuralism for questions of ethics (see Jones, 2003a, 2003b, 2004a, Jones *et al.*, 2005; Munro, 1998). Others still have stressed the need to take poststructuralist theorists seriously on their own terms, without the reductive tendency of commentary (see Jones, Sørensen, in this volume). The inheritance of poststructuralism is far from decided. Some have turned instead to the work of more recent theorists, such as Butler, Serres and Agamben (see, respectively, Borgerson, Brown, ten Bos, in this volume), while others have revisited earlier traditions, such as the Marxist tradition of the critique of capital, in the light of recent thinking (see Mandarini and Böhm and De Cock, in this volume). Moves such as these hold the prospect of not simply a new relation to poststructuralism, but also a broadened understanding of the very project of organization theory.

Selecting theorists

As already indicated, this collection swims against the tide of the recent collections that propose to capture, and constrain, the domain of organization theory that can be seen in recent years a number of handbooks or other compendia of organization.[4] What is concerning about previous collections is the authority with which they set themselves the task of describing the territory. The very fact that they describe organization theory in such different ways from each other should be indicative of the problems of description. They are describing something that is obviously contested. Language that attempts to be descriptive will always involve what Austin (1962) calls 'performative' consequences. Even the most innocent attempt to describe what organization theory is will involve normative assumptions. What is interesting is the way these collections largely forget this and rather see this contest as something that happens 'out there' in this thing organization theory, as if they – the judges – are not involved in that contest.

The politics of prescribing what is 'proper' to organization theory (a process of also excluding considerable bodies of theory that it proposes to disown) has long vexed the subject area. With this collection we make no claim to be comprehensive in selection of the theorists we have written about, and make no claim that our selection is definitive. There are many theorists that we could have included, and many readers would have their own preferences, often with good reason. All we claim is that our selection is one possible representation of developments in contemporary organization theory.[5]

Beyond this kind of issue about different names, there is a question of whether or not to include authors who have written theory about organization but would not typically be included, or would not include themselves, as organization theorists. Exemplary here is someone such as Marilyn Strathern (see Munro, in this volume). So, too, Robert Cooper has written on organization, and on related matters such as information, but absolutely refuses the title of 'organization theorist' and, in fact, much of the idea of an organization theory (see Spoelstra, in this volume). Relatedly, there are others like Knights and Willmott who have written prolifically about the field of management, as well as the labour process. Should this work be included under the rubric of organization? Some would argue not, particularly in the light of a continuing tendency to treat organization simply as a matter of management.

Similar issues arise in respect of the space of 'philosophy'. One might expect to find discussion in philosophy ablaze with ideas of organization. Yet, beyond claims that institutions such as universities are likely to trigger accusations of 'category errors' and a recognition that institutions like marriage require 'performative' acts (Austin, 1962, see also Borgerson, in this volume), the analytical school is almost entirely silent on matters germane to organization. European philosophy has taken a very different tack, which is perhaps why continental philosophers have more to say to organization theory, even though we should recall that, since Heidegger, many 'philosophers' have tended to eschew the title of philosophy. It is salutary, for example, that writers such as Judith Butler, who we have included in this volume, styles herself not simply as a 'philosopher', but as a 'theorist', and someone working 'with' philosophy but not only that (see Butler, 2004).

For the purposes of the present volume we have also deliberately included several authors whose work normally falls best under the rubric of social theory, or who might be called 'philosophers' or simply 'theorists'. The boundary between organization theory and social theory is difficult at the best of times. But as editors we have particular reasons for thinking that it is over their grasp of social theory that debates on organization most often flounder. Equally, in the other direction, many otherwise impeccable social theorists are at their most banal when it comes to their accounts of organization.

Our view is that organization theory is still a young field, as full of promise as it is of wrong directions. Thus, as well as wishing to include authors who might rather call themselves social theorists than organization theorists, we want to distance ourselves from the normative criteria for inclusion that have pervaded previous volumes.[6] In assembling the materials for this current volume, we have been wary of paying too great a heed to whether or not something is 'really' organization theory, or even to whether or not it is usually considered to be organization theory at all. Instead, we set ourselves the task of trying to identify a collection of writers who have, deliberately or not, made a sustained or sustainable contribution to the theory of organization. So in this book you will find some writers who will be immediately recognized as organization theorists, but some about whom this naming might at first appear rather strange. We have consciously made these selection decisions in order to contest the artificial reification of 'organization theory' as a canonically and topographically predetermined terrain.

There are at least three ways of relating to organization theory. First, there are writers who are comfortable in describing themselves as organization theorists. Second, there are those who would not typically call themselves organization theorists but who theorize directly on organization. Third, there are those who neither describe themselves as organization theorists, nor theorize directly on organization, but whose thinking has implications for the wider understanding of organization.

One might be tempted to organize the chapters of this book in accordance with this tripartite distinction. We could then say that we have half a dozen candidates for each of the three sections. The 'organization theorists' would be Gibson Burrell, Marta Calás and Linda Smircich, Stewart Clegg, Robert Cooper, David Knights and Hugh Willmott, and Karl Weick. The 'theorists of organization' would be Zygmunt Bauman, André Gorz, Niklas Luhmann, Antonio Negri, Gayatri Chakravorty Spivak and Marilyn Strathern. The 'theorists with concepts for understanding organization' would be Giorgio Agamben, Judith Butler, Gilles Deleuze and Félix Guattari, Bruno Latour,

Michel Serres and Slavoj Žižek.[7] Such partitioning would break the book into three parts, 'organization theory', 'theory of organization' and 'theory for organization'. It would tidily summarize the most significant contributors to each of these three domains over the past twenty years.

The problem with such an ordering should be clear. Organizing the material in this way would repress the fact, for example, that Cooper explicitly eschews the label 'organization theory', and has written in many other areas. So, too, Latour and also Deleuze and Guattari have quite explicitly developed concepts of organization. And Žižek speaks directly to many of the concerns of organization theorists and theorists of organization. To attempt to fit these writers into the Procrustean bed that we are creating is to perform what is, perhaps, the fallacy of all attempts at organization. Doing so we deny what Agamben calls the 'irreparable' nature of the world, and tend towards what what René ten Bos and Ruud Kaulingfreks (2001) have identified as the tendency of the 'hygienic' temptation of contemporary culture, organization and thinking. To resist this temptation is not to make a case for things being as they are. Rather, it is to recognize the intractability of the human, and to see that the disorganization is not always simply lack, a failed state awaiting proper organization.

The fiction of the author

There are clear limits, at least for the moment, to the way in which diverse theories can be brought together. We have therefore made no effort to structure the contributions to this book into paradigms or perspectives. Likewise we see little that is to be gained by setting up monolithic blocks of those 'for' or 'against' a particular issue or practice (cf. Westwood and Clegg, 2003). These usually are weak ways of relating to concepts and lazy ways of doing theory. We have, in contrast, organized the book in terms of the fiction of 'authors', and have structured the authors of contemporary organization theory alphabetically in the book. But this will require a little further justification, given the risk of prioritizing the author as the origin of concepts of organization and therefore of organization theory.

Organizing this book around authors, but recognizing the limits of thinking in terms of authors, we have set out to use the subjects of this book as self-conscious instruments for a particular thinking of organization theory. We want, at the outset, to acknowledge the contribution someone can make by finding a 'place' or 'position' from which they can articulate issues and ideas few others can see. This said, each of the subjects of this book, from Agamben to Žižek, is not something autonomous or individually creative. In much the same sense that Homer is a fabrication, but we can still speak of Homer, we use the names of authors here as convenient symbols. Their names serve as placeholders for a set of ideas. The names 'Knights and Willmott', for example, serve to represent

9

something that exceeds both the individual and the joint productions of these authors (see O'Doherty, in this volume).

How, then, can we speak of authors? Can we ever use proper names to refer to the producers of books? First of all, we should recall, after all of the talk of the 'Death of the Author' and the 'Death of Man', taken from 1960s Paris and surfacing in organization theory in recent years, that these are grand overstatements.[8] Foucault, for instance, later speaks of his declaration of the 'death of man' as 'confused, simplifying and a bit prophetic' (1991: 124, cf. 1970: 385). Such overstatements are sometimes useful to break a previous concept and to think again, and thinking again about the subject and the author is one of the gains of a thinker such as Foucault. But we should recall also Foucault's insistence that 'the subjected should not be entirely abandoned. It should be reconsidered, not to restore the theme of the originating subject, but to seize on its functions, its intervention in discourse, and its system of dependencies' (1977: 137).

At the same time that we insist on the importance of being careful to not valorize the individual as producers of theory, we want to make something of a case for analysis of texts organized around self-consciously fictional conceptual personae. In contrast with other disciplines in the social sciences, a long tradition of commentary in which advances in theory take place in relation to the work of contemporary writers has been notably absent in the study of organization. Developments in organization theory tend to be presented thematically, rather than through an assessment of the theoretical contribution of major figures. Criticism is thus relegated to secondary status and there is currently no single volume that comments directly on the approach of those writers who have contributed most to the recent study of organization.

One major advantage of looking at theoretical contributions in terms of the work produced by conceptual personae is the ability to subject their ideas to critical scrutiny. This means to test their limits and identify their deficiencies. Of course, readers often find that 'the author' is ahead of them here, restlessly subjecting their previous ideas to new material, different pastures. In helping identify the key shifts in ideas, methodologies, proclamations and practices, the modest hope is to put an end to the regrettable tendency in organization theory to make prescriptions that pronounce unequivocally, under the guise of description, that 'Foucault said this', or 'Marx said that', as if this or that is something that each might *always* say. The task, instead, is to see how far we can take these authors, and see how much further we can move and think with them; even also beyond them. Because good theory is not about creating a mirror to the world: it is what helps to open up a field, not to close it down.

Notes

1 In addition to books working in such a way (see Hassard and Parker, 1994; Hassard and Pym, 1990; Linstead, 2004; Reed and Hughes, 1992) there are many journals that explicitly commit

themselves to developing *theory* in relation to organization. We could think of the issues of journals such as the *Academy of Management Review* and *Administrative Science Quarterly* that regularly feature issues on 'theory development', and also newer journals expressly devoted to such issues, such as *Organization*, subtitled 'the critical journal of organization, theory and society' and *ephemera*, subtitled 'theory and politics in organization'.

2 While organization theory has often been 'derivative' in the sense that it has borrowed widely from other disciplines for theory, not all the traffic has been one way. Previous volumes in this series of Sociological Review Monographs have drawn on some of the new thinking on organization in such volumes as *Power, Action and Belief* (Law, 1986), *A Sociology of Monsters* (Law, 1991), *The Cultures of Computing* (Star, 1995), *Consumption Matters* (Edgell, Hetherington and Warde, 1996) and *Actor Network Theory and After* (Law and Hassard, 1999). Other Sociological Review Monographs have reworked existing sociological tropes such the 'labour of division' in *Ideas of Difference* (Hetherington and Munro, 1997), mass consumption in *The Consumption of Mass* (Lee and Munro, 2001), and utopia in *Utopia and Organization* (Parker, 2002). The ambition in these texts has been to draw wider attention to advances in the thinking of sociologists concerned with the topic of organization.

3 The running conflation between postmodernism and poststructuralism has befuddled the easy prospect that organization theory would be reinvigorated by this theoretical turn. Certainly some, notably Paul Thompson and Stephen Ackroyd (1995), have criticised the kind of turn in organization theory that would deny attention to workplace conflict, exploitation and resistance. What seems a little strange about such responses, though, is the sharp dividing line that is being drawn between theory, on the one hand, and politics on the other.

4 For a selection of this vast surge in publication of handbooks see, for example, Ackroyd *et al.* (2004), Baum (2002), Clegg (2002), Clegg, Hardy and Nord (1996), Sorge and Warner (2000), Tsoukas and Knudsen (2003), WOBS (2001). On these handbooks, and more generally on the idea that a single handbook might capture organization theory in a tidy, easy to use location, see Jones and Böhm (2004).

5 In addition to the usual issues of selection for assembling this collection, we therefore faced the issue of naming 'organization theory'. As well as sociology having its own distinctive sub-discipline in the sociology of organization, a number of quite different words are used to describe the generic area. These include organization theory, organization studies, organizational analysis, organizational behaviour, organization science, institutional theory, administrative theory, management theory and management studies. These labels are extraordinarily loose and mobile, to the point that they can sometimes even surprise the authors who use them (see Jones, 2004b).

6 Arguably, what can be called this 'policing' of the field has not served organization theory well. We can see such acts of policing in extreme form, for example, in Lex Donaldson's *Defence of Organization Theory* (1985). This naked attempt to valorize a limited and naïve inheritance of 'structure' from administrative theory ends up dismissing a vast body of social theory on the basis of what appears to be a personal taste preference, but justifies this preference in terms of what a 'proper' organization theory should look like. We can see a similar tendency to policing in collections such as the well-known collections on *Writers on Organizations* edited by Derek Pugh and colleagues. The idea that they can justify themselves by recourse to what they called 'theory' (Pugh *et al.*, 1971: 13) is mistaken. Their generalizations about structure and function, often attributed to Weber's writings on bureaucracy, did not rest on 'theory' as claimed – the problem was that their administrative theory reflected asymmetries of interest, narrowly focussed around the managerial imperatives of co-ordination and control.

7 For those who are immediately searching for exclusions, we should stress again the difficulty of making these selections. Still restricting ourselves to the past twenty years, we could easily have included chapters on organization theorists such as Mats Alvesson, Joanne Martin, George Ritzer or Richard Sennett; theorists of organization such as Arlie Hochschild, Naomi Klein, Peter Miller or Nikolas Rose; and theorists with concepts for the understanding of organization such as Pierre Bourdieu, Luce Irigaray, Jean-Luc Nancy and Samuel Weber. And many, many more. Arranged into the three categories as we have listed them here, or arranged differently.

8 This was based in a recognition that to speak of a singularized, isolated individual 'author' is to invite all manner of difficulties. The criticism of the idea of the author that we find in Barthes and Foucault drew sharp attention to the tendency, in commentary on literary texts and also more generally in modern culture, to explain discourse in terms of the utterances and intentions of individuals. This causes all manner of difficulty: first of all because intentions are rather hard to get a hold of, but further because individuals always produce concepts with others and in relation to others. The idea that an individual as an isolated author is the creator of concepts is at best misguided and at worst is a result of the kind of fetish of the individual that has marked Western culture for at least the past two hundred years.

References

Ackroyd, S. and P. Thompson (1999) *Organizational* Mis*behaviour*. London: Sage.

Ackroyd, S. and S. Fleetwood (eds.) (2000) *Realist Perspectives on Management and Organizations*. London: Routledge.

Ackroyd, S., R. Batt, P. Thompson and P. Tolbert (eds.) (2004) *The Oxford Handbook of Work and Organization*. Oxford: Oxford University Press.

Alvesson, M. (1987) *Organization Theory and Technocratic Consciousness: Rationality, Ideology and the Quality of Work*. Berlin: de Gruyter.

Alvesson, M. and H. Willmott (eds.) (1992) *Critical Management Studies*. London: Sage.

Alvesson, M. and H. Willmott (1996) *Making Sense of Management: A Critical Introduction*. London: Sage.

Alvesson, M. and H. Willmott (eds.) (2003) *Studying Management Critically*. London: Sage.

Austin, J. L. (1962) *How to Do Things with Words*. Oxford: Clarendon Press.

Barthes, R. (1977) 'The death of the author' in *Image, Music, Text*, trans. S. Heath. New York: Hill and Wang.

Bittner, E. (1970) 'The concept of organization' in G. Salaman and K. Thomson (eds.) *People and Organizations*. London: Longman.

Böhm, S. (2005) *Repositioning Organization Theory*. Basingstoke: Palgrave.

Boje, D. (2001) *Narrative Methods for Organizational and Communication Research*. London: Sage.

Brewis, J. and S. Linstead (2000) *Sex, Work and Sex Work: Eroticizing Organization*. London: Routledge.

Burrell, G. (1988) 'Modernism, post modernism and organizational analysis 2: The contribution of Michel Foucault' *Organization Studies*, 9(2): 221–235.

Burrell, G. (1994) 'Modernism, post modernism and organizational analysis 4: The contribution of Jürgen Habermas' *Organization Studies*, 15(1): 1–19.

Burrell, G. and G. Morgan (1979) *Sociological Paradigms and Organizational Analysis: Elements of the Sociology of Corporate Life*. London: Heineman.

Butler, J. (2004) 'Can the "other" of philosophy speak?' in *Undoing Gender*. London: Routledge.

Calás, M. and L. Smircich (1999) 'Past postmodernism? Reflections and tentative directions', *Academy of Management Review*, 24(4): 649–671.

Calás, M. and L. Smircich (eds.) (1997) *Postmodern Management Theory*. Aldershot: Ashgate/Dartmouth.

Case, P., S. Lilley and T. Owens (eds.) (forthcoming) *The Speed of Organization*. Copenhagen: Copenhagen Business School Press.

Clegg, S. (1989) *Frameworks of Power*. London: Sage.

Clegg, S. (ed.) (2002) *Central Currents in Organization Studies* (8 vols.). London: Sage.

Clegg, S., C. Hardy and W. Nord (eds.) (1996) *The Handbook of Organization Studies*. London: Sage.

Cooper, R. (1989) 'Modernism, post modernism and organizational analysis 3: The contribution of Jacques Derrida' *Organization Studies*, 10(4): 479–502.

Cooper, R. and G. Burrell (1988) 'Modernism, postmodernism and organizational analysis: An introduction' *Organization Studies*, 9(1): 91–112.

Czarniawska, B. (1999) *Writing Management: Organization Theory as a Literary Genre*. Oxford: Oxford University Press.

Czarniawska-Joerges, B. (1998) *A Narrative Approach to Organization Studies*. London: Sage.

Czarniawska-Joerges, B. and P. Guillet de Monthoux (1994) *Good Novels, Better Management: Reading Organizational Realities*. Chur: Harwood.

Davis, G., D. McAdam, W. R. Scott and M. Zald (2005) *Social Movements and Organization Theory*. Cambridge: Cambridge University Press.

Donaldson, L. (1985) *In Defence of Organization Theory: A Reply to the Critics*. Cambridge: Cambridge University Press.

Edgell, S., K. Hetherington and A. Warde (eds.) (1996) *Consumption Matters: The Production and Experience of Consumption*. Oxford: Blackwell.

Ferree, M. M. and P. Y. Martin (1995) *Feminist Organizations: Harvest of the New Women's Political Economy*. Philadelphia: Temple University Press.

Foucault, M. (1970) *The Order of Things: An Archaeology of the Human Sciences*, trans. A. S. Smith. London: Routledge.

Foucault, M. (1977) 'What is an author?' in D. Bouchard (ed.) *Language, Counter-Memory, Practice: Selected Essays and Interviews*, trans. D. Bouchard and S. Simon. Ithaca, NY: Cornell University Press.

Foucault, M. (1991) *Remarks on Marx: Conversations with Duccio Trombadori*, trans. J. Goldstein and J. Cascaito. New York: Semiotext(e).

Gabriel, Y. (2000) *Storytelling in Organizations: Facts, Fictions and Fantasies*. Oxford: Oxford University Press.

Grant, D. and C. Oswick (eds.) (1996) *Metaphor and Organizations*. London: Sage.

Grant, D., C. Oswick, C. Hardy and L. Putnam (eds.) (2004) *Handbook of Organizational Discourse*. London: Sage.

Grant, D., T. Keenoy and C. Oswick (eds.) (1998) *Discourse and Organization*. London: Sage.

Grint, K. and S. Woolgar (1997) *The Machine at Work: Technology, Work and Organization*. Oxford: Polity.

Hancock, P. and M. Tyler (2001) *Work, Postmodernism and Organization: A Critical Introduction*. London: Sage.

Harney, S. (2002) *State Work: Public Administration and Mass Intellectuality*. Durham: Duke University Press.

Harney, S. (forthcoming) *Management and Fugitivity: A Critique of Immaterial Political Economy*. New York: Routledge.

Hassard, J. and D. Pym (eds.) (1990) *The Theory and Philosophy of Organizations: Critical Issues and New Perspectives*. London: Routledge.

Hassard, J. and M. Parker (eds.) (1993) *Postmodernism and Organizations*. London: Sage.

Hassard, J. and M. Parker (eds.) (1994) *Towards and New Theory of Organization*. London: Routledge.

Hassard, J. and R. Holiday (eds.) (1998) *Organization-Representation: Work and Organizations in Popular Culture*. London: Sage.

Hassard, J., R. Holiday and H. Willmott (eds.) (2000) *Body and Organization*. London: Sage.

Hearn, J. and W. Parkin (eds.) (2001) *Gender, Sexuality and Violence in Organizations*. London: Sage.

Hearn, J., D. Sheppard, P. Tancred-Sherriff and G. Burrell (eds.) (1989) *The Sexuality of Organization*. London: Sage.

Hetherington, K. and R. Munro (eds.) (1997) *Ideas of Difference: Social Spaces and the Labour of Division*. Oxford: Blackwell.

Jermier, J., D. Knights and W. Nord (eds.) (1994) *Resistance and Power in Organizations*. London: Routledge.

Jones, C. (2003a) 'As if business ethics were possible, "within such limits" . . .' *Organization*, 10(2): 223–248.

Jones, C. (2003b) 'Theory after the postmodern condition' *Organization*, 10(3): 503–525.

Jones, C. (2004a) 'Jacques Derrida' in Stephen Linstead (ed.) *Organization Theory and Postmodern Thought*. London: Sage.

Jones, C. (2004b) 'The archive and its other' *ephemera: theory and politics in organization*, 4(1): 50–58.

Jones, C. and S. Böhm (2002) 'Hors d'oeuvre' *ephemera: critical dialogues on organization* 2(4): 277–280.

Jones, C. and S. Böhm (2004) 'Handle with care' *ephemera: theory and politics in organization* 4(1): 1–6.

Jones, C., M. Parker and R. ten Bos (2005) *For Business Ethics*. London: Routledge.

Kilduff, M. and A. Mehra (1997) 'Postmodernism and organizational research', *Academy of Management Review*, 22(2): 453–481.

Knights, D. and H. Willmott (1999) *Management Lives: Power and Identity in Work Organizations*. London: Sage.

Latour, B. (1993) *We Have Never Been Modern*. London: Harvester Wheatsheaf.

Law, J. (ed.) (1986) *Power, Action, and Belief: A New Sociology of Knowledge?* Oxford: Blackwell.

Law, J. (ed.) (1991) *A Sociology of Monsters: Essays on Power, Technology and Domination*. Oxford: Blackwell.

Law, J. (1994) *Organizing Modernity*. Oxford: Blackwell.

Law, J. and J. Hassard (eds.) (1999) *Actor Network Theory and After*. Oxford: Blackwell.

Lee, N. and R. Munro (eds.) (2001) *The Consumption of Mass*. Oxford: Blackwell.

Lilley, S., G. Lightfoot and P. Amaral (2004) *Representing Organization: Knowledge, Management and the Information Age*. Oxford: Oxford University Press.

Linstead, A. and S. Linstead (eds.) (2005) *Organization and Identity*. London: Routledge.

Linstead, S. (ed.) (2004) *Organization Theory and Postmodern Thought*. London: Sage.

Linstead, S. (ed.) (2005) *Text/Work: Representing Organization and Organizing Representation*. London: Routledge.

Linstead, S. and H. Höpfl (eds.) (2000) *The Aesthetics of Organization*. London: Sage.

Mangham, I. and M. Overington (1987) *Organizations as Theatre: A Social Psychology of Dramatic Appearances*. Chichester: Wiley.

Monin, N. (2004) *Management Theory: A Critical and Reflexive Reading*. London: Routledge.

Morgan, G. (1986) *Images of Organization*. London: Sage.

Munro, R. (1996) 'A consumption view of self: Extension, exchange and identity' in S. Edgell, K. Hetherington and A. Warde (eds.) *Consumption Matters: The Production and Experience of Consumption*. Oxford: Blackwell.

Munro, R. (1998) 'Ethics and accounting: The dual technologies of self' in M. Parker (ed.) *Ethics and Organizations*. London: Sage.

Munro, R. (2001) 'Calling for accounts: Numbers, monsters and membership' *Sociological Review*, 49(4): 473–493.

Parker, M. (1992) 'Post-modern organizations or postmodern organization theory?' *Organization Studies*, 13(1): 1–17.

Parker, M. (2002a) *Against Management*. Oxford: Polity.

Parker, M. (ed.) (2002b) *Utopia and Organization*. Oxford: Blackwell.

Parsons, T. (1956a) 'Suggestions for a sociological approach to the theory of organizations, part I' *Administrative Science Quarterly*, 1: 63–85.

Parsons, T. (1956b) 'Suggestions for a sociological approach to the theory of organizations, part II' *Administrative Science Quarterly*, 1: 225–239.

Prasad, A. (ed.) 2003) *Postcolonial Theory and Organizational Analysis: A Critical Reader*. Basingstoke: Palgrave.

Pugh, D. (1971) 'Introduction' in D. Pugh (ed.) *Organization Theory: Selected Readings*. London: Penguin.

Pugh, D. S., D. J. Hickson and C. R. Hinings (1971) *Writers on Organizations* (second edition). Harmondsworth: Penguin.

Reed, M. and M. Hughes (eds.) (1992) *Rethinking Organization: New Directions in Organization Theory and Analysis*. London: Sage.

Rehn, A. (2001) *Electronic Potlatch: A Study of New Technologies and Primitive Economic Behaviors*. Kungl Tekniska Högskolan.

Rhodes, C. and R. Westwood (forthcoming) *Critical Representations of Work and Organizations in Popular Culture*. London: Routledge.

Scarborough, H. and M. Corbett (1992) *Technology and Organization: Power, Meaning and Design*. London: Routledge.

Smith, W., M. Higgins, M. Parker and G. Lightfoot (eds.) (2001) *Science Fiction and Organization*. London: Routledge.

Sørensen, B. M. (2004) *Making Events Work, or, How to Multiply your Crisis*. Copenhagen: Samfundslitteratur.

Sorge, A. and M. Warner (2000) *The IEBM Handbook of Organizational Behavior*. London: Thomson Learning.

Star, S. L. (ed.) (1995) *The Cultures of Computing*. Oxford: Blackwell.

Strati, A. (1999) *Organization and Aesthetics*. London: Sage.

Sudnow, D. (ed.) (1972) *Studies in Social Interaction*. New York: Free Press

ten Bos, R. (2000) *Fashion and Utopia and Management Thinking*. Amsterdam: Benjamins.

ten Bos, R. and R. Kaulingfreks (2001) *De hygiënemachine: Kanttekeningen bij de reinheidscultus in cultuur, organizatie en management*. Kampen: Agora.

Thomas, R., A. Mills and J. H. Mills (2004) *Identity Politics at Work: Resisting Gender, Gendering Resistance*. London: Routledge.

Westwood, R. and S. Clegg (eds.) (2003) *Debating Organization: Point-Counterpoint in Organization Studies*. Oxford: Blackwell.

Westwood, R. and S. Linstead (eds.) (2001) *The Language of Organization*. London: Sage.

Whipp, R., B. Adam and I. Sabelis (eds.) (2002) *Making Time: Time and Management in Modern Organizations*. Oxford: Oxford University Press.

Giorgio Agamben and the community without identity

René ten Bos

Introduction

The Italian philosopher and philologist Giorgio Agamben has been on the scene now for more than twenty years, even though most of his work has only been available in English for a decade or so. Perhaps, it might strike you, the reader, as somewhat strange to have a thinker like Agamben in a book on theorists of organization. While it is true that his work is characterized by a profound interest in human beings, which is, I believe, how most organizational scholars would characterize themselves as well, the kind of human beings portrayed by Agamben are probably not the kind of human beings you are likely to encounter in and around organizations (managers, shareholders, workers, and so on). On the contrary, Agamben's work seems to focus on those who are, for many different reasons, *excluded* from these seemingly well-ordered places. If, for a single moment, Agamben does seem to speak about people working in organizations, then his attention will always be rapidly diverted towards those who have, for reasons that must remain obscure for all the people who continue doing their jobs, stopped working – as is the case, for example, in his splendid analysis of Melville's short story about a scrivener called Bartleby (Agamben, 1999a: 243–271; see also ten Bos and Rhodes, 2003). The truth about human beings, Agamben seems to suggest, is, if anywhere, surely not to be found in organizations that put people to work.

In the next section, I will argue that Agamben opens up to a concept of organization as a *threshold*, that is, a zone of indifference between work and non-work, humanity and bestiality, culture and nature. These insights are subsequently linked to a dramatic and gloomy understanding of contemporary USA-dominated politics that might, I will argue, be pertinent to the work of organization theorists as well. While I am broadly sympathetic to Agamben's work, it is in the sections called 'Prophecy' and 'Melancholia' that I will raise some critical issues. These are related to Agamben's sometimes astonishing understanding of bourgeois consumers and to his denial of melancholia as a source of the coming politics. Yet, accusations that Agamben's work is unrealistic miss the point. Here is a *philosopher* at work and in the final two sections of the chapter, I will show that Agamben's understanding of what a philosopher should do is intimately related to his analysis of contemporary capitalistic organization.

Threshold

The human beings figuring in Agamben's texts are refugees, tramps, migrants, angels, poets, patients, sub-proletarians, the inmates of concentration camps and others who are generally only noticed for their uselessness with respect to the dictates of labour. These people generally appear to us as if they are coming from places where something called organization has been perverted – which is the reason why the very presence of these people is considered to jeopardize the normal civil order and the categories of classification that go with it ('being British', 'being an employee belonging to firm X', 'being a citizen with a social security number', 'being a customer with a special customer number', and so on). Nevertheless, it is always some sort of organization that excludes these 'less-than-humans'. That is to say, the places from which they speak to us in hardly audible voices are neither pristine nor natural, but are themselves creations of order and organization: camps like Auschwitz and Guantanamo Bay are, for all their mutual differences, the result of well-organized political efforts to pervert order and organization.

How are we to understand these perversions? In camps, Agamben explains, human beings live detached from soil and are therefore placed beyond any constitutional or civil order, they live there as 'naked bodies' without a shimmer of the privacy warranted elsewhere, and so on. Agamben's tone when invoking the idea of the camp is, if anything, alarmist: he wants us to believe that today 'it is not the city but rather the camp that is the fundamental biopolitical paradigm of the West' (1998: 181). This paradigm, Agamben goes on, 'throws a sinister light on the models by which social sciences, sociology, urban studies, and architecture are trying to conceive and organize the public space of the world's cities without any clear awareness that at their very centre lies the same bare life (even if this has been transformed and rendered apparently more human)' (1998: 181–182). This may all be somewhat exaggerated – for example, do we organize camps for poets or tramps? Or is a hospital a camp for patients? Is a prison a camp for its inmates? But Agamben also uses less-alarmist concepts that might convince even the most persisting sceptic that what he has to say is as important as it is disquieting.

More particularly, he describes efforts to pervert order and organization also in terms of 'sovereignty' and 'law': the political sovereign can, in an act of great arbitrariness, decide to suspend the law, for example, in order to fight a dangerous enemy (e.g., Hannibal and his elephants or Osama Bin Laden). Necessity knows no law: you may have to suspend the law just in order to paradoxically save it. In this way the sovereign creates a 'state of exception': a situation where law and order are put into action in order to place human beings outside law and order. Where 'states of exceptions' were once, for example, during the Roman Empire, very rarely 'used' by the political sovereign, nowadays the state of exception has become the rule. The disquieting suggestion made by Agamben is that the normal and civil order in which we, as average citizens of our late-capitalistic society, might feel so protected and secure might easily turn into a perverted order where the law is suspended and where we lose our civil status and become, indeed, less-than-human. If we are to believe Agamben, the likelihood that this happens to the citizens of our precious democracy has never been bigger.

Indeed, when he writes that his work must be seen as 'a response to the bloody mystification of a new planetary order' (1998: 12), it becomes dramatically clear that Agamben is very serious in his efforts to convey a sense of urgency to his readership. He explicitly argues that the concepts of the social sciences, 'from law to anthropology', must be 'radically revised' in light of the 'urgent catastrophe' (ibid.). If we are not willing to do this, we are complicit in the drama that unfolds right now. It is true, Agamben's own sense of urgency has seduced him to write in perhaps overly dramatic and alarmist tones about camps as paradigms for political organization. Yet, it is not difficult to see how concrete the dangers really are. In a book, eight years after *Homo Sacer*, Agamben is much less dramatic and perhaps therefore much more explicit. At the end of a very disconcerting historical survey about how often in the past two centuries modern democracy has resorted to the state of exception, he points out that George W. Bush, who after 9/11 made himself the 'Commander in Chief of the Army', 'is attempting to produce a situation in which the emergency becomes the rule, and the very distinction between war and peace (and between foreign and civil war) becomes impossible' (2005: 22).

This is not the place to go into details about the War on Terrorism, the Patriot Act, Guantanamo Bay, putatively preventive wars in the Middle-East, or the repeated threats to the International Court of Justice in The Hague – to mention just a few examples – but, in Agamben's view, all these events show that the state of exception, arbitrarily created by the sole contemporary superpower, has become a planetary issue. How does organization fit in with this? First of all, it should be clear that business organizations worldwide should be able to finance the American political and military hegemony. This is why the USA, as was pointed out by Tariq Ali (2004), have been so keen to export their version of democracy: business companies all over the world should be able to finance the incredibly expensive military aspirations of American neo-conservatives. Secondly, and perhaps more importantly in the context of this chapter, Agamben shows that the very idea of organization is disturbingly indifferent to our identities, to what we want to become, to our happiness, to our love-life, to our civility, that is, to our entire life. Organization, it is true, might help us to attain a civil status, a secure income, or a clear-cut identity, but it might also cause us to topple down to the other side of this seemingly well-entrenched order. Organization is not a citadel of order but rather a 'threshold' where people routinely pass from order into disorder and from disorder into order. From this perspective, there is only a difference of degree between sacking a person on the one hand and in holding him or her in a prison camp on the other. Under capitalistic conditions, most of us have grown accustomed to the idea that the first alternative might sooner or later apply to us, but if this is the case, how far away is the second alternative?

The concept of the 'threshold' is central to Agamben's project and he uses it (or alternatives such as 'zones of indifference') to make clear that nobody is safe from the other side of order and civilization and that we may therefore have to face it right away. This implies not only an ethics about the other but also an ethics about the self, for it is the self that might easily pass the threshold and turn into the other. In this respect, it is noteworthy that Agamben has written extensively on werewolves, centaurs, ape-men, and other creatures that seem to blur the distinction between the human and the animal (1998: 104–111; 2004: 33–38). Questioning this distinction implies a questioning of a number of other distinctions as well: culture and nature, city and country, public and private, *and*, indeed, organization and disorganization. In our contemporary society, threatened by the catastrophe of American corporate and military hegemony, these distinctions have become thresholds or zones of indifference. Only when we understand that we can become like them (animal, inmates, less-than-humans) as well, that is to say, only when we understand that politics should be about a communality with the other side, are we able to envisage that this threshold is not only a danger but perhaps also, against all odds, an opportunity.

The key word in Agamben's analysis is *'homo sacer'*, the sacred and cursed man. This is the human being who is stripped bare of all his mundane qualities simply to become reduced to his bodily existence, which, isolated from community and organization, is waiting for whatever it is that those who have banned his body plan to do with it (Agamben, 1998). The sacred man appears as a non-person who can be sacked, enslaved, deported, mistreated, killed, and so on, without any risk of punishment. In horrific cases such as the *Muselmänner* in Auschwitz, the sacred are not even really killed when they are killed: the horror of Auschwitz is that their death is not death and that their corpses are not really corpses but, as the SS had it, 'figures' (1999b: 70). Against this tendency towards the extremity of violence, Agamben insists on the *Dasein*, on the being *in this world*, of sacred people and he even goes so far as to argue that if we are to understand what human being-in-the-world is we had better look at those whose presence apparently defies order. His claim is even stronger: the truth about who we are *cannot* be found in organized and well-ordered places, or more precisely, we cannot understand human nature if we do not understand that the symbols of our order – civility, law, organization, and so on – in fact refer to a threshold between order and disorder, a threshold that we are all sooner or later destined to pass by. If Agamben is right, then all understandings of human beings in the context of order and organization can only be based on a mystification if they do not take into account the other side. What is organization if it denies the ruins that it causes? Or analogously, what are democracy and freedom of trade if they deny, as is routinely done by Western media

(Ali, 2004), the hundreds of thousands of victims of 'benevolent' violence in Asia and elsewhere?

There are, admittedly, quite a few contributions in organizational theory that would probably acknowledge these problems with organization, democracy, and capitalism. I think here, for example, of Burrell (1997) who has alerted us to the fact that most people in this world are still poor farmers rather than well-organized factory workers, let alone managers. One might also think of Brewis and Linstead (2000) who have proposed that in order to understand what trust in economic relationships might mean you had better look at people who have to do their work in lawless and disorganized circumstances – street prostitutes picked up by car drivers are their preferred example – rather than at people who know right from the start that their trust in someone is backed-up by law and contract. And the issues raised by global capitalism have been dealt with in ways that sometimes seem to resonate fairly well with Agamben's work (see, for example, Korten, 1995; Jones, Parker, and ten Bos, 2005). In spite of some of these and other exceptions, however, it is fairly safe to assume that the bulk of organizational theory as we know it today, even its allegedly critical varieties, is complicit in upholding the political mystification envisaged by Agamben. The new politics about which he muses so much and to which I will return below requires a disorganization which transforms us into who *they* are rather than them into who *we* are:

> Only in a world in which the spaces of states have been thus perforated and topo-logically deformed and in which the citizen has been able to recognize the refugee that he or she is – only in such a world is the political survival of humankind today think-able. (Agamben, 2000b: 26; see also Agamben 2002a).

This is, I would like to add, surely not the kind of integration that most con-temporary politics and managements have in mind. Integration can only take place in zones of indifference and not by inviting people to change who they are and to become like us.

Prophecy

So then, we must think a 'community' without exclusion, inclusion, violence, discrimination, abandonment, and so on. The controversy in Agamben's writing lies precisely here: he thinks that current concepts of belonging, togetherness, and community are misguided, and he develops a plethora of concepts and terms that all serve the purpose of finding new articulations of a community without exclusion and inclusion, without violence and negativity, without sub-stance and identity. What does this all mean? And, is this community of which it is announced that it is 'coming' really coming?

When reading Agamben, one is often struck by the extremities of his style: on the one hand, we read dark and disconcerting prose about naked people, bare life, camps, and states of exceptions and on the other hand his texts sometimes seem to wallow in a kind of 'messianic' optimism. In a comment on the Roman Letters (2000a: 60–84; see also 2002b), Agamben defines 'messianic time' as the time that is still left, that is to say, the time between now and the end of time. Hence, it is not the time that is foretold by prophets who say things about the future. Neither is it the time of the apostles for they know about the Messiah and, with the exception of St. Paul, already experienced time with him. So, if we are to understand Agamben's ideas about the 'coming' as messianic, then we should bear in mind that it is neither as a straightforward prophet (who has caught a glimpse of the future) nor as an apostle (who has witnessed what we apparently did not) that he speaks to us.

Still, I want to suggest that there is something prophetic, in a very special sense of the word, about Agamben's work. I think here of what Baudrillard (1998) has in mind when he argues that apparently future-oriented activities such as planning and prediction do not generally speak about the future but rather signify the possibility of a symbolic break in time that eventually might engender a symbolic break in the mind. In other words, '[t]he only thing we try to imagine is how to get rid of our history which weighs so much and then start all over again.' Similarly, a prophet might be seen as someone who does not speak about a future reality but rather calls for the end of what has always been going on. In this sense, a prophet appears as someone who accuses his/her contemporaries of being unable to put an end to this and also of being unable to look beyond that end. Only in this sense, I suggest, can we understand Agamben's work as prophetic.

Thus, the obvious analogy with religious people who believe, for example, that the kingdom of Jehovah will 'come' simply collapses when one takes a closer look. To be sure, Agamben believes in things to come: he talks about the 'coming' community, the 'coming' philosophy, or the 'coming' politics. But we should bear in mind that he has repeatedly referred to himself as a philosopher of the possible, that is, as a philosopher whose major interest lies in the analysis of the functions of the verb 'can' and its negative 'cannot' (1999a: 177). In other words, the things which Agamben sees as 'coming' are to be seen not as inevitabilities, which is probably how they are viewed by religious zealots, but as (im)possibilities: the coming community *might* happen if and only if we do not let slip away certain opportunities and it *might not* happen if we do let them slip away. To put it succinctly, the coming community is a possibility rather than a certainty, and the thing about possibilities is that some of them, perhaps many of them, will never be actualized. These possibilities persist, as it were, in their being a potency and nothing else.

It is clear therefore that Agamben, while refusing to abandon hope, does not offer any straightforward salvation or redemption:

> We can have hope only in what is without remedy. That things are thus and thus
> – this is still in the world. But that this is irreparable, that this *thus* is without
> remedy, that we can contemplate it as such – this is the only passage outside the
> world. (The innermost character of salvation is that we are saved only at the

point when we no longer want to be. At this point, there is salvation – but not for us.) (1993a: 102)

Rather surprisingly, given his predilection for the banned and excluded, Agamben claims that it is the 'planetary petty bourgeois' who may hold the seed for the community that comes, for it is here, in a sense against all odds, that we may at last encounter a shimmer of the non-exclusiveness stressed in his work. To use the complex language Agamben oftentimes uses: if the petty bourgeois is willing to stop looking for 'a proper identity in the already improper and senseless form of individuality', here conceived as either a 'me' or a 'we' (something to which Nancy has referred as 'immanentism', that is, a political craving for a completed social identity that functions as an absolute horizon for those who are going to bear it and that can only be achieved by means of myth and sacrifice; see: Nancy, 1991: 12; 56–57; Nancy 2003: 74) *and* if the bourgeois accepts his or her 'proper being-thus' not as belonging to an identity but as a 'singularity without identity', then and only then might there be a chance that this bourgeois will 'enter into a community without presuppositions and without subjects' (1993a: 65). Agamben's point is based on what he understands to be the classlessness of the bourgeoisie who are, in the sense that they refuse (or, perhaps better, have the possibility to refuse) any straightforward or recognizable social identity (Agamben, 1993: 63), the true successors of the sub-proletarians that figure as heartbreaking non-identities in the films of Pier Paolo Pasolini (see also Vighi, 2003). Global capitalism is indifferent to whether products are being sold to Moslems, Christians, Buddhists, Hindus, or atheists. It is also indifferent to national or political identities. It only takes an interest in anonymous and acquisitive citizens. Agamben locates, somewhat surprisingly perhaps, an (im)possibility in the bourgeois consumer that is so essential to global capitalism. He bases his hope in part on the loss of tradition and 'immanence' that is consequential upon capitalistic organization and disorganization.

Melancholia

But again, this hope is neither a prediction nor a prophecy. Melancholia is just one serious danger. It is arguably a corollary effect of globalization (Sloterdijk, 1999): the more corporations and money markets seem to defy any appeal to identity and togetherness (and, hence, undermine all claims to immanence), the more we see citizens and politicians all over the world being subjected to various kinds of melancholic desires, one of which is the desire for an allegedly lost identity or community (the British identity, the French identity, the Dutch identity). In an older work, Agamben maintains that melancholia is always about possession and loss at the same time (1993b: 21): the melancholic individual can only possess the desired object while losing it. I think this subtle phrasing, which relies heavily on what Freud once wrote in *Mourning and Melancholia* (originally published in 1914), shows, if anything, the tenacity of the melancholic sentiment. The craving for a loved person – and love is just another kind of togetherness about which Agamben has written extensively (eg, 1993a: 2; 1993b: 109–123; 1995: 61) – cannot be simply overcome by getting what one is longing for. As Robert Walser, a novelist who figures prominently in the book on the coming community, writes in a novel set in a German boarding-school where emotions are rigidly suppressed:

> For example, not being allowed to cry, well, that increases crying. To do without love, yes, means to love. If I should not love, my love will be tenfold. All that is forbidden lives in hundredfold ways; hence, what should be dead, lives its life only more vivaciously. (Walser, 1985: 105; my translation)

Melancholy is not simply something that can be suppressed and I am quite sure that Agamben would acknowledge this. Yet, he seems to deny it when he writes about bourgeois forms of melancholy. Indeed, he boldly claims that what has been valuable for peoples and generations in the history of our planet – ways of life, languages, senses of belonging, race, and so on – has simply lost all meaning for the bourgeoisie (1993a 62). Hence, all melancholy and pathos can be pushed away into the 'phantasmagorical vacuousness' of this bourgeoisie. It is as if a sigh is heaved: 'If only we can make them understand that this is an enormous opportunity . . .'

This is perhaps an ingredient of the task to come for philosophers whose primary concern should be the community of all (rather than a few pro-American) human beings? My point is simply that an awful lot of convincing is to be done if the bourgeoisie, petty as it is, is ever to rejoice in this vacuity. Not only do I think that the coming community might be a little bit too philosophical or, perhaps better, too cerebral, for the liking of the average bourgeois, but – and this matters much more – I do not see how he or she can emancipate themself from this melancholic craving for community and identity. To be sure, the above quoted passage about the refugees that we should all become is enchanting, but will it convince the bourgeois? Is he or she willing to live the life of a refugee?

Elsewhere in his work, Agamben seems to be in doubt and admits – in line with his understanding of the 'possible' – that the 'planetary masses of consumers' may fall back in the 'old ethnic and religious ideals' (2000b: 114). The myth of an integral and inviolate self from which melancholia feeds itself might turn out to be very persistent, even among members of the bourgeoisie. That it is suppressed by current developments in our society (migration, globalization, the opening of borders, and so on) is not to say that it will disappear. On the contrary, the danger is that this myth will only become more powerful, for we should not forget that those who believe in it do not depart at all from an identity but from a non-identity. To put it differently, the stronger the belief in the myth of an integral and violate self, the more certain you can be that this self is painfully absent. The myth about what is there only reveals its absence.

Can we therefore seriously ask people to forfeit the security of their imaginary integrity, identity, home, race, class, and so on? And, assuming that we have

done this, how are we then to proceed? Are we then asking them to happily identify with the loss of myths? And is it possible to identify with this loss without
having myths – old myths, new myths – overwhelming them once again? As
Anne Cheng has argued in her penetrating study on the melancholy of race, we
would simply expect people to become versed in 'the art of losing' (2001: 175).
The problem therefore remains 'whether there can be a progressive politics that
recognizes, rather than denies, the . . . subject's melancholic desires' (Cheng,
2001: 127).

Philosophy and language

Now that I have explained some of my reservations with respect to Agamben's
enterprise, I will try to shed light on some central themes in his work in order
to see what he believes is an alternative to the myth and melancholy that surrounds so much contemporary thought about the community. I take as a starting point an article, published for the first time twenty years ago, in which he
speaks about 'the tasks of the coming philosophy' (1999a: 38). He argues that
this task has a double edge: first, the coming philosophy is supposed to 'restore
the thing itself into its place in language'; second, it should also 'restore the difficulty of writing, the place of writing in the poetic task of composition'. What
does this mean?

Agamben's ideas about the difficulty of writing, a topic that pops up over
and over again in his work, relates to the solitary and isolated nature of philosophical writing. While, according to Agamben, it cannot be maintained that
philosophers unproblematically dip their pen in thought, as was once said of
Aristotle, it should be admitted that they have only their pen with which to create
letters, words, and texts, and it is only by means of the solitary activity of writing
that they can paradoxically contribute to the struggle against solitude. In other
words, they serve togetherness and community by choosing loneliness and isolation. This has been their task forever, although most philosophers seem to have
forgotten about it and have, on the contrary, tried to 'isolate' or even 'individu-
alize' the human being (the Cartesian cogito, the subject of human rights, and
so on). This is why Agamben wants to insist on a rehabilitation of this
quintessentially philosophical task: *to think community in the most abstract and
general sense of the word, that is to say, not this or that community but perhaps
community as such.* In this respect, Agamben clearly sides with people like Nancy
(1991) against communitarians such as Anscombe or MacIntyre who only think
about particular (for example, catholic or Franciscan) communities.

The remarks about the 'difficulty of writing' indicate that Agamben's ideas
about the community are profoundly 'philosophical', *both* in the sense that he
considers it the natural task of philosophers to contribute to community *and* in
the sense that the community he wants to bring about is a community envisaged
by a philosopher rather than a politician or, let us say, a member of an already
existing community (which a philosopher apparently is not). The rehabilitation

of the philosopher as the one who opens a perspective on the most general being-in-common that human beings are capable of is closely linked to the nature of language. This observation takes us back to the first element of the double-edged task of the coming philosophy. It is not only a matter of rehabilitating an old task of the philosopher, it is also a matter of an old understanding of language, one which has long since been forgotten. What Agamben wants to remind us of is a time when philosophers worried not so much about the capacity of language to refer to an external world or, to invoke some post-Kantian imagery, about language's indelible strangeness with respect to the thing-in-itself, but about an understanding that *the saying itself remains unsaid in what is being said* (1999a: 33).

Now, this is a complicated idea, one which is strongly indebted to Benjamin's conceptualization of 'language as such' not as something with a content or as a means to communicate something non-linguistic, but as what communicates itself. Language is a medium or a middle rather than a means (Benjamin, 1978; see also Agamben, 1999a: 52–54). Here is not the place to pursue in great detail the influence of Benjamin on Agamben's work. It suffices to indicate that Benjamin's ideas about language as well as about the task of the coming philosophy are towering over Agamben's entire enterprise with respect to the community, something which the Italian professor readily admits (1999a: 58; see also 1993b, *passim*).

Another important source of inspiration in this discussion is Plato who has claimed, according to Agamben, that the most important philosophical task is to help language to become language (1999a: 35). Agamben comments on this that such a task implies that language should be rendered presupposition-less. In other words, philosophy has the task to make clear that there is no thing-in-itself that is presupposed to be behind or beyond language, no subject behind all subjects, no outside world that is assumed to bestow upon our words a variety of meanings. If the thing-in-itself does exist at all, it must be as a linguistic entity in the sense that we can only conceive of this allegedly 'extra-linguistic' being in terms of language. Plato's conceptualization of the idea or the form is, of course, a case-in-point: it is not beyond or outside language but itself a linguistic entity, a *logos* (1999a: 58–59). What we should be worrying about, according to Plato, is not so much the relationship between language and what is outside language (since there is no outside language or, rather, reality is language), but the fact of language itself, that is, its very 'sayability'. If it makes sense to speak about a 'thing-in-itself' at all, then such an expression or concept is perhaps best associated with the 'sayability' of language.

Agamben refers to it in terms of a linguistic openness which, for him, constitutes *the idea of language* (1999a: 47). Elsewhere, in *Idea of Prose*, he links this openness to silence, not in the sense that all discourse is suspended (which would be the case when nobody speaks anymore and that would hardly be an openness) but in the sense that the words that are spoken are themselves silent. It is in its silence that the word itself becomes visible. In a passage which nicely illustrates how Agamben has mastered the art of giving lyrical twists to apparently commonplace expressions, he explains how this silence and visibility of the word, that is, its openness, might be interpreted:

> Only the word puts us in contact with mute things. While nature and animals are forever caught up in a language, incessantly speaking and responding to signs even while keeping silent, only man succeeds in interrupting, in the word, the infinite language of nature and placing himself for a moment in front of mute things. The inviolate rose, the idea of rose, exists only for man. (1995: 113)

Contrary to classical definitions of man as the speaking animal, Agamben insists that it is not the capacity for language that makes him/her a unique creature but rather *the ability to make language visible by silencing it*. And it is only this ability – the ability to isolate the rose from the language of nature and hence to turn it into a mute object – that allows man to become object-oriented or, to use Heidegger's terminology, world-forming. Animals are not world-forming in this sense simply because they are 'withheld' by the ongoing chatter that makes up nature (2004: 53).

We can now understand what Agamben has in mind when he argues that it is the task of the coming philosophy to present us the idea of language. This task implies nothing less than an ongoing commitment to show what all human beings have in common – their linguistic openness to the world – and therefore to show the humanity of all human beings (including those who are excluded). That we can all speak is what ultimately matters much more than the *quid* about which or from which we are supposed to speak. Agamben (2000b: 116; 1999a: 66) refers to the fact that there is speaking or that there are speakers as the *factum loquendi* and philosophy should be concerned with this fact. It is therefore very different from a science such as linguistics which tries to identify the real properties of language in order to determine the essence of language. The philosopher's task, on the other hand, is 'exhausted in the presentation of the existence of language' (1999a: 67) and in doing this, she or he attempts to 'define categories and modalities in such a way that being is not *presupposed* but rather *exposed*' (1999a: 76, emphasis added).

Community and happiness

Agamben's central claim is that both community and tradition find their condition of possibility in the *factum loquendi*, in the '*sayability*' of language, in our-being-in-language. More accurately, the presupposition of language, which resides in its 'sayability', is in fact the very structure of tradition and community. It is only by means of language that we are able to presuppose, to pass on, to convey and, indeed, to 'betray the thing itself in language, so that language may speak about something' (1999a: 35). In Agamben's opinion, it is the 'sayability' of language that is *betrayed* in tradition and community rather than who we are, where we are, and so on. 'Tradition' and 'betrayal' are words with a similar etymological origin which is related to the verb 'to pass on'. Agamben wants us to understand that tradition as he sees it does not pass on a belonging to this or that group, nation, soil, God, class, or municipality. It rather passes on the plain fact that we can speak and hence can be open to other speakers and can be open to the entire world. Any conceptualization of tradition or community that does not acknowledge this openness indeed invokes an appeal to substance, classification, organization, or any other kind of 'container' and *must* betray tradition as well as the community of all human beings. In this sense, the philosopher's task is profoundly political: by bringing the thing itself into language and by constantly reminding us about what this thing itself is, she or he contributes to the tradition and community of all (rather than a few) human beings. The philosopher can thus be seen – in a very special sense of the word – as the protector of a *universal* tradition.

It is not a property, a nature, a voice, a vision, or, indeed, a particular language that unites human beings in this tradition but the 'vision of language itself and therefore the experience of language's limits, its end'. And, having arrived at this point, so to speak at the end of language, Agamben adds that 'a true community can only be a community that is not presupposed' (1999a: 47). But what does this mean? How are we to conceive of a community without a particular vision or voice, without any reference to a provenance or descent? In another book crucial for his understanding of community, *Language and Death: The Place of Negativity* (1991), Agamben makes clear that he is driven by a desire to eliminate all negativity from conceptualizations of community and tradition, a negativity that he locates in the myths of immanentism that prevail in contemporary politics. It is the state, the nation, or the capitalistic organization that preserves from language only a voice which functions as the myth that must include by excluding and exclude by including. Bush: 'You are either for us or against us.' This voice, magical as it may be, finds its sole source of inspiration in nihilism and negativity. The point of Agamben's intervention in the debate about community becomes now clear: he wants to silence this voice of negativity that permeates not only our thinking on communities but also these communities as praxis (1991: 94–95) and, in order to do this, he tries to think the thing itself of language rather than a particular language that comes from somewhere or that has a distinct identity.

The coming politics to which his philosophy of language opens a perspective is therefore a fight not only against American hegemony but also against the nation-state and, I would like to add, against all organization and management. More accurately, it is a fight between humanity and state/organization – and humanity is understood here not in terms of people who have inalienable human rights but in terms of singularities that 'cannot form a *societas* because they cannot possess any identity to vindicate nor any bond of belonging for which they seek recognition' (1993a: 86). What is important for the state and its organizations, is that all these 'singularities' – which Agamben defines as beings such as they are, that is, as beings that are 'indifferent with respect to a common property' (1993a: 1) – cannot be accepted as such and should be either included in some 'representable identity' or be violently excluded or banned in nowhere lands (camps, seas, limbos, asylums, forests, and so on) (1993a: 86). Singularities, that what people are when they are not subordinated into classes or sets, are the State's principal enemies and wherever these singularities will come to the fore and demonstrate their 'being-in-common', which happened, for example, on Tiananmen Square in Beijing 1989, but which is also happening every day at the borders of our countries where the gathering of refugees puts the very concept of a border or a nation-state into question – weapons will appear sooner rather than later.

Agamben's radical claim is that philosophy should take sides with these singularities and should reflect the most general being-in-common of human people. It should try to make thresholds visible everywhere, even in the system that is based on dangerous mystifications. This implies a kind of reflection that religion, science, and politics, as they are currently practiced, cannot provide anymore. There is no doubt that this philosophical endeavour betrays a certain political hubris, but it is a hubris that feeds itself not only from a profound solidarity with the repressed and the banned but also from an understanding that a crucial task of philosophy has always been quite simply to ponder the possibilities of a happy life, a life that is not guaranteed any more by a politics of sovereignty that of necessity resorts to violence and exclusion when challenged (2000b: 114–115). Agamben's philosophy makes us aware that this old task – reflecting happiness – is not to be banned to the domain called *Lebenskunst* (the art of life), as if this is an area that can be nicely isolated from the areas of production and work and therefore from politics itself; on the contrary, this ancient task is to be rehabilitated by allowing it to take once more a central place in political thought. Only when we understand that politics and art of life are not separated anymore, only when we see that politics is intimately related with what happens when people are not subjected to working organizations and are in this sense inactive (2000b: 141; see also Nancy, 1991: 31, 72–74 and Wall, 1999: 87, 132), are we able to grasp that politics is about happiness and the manifold ways that we communicate about this.

Agamben dares to dream about a politics of thought, in other words, a life-form that takes as its starting point not our belonging to a particular community but communicability itself. This is a politics that resists our seemingly unstoppable actualizations and instead always stresses potency and possibility, for all human beings can only communicate and be in common when they are aware that *it is only potency and not actualization that can be truly shared*. I have indicated that I am unsure whether this is a viable starting point for a progressive politics to come, but if Agamben is right in claiming that philosophic thought should be about the possible rather than about the actual, then he has done – as a philosopher – simply what he had to do: trying to open the way for an alternative politics that defies the logic of actualization that characterizes capitalist organization.

References

Agamben, G. (1991) *Language and Death: The Place of Negativity*, trans. K. E. Pinkus and M. Hardt. Minneapolis: University of Minnesota Press.

Agamben, G. (1993a) *The Coming Community*, trans. M. Hardt. Minneapolis: University of Minnesota Press.

Agamben, G. (1993b) *Stanzas: Word and Phantasm in Western Culture*, trans. R. L. Martinez. Minneapolis: University of Minnesota Press.

Agamben, G. (1995) *Idea of Prose*, trans. M. Sullivan and S. Whitsitt. Albany, NY: State University of New York Press.

Agamben, G. (1998) *Homo Sacer: Sovereign Power and Bare Life*, trans. D. Heller-Roazen. Stanford, CA: Stanford University Press.

Agamben, G. (1999a) *Potentialities: Collected Essays in Philosophy*, trans. D. Heller-Roazen. Stanford, CA: Stanford University Press.

Agamben, G. (1999b) *Remnants of Auschwitz: The Witness and the Archive*, trans. D. Heller-Roazen. New York: Zone Books.

Agamben, G. (2000a) *Il tempo che resta: Un commenato alla Lettera di Romani*. Torino: Bollati Boringhieri.

Agamben, G. (2000b) *Means Without End: Notes on Politics*, trans. V. Binetti and C. Casarino. Minneapolis: University of Minnesota Press.

Agamben, G. (2002a) 'Security and terror' *Theory & Event* 5(4).

Agamben, G. (2002b) 'The time that is left' *Epoché*, 7(1): 1–14.

Agamben, G. (2004) *The Open: Man and Animal*, trans. K. Attell. Stanford, CA: Stanford University Press.

Agamben, G. (2005) *State of Exception*, trans. K. Attell. Chicago: University of Chicago Press.

Ali, T. (2004) *Bush in Babylon: The Recolonisation of Iraq*. London: Verso.

Balibar, E. (2004) *We, the People of Europe? Reflections on Transnational Citizenship*, trans. J. Swenson. Princeton, NJ: Princeton University Press.

Baudrillard, J. (1998) 'In the shadow of the millennium (or, the suspense of the year 2000)' *CTheory*, online at: http://www.ctheory.net/text_file.asp?pick=104 (accessed 25 Feburary 2005).

Benjamin, W. (1978) 'On language as such and on the language of man' in Peter Demetz (ed.) *Reflections: Essays, Aphorisms, Autobiographical Writings*. New York: Shocken.

Brewis, J. and S. Linstead (2000) *Sex, Work, and Sex Work*. London: Routledge

Burrell, G. (1997) *Pandemonium: Towards a Retro-organization Theory*. London: Sage

Cheng, A. A. (2001) *The Melancholy of Race: Psychoanalysis, Assimilation, and Hidden Grief*. Oxford: Oxford University Press.

Jones, C., M. Parker and R. ten Bos (2005) *For Business Ethics*. London: Routledge.

Korten, D. (1995) *When Corporations Rule the World*. London: Earthscan.

Nancy, J.-L. (1991) *The Inoperative Community*, trans. P. Connor and C. Fynsk. Minneapolis, MN: University of Minnesota Press.

Nancy, J.-L. (2003) *A Finite Thinking*, trans. S. Sparks. Stanford, CA: Stanford University Press

Sloterdijk, P. (1999) *Sphären I & II*. Frankfurt: Suhrkamp.

ten Bos, R. and C. Rhodes (2003) 'The game of exemplarity: Subjectivity, work and the impossible politics of purity' *Scandinavian Journal of Management*, 19(4): 403–423.

Vighi, F. (2003) 'Pasolini and exclusion: Žižek, Agamben and the modern sub-proletariat' *Theory, Culture & Society*, 20(5): 99–121.

Wall, T. Carl (1999) *Radical Passivity: Levinas, Blanchot, and Agamben*. Albany, NY: State University of New York Press

Walser, R. (1985) *Jakob von Gunten*. Frankfurt am Main: Suhrkamp.

Are we all good? Zygmunt Bauman's response to Hobbes

Ruud Kaulingfreks

Introduction

Business ethics is topical. We expect organizations to be concerned about ethics and to show their goodness. Managing should be ethically sound and moral codes of conduct for organizations are the subject of widespread debate. Corporate social responsibility is rapidly becoming a distinguishing characteristic of organizations. When one is thinking about the relation between organizations and ethics, the work of Zygmunt Bauman catches the eye. He does not search for an ethical way for organizations to behave but questions the morality of organizations themselves by suspecting the moral grounds of organization.

The work of Zygmunt Bauman can be seen as a strong argument against the justification of organizations and as a critique of the morality of organizations. Bauman attacks Hobbes' problem of order and the consequential image of human beings in Enlightenment. In this chapter I present Bauman's ideas on ethics and morality in relation to organizations and management. First I will present the two ideas Bauman opposes: Hobbes' problem of order and the Promethean idea of transforming the world. From there we will go into Bauman's work and finally a relation will be drawn between Bauman's ethics and some ideas from aesthetics. His concept of morality is best to be understood as an aesthetic category. By so doing we obviate some problems arising from his ideas.

Although he is a prolific writer with more than 25 books and hundreds of articles, I concentrate here on his early work because I think in this work he lays the foundations for his thinking. Given the limited space of this chapter I concentrate on a couple of arguments that I think are essential for his thinking. This chapter is in this sense not an exhaustive account of his ideas but aims to give the reader an engagement with some basic problems Bauman puts forth.

Hobbes' problem of order

According to Talcott Parsons (1949) the ultimate condition for social life is the problem of order, as it was put forth by Hobbes in 1651. On this view, man is guided by passions and reason acts as a servant of passions – it is the faculty of devising ways and means to secure what one desires. Because desires are random, there is nothing to prevent conflict. Because the means are limited, the pursuit of desires results in a power struggle over the means for realization. In the absence of control men adopt force and fraud to attain the most efficient available means. Hence the result is a war of all against all. But this state of war is not in conformity with human nature. The fear of such a state of war calls for a social contract by which 'men agreed to give up their natural liberty to a sovereign authority which in turn guarantees them security, that is immunity from aggression by the force of fraud of others' (Parsons, 1949: 90). It is by this contract that order and security is maintained.

In Hobbes' system people are rational but they are only rational with respect to means. The goals of action are passionate. For Hobbes the problem of order is the problem of attaining satisfaction in a social situation. People need others in order to attain goals. But the other is also recognized as a goal. The other is recognition and service. The best way to secure the realization of desires is by exerting power. But this brings us in a state of war. Hobbes solves the problem of order by the Leviathan (see also Fleming and Spicer, in this volume). That is, by stretching the rationality to the point that people give up their desires in order to create order. Hobbes believes in an innate egoism that makes us seek fulfilment at any price. For him, according to Parsons, 'the actions of men should be potential means to each others' ends. Hence . . . all men should desire and seek power over one another' (1949: 93). A rational society is centred on a power struggle, or, the problem of order leads to a power problem. A strong government is needed to prevent society from falling into chaos.

Under the Leviathan, society is justified and grounded in a rational way. We give up some of our passions for a greater good and freely accept the coercion of our desires in order to attain security and stability. Although according to Parsons, Hobbes in no way solved the problem of order, his idea of the necessity of a Leviathan has become widely accepted. In Parsons' view the social contract stretches rationality too far, 'to a point where actors come to realize the situation as a whole instead of pursuing their own ends in terms of their immediate force and fraud, and, purchasing security at the sacrifice of the advantages to be gained by their future employment' (1949: 93). This means that Hobbes formulated not a descriptive but a normative theory. There is no reason why people would choose an uncertain future. Still, Hobbes' solution to the problem of order has become widely accepted and forms nowadays the basic justification of institutions and hence of organizations. We need organizations in order to prevent us from fraud and force. Here the argument also turns itself inside out.

Let us rehearse the familiar arguments. Organizations justify themselves as being the most rational answer to egoistical human nature. Society needs to be organized in such a way that people are prevented from pursuit of their passions. Organizational order forces us away from our desires into a productive, future-oriented order and security. Organizations – the order that produces the different organizations, however different the one may be from the other – discipline us and in return we obtain prosperity and a secure living. Organizations thus have an intrinsic social value. Even more, society depends on them. In order for society to have security and order it must be organized and structured in institutions or different organizations. Organizations are moral in themselves; if they did not exist, anomie and chaos would reign. Our social actions are social because of our power to organize ourselves and to set aside our egoistic nature, to set aside our passions in order to become productive. It is because of institutions that we become social and learn to postpone our passions for a greater common good. Organizations are in this view justified by the morality of Enlightenment. As Max Weber stated (1978) they are iron cages wherein we attain goal rationality. They provide the most rational way to act and are themselves the product of our rationality. Hence it is assumed that they are intrinsically good and produce good. They make us good. We need them.

It is this conception of people, organizations and society that has become predominant in modern society to the point that it has become a truth in itself. Organizations are the natural way in civil society wherein men work together. Little or no critique is heard of these basic grounds. Still, as Parsons rightly argued, if man is 'each pursuing his own ends independently of the others' (1949: 95), how is it possible they agree in such a suspension of their individuality in order to have a social contract where it is by no means certain it will give them the desired satisfaction? This is only possible because Hobbes introduced a normative principle. Men *should* have a social contract. Or, we are not all that egoistic and individual and have some innate sociability. According to Locke (1690/1966) it is because of this innate peacefulness that we agree to a government that must preserve the peace by preventing one individual from acquiring too much power over others. The state is to preserve peace. Individuals will control the state making it impossible for a ruler to exert power over individuals. The state is just a legislator – and executor – of the sovereign will of the people. People decide the rules of the state by majority and are entitled to revolt if the state takes too much power. Still, questions remain even after Locke's alteration of Hobbes: why a war of all against all?

Not only is this idea of a natural war of all against all theoretically strange as a starting point of modern society and as a justification of organizations, but it also gives rise to difficult moral questions. If our nature is egoistical then all sociability is forced upon us and all our altruistic or social feelings of togetherness and association are disciplined. We only deal with others in pursuit of self-interest and no love is innate (even for Locke the state of nature is changed into a social contract because individuals impose power over others and start the war of every man against every man). On this view, society exists only because of disciplinary forces and we assume we should mistrust all emotions of mutual understanding. But there is no justification whatsoever for such an argument. The opposite axiom of an innate altruism in men is also possible as it was put forth by Rousseau (1762/1968). He grounded the social contract as a way to secure altruism. Both points are possible and the consequences are crucial. If people are egoistic we need organizations. If men are in essence good organizations may not be needed, or they might not be as good as we think they are. It is precisely at this point that Bauman directs his thoughts by putting forward the case that organizations may not be all that morally good.

Prometheus

Before going into Bauman's work there is another fundamental thought that he questions. This is the Promethean idea that in order to live a prosperous life we need to take actions. The Titan who stole the fire from the Gods gave humanity not only civilisation but mostly the need to change the world and not accept the given. Prometheus is about perpetual progress, as Gehmann explains in his remarkable article:

> The Promethean mythology is one devoted to the deed. The progress forever, to the mythic hope of the individual's enduring, and eternal, liberation from the chains of the world 'as it is'. A mythology of expansion and omnipotence steered by the striving for immortality. Culminating in the myth of modernity: that in everything what can be done has to be done, also, has to be realised . . . no matter the cost or consequences . . . The world 'as it is' in its respective primordial shape . . . has to be encountered by us – reshaped, re-arranged, put in line with our wills and conceptions: transformed. (2003: 96)

The heritage of Prometheus is that we have to reorganize the world, transform it into our own world. The given world 'as it is' is unacceptable and deeply mistrusted. Only by managing it does the world become bearable. Therefore everything is encountered as a matter to be managed, to be rearranged, to be pulled inside our sphere of influence. It is perfectly clear that this means a destruction of the given. By transforming the given into matter we destroy it, we devoid it of meaning in order to impose our own. The world is an artefact. This is all necessary in order to grow, to develop. If we were pleased with the world as it is, we would not grow or expand. Expansion is necessary in order to change, to manage the world. We get entangled in a process of continual rearrangement and of reorganization after reorganization (see Heidegger, 1977, see also 1972 and 1978b). So in the end, matter indeed depends on us. Once we have created an artificial world of our own we have to maintain the artificiality and management. In other words we become the prisoners of our own expansion. We depend on it. In the eyes of the gods this can only be defined as hubris. No wonder Prometheus got punished.

Hubris

The Hobbesian concept of human beings and the Promethean view of the world justify organizations in the modern world and have put forth a moral view of organizations. Both are needed in order to have prosperity and a stable society. But they also have some other implications beside the already mentioned. One of them is the disdain for the present. From the Enlightenment on we have to reach for the future, get away from the given situation. Only because humanity is able to surpass the present is the social contract possible. Only because we are Prometheans can we have an orderly society. This turning away from immediacy means also turning away from our sensibility. Reaching for the future is also a turn into abstraction, into a dream of future happiness: one day the world will be exactly as we like it. One day the planning will mean a transparent world, or as Hegel said, spirit will fall together with the sensible. We will be gods. Only then will we be totally free and the perfect organization will exist. Rationality will be total and all calculations of the planning will come out perfectly. The world will equal the calculations. In the meantime we plan and trust reason to the detriment of the senses. Aesthetics as the field of the sensible is marginalized to the fringe of social life, to the spare time, enclosed in museums for instance. We become a kind of Mrs Tittle-Mouse from Beatrix Potter, who is always cleaning up and tidying her house to the point that it is not possible to be in the house. Heidegger of course explained very clearly that by progressing and trusting technology, we hand ourselves over to technology and become more and more imprisoned in a technical world, we depend on technology (Heidegger, 1977) and logic becomes logistic (Heidegger, 1955: 47, see also 1978c). Only planning and accounting in an abstract world of numbers counts, and everything is subordinate to planning, even morals. This is exactly what is called hubris.

The moral impulse

Now it is time to turn our attention to Bauman. He starts from the opposite idea of Hobbes. This is from an innate pre-social moral impulse of closeness. I am always with the Other and for the Other. The starting point is not a different I who associates with the other but a fundamental association of togetherness. Drawing heavily on Levinas (see Levinas, 1969), Bauman explains that this primordial relationship is not a reciprocity but togetherness:

> Moral stance begets an essentially *unequal* relationship; this inequality, non-equity, this not-asking-for-reciprocation, this disinterest in mutuality, this indifference to the 'balancing up' of gains and rewards – in short, this organically 'unbalanced' and hence non-reversible character of 'I versus the Other' relationship is what makes the encounter a moral event. (Bauman, 1993: 48)

The Other is encounter for the Other's sake and as an end in itself. In this sense the moral impulse is in no way a contract (1993: 58) because there is no expectation. I am directed to the Other regardless of what the Other does. I don't expect anything of the Other. Nothing is agreed in advance, it is not a transaction (1993: 56) and it even does not have a purpose (1993: 54) because we don't expect retribution. It is a moral impulse and not a moral rule in the sense that it presupposes an universality: 'I suggest that morality is endemically and irredeemably *non-rational* – in the sense of not being calculable, hence not being presentable as following impersonal rules, hence not being describable as following rules that are in principle universalizable' (1993: 60). The moral impulse is a responsibility towards the Other. Not a rule but indeed an impulse; it is there before I think, before I am even aware of it. It happens in the face of the Other. This responsibility is proximity. Not in the sense of spatiality physical or social but as the suppression of distance in an immediacy of forgetting reciprocity, or, borrowing a term from Blanchot; an attention (1993: 87). It is in short a 'state of permanent attention come what may' (1993: 88). It is proximity because it does not merge, it does not swallow, absorb or identify; it stays near.

The moral impulse does not mean it is all love and understanding. Although it is a form of love it is mainly characterized by uncertainty: I am never sure I am doing the right thing. The moral impulse is a moral anxiety because I act before knowing, before thinking even; it is an urge to do (1993: 80). This means that the moral impulse involves an aporia. The anxiety of proximity, the stretching of not transgressing the attention into incorporation makes responsibility almost unendurable and the urge to escape is gigantic (1993: 89). It becomes very difficult to deal with the ambivalence of morality. The ambivalence of being myself insofar as I am directed to the Other, of being in attention and not interfering.

Rational ethics

For Bauman it is from the moral impulse that we act and we create society: 'We are not moral thanks to society (we are only ethical or law-abiding thanks to it); we live in society, we *are* society, thanks to being moral' (1993: 61, emphasis in original). The difference between morality and ethics is at the core of Bauman's critique of Hobbes and Enlightenment philosophy. According to Bauman the Enlightenment project was directed to suppress the moral urge, or better to create distance. Enlightenment philosophers sought after a way to ground existence on reason. Morality's ambiguity was something that they could not accept. So they searched for a rational law to explain morality. Therefore the code had to be universal. This they found in an ethics for the Other. Doing good is something one does to others; it brings benefits. It justifies itself as a rational choice. As a choice then, the nature of humanity is to be egoistic. Only by surpassing our natural state, by exerting our reasonable faculties, we chose to be good. This is in Bauman's eyes the reason why Hobbes starts with a war of all against all. In this process, ethics reserves a great role to the state as educator and disciplinary force, and as a result the ethical code became an instrument of social domination (1993: 28). From the perspective of a rational order, morality is in essence dangerous because of its irrational character:

> For every social totality bent on uniformity and the soliciting of the disciplined, co-ordinated action, the stubborn and resilient autonomy of the moral self is a scandal. From the control deck it is viewed as the germ of chaos and anarchy inside order; as the outer limit of what reason can do to design and implement. . . . [Moral impulses] have to be, therefore, tamed, harnessed, and exploited, rather than merely suppressed or outlawed. (1993: 13)

The theorists of civil society changed everything into reason and rational laws. Therefore they made ethical codes take the place of morality. By so doing we lost sight of our moral impulse and solved the ambivalence and apprehension of it with universal rules that create distance between self and Other. From now on I have to think before I act and proximity becomes a contract. In postmodern society there is a crisis in the rules or metanarratives, the rational arguments become entangled in themselves. It seems then that the resulting crisis in ethics is also a moral downfall. But Bauman advocates the opposite: a rebirth of morality without ethical rules. He wants to bring proximity to the fore. This means that morality becomes a contextual matter. Morality is not universal in the sense that it provides universal maxims. As we saw above, morality for Bauman is pre-rational; an impulse before we think of it. This means that we cannot say much about it. It just happens. Once I start to think about it I inevitably fall into a consciousness trap that makes me universalize the impulse and from thereon make rules. Bauman emphasizes the aporetic and ambivalent character of the moral impulse. It is ambivalent because I never know beforehand how I will react and every time I think about it I create a distance. Moreover, the moral impulse does not mean we are all good. It is not a mechanical impulse in the sense that every time I encounter the Other there is proximity. Even more it isn't even clear that I understand the Other. My actions can cause harm; can go against the interest of the Other. I can cause evil. So what does it mean to live from morality but not from ethics? It means 'life in fragments' (Bauman, 1995) or living in the contextuality of the ambivalence. We will return to this later on.

Bureaucracy

Rational laws and ethical codes organize modern society. As argued above, Hobbes' problem of order opens the ground for rational institutions. In Bauman's view institutions suppress the moral urge. They divert attention from the Other to the rules of institutions by underlining the technical goal of the institution. We engage with planning of institutions, the business at hand, and not with the Other. In his most famous book: *Modernity and the Holocaust* (1989) he analyses the holocaust from a sociological perspective and develops the thesis that the holocaust was carried out by perfectly ethical people. This is due to the bureaucratic organization of Nazi Germany. The book is not so much a study of Nazism as a research into bureaucracy in action, or better, into bureaucratic mentality. Bureaucracy demands commitment of bureaucrats, who are asked to obey orders at all times. Questions about order are not posed because the bureaucrat is continually engaged in solving technical problems. Obedience is guaranteed because of a hierarchy based on means rationality. Bureaucracy is there to solve technical problems in an efficient manner.

> Bureaucracy is programmed to seek the optimal solution. It is programmed to measure the optimum in such terms as would not distinguish between one human object and another, or between human and inhuman objects. What matters is the efficiency and lowering of cost of their processing. (1989: 104)

This it does by dissociating business from any goal-rationality, which is divorced from any moral evaluation of ends. These are considered outside the scope of bureaucracy. This separation is possible because of two parallel processes: a meticulous functional division of labour and a substitution of a moral for a technical responsibility. Each bureaucrat deals only with a small portion of the business and usually does not have full knowledge of the effects of their work. The bureaucrat is devoted to one assigned fragment. This can be done because the work is abstracted into statistics and measures, into numbers and graphs. The targets are numbers detached from reality. Bureaucrats work from a distance to reality. Only in this way is an optimum of efficiency attained. The result is a moral indifference and a lack of moral responsibility. Bureaucrats are only responsible to their technique, to the statistics they deal with. The numbers only measure the progress of the task, they say nothing about the nature of the work. In this way 'the bureaucrat's own act becomes an end in itself. It can be judged only by its intrinsic criteria of propriety and success . . . To put it bluntly, the result is the irrelevance of moral standards for the technical success of the bureaucratic operation' (1989: 101).

Bureaucracy works by creating distance and by denaturing and dehumanizing the objects of their dealings. This is exactly what happened in Nazi Germany. As Bauman states in the beginning of his book: 'Modern civilization was not the Holocaust's *sufficient* condition; it was, however, most certainly its *necessary* condition. Without it, the Holocaust would be unthinkable. It was the rational world of modern civilization that made the Holocaust thinkable' (1989: 13, emphases in original). According to Bauman, Nazi bureaucrats planned and organized the Holocaust yet were sympathetic to Jews they personally knew. They never made the connection. They were only dealing with abstract concepts, solving small technical problems. It is in this sense that bureaucracy is the result of a Promethean view that makes an abstract world of technical domination where everything is manageable regardless of the intrinsic value of things. Bureaucrats suppress their moral responsibility in order to attain efficiency. Bauman shows the danger of the Promethean view and he argues strongly against Hobbes solution for the problem of order. Technique and institutions create distance between people and a subsequent dehumanization and lack of moral responsibility. They create moral indifference or, in other words, they negate the presence of the Other. And this goes as far as the Holocaust.

The stranger

These disturbing thoughts point towards a fundamental critique of our civilization. Institutions numb our moral impulses and dehumanize us. They make us forget ourselves in order to rely solely on rules and obedience to laws and management experts. But is Enlightenment to be blamed for creating a disciplinary society? Not at all. Bauman is not so naive as to say that man is good and institutions make them evil. There is no evil strategy of submission and discipline in Bauman's thought. Bureaucracy does not lead inevitably to the Holocaust. It is a necessary condition, but by no means a sufficient condition. How is it possible then that we become moral indifferent and we forget about our moral responsibility towards the Other? How is it possible we become calculating Prometheans? This is because of the ambivalent and aporetic nature of morality.

The main problem of morality is the existence of the third. Society does not consist of moral parties of two. There always is a third involved. This third has no voice but is there. My actions have consequences for a third and then my moral impulse is baffled, confused, lost. The third introduces distance, is distance as opposed to the proximity of the Other. I cannot stay in the moral party of two because this moral realm has outgrown itself into the stranger. The one is left behind but always there. It is because of the third that we enter the realm of justice and social order and that we leave the realm of morality. Because the third is always a disinterested party it introduces objectivity. The moral party, my relation to the Other, my responsibility is now seen as a group: a totality that is greater than the sum of its parts. 'Thus simultaneously, the selves become comparable, measurable, amenable to be judged by extra personal, 'statistical average' or normative standards – and the third is firmly placed in the position of the judge, umpire, he-who-passes-the-verdict' (1993: 114). The passion of morality now gives way to reason; we have to take into account the consequences towards a group, towards the Many. Now the Other is not a face anymore but a mask. I don't know who the Other is and anxiety takes charge because I live in the uncertainty of not knowing who the Other is, in the ambivalence of trust and distrust. In front of the Many, in society, we need guidance in order to cope with the faceless others, with the stranger or the third. We therefore need rules. Only by organizing the world we can live amongst strangers. In the end we create ethics and we live at a distance to the Other. We manage society.

Societas and communitas

What Bauman introduces here is the impossibility of living in an impulse, in a passion. In society we live not only with trusted and beloved ones, but also with passers-by. We therefore need structures and rules. So we have a new ambivalence in the coexistence of two separate domains. Borrowing from Victor Turner (1969) he makes a modification of Tönnies' famous dichotomy of *Gesellschaft* and *Gemeinschaft*, and proposes two models of interrelatedness: *societas* and *communitas*. The first being a structured, differentiated, hierarchical system characterized by heterogeneity, inequality, status and economic position, while the latter is unstructured, undifferentiated, homogenous, characterized by equality and absence of status. Against Tönnies' ideas these two types are not a historical succession and definitely not exclusive but they alternate and interpenetrate each other, Bauman argues:

> The condition of *communitas* is dissipation or suspension or temporary cancellation of the structural arrangements which sustain at 'normal times' the life of *societas*. . . . In other words, *communitas* melts what *societas* tries hard to cast and forge. Alternatively *societas* moulds and shapes and solidifies what inside *communitas* is liquid and lacks form. (1993: 117, emphases in original)

These two modes should be seen, according to Bauman, as processes of *socialization* and *sociality*. 'Socialization aims at creating an environment of action made of choices amenable to be 'redeemed discursively', which boils down to the rational calculation of gains and losses. Sociality puts uniqueness above regularity and the sublime above the rational' (1993: 119). Sociality is the domain of moral impulses and proximity. Socialization is the replacement of morality by discursive rules; it is the domain of management while morality is a matter of spontaneity. It is important to remember that both these processes coexist, we constantly change from the one into the other. It is because of these two modes that morality is replaced by ethics and that our society is organized. Bauman's point is not that the Promethean mentality should be abolished and that institutions are evil by nature, but that there always is a realm of proximity and spontaneity that counterbalances the organized world. It is Bauman's firm belief that morality is in the end the thriving force of humanity. It is in the moral responsibility that we find meaning for our lives. Management, though needed, should take into account that there is community and sociality. Prometheus will never have the last word and Hobbes was wrong with his war of all against all. If this nevertheless happens, the conditions for a Holocaust are given. Bauman advocates a moral space where we can live in the proximity of the Other, that is, switching from organization to interaction and living according to one's private morality (which is essentially social in nature: it is directed to the Other). In a sense Bauman's morality is a reminder that whatever we socially achieve, we remain human in communion with others and we should never be seduced by the distance that organizations offer. It is an appeal to remain in the microclimate of the face-to-face encounter and not to be blinded by the status of efficient business and abstract numbers. In this sense his appeal for morality is a very strong critique of the very justification of organizations.

In praise of bureaucracy

Bauman's work has had a great influence in organization theory. His advocacy of ambiguity, ambivalence, uncertainty, the aporetic nature of morality and the lack of a universal and rational foundation for morality, in detriment of clear ethical rules, gave a strong impulse on thinking about ethics in postmodern society. The disturbing thought that bureaucracy dehumanizes by creating distance and defacing the Other has of course met some considerable criticism. Bauman comes very close to a romantic and simplistic view of organization being evil and man being essentially good as long as he stays in the proximity of the Other. It comes very close to a romanticism of emotions, impulses, spontaneity and passions versus the distance of reason and calculated behaviour (see, for example, ten Bos and Willmott, 2001).

A serious critique is offered by Paul du Gay's book *In Praise of Bureaucracy* (2000). Du Gay stretches the importance of bureaucracy for representative democracy by re-reading Weber. He focuses on two points. The first is that bureaucracy is a specific ethical domain in its own right and the second is the specific competence of the bureau *vis-à-vis* entrepreneurs.

Du Gay notes that bureaucracy was originally envisaged in order to prevent public administrators from following their own agendas. Bureaucracy is the most powerful weapon against the partialities of patronage and the dangers of corruption. It is because bureaucrats are devoted to their bureaucratic rules of formal treatment that social equality is achieved. The bureaucratic rule of depersonalizing matters is in effect a moral value that makes social justice and proper administration possible. For Weber it was perfectly clear that bureaucracy should be differentiated from politics. It is politicians that make decisions about the direction of government, and bureaucrats only realize these decisions. It is politicians who are accountable by being elected and representing people. The bureaucrat should stick to the rules. If these two intermingle then democracy is jeopardized. Nazi Germany politicized bureaucracy, according to du Gay, is asking the bureaucrats to be loyal to the party above their administrative duties. Bauman does not seem to realize the moral value of bureaucracy:

> Bauman's concern with the 'whole person' registers his inability to come to terms with the plural, differentiated nature of personhood in modern societies. For . . . the highly specialized spheres of life characteristic of modern societies involve an abstraction from and indeed, indifference to, multiple aspects of the lives of concrete individuals. Thankfully, we do not depend upon the personal moral propensities of our postmen and women to ensure that our mail is delivered, but rather on . . . a set of abstract 'membership rules' that link wage remuneration with a codified set of professional obligations. (du Gay, 2000: 56–57)

Bureaucracy must not only be distinguished from politics but also from entrepreneurship. Bureaucrats are directed to the public good and should be conscious of their duty to democracy. Entrepreneurs can take risks by compensating their losses when cutting a good deal afterwards. If Bureaucrats act as entrepreneurs and the public is treated as customers then the realm of making profits and the realm of justly distributing wealth melt together with dangerous consequences for society.

This is not the place to go deeper into du Gay's thinking (but see Kaulingfreks and ten Bos, 2005). Here, it suffices to say that he has a strong point. We need bureaucracy in order to have a just society. The question is whether or not Bauman would disagree with this praise. To a certain extent he would not. As said, he realizes that we cannot live on the moral impulse alone. There is *societas* and *communitas* and they alternate constantly. We are ambivalent towards bureaucracy but that's precisely Bauman's point: the fundamental ambivalence and disturbing nature of morality. There is always a stranger we have to take into account.

Misanthropy

Du Gay's critique is not entirely beside the point. Bauman realizes the need for an organization and management of society but his emphasis is on the moral responsibility of proximity and the moral indifference caused by organizations. As long as we are in the process of sociality and away from socialisation we are in a state of morality or in other words we are doing good, no matter how confused we can be. There is very little, if at all, of possible feelings of hate in Bauman's proximity. In the face of the Other I am instinctively directed to the Other, and do good. Of course I never know if I do really good, but that's not the point here. The point is the absence of the possibility of hate or *dégoût* as for instance, was put forward by Camus. In *L'etranger* (1942) he describes the passionate hate for somebody and the consequent murder at the moment the sun reflected on the knife. French existentialists considered the Other as opposed to the I. Being face to face to the Other arouses hate or nausea. Sartre's idea that 'hell is other people' epitomizes this idea.

Being with the Other does not always imply an opening but it may as well arouse the opposite. A violent impulse – as pre rational as Bauman's moral impulse – of *dégoût* of sickening. Misanthropy is an existing impulse or passion. Besides Camus, Celine or Genet show very convincingly the existence and influence of this impulse. It is the same impulse that in Sartre (1938/1990) leads to a nausea about the whole of existence: just being fed up with everything and everybody. French existentialist thinking calls on us to not deny this feeling and even to act accordingly.

I'm not saying that one should be a misanthrope. I am just pointing to the existence of this impulse. It is, among others, from the dangers of misanthropy that ethical rules come to the fore. Bauman does not say anything about misanthropy or nausea. But then the world according to Bauman is not absurd at all – as long as we are in the moral party of two, that is. Misanthropy, so it seems, would in Bauman's eyes come from the distance between people. It is very unclear if this distance is related to organizations or that it just exist as a human impulse. He only talks about the moral indifference caused by organizations.

What I am trying to point out here is not an anthropological discussion but to stretch the ambiguity of morality even further than Bauman. One could argue that precisely because of the ambiguity and aporetic nature of morality organizations are needed. That we are always placed in the in-between of a moral impulse and sociability. Bureaucracy represses our morality but it also makes our democratic society possible. We dislike the impersonality and 'red tape' mentality in our civil servants; we even consider it unethical to transform real people into cases and to denature people. But, as du Gay notes 'The citizen who scoffs at the elaborate record keeping undertaken by government offices might as well be equally annoyed should an official lose track of her affairs through relying on memory and telephone conversations' (2000: 1). In the end we all want the trains to be on time. The point is not whether Bauman or du Gay are right. They both are right. We are constantly thrown between our rational world and the empathy of morality. This ambiguity makes our lives. Some people we relate and we feel responsible for, others we dislike. It is thanks to rational order that we cope with the people we dislike and also that there will be distance with the people we relate to.

Aesthetics

In this sense Bauman's morality is much closer to aesthetics than he is prepared to accept. His whole enterprise is directed to rescue morality from those critics that proclaim the substitution of aesthetics for ethics (see Bauman, 1993: 2). And he even considers aesthetics as the space wherein one is just an unrelated spectator in control of life, in other words aesthetics is another form of creating distance and not relating to others (Bauman, 1993: 168–169). Aesthetics, as the realm of empathy, of forms of knowledge and relationship outside strict intellectual rationality, deals with exactly the same questions Bauman is trying to answer with the aid of morality. What happens when I like or dislike something? How do I relate to objects?

True, aesthetics deals primarily with objects or nature and not with people. But there is no reason not to apply aesthetic principles to our social world. Consider, for instance, Walter Benjamin's famous thesis on the work of art in the age of mechanical reproduction (Benjamin, 1968: 217–251). Because of reproduction techniques the value of a work of art has changed from the use or cult value of a work to their exchange or exhibition value. This is because the work of art has lost its aura, which is its value as a unique object, as something to be venerated because it has some intrinsic power. Benjamin defines the aura as: 'the unique phenomenon of a distance, however close it may be. If while resting on a summer afternoon, you follow with your eyes a mountain range on the horizon or a branch which casts its shadow over you, you experience the aura of those mountains, of that branch' (1968: 222–223). In a footnote he explains that it is distance because of inapproachability, while in closeness we enforce our self to it, or we use it, we integrate it in our daily exchange. This explanation is remarkably similar to Bauman's explanation of proximity:

> Proximity is neither a distance bridged, nor a distance demanding to be bridged; not a preambula to identification and merger, which can, in practice, only be an act of swallowing and absorption. Proximity is satisfied with being what it is – proximity. (Bauman, 1993: 88)

Although both thinkers use very different concepts, they share the preoccupation of leaving the object or the Other in their autonomy and colonizing them by our influence. It is this relation of farness or autonomy which is at the core of the aesthetic experience and that is defined by Heidegger as the truth of art. The work of art being a thing sets up a world (Heidegger, 1978a: 170) it does not integrate into our sphere of influence, it cannot be used to our purposes, we cannot do anything with it. In so doing it opens up a space wherein we just see the work. The work makes a world and does not integrate into our world. Our reaction is then one of a shock, or as Vattimo explains:

> Whilst single things belong to the word insofar as they are inserted in a referential totality of significance, the world as such and as a whole does not refer and thus has no significance. Anxiety is a mark of this insignificance, the utter gratuitousness of the fact that world is. The experience of anxiety is an experience of 'uncanniness'. (Vattimo, 1992: 50)

We encounter a work of art, a thing, we cannot put into place except as a work of art. We feel related to it but cannot grasp it. The result is a shock or uncanniness or anxiety, which is also ambivalence and ambiguity: we do not know how to react. Here we experience a space, an opening, something we cannot understand or deal with. We are confronted with strangeness but a related-strangeness because it reveals something essential about ourselves. It shows my condition: who I am, and by this alone I change. In a sense I come under the influence of the work. This openness is what Heidegger calls truth. The truth of art (or to say it technically: the setting-to-work of truth) is in this respect a moral happening. It changes us but it changes us in ambiguity and even uncanniness. At the same time it is a relation of proximity in the above-mentioned meaning: near and far, or, as Benjamin puts it, farness in closeness. We cannot say anything about what the work will do to us, but it will do something. As Gadamer explained, it is impossible not be seized by the work, like spectators of a tennis match cricking their necks (Gadamer, 1986: 24).

Aesthetics is not about pleasure and amusement but has profound implications for the way we deal with the world and with objects and people. Aesthetics is profoundly moral and comes very near Bauman's moral impulse but modifies it into the ambiguity of uncanniness. Even more, aesthetics sets a place where ambiguity and uncanniness are constitutive of ourselves and of our world. Aesthetics opens up a relation with things or people who can (even at the same time) be of joy and proximity as well as sickening and repulsive. We cannot say that a work of art is good or bad. It is always both, and even our reaction towards one and the same work can change. But we always will react. We learn form the aesthetic experience that the world is unsettling and not at all predefined, that everything is ambiguous, even the Other.

Conclusion

An aesthetic approach to morality, contrary to Bauman's position, underlines the ambiguity of morality. It does not attack Bauman but corrects what ten Bos and Willmott (2001) call a humanistic tendency, that is that for Bauman the moral party of two is always good. That misanthropy does not exist there. An aesthetic approach reveals a fundamental ambiguity at the heart of reality. That the Other is ambiguous as well and that we live in uncanniness, the world is unsettling. In this respect aesthetics shows an attitude very different from Hobbes' problem of order. It calls for a way of living in the uncertainty of not being the centre of the universe. It shows us that Prometheus is not the only way of dealing with the world and technology.

Still, Bauman's work is a very strong invitation to start thinking about the moral value of organizations, that is, about the moral value of the organizational order. The need to have everything structured in a planned way, to have the world subsumed to rational institutions. Bauman reminds us that behind the organized world there must be a morality of belonging, a pre-rational moral impulse of being with the Other. It is this morality that is a strong counterforce to the hubris of planning.

References

Bauman, Z. (1989) *Modernity and the Holocaust*. Cambridge: Polity
Bauman, Z. (1993) *Postmodern Ethics*. Oxford: Blackwell
Bauman, Z. (1995) *Life in Fragments*. Oxford: Blackwell
Benjamin, W. (1968) 'The work of art in the age of mechanical reproduction' in H. Arendt (ed.) *Illuminations*, trans. H. Zohn. New York: Schocken
Camus, A. (1942) *L'etranger*. Paris: Gallimard.
du Gay, P. (2000) *In Praise of Bureaucracy*. London: Sage
Gadamer, H. G. (1986) *The Relevance of the Beautiful and Other Essays*, ed. R. Bernasconi. Cambridge: Cambridge University Press.
Gehmann, U. (2003) 'Prometheus' *ephemera: theory and politics in organization*, 3(2): 95–114.
Heidegger, M. (1955) *Was ist Metaphysik?* Frankfurt: Klostermann
Heidegger, M. (1972) *What is Called Thinking?* trans. J. Gray and F. Wieck. New York: Harper & Row.
Heidegger, M. (1977) *The Question Concerning Technology and Other Essays*, trans. W. Lovitt. New York: Harper & Row.
Heidegger, M. (1978a) 'The origin of the work of art' in D. F. Krell (ed.) *Basic Writings*. London: Routledge.
Heidegger, M. (1978b) 'What calls for thinking?' in D. F. Krell (ed.) *Basic Writings*. London: Routledge.

Heidegger, M. (1978c) 'What is metaphysics?' in D. F. Krell (ed.) *Basic Writings*. London: Routledge.

Hobbes, T. (1651/1985) *Leviathan*. London: Penguin.

Kaulingfreks, R. and R. ten Bos (2005) 'In praise of blowjobs' in J. Brewis, S. Linstead, D. Boje and T. O'Shea (eds.) *The Passion of Organizing*. Oslo: Abstrakt.

Levinas, E. (1969) *Totality and Infinity*, trans. A. Lingis. Pittsburgh: Duquesne University Press.

Locke, J. (1690/1966) *Two Treatises on Government*. New York: Cambridge University Press.

Parsons, T. (1949) *The Structure of Social Action*. Glencoe, ILL: The Free Press.

Rousseau, J.-J. (1762/1968) *The Social Contract*, trans. M. Cranston. London: Penguin.

Sartre, J.-P. (1938/1990) *Nausea*, trans. Robert Baldick. London: Penguin.

ten Bos, R. (1997) 'Business ethics and Bauman ethics' *Organization Studies*, 18(6): 997–1014.

ten Bos, R. (2003) *Rationele Engelen, moraliteit en management*. Amsterdam: Boom.

ten Bos, R. and H. Willmott (2001) 'Towards a post-dualistic business ethics: Interweaving reason and emotion in working life' *Journal of Management Studies*, 38(6): 769–793.

Turner, V. (1969) *The Ritual Process: Structure and Anti-Structure*. London: Routledge.

Vattimo, G. (1992) *The Transparent Society*, trans. D. Webb. Cambridge: Polity.

Weber, M. (1978) *Economy and Society: An Outline of Interpretive Sociology*, ed. G. Roth and C. Wittich. Berkeley: University of California Press.

Gibson Burrell: Diabolical architect

Philip Hancock and Melissa Tyler

Introduction

Gibson Burrell's reputation as a heterodox and iconoclastic thinker, combined with his talent for making incisive and timely interventions into the intellectual arena, has made him a significant figure in the field of contemporary organization theory. Indeed, it is probably not unfair to claim that at least several of the authors within this particular collection have, in one way or another, benefited from the relative openness that characterizes the field today; an openness which undeniably owes much to his efforts over the years.

In a series of assorted publications he has consistently contributed to the act of remembering that organization theory remains an essentially social scientific undertaking and, as such, its practitioners should not distance themselves from those philosophical questions and debates (see, for example, Burrell, 1989) that define the vibrancy and continued relevance of the social scientific endeavour. As a founding editor of the international journal *Organization*, he has also played a vital role in ensuring the accessibility and relevance of the kind of inter (or indeed neo) disciplinary work he champions.

More than this, however, from his early collaborative work with Gareth Morgan, through a series of seminal articles introducing the 'idea of the post-modern' (Bertens, 1995) to organization theory, to his most recent writings on the significance of organized spaces, what appears to drive Burrell is a desire to build alternative ways of thinking about and doing organization. Deeply influenced by the radical, post-Enlightenment writings of figures as diverse (yet in many ways closely related) as Adorno, Marcuse, Foucault and Derrida, as well as the more commonly acknowledged triumvirate of Marx, Weber and Durkheim, Burrell always recognizes the historical and economic situatedness of organization both as a practice and an ideology, and its role in the propagation of what he considers to be the essentially coercive rationality of modernity's 'impure reason' (McCarthy, 1990).

Thus, while his tendencies may be postmodern for some, his influences are also those of a far more established and more ambivalent critical tradition, especially in relation to the question of rationality, organization and modernity. Certainly, one element that has remained relatively constant within Burrell's work has been a commitment not only to iconoclasm but also to the exposure of the machinations of the dominant organizational order and its abuses of power and command. A commitment that is born from a belief in the power and necessity of permanent opposition, but which strives to stand firm against the debilitating consequences of the pessimism such an endeavour can so often engender (WOBS, 2000; Burrell, 2001).

Integral to this intellectual and political project (though such a distinction, in the notable tradition of critical social theory, makes little sense when referring to Burrell's work) has been a desire not only to expose but also to valorize the negative dialectic of rationality and irrationality, permanence and flux, and order and disorder that characterizes the very fabric of organizational life. Further-more, it is this very same dialectic that also constitutes perhaps one of the most interesting features of Burrell's writing; his simultaneous desire to embrace the radical opportunities offered by an acceptance of disorder and disorganization while at the same time invoking these as the principles upon which we believe – despite Burrell's (2001) own protestations to the contrary – an emancipatory body of organization theory might (albeit temporarily) be established.

While Burrell's published output has been relatively slim, due to the limita-tions of space we still do not attempt an exhaustive commentary on every aspect of his work. Nevertheless, we have sought to present what we consider to be the main themes that have inhabited his thinking over the past three decades. Com-mencing with a review of his collaborative work with Gareth Morgan and his solo promotion of the idea of a radical organization theory, we then explore Burrell's contribution to the popularization of postmodernism. Our attentions are then turned to the themes of sexuality and pleasure which appeared in a number of his writings around the same time, themes which found perhaps their fullest expression in his only sole-authored book to date, *Pandemonium*, which then becomes the primary object of our considerations. Finally, future direc-tions in his work are anticipated, in particular his ongoing fascination with the aesthetics and architecture of organizational spaces.

Four equally sized rooms

It is now over twenty years since Burrell co-authored with Gareth Morgan what remains the highly influential *Sociological Paradigms and Organizational Analy-sis* (1979). Drawing rather loosely on Thomas Kuhn's (1962) paradigmatic con-ception of science, the most immediate idea offered by the authors was that it is possible to divide sociological and thus organizational theory into four dis-tinct paradigms – that is, ways of conceptualizing and knowing organizational forms – each one incommensurable with the others.

Each paradigm is described by the authors as offering a series of shared philosophical – ontological, epistemological and normative – assumptions, each one underpinning 'the frame of reference, mode of theorising and *modus operandi* of the social theorists who operate within them' (Burrell and Morgan,

1979: 23, emphasis in original). The concept of incommensurability further suggested however, that each paradigm must be understood as representing a distinctive worldview in relation to any of the others. Thus, researchers deemed to be working in one paradigm may not even be aware of the existence of work being undertaken in any of the alternatives and even if they were, it would take a conversion of major proportions to enable constructive (rather than colonizing) communication to take place between them. Thus, as Carter and Jackson (1991: 115) observe, while the Kuhnian ideal of the relationship between paradigms is ultimately a divergent one, this is not the case for Burrell and Morgan.

On one level, what was important to this endeavour was a desire on the part of the authors to encourage those partaking in research into organizational life to acknowledge and face the philosophical implications of their chosen research strategies rather than simply accept them as some universal, *a priori* set of immutable givens. Yet while few disputed the idea that organizational researchers should be aware of the often unspoken philosophical assumptions that underpinned their work, as Burrell (1999) himself has subsequently acknowledged, the book did draw significant critical attention to the implications embedded within the proposition that the complexities of social theory could somehow be reduced to the form of a 2x2 matrix and, perhaps even more disturbing, that a state of incommensurability could be said to exist between each compartment within it.

Leaving to one side more conservative defences of the innate superiority of the functionalist paradigm such as that made by Donaldson (1985), the main front of this assault came from those who, while broadly sympathetic to the efforts Burrell and Morgan had made to reintegrate philosophy and social theory into the field, shunned their incommensurability thesis as both conservative and potentially divisive. Thus, notable fellow theorists such as Clegg (1982), Reed (1985) and Hassard (1993) all expressed a marked unease with any framework apparently designed to restrict rather than encourage what they considered to be the necessity of greater pluralism within organization theory.

As Burrell both then and subsequently (1999) has argued, however, the principle underlying the recognition of such incommensurability was not one grounded in a belief in an already existent level playing field as perhaps inferred by his critics, but rather in a realization that the ongoing dominance of the functionalist paradigm operated as an obstacle to the emergence of alternative strategies of organizational analysis. Incommensurability was thus as much a political declaration as it was a philosophical one – aimed at the reclamation of a conceptual and indeed institutional space within which critical organizational research could operate free of the potential tyranny of dialogue with more powerful voices of opposition (Burrell, 2001).

Nevertheless, despite such political aims and the later declaration by Morgan that the selection of the term 'paradigm' was probably an error of judgment (Morgan, cited in Mills, 2001: 3), this does not entirely mitigate against the very real philosophical problems such a schema raises for those approaches which, in a way that is integral to their very radicalism, deliberately seek to overcome the kinds of dualistic thinking that such a paradigm model appears to sustain. As Willmott (1990) observed in this respect, self-professedly radical social theories such as Berger and Luckmann's social constructionism (1967) approach, or Giddens' structuration theory (1986) would both fall foul of such a restriction on the dialectic of subject and object which constitutes Burrell and Morgan's vertical axis. As such, from this perspective, such incommensurability actually runs the risk of undermining the very critical or emancipatory project its authors seemingly wished to propagate.

As to whether one is able to adjudicate on the ultimate value of *Sociological Paradigms*, particularly as a radical contribution to the field remains, nevertheless, a vexed question. Certainly Burrell himself displays a somewhat ambivalent attitude towards the legacy of this particular work. On the one hand he is openly prepared to defend the likes of Jackson and Carter (1993) whose appeal to the protective embrace of incommensurability is one which perhaps continues to resonate with those eager to take an unorthodox or critical stance in their work. On the other hand, he is clearly conscious of the limitations such a framework places on the valency of critical thought, aware that it is perhaps now time that he left 'the four equally sized rooms he has been stalking' (Burrell, 1997: 25) and embrace an altogether more open-plan intellectual habitat.

In praise of armchair theory

Whatever conclusions one is tempted to draw about *Sociological Paradigms*, it provided a launching pad for Burrell's academic reputation. Nor did its relative success detract from his continuing to pursue what was an essentially Marxian agenda in relation to the role and functioning of organizations within a capitalist environment. A prime example of this stage in Burrell's thinking is reflected not only in Chapter 11 of *Sociological Paradigms*, but somewhat more explicitly in his 1979 essay, 'Radical Organization Theory'.

Central to this period of Burrell's work, and to this essay in particular, was the proposition that if a radicalized organization theory were to represent an effective bulwark against the erosive tide of functionalist orthodoxy within the field, it must seek to move beyond its mere critical negation and endeavour to construct a 'genuine alternative' (Burrell, 1979: 91) able to generate real insights into the ways in which contemporary organizations serve to maintain and propagate the repressive totality of capitalist socio-economic relations. 'Alternative' should not be taken to mean a search for alternative modes of organizing, therefore, but rather the pursuit of a coherent theory of organization specifically directed at enhancing our understanding of its historical specificity and the role it plays in sustaining asymmetrical socio-cultural and economic relations.

One important dimension of such a theory for Burrell is that it should seek to withdraw from those philosophies of science which, by virtue of their epistemological commitment to a representational theory of knowledge and the largely empirical methodology that arises from this, can achieve little more than the reproduction of those common-sense observations about the world which in fact provide an ideological blockade against the very notion that things could be other than they seem. In doing so, however, Burrell made what in hindsight might appear to have been something of an uncharacteristic appeal to the tradition of 'transcendental', or as it has more commonly come to be termed 'critical' realism (see Bhaskar *et al.* 1998; Ackroyd and Fleetwood, 2000). For despite its unequivocal dualistic commitment to an external and intransitive reality, external to the perceiving subject, Burrell considered its capacity to accommodate the practice of abstract theorizing as a legitimate epistemological pursuit as an important ally in any radical alternative to the empirically dominated functionalism of traditional organization theory.

Abstract or 'armchair' (Burrell, 1979: 96) theorizing, protected by paradigmatic closure, thus became for Burrell the basis of a possible radical organization theory, one capable of engaging critically with the practices and processes of organization. Of course how literally we should continue to take Burrell's claim that organization theory should entirely abandon its empirical dimension remains open to question and very much depends on how one tends to define the empirical. Indeed, as Stablein (1999: 255) notes, the study of organizations:

> is necessarily an empirical study, exploring attitudes, behaviours, experiences, artefacts, symbols, documents, texts, feelings, beliefs, meanings, measures, facts and figures. Even the armchair/conceptual theorist must muse on empirical data.

Perhaps then, the question is not so much that of empirical material itself, which is in effect necessary for us to make even the most basic judgments about the world in which we live, but rather the epistemic, and arguably ethical primacy that empiricism has acquired within the field of organization theory as well as a rejection of its logocentrism, and the ideology of disinterested neutrality that underpins its claims to methodological coherence.

Like a (post) postmodern man

Considering Burrell's public rejection of empiricism and the importance he placed on the need to construct a radical approach to organization theory that paid close attention to theoretical and philosophical developments within the social sciences more generally, his subsequent identification with the popularization of postmodernism within the field should come as no surprise. Still one of the most cited articles within organization theory, 'Modernism, Postmodernism and Organizational Analysis: An Introduction', published in 1988 and co-authored with Robert Cooper (see Spoelstra, in this volume), introduced postmodernism to its widest organization theory audience yet, and still remains a touchstone for organizational scholars adopting the language and ideas associated with it. The first of several planned articles, it established a close relationship between postmodern discourse and the pursuit of an anti-systemic approach to organization theory which diametrically opposed itself to the performative rationality of capitalist organization.

Perhaps most influentially, the article established a series of conceptual distinctions, firstly between what the authors termed systemic and critical modernism, and then between the latter of these and postmodernism. The first distinction perhaps reflected Burrell's recognition of the critical capacity already embedded within the modernist idealization of emancipation through reason, though it was clear that he was now coming to adhere to an altogether more sceptical view of whether or not such an ideal could still be realized within the confines established by the systemic hegemony. Thus, in contrast to the critical modernism of, say, Habermas, Burrell starts to place perhaps greater faith in the potential of postmodern thought, with its emphasis on the acceptance of disorder and indeterminacy, not only as a means of recognizing the artificiality of modernist discourses on the essential qualities of organization but also as an intellectual means of destabilizing their continued socio-cultural legitimacy.

Drawing on the ideas of Foucault and Derrida in particular, Cooper and Burrell's opening paper is notable in that it posits a clearly radical agenda for a postmodern organization theory; one that establishes at its core a critique of the formalizing tendencies of modern organization (and organization theory) which correspondingly results in a suppression or marginalization of the informal, spontaneous and everyday life of organizations. Furthermore, in recognizing the fundamentally constitutive nature of organization as a process of formalization, Cooper and Burrell bring the very ontology of organization radically into question:

> we need to see organization as a *process* that occurs within the wider 'body' of society and which is concerned with the construction of objects of theoretical knowledge . . . It becomes a question of analysing, let us say, *the production of organization rather than the organization of production* (1988: 105–106, emphasis added).

Note, however, that despite the obviously sympathetic attention being made to the fragmented ontological claims of postmodernism, even here there remains an acknowledgement of the need to retain some notion of the totality, a theme that was also present within Burrell's earlier, more Marxian and indeed realist-inspired writings.

In the second article within the series, Burrell (1988) developed many of these ideas and themes into a study of the particular relevance of Michel Foucault to the radical theorization of organization. Itself 'organized' around a tripartite historical delineation of the archaeological, the genealogical and the ethical in his work, Burrell's article clearly locates Foucault within that critical discourse of modernity that has, correctly or not, come to be labelled postmodernist. And while some of Burrell's opening claims about Foucault's own epistemological disposition reflect his own confusions about the quality of the empirical and the nature of idealism identified in some of his earlier work, he does succeed in conveying the essentially 'iconoclastic' and as Burrell (1988: 222) puts it, 'suggestive' style of Foucault's concerns and writings.

As such, Foucault's recognition that organization must be understood not simply as a universal descriptor, reducing difference to sameness, but that at the same time realizing that there is an underlying dynamic of discipline that increasingly organizes all aspects of social life, offers for Burrell what appears to be a valuable contribution to a radical theory of organization. Rather than simply violating the experience of difference within some proto-positivistic classificatory framework, or conversely elevating the celebration of difference to such a degree that it blinds one to the underlying ubiquities of control and order, such an approach – shorn of the restrictions of the formal logic of modernity – is able to grasp the simultaneous coexistence of both realities.

What Burrell seems to find himself struggling with in particular in this article, however, is his apparent desire to continue to pursue the development of a politically potent critical theory of organization, and what he believes are the potential dangers posed to this by an overly enthusiastic reconciliation with the anti-epistemic character of Foucauldian thought. For as knowledge is itself performative in and through the realm of discourse, for Foucault any attempt to conceptualize and communicate fixed representations of organization merely serves to propagate its socio-cultural ubiquity and disciplinary efficaciousness. As Burrell himself cautions in this regard:

> It is important to know that the reality of organizations is that they reflect and reproduce a disciplinary society. But to talk about them, to develop discourses and classification schemes for their analysis actively contributes to the reproduction of this discipline. Reality, and our discourse about reality, are both ever more closely confining. (1988: 233)

In an attempt perhaps to address this postmodern paradox, Burrell's next and indeed final contribution to this series of articles engages albeit somewhat more critically with the work of Jürgen Habermas, perhaps the most prominent representative of what Cooper and Burrell termed critical modernism. As with the previous papers in this series, Burrell presents a balanced account of many of the key ideas associated with the work in question, yet unlike the previous articles he is far less sympathetic to the work he is considering (Burrell, 1994: 3). Habermas is thus portrayed, perhaps not all together unreasonably, as a thinker who is unable to recognize the possibility that the shifting cartography of contemporary society renders the basic principles of his vision of an emancipatory project if not obsolete, certainly in urgent need of rethinking.

Yet despite this, and other criticisms, Burrell is unable to entirely dismiss Habermas or the ideas he represents. Even his highly apposite observation that Habermas's tendency to shift between philosophical and social scientific propositions – see for example his discussion of the basis of 'knowledge-constitutive interests', or the transcendental presuppositions which underpin his account of the 'ideal speech situation' – often leads to claims that cannot be justified within the scope of either tradition is not sufficient to deter him entirely. As Burrell himself notes, in pursuing this project of reconciliation, Habermas is perhaps merely seeking to enter a territory 'where organization studies at some point, sooner or later, must go' (Burrell, 1994: 8), and one into which Burrell has himself already made several inroads.

Indeed, what is evident in much of this period of Burrell's work is a deep-seated ambivalence towards postmodern ideas, welcoming them only in so far as they may be able to contribute to the dethroning of mainstream (and thus predominantly systemically modernist) ideas about organization. On the subject of labour (Burrell, 1990) for example, while professing allegiance to a modernist production of meta-narratives which may be able to grasp the fragmentation of contemporary capitalist societies in their totality and the various modes of labour this has formed, Burrell also demands that such meta-narratives do not aspire to universalistic status. Thus the modernist meta-narrative is tempered by the postmodern recognition of its contingency and the caveat that better meta-narratives will be judged as such, 'not because they will be believed by all who hear them but because they excite, titillate and amuse small numbers of interested parties' (Burrell, 1990: 293).

Equally, when it comes to the relationship between time and its dominant conceptualization within organization and management studies (Burrell, 1992a), a similar story unfolds. While the unreflexive acceptance of a systemically modernist understanding of time as a linear and fundamentally progressive process is rejected, the need to grasp the problem of temporality in a critical and ultimately rational manner is not. Other possibilities exist, then, and these should be embraced in the search for a richer, if never final, understanding of the dynamics of organized existence.

Beyond the pleasure dome

Around the same period a more substantive, though still primarily theoretical, topic of interest for Burrell was that of the relationship between organization and sexuality. Evocative of both his pioneering predilections to take organization theory into uncharted territories and indicative of his ongoing attempts to create a disruptive critical theory of organization, what he called 'organization sexuality' – a 'frontier' of control and resistance (Burrell, 1984: 102) – allowed him to experiment with a synthesis of both Foucauldian post-structuralism and Marcusian Hegelian-Marxism in an attempt to elevate sexuality to a position of both theoretical and empirical significance.

Burrell's (1984) initial argument was that, far from being beyond (or beneath) the managerial gaze, management has been concerned since its inception with expunging manifestations of sexuality and the expenditure of energy on sexual rather than productive activities from the workplace. He suggested that following the advent of the industrial revolution, sexuality has been regarded as incompatible with organization; as disruptive of production processes and as a threat to accumulation imperatives. Accordingly, the suppression of sexuality, he argued, had always been a discernible managerial preoccupation; one integral to the rise of industrial capitalism.

In particular, the modernist organization of time and space were crucial for what Burrell (1984: 108) termed 'the desexualization of labour'. Invoking Elias's (1978) account of the civilizing process and also Foucault's (1977, 1979) concern with discipline, he emphasizes that processes of industrialization and urbanization both enabled and demanded the exercise of tighter disciplinary controls over the workforce. Hence, the modernist sexual sensibility came to be that 'sex had its place but not within the walls of the factory' (Burrell, 1984: 108).

Drawing promiscuously on Weber, Elias, Foucault and Marcuse amongst others, Burrell (1984, 1992b) conceptualized the organization of sexuality largely in terms of a gradual process of desexualization and 'a managerial effort to repress sexual relations and expel them from the organization into the 'home' (1992b: 70). Shaped by a combination of religious morality, bureaucratization and ever more sophisticated technologies of surveillance, the rationale for desexualization took several forms including medical advice given to employers based on a theory of equilibrium of bodily fluids; religious beliefs, and those social norms associated with the civilizing process as well as the discourse of (self) 'discipline' (Foucault, 1977).

Burrell's desexualization thesis was thus predicated on the contention that organization sexuality is the outcome of a dual process of eradication (of sexuality from work organizations) and containment (of sexuality within the non-work sphere). To conceptualize organization sexuality solely, or even largely, in terms of exclusion would, however, be a mis-reading of his account. For, as he also observed, the modernist desexualization of work organizations also involved a related process of 'over-inclusion', based on the co-option and commodification of sexuality. In particular, Burrell identified the ongoing relationship between 'over-included' organization sexuality and patriarchal power, emphasizing for instance that 'organizations . . . [are] sites of sexual harassment in which patriarchy and the control it gives over women is reflected in, and enhanced by, sexual harassment' (Burrell, 1984: 101), a theme particularly developed in collaborative (editorial) work with Jeff Hearn (Burrell and Hearn, 1989) and in Burrell's analysis of the organization of pleasure (1992b).

It is in this later work that he focuses not only on the theme of desexualization, but also, turning once more to the critical modernism of Marcuse, on the radical potential of re-eroticization as a counter-strategy to the rationalization process. In doing so Burrell emphasizes not only that managerial efforts to eradicate, contain, co-opt and commodify sexuality are never 'total', but also that sexuality represents a powerful site of potential resistance to the rationalization process. As such, Burrell advocates – through a critique of what he calls 'Heathrow Organization Theory' and a discussion of Orwell's *Nineteen Eighty-Four* – a re-eroticization of work organizations, albeit one premised on his rather romantic vision of

> A more joyous, playful attitude to life and to fellow humans, where sensuality and feeling are enhanced and where the erotic plays a more central role in our day-to-day lives. (Burrell, 1992b: 78)

For Burrell, re-eroticization is the antithesis of desexualization and therefore formal or instrumental rationalization. Thus, while his critique is premised in many respects on Foucauldian post-structuralism his posited response (its underlying 'face') is one of a Marcusian ideal of non-repressive desublimation and a touch of reaestheticization. As Brewis and Grey (1994: 71) put it in their critical engagement with Burrell's ideas, in essence it involves an attempt to advocate an alternative to 'the managerialist appropriation of sex and sexuality by recognizing, allowing and playing with the pluralistic erotics of organizations outside of the instrumental control of management'.

Even at his most celebratory, though, Burrell is clearly aware of the extent to which a re-eroticization of the workplace potentially opens up the way for increased sexual co-optation and commodification, and for abuses of power relations. As such, he makes it clear that he is not implying a re-sexualization of organizations where this merely involves an increase in sexual relations embedded within established power structures. Instead, he proposes a radical restructuring of erotic energies, evocative of Bakhtin's carnivalesque, in which 'the hierarchy of the official order is overturned and the lowly are able to mock the high' (Burrell, 1992b: 80). Yet despite such caveats, as Brewis and Grey (1994: 73) observe, 'little detail is given . . . as to what the erotic workplace would actually look like', leaving them concerned not only about the essentialist version of the feminine in re-eroticization as well as its 'quasi-humanistic emancipatory promises', but also the endorsement of potentially violent forms of sexuality. For them, 're-eroticization theorists are . . . mistaken in their evocation of a sexual Utopia free from the workings of power' (Brewis and Grey, 1994: 80).

Indeed, Burrell has since questioned (with characteristic reflexivity) his erotic visions, reflecting on their utopianism and acknowledging the extent to which they may be as much the outcome of a phallocentric worldview as the ideas they sought to displace. Concluding that it is 'extremely difficult to see how re-eroticization should be progressed', he confesses to 'middle-aged thinking' and the view that 'it may be time to abandon' his earlier ambitions in this respect (Burrell, 1997: 236).

Ramblings in hell

Excluding more mischievous interventions, such as his collaborative essay which dwelt on the possibility of middle-managers forming a new kleptocratic class (Scarborough and Burrell, 1996), the latter years of the 20th century were dominated for Burrell by the publication in 1997 of what was to be his most substantial work since *Sociological Paradigms*. Representing, as a number of Burrell's fellow academics have noted, perhaps the closest attempt yet to building a postmodern theorization of organization, this was a book long in the making, drawing as it did on many of the themes and critical questions raised throughout his previous work. Time, sexuality, and the role and status of organization theory all featured heavily in its pages, brought together in an attempt, if not to shatter then forcibly to rattle the windows of the purveyors of mainstream organization theory. This much was evident at least from its title *Pandemonium: Towards a Retro-Organization Theory.*

Pandemonium, the capital of Hell in Milton's *Paradise Lost*, refers largely to chaos, disorder, noise and confusion; in other words, to the antithesis of organization as we have come to understand it according to established frameworks of thinking and being. And it was these very frameworks that Burrell once again sought to deconstruct, circumvent or undermine (depending on which review you read). Yet it was not only in the form of argumentation that Burrell sought to achieve this. In creating *Pandemonium* Burrell also understood, as the likes of Nietzsche, Marcuse, Lyotard and many others had before him, that transgression can be an aesthetic as well as an intellectual act. Indeed, he had already considered at some length in his 1993 essay, (again somewhat playfully) entitled 'Eco and the Bunnymen', the transgressive role that alternative styles of presentation could play within the field, as well as, it should be noted, the wrath such a strategy might incur, especially from those whose self-identities are closely enmeshed in the kudos of academia.

Nevertheless despite such risks, *Pandemonium* was without doubt an attempt to develop an aesthetically as well as an intellectually transgressive work. After working with a somewhat traditional layout for the first 33 pages, it dispenses with textual conventions and for the rest of the narrative, divides every page into two: an upper part that reads from left to right, and a lower part that flows in the opposite direction, so that the two parts taken together navigate a circular route. Hence, much like the poem from which it takes its title, *Pandemonium* beging *in medias res.*

Such aesthetic unorthodoxy should not be taken simply to reflect an idiosyncrasy on the part of the author, however, or be seen solely as an attempt to shock and disturb *à la* Dadaism (though undoubtedly both of these factors played their part). Jones (1998) sums this up in his review of the book when he describes it as an 'effort', seemingly emphasizing the extent to which it is both an attempt (on Burrell's part) to consolidate a number of significant contributions to the development of a radical organization theory, and a demanding text (on the part of its reader) not least in terms of the range of sources and ideas it draws on, but also in relation to its presentation. Hence, as Burrell himself puts it, the book 'is meant to escape from the normal conventions of textual presentation which pass for common sense within Western social science . . . the text is designed to be disruptive, randomizing and reliant upon the reader's creativity' (Burrell, 1997: 1–2).

Pandemonium is not, however, solely an exercise in transgressive aesthetics. In seeking to undermine the validity claims of modernity, Burrell also presents the reader/traveller with what he describes as a *retro-organization theory*. That is, one that is prepared to plunder the past, present and future in an attempt to expose the forgotten continuities of contemporary organization and the often horrific consequences of those actions undertaken in its name. As such, we are led through ancient Greek mythology, paganism and the European baroque into the everyday world of the pre-modern peasantry, each step exposing us to the often forgotten underside of a sterile modernity. We then head to Canada's West Edmonton Mall and America's Disneyworld where modernity and pre-modernity fold into one another and where we are reminded of the four humours (phlegm, blood, choler and black bile) and, through glimpses of abattoirs, the Holocaust, witchcraft and also the 'death service industry', modernity's many necrotic detours.

Despite its appeal to chaos and disorder, therefore, *Pandemonium* is more than a place of postmodern smoke and mirrors. Rather, it is ultimately envisaged as a site of theoretical reinvigoration and reconstruction, albeit one which casts aside the rules and expectations of modernity and its linear conception of progress. And it is in the final chapter (for even in Burrell's non-linear endeavour such a place still exists) that the project of reclaiming organizational thinking 'as a branch of social theory' in the form of 'retro-organization theory' takes place. Thus, in an attempt to 'make history bend and groan', he denounces the modernist assault on the peasantry and warns us (once again) against the dangers of Enlightenment linearity, describing retro-organization theory as:

> A form of analysis which seeks to underplay the importance of developing an argument in a linear, logical way. There is a rejection of beginning at the beginning and claiming that the conclusion which falls at the end (of course) represents progress and enlightenment ... It values pre-modern history, particularly pre-Enlightenment history, in so far as this study can help us understand the modern and the postmodern but it also plunders history for insight and data, not mindful of chronology, anachronisms, the respect for meta narrative or story. (Burrell, 1997: 27)

Despite such ultimately lofty goals, however, *Pandemonium* received a mixed response. So while Corvellec (2002), for example acknowledged its originality and ability to remind us of the potential diversity and richness of organization, it was equally denounced for failing to move beyond the limitations of what the reviewer considered to be a piece of intellectual autobiography, albeit one that incorporates a wealth of related reflections on organizations scattered throughout the text.

In a similar vein, Jones (1998) although prepared to emphasize the radical potential of *Pandemonium* to initiate a critique of the logocentric conventions of organization theory and its practices of textual closure, ultimately views it as a frivolous work which, instead of providing a sustained critique of the politics of textual practice, tends rather to parody those varieties of organization theory that rest on a naïve view of language as representational in a way that Jones variously describes as 'disappointing', 'frustrating' and 'inadequate'. Other reviews (see Jackson, 1998; ten Bos, 1998; O'Doherty, 1999) set a similarly ambivalent tone, but what is perhaps most telling is that apart from the occasional reference to the relationship between *Pandemonium* and postmodernism (see for example Hancock and Tyler, 2001; Carter and Jackson, 2004), there has subsequently been a notable lack of substantial critical engagement with the ideas presented in what is, after all, Burrell's most sustained 'position piece' to date.

Certainly retro-organization theory, while never convincingly developed (though in many ways illustrated) in the pages of *Pandemonium*, has failed to make anything in the way of a consistent impact on subsequent work within the field (for a notable exception see Case and Philipson, 2004). Nor can one deny, as so many of its critics have argued, that it is a self-indulgent and 'empirically inadequate' book (ten Bos, 1998: 603) if one wishes to identify the empirical with the narrow worldview of the sciences. Yet in a more general sense it is also an incredibly extensive empirical text, providing a rich background of historical illustrations and insightful observations about the realities of everyday organizational life. Yes, in doing so it might 'take liberties with history' (Rowlinson and Carter, 2002: 540), but in no sense is this unique to *Pandemonium*.

Indeed, as Burrell himself openly states in *Pandemonium*, 'you are invited not to treat it seriously but to look for enjoyment and pain where you can' (1997: 28). Such criticisms, therefore, while more than justified, may well say more about the imaginative limitations of those (of us) who are unable to step outside of the somewhat myopic conventions of academia than it does about the aspirations and abilities of the author, or of this particular text.

Building new horizons

Nevertheless, while *Pandemonium* will undoubtedly remain a lasting monument to Burrell's critical ambitions, it is probably fair to say that it failed to have the impact on the field that he might have hoped for. Not that this has entirely dampened Burrell's continuing ambitions to construct a viable and potent critical theory of organization. What it has done, however, or so it would seem, is led him to revisit several of his older intellectual haunts, including the somewhat more Marxian-inspired work of the Frankfurt School, in his search for a sufficiently flexible foundation for his endeavours. This is not to suggest that he has somehow abandoned the more postmodern strains within his thinking that were clearly so important in the building of *Pandemonium*. Nor has he entirely jettisoned the ideals that underpinned his albeit loose formulation of a retro-organization theory. Rather, these have coalesced around a new concern; namely, the relationship between power, aesthetics and the architecture of organizational space.

The proposition that the aesthetics of the physical environment itself contributes to 'ideological, political and economic structures of domination' (Dale and Burrell, 2003: 155) is not within Burrell's work an entirely new one, contributing as it did both a thematic and, in small part, substantive dimension of *Pandemonium*. Indeed, the organization of space came to play an important metaphorical function for Burrell around this time as illustrated in his (2002) paper exploring the shifting quadrilateral relationships between 20th century society's four leading organizational groups (professionals, owners, managers and the aristocracy).

It is, however, in collaboration with Karen Dale that the physical component of the administration and organization of everyday life has taken up a much more prominent position within his thinking (Burrell and Dale, 2002, 2003; Dale and Burrell, 2000, 2003), as has a renewed interest in the work of the first generation of Frankfurt School scholars including Adorno and Benjamin. Whatever tradition Burrell chooses to cite, what is evident however, is that his most recent work has lost none of its radical intent. Even its apparent shift out of the armchair and into the materiality of the everyday (Burrell, 2003) has done nothing to attenuate its critical engagement with taken-for-granted assumptions about the relationship between space and agency, aesthetic and anaesthetic stimuli and even the vexed questions of progress and emancipation (Burrell, 2001). For example, in the essay 'An-Aesthetics and Architecture' (Dale and Burrell, 2003), Walter Benjamin's conception of the dazzle is utilized critically to interrogate the increasing ubiquity of visual stimulation in certain styles of corporate architecture and its potentially anaesthetizing consequences for other aspects of human sensory reception amongst a range of interested groups. The aesthetic is understood, therefore, not simply as a potential source of pleasure or even liberation, but one that remains equally as vulnerable to control and manipulation as any other dimension of human experience.

What this essay also represents, however along with other examples such as Burrell and Dale (2003), and a forthcoming co-authored book on organization, space and architecture, is a reaffirmation of the contribution a critical organization theory is capable of making to the social scientific understanding of the configurations and trajectories of contemporary society. More than this though, we would continue to contend that despite the negativity of its dialectic, Burrell's work remains an expression of a profoundly, if deeply guarded, emancipatory vision. One that is guided not by the unreflexive prescription of solutions or particular agendas for change, but by the spirit of an Enlightenment radicalism that continues to view reason not simply as a tool of order and control, but rather as a catalyst for the adventurous denial of mythology and the quest for a knowledge that, while aware of its own limitations, continues to build new horizons of possibility before bringing them simultaneously into focus and question.

Concluding thoughts

In this chapter we have, albeit briefly, characterized many of Burrell's endeavours in relation to a desire to tear down the stifling edifices of orthodoxy within organization theory while, at the same time, tentatively constructing an alternative body of ideas and impetus for critique. Perhaps somewhat ironically, however, this is no longer purely a theoretical project but one that has taken on a profoundly material character. Recently appointed as director of the

Management Centre of the University of Leicester in the UK, Burrell has set out to build a department dedicated to the realization of this goal. Drawing together critical organization and management theorists from across the UK and further afield, he is creating what appears to be his ideal of a 'neo-disciplinary' and 'robust but less disciplined community of scholars' (Burrell, 2003: 532), in an attempt to challenge, from a position of institutional strength the instrumentalism and often intellectual vacuity that seems to characterize so much management and business scholarship and education.

Not that this will be an easy task. Such a project contains a number of tensions at both the institutional and theoretical level, tensions which are all too evidently displayed within the Centre's own research strategy:

> Our overarching aim is that research in the Management Centre should encourage critical and heterodox work of international standing, and hence contribute to the re-thinking of management, business and organization. In order to do this we want to maximize the academic quality and external visibility of our research, stimulate the generation of external grant income from a variety of sources, and co-ordinate a well-resourced and competitive PhD programme.

Just how far this demand for heterodoxy can be reconciled with the bottom line requirements of the contemporary higher education sector in the UK is yet to be seen, particularly in an environment as competitive and, in its own way, deeply conservative as business education. Undoubtedly compromises will have to be made along the way, and despite his Mulciberesque aspirations, it is unlikely that Burrrell's *Pandemonium* will ever be realised in Leicestershire's green and pleasant land. Nevertheless, if in both his institutional role and his academic endeavours Burrell continues to ask awkward questions, to champion the critical exploration of resources beyond the traditional confines of the field and, ultimately, to embrace the negativity of this particular dialectic in an optimistic and generous way then no doubt such compromises will if not be forgotten, then quickly forgiven.

References

Ackroyd, S. and S. Fleetwood (eds.) (2000) *Realist Perspectives on Business and Organization*. London: Routledge.

Berger, P. L. and T. Luckmann (1967) *The Social Construction of Reality*. Harmondsworth: Penguin.

Bertens, H. (1995) *The Idea of the Postmodern: A History*. London: Routledge.

Bhaskar, R., M. Archer, A. Collier, T. Lawson and A. Norrie (eds.) (1998) *Critical Realism: Essential Readings*. London: Routledge.

Brewis, J. and C. Grey (1994) 'Re-eroticizing the organization: An exegesis and critique' *Gender, Work and Organization*, 1(2): 67–82.

Burrell, G. (1979) 'Radical organization theory' in D. Dunkerley and G. Salaman (eds.) *The International Yearbook of Organizational Studies*. London: Routledge and Kegan Paul.

Burrell, G. (1984) 'Sex and organizational analysis' *Organization Studies*, 5(2): 97–118.

Burrell, G. (1987) 'No accounting for sexuality' *Accounting, Organizations and Society*, 12(1): 89–101.

Burrell, G. (1988) 'Modernism, postmodernism and organizational analysis 2: The contribution of Michel Foucault' *Organization Studies*, 9(2): 221–35.

Burrell, G. (1989) 'The absent centre: The neglect of philosophy in Anglo-American management theory' *Human Systems Management*, 8(4): 307–342.

Burrell, G. (1990) 'Fragmented labours' in D. Knights and H. Willmott (eds.) *Labour Process Theory*. Basingstoke: Macmillan.

Burrell, G. (1992a) 'Back to the future: Time and organization' in M. Reed and M. Hughes (eds.) *Rethinking Organization: New Directions in Organization Theory and Analysis*. London: Sage.

Burrell, G. (1992b) 'The organization of pleasure' in M. Alvesson and H. Willmott (eds.) *Critical Management Studies*. London: Sage.

Burrell, G. (1993) 'Eco and the Bunnymen' in J. Hassard and M. Parker (eds.) *Postmodernism and Organizations*. London: Sage.

Burrell, G. (1994) 'Modernism, postmodernism and organizational analysis 4: The contribution of Jürgen Habermas' *Organization Studies*, 15(1): 1–45.

Burrell, G. (1997) *Pandemonium: Towards a Retro-Organization Theory*. London: Sage.

Burrell, G. (1999) 'Normal science, paradigms, metaphors, discourses and genealogies of analysis' in S. Clegg and C. Hardy (eds.) *Studying Organization: Theory and Method*. London: Sage.

Burrell, G. (2001) 'ephemera: critical dialogues on organization' *ephemera: critical dialogues on organization*, 1(1): 1–29.

Burrell, G. (2002) 'Twentieth-century quadrilles: Aristocracy, owners, managers and professionals' *International Studies of Management and Organization*, 32(2): 25–50.

Burrell, G. (2003) 'The Future of Organization Theory: Prospects and Limitations' in H. Tsoukas and C. Knudsen (eds.) *The Oxford Handbook of Organization Theory: Meta-Theoretical Perspectives*. Oxford: Oxford University Press.

Burrell, G. and K. Dale (2002) 'Utopiary: Utopias, gardens and organization' in M. Parker (ed.) *Utopia and Organization*. Oxford: Blackwell.

Burrell, G. and K. Dale (2003) 'Building better worlds?: Architecture and critical management studies' in M. Alvesson and H. Willmott (eds.) *Studying Management Critically*. London: Sage.

Burrell, G. and J. Hearn (1989) 'The sexuality of organization' in J. Hearn, D. Sheppard, P. Tancred-Sheriff and G. Burrell (eds.) *The Sexuality of Organization*. London: Sage.

Burrell, G. and G. Morgan (1979) *Sociological Paradigms and Organizational Analysis*. London: Heinemann.

Carter, P. and N. Jackson (2004) 'Gilles Deleuze and Felix Guattari' in S. Linstead (ed.) *Organization Theory and Postmodern Thought*. London: Sage.

Case, P. and G. Philipson (2004) 'Astrology, alchemy and retro-organization theory: An astro-genealogical critique of the Myers-Briggs Type Indicator®' *Organization*, 11(4): 473–495.

Clegg, S. (1982) 'Review of Burrell and Morgan (1979)' *Organization Studies*, 3(4): 380–381.

Cooper, R. and G. Burrell (1988) 'Modernism, postmodernism and organizational analysis 1: An introduction' *Organization Studies*, 9(1): 91–112.

Corvellec, H. (2002) '*Pandemonium: Towards a Retro-Organization Theory* – A review' *Scandinavian Journal of Management*, 18(2): 255–258.

Dale, K. and G. Burrell (2000) 'What shape are we in? Organization theory and the organized body' in J. Hassard, R. Holliday and H. Willmott (eds.) *Body and Organization*. London: Sage.

Dale, K. and G. Burrell (2003) 'An-aesthetics and architecture' in A. Carr and P. Hancock (eds.) *Art and Aesthetics at Work*. Basingstoke: Palgrave. pp. 155–173.

Donaldson, L. (1985) *In Defence of Organization Theory*. Cambridge: Cambridge University Press.

Elias, N. (1978) *The Civilizing Process*. Oxford: Blackwell.

Foucault, M. (1977) *Discipline and Punish: The Birth of the Prison*, trans. A. Sheridan. London: Allen Lane.

Foucault, M. (1979) *The History of Sexuality Volume One: The Will to Knowledge*, trans. R. Hurley. London: Allen Lane.

Giddens, A. (1986) *The Constitution of Society: Outline of the Theory of Structuration.* Cambridge: Polity.

Hancock, P and M. Tyler (2001) *Work, Postmodernism and Organization: A Critical Introduction.* London: Sage.

Jackson, N. (1998) 'A review of *Pandemonium: Towards a Retro-Organization Theory* by G. Burrell' *British Journal of Industrial Relations*, 36(2): 325–328.

Jackson, N. and P. Carter (1991) 'In defence of paradigm incommensurability' *Organization Studies*, 12(1): 109–127.

Jackson, N. and P. Carter (1993) 'Paradigm wars: A response to Hugh Willmott' *Organization Studies*, 14(5): 727–730.

Jones, C. (1998) 'A review of *Pandemonium: Towards a Retro-Organization Theory* by G. Burrell' *The Electronic Journal Of Radical Organization Theory*, 4(1).

Kuhn, T. (1962) *The Structure of Scientific Revolutions.* Chicago: University of Chicago Press.

Marcuse, H. (1962) *Eros and Civilisation: A Philosophical Inquiry into Freud.* Boston, MA: Beacon.

McCarthy, T. (1990) 'The critique of impure reason: Foucault and the Frankfurt School' *Political Theory*, 18(4): 437–469.

Mills, A. (2001) 'Gareth Morgan: *Sociological Paradigms And Organizational Analysis*' *Aurora Online:* Online at: http://aurora.icaap.org/archive/morgan.html

O'Doherty, D. (1999) 'A review of *Pandemonium: Towards a Retro-Organization Theory* by G. Burrell' *Journal of Management Studies*, 36(7): 1033–1035.

Rowlinson, M. and C. Carter. (2002) 'Foucault and history in organization studies' *Organization*, 9(4): 527–547.

Scarborough, H. and G. Burrell. (1996) 'The axeman cometh: The changing roles and knowledges of middle managers' in S. R. Clegg and G. Palmer (eds.) *The Politics of Management Knowledge.* London: Sage.

Stablein, R. (1999) 'Data in organization studies' in S. R. Clegg and C. Hardy (eds.) *Studying Organization: Theory and Method.* London: Sage.

ten Bos, R. (1998) 'A review of *Pandemonium: Towards a Retro-Organization Theory* by G. Burrell' *The Sociological Review*, 46(4): 889–890.

Willmott, H. (1990) 'Beyond paradigmatic closure in organizational enquiry' in J. Hassard and D. Pym (eds.) *The Theory and Philosophy of Organizations.* London: Routledge.

WOBS (Warwick Organizational Behaviour Staff) (2000) (eds.) *Organizational Studies: Critical Perspectives* (4 vols.). London: Routledge.

Judith Butler: On organizing subjectivities

Janet Borgerson

Introduction

Judith Butler offers some of the most complex, rhetorically brilliant and diligently comprehensive contemporary theory, although her theoretical and philosophical depth often evades researchers who look to her work with preconceived notions of her contribution. Examining bibliographies 'of Butler's works and those which reference or draw from her (there are literally hundreds of the latter), reveals the extent of her influence in, among other fields, queer theory, feminist theory, "race" studies, film studies, literary studies, sociology, politics, and philosophy' (Salih, 2004: 13). Butler's work stands against essentialist understandings of identity and existence; culture and biology; and relationships between gender and sex – that is, femininity's link to the female, and masculinity's link to the male. As useful and sympathetic as such conceptual notions may appear to organization theory's concerns, however, engagement with a developed notion of Butler's philosophical thought (eg, 1987/1999, 1990, 1993, 1997, 2004a, 2004b) has been scant. For notable exceptions, see Ford and Harding (2004) and Hodgson (2005), and for discussion of Butler's concepts, often in the context of poststructuralist understandings of gender and queer theory see, for example, Bowring (2004), Brewis (2002), Brewis and Linstead (2000), Fournier (2002), Gherardi (1995), Knights (1992, 1997) and Parker (2002). I aim to rectify a lingering and fundamental miscomprehension and underestimation of her thought.

Common discourse suggests that Butler's writing demands more than many readers are willing to give. I believe that some of the perceived difficulty in reading, understanding, and drawing upon Butler's work emerges from a misapprehension of her project. In other words, if readers understood Butler's philosophical background and context better, her work would link clearly with more familiar traditions in organization theory, explicating, as well, connections to theorists, such as, Foucault and Derrida, but also, for example, Spivak and Žižek (see Jones, and Böhm and De Cock, in this volume). Crucially, she concurs with co-authors Ernesto Laclau and Slavoj Žižek – and with basic tenets of phenomenology (eg, Zaner, 1970; cf Deleuze, 1991) – that:

any effort at empirical description takes place within a theoretically delimited sphere, and that empirical analysis in general cannot offer a persuasive explanation of its own constitution as a field of enquiry [and] that theory operates on the very level at which the object of inquiry is defined and delimited, and that there is no givenness of the object which is not given within the interpretative field – given to theory, as it were, as the condition of its own appearance and legibility. (Butler, 2004d: 274)

Some of the potential implications of this have been considered by Czarniawska and Höpfl (2002) and Wray-Bliss (2003). Emerging, then, is a crucial, long-standing anxiety and debate around the conflict between empiricism and phenomenology that impacts, usually implicitly, upon organization theory, and to the essentials of which I will return shortly.

In this chapter I explore Butler's *potential* contribution, providing a broad frame for her work. I focus on specific concepts from her writings – performativity, iteration, and foreclosure – that have profound implications for organization theory. Introducing and contextualizing these concepts and Butler's background, I call Butler's transformative theoretical possibilities more fully into organization theory. I also point to philosophers working in the phenomenological tradition in which Butler trained, including influential precursors, colleagues and contemporaries, to establish how issues raised in organization theory – for example, the virtue of engaging otherness, rather than difference (Fournier, 2002) – can be recognized and comprehended in relation to philosophical phenomenology more generally.

Compared with theoretical understandings attributed to, and adapted from, Foucault and Derrida, one might identify in organization theory a resistance to adopting Butler's work and fully comprehending the phenomenological philosophical training's impact on her choice of topics and modes of explication. Some researchers may feel comfortable with certain ways of understanding Butler – and, perhaps more precisely, limited ways of applying Butler's theory to issues relating to organization theory. Butler writes, 'In a sense, all of my work remains within the orbit of a certain set of Hegelian questions: What is the relation between desire and recognition, and how is it that the constitution of the subject entails a radical and constitutive relation to alterity' (Butler, 1987/1999: xiv). In other words, Butler seeks to explore and elaborate upon one of Hegel's most fundamental concerns – the way in which any Self, or subject position, requires an Other, or alterity, for its own constitution and existence. Thus, marking genealogical stepping-stones from Butler's theoretical heritage makes her more understandable, exploits opportunities for profound insights and, furthermore, seeks to assist organization theorists in recognizing philosophical interconnections that impact on the coherence of relevant arguments and conclusions.

Butler's philosophical background

As suggested above, Butler's work, radical as it may seem, responds to classic questions of ontology, philosophy of language, and epistemology. After studying philosophy as an undergraduate at Bennington College in Vermont and Yale University in the 70s, Butler travelled on a Fulbright Scholarship to Germany, attending the lectures and seminars of Hans Georg Gadamer. Back at Yale for graduate training in philosophy, she occasionally – not without ambivalence – attended lectures by Jacques Derrida and Paul de Man (Butler, 1987/1999, vii–viii; 2004b: 242). Butler earned her PhD in Philosophy in 1984 at Yale University under advisor Maurice Natanson, an influential and well-respected phenomenologist and Husserl scholar (Natanson, 1973). Natanson, in turn, studied with Alfred Schutz and published books on 'the social role' (Natanson, 1970) and the problem of anonymity – being treated as indistinguishable from and replaceable by anyone else of a similar 'kind' (Natanson, 1986). Deeply steeped in continental philosophy, Butler joined the ranks of others in the phenomenological tradition who have explored binaries, such as, the finite and infinite (Hartmann, 1966), being and nothingness (Sartre, 1956), typicality and anonymity (Natanson, 1986), Self and Other (Levinas, 1969), and black and white in an 'antiblack' world (Gordon 1995a). Driven by similar theoretical concerns, Butler has sought to understand the paradoxes and complexities of poles of meaning and being, the role of ideal instance and particular experience, and the interrelations between them, often in relation to gender or modes of masculinity and femininity (eg, Butler, 1987/1999,1990, 2004a).

Butler became notorious for *Gender Trouble* (1990), a founding text in what has become known as queer theory, which was adopted by many as an argument for understanding gender as a performance – and hence worn, or not, rather like a particularly theatrical concatenation of clothing. Nevertheless, she remains, regardless of her theory's evocativeness for gender fluidity and drag performances, not primarily a queer theorist, but a phenomenologist (Butler, 1987/1999; 2004b: 232–250; Salih, 2004: 4–5). In her writings, masculinity and femininity perform much the same role as concepts of subject and object; mind and body; and time and space in the history of phenomenology's development. We see this clearly in the early pages of *Bodies That Matter: The Discursive Limits of 'Sex'* (1993). In interrogating the way 'constraints' produce domains of intelligibility and domains of the unthinkable, Butler writes 'This latter domain is not the opposite of the former, for oppositions are, after all, part of intelligibility; the latter is the excluded and illegible domain that haunts the former domain as the spectre of its own impossibility, the very limit of intelligibility, its constitutive outside' (1993: xi). Thus, positions recognizable in these dualisms form in relation to each other, form interrelations and manifest limits and boundaries; but always contingently and within time's spectrum.

The temptation in articulating Butler's contribution to theorizing organization is to focus on gender, as her work here has been so influential. Whereas I turn to gender, often as an exemplar, much is gained by development elsewhere, particularly so that gender will not be misconstrued as her fundamental concern. At the same time, although often critical of legitimating institutions (Butler, 2000a; 2002; 2004a; 2004b: 102–130), Butler rarely discusses business or management and organization issues *per se*. Indeed, in *Contingency, Hegemony,*

Universality's collaborative questioning around democratic political articulation and radical democracy, Butler assents somewhat uncertainly: 'a critique of the market economy is not found in these pages' (2000b: 277). Her lack of direct attention to such a delimited subject should not dissuade those in organization theory, however. As realized by researchers such as those cited above, engaging with Butler's insights and concepts, much as with those of Hegel, can be inspiring and productive – whether one ultimately agrees with her or not.

Currently the Maxine Elliot Professor of Rhetoric and Comparative Literature at the University of California at Berkeley, Butler stands outside her academic home field of philosophy and writes, arguably, for a broader audience. She is also on the faculty of the European Graduate School, and held the Spinoza Chair at the University of Amsterdam. Butlerian websites, fanzines, university courses and PhD theses abound – dedicated to her ideas and the possibilities people have derived from her work. In proposing – and composing – Butler for organization theory, I draw upon my own training in philosophy, particularly post-doctoral study in existential phenomenology with Lewis R. Gordon, another student of Natanson's, as well as several seminar discussions with Butler over the last decade.

Visualizing the tropological inauguration of the subject

Imagine a motion, a movement, perhaps mesmerizing and repeated, or a unique, one time only instance of going out and coming in – the tides; a reader's glance to the horizon and back to her book; the dancer's graceful gesture of a relaxed hand held near the body, then drifting out and away, then brought near again. Now abstract this gesture – it is not the hand, eye, or sea – seen as motion in the mind's eye, out and back. There! That's it! Imagine this gesture belonging to no one in particular, produced by no one in particular, but turning at a limit and returning. The limit, the point or moment of turning back transforms the going out to the coming in. The limit – imagined from a human perspective, perhaps, as bumping up against another human being apparently not oneself; feeling breath not one's own against the skin; or one's hand grasped, stopping one's hand from grasping . . . something; or understood psychically, as Butler encourages us to do, through consciousness – gives form, spurs a shift, perceptually imagined and recognized, perhaps, as a change of direction.

Call this subjection, the founding of subjectivity. The turn, or 'trope' (Butler, 1997: 3–4) – this gesture's formation at a limit – gives definition and boundary to what would be otherwise endless drifting. Do we have domination here? Do we have power? Do we have a human subject? The motion, movement, or gesture's shape itself sparks controversy. Derrida describes a more circular dialectical movement in 'The Pit and the Pyramid' (1982a); yet, in that case, Butler herself questions Derrida's assumption that 'Hegel's system, understood in terms of his semiology, is completed and self-sufficient' – thus, the closed circle – arguing that 'it is precisely that assumption that first requires clarification' (Butler, 2004: 86n2.) In any case, what we have is a model of motion influencing, evoking, and provoking theory, at least, since Hegel's permutations in *Phenomenology of Spirit* and Kant's articulation of imagination in *Critique of Judgment*. For example, Kant writes, 'The imagination attains its maximum, and in the effort to go beyond this limit sinks back into itself, and in so doing is displaced into a moving satisfaction' (Kant, 1951, §26,174: 91; see also Nancy, 1993: 40). This turning motion has been observed, mutated, delineated, and evaluated over and over again, its potential sometimes rejected, yet nevertheless mined for insight into history, human labour, difference, human agency, subjectivity, and the potential for resistance through contingency. An impressive quantity of deliberation and insight, spanning centuries! Imagine a gesture!

Theorists and philosophers for centuries have invoked this trope, or turning; and they have given the limiting boundary, or realm, names such as Other, power, or the unknowable, often as if inaugurating entities. In turn, these hypothesized entities and their implied effects, such as, subjection or reflexivity, open as lenses onto human life processes, subjectivities, and potential actings and interactings. Researchers writing in organization theory have called upon insights derived from models that have grown up around the limit spurring turning, as in Jones and Spicer's (2005) discussion of Althusser's interpellation and Žižek's encounter with the Real; but also often Foucault's notion of productive power. So, what makes Butler's contribution in using the trope to develop insights into subjectivity, subjection, and intelligibility different from, for example, those of Foucault or Žižek or Derrida or Levinas? Core ideas and rallying points from many such thinkers could be usefully explicated around the subject's tropological inauguration; however, one takes to different subjectivities differently, one learns differently from each, and a point made differently is just that, different.

Butler reminds us throughout our engagement with her work that there is no subject to engage in mutual recognition in the inaugural moment of recognition, subjection, and turning. To put this another way, 'the turn appears to function as a tropological inauguration of the subject, a founding moment whose ontological status remains permanently uncertain' (1997: 4). She writes, 'The paradox of subjection implies a paradox of referentiality: namely, that we must refer to what does not yet exist. Through a figure that marks the suspension of our ontological commitments, we seek to account for how the subject comes to be' (Butler, 1997: 4). In signature relentless questioning, she asks, 'Does subjection inaugurate tropology in some way, or is the inaugurative work of tropes necessarily invoked when we try to account for the generation of the subject?' (1997: 4). Her analysis of this 'rhetorically, performatively spectacular' turn reinforces the point that this figure of turning 'operates as part of the explanation of how the subject is produced, and so there is no subject, strictly speaking, who makes this turn' (Butler, 1997: 3–4). The subject, and subjectivity, come into being. From this critical interrogation a related question arises: How can we explain the materiality of sex without resorting to notions that sex is beyond the realm of discursive construction?

Similarly, our enthusiasm for delimiting the workings of power should never eclipse power's own ontological uncertainty: power itself should not be placed in a subject position, as if an agent of action. The workings of power are also contingent. Butler builds upon Foucault, certainly, but demands further 'thinking the theory of power together with a theory of the psyche' (Butler, 1997: 3). 'What is the psychic form power takes?' she asks, calling time and trope fully into the considerations. Acknowledging temporal contingencies demands a designation of the before and after, yet an acceptance of the forever unknowable prior, and animates an investigation of how the subject might engage the moment of turning when there is, yet, no subject.

The subject takes form from language and gestures – produced with body positions, speech acts, reflective processes, and other performative behaviour, including consumption and production itself – given, or normatively imposed, as limits that at the same time offer and foreclose. Butler articulates the subject as follows:

> The genealogy of the subject as a critical category, however, suggests that the subject, rather than be identified strictly with the individual, ought to be designated as a linguistic category, a placeholder, a structure in formation. Individuals come to occupy the site of the subject (the subject simultaneously emerges as a 'site'), and they enjoy intelligibility only to the extent that they are, as it were, first established in language. The subject is a linguistic occasion for the individual to achieve and reproduce intelligibility, the linguistic condition of its existence and agency. (Butler, 1997: 10–11)

One recognizes here the fundamental role of semiotics and other theories of language – conjoined with notions of subjection's psychic forms – in building a cohesive and coherent model of subject formation. Moreover, the subject's intelligibility or legibility is limited by the available, and simultaneously foreclosed, repertoires of what Butler calls performative iterations. The turning gesture grounds an understanding of Butler's organizing subjectivity, including her conceptual work on performativity, iteration, and foreclosure discussed below.

Performativity, iteration, foreclosure

Butler's (1990) work on subject identity constitution through performative iterations – of gendered gestures and roles – demonstrates fundamental aspects of her theoretical perspective. She requires that we note reproduction, but also *potential production of difference* emerging from required modes of behaviour – not necessarily to be understood as intentional resistance. Performative iterations are not simply the acting out of ways of being in the world: rather each iteration, 'a regularized and constrained repetition of norms' (Butler, 1993: 95), plays the role of producing identities and foreclosing others, maintaining the illusion of natural categories of behaviour, including gender.

Butler's potential impact in organization theory can be articulated through the sympathy of her own work with Hegel's: for example, organization researchers Hancock and Tyler (2001) recognize the potential of the Hegelian notions that Butler draws upon and develops. They utilize their 'understanding of Hegel's ontology of the subject; that is, the phenomenological process through which subjectivity evolves' in examining 'managerial interventions into the process of subjectivization' (Hancock and Tyler, 2001: 570). By focusing upon the creation of institutionalized embodied subjectivities within the organization environment, they are able to point out the absence of non-colonized bodies capable of intersubjective exchange and growth. The body – Hegel's 'primary medium through which inter-subjective mutual recognition occurs' (Hancock and Tyler, 2001: 575) – disciplined by organizational management's 'corporate culturalism' that cannot support fully human relations, fails to fulfil its role. Hancock and Tyler observe that the alienated organizational intersubjectivities of 'corporate culturalism' require particular modes of dress and behaviour, and repetitions in reference to these. Butler allows us to see that organizational environments serve as contexts for iteration of whatever is demanded within such a space, creating and controlling subjectivities and relations among these. Alienating iterations infect intersubjectivity and the potential for mutual recognition.

Their compelling and insightful argument, nevertheless, slips between levels of theory. Human selves as performative bodies in an organizational environment are rather unproblematically represented here, existing prior to engagement for recognition. Reflection upon Butler's tropological inauguration reminds us of the 'paradox of referentiality', that at the founding moment of the subject, there is no possibility of mutual recognition. Of course, a vision of bodily intersubjectivity in everyday life, even if it begins with an engaging subject has much to recommend it; yet, if Hancock and Tyler's goal is to avoid the non-processual self that they attribute to Marxist labour process interventions, such as Knights and Willmott's (see O'Doherty, in this volume), then we must return to Butler's inquiries. Furthermore, disciplinary demands create a context not only for reproduction and repetition, but iteration's process offers the potential production of difference, as noted above. These analytic problems emerge under a Butlerian lens.

The performative's role – constructing what it purports to be, creating a referent it appears to represent – is to deliver the organized subject. Butler's use of the term performative remains technical, derived from semiotic insights into the linking of words and things or, lacking things, linking between words and other signs (Austin, 1962; de Saussure, 1972). Indeed, the function that the performative plays cannot be captured by the word 'performance'. Of course, the performative does perform, just as it may be said that people perform aspects of their gender; however, these uses do not capture the technical productive function of the performative.

'Performativity is neither free play nor theatrical self-presentation; nor can it be simply equated with performance' (Butler, 1993: 95). She continues, 'performativity cannot be understood outside of a process of iterability, a regularized and constrained repetition of norms. And this repetition is not performed *by* a subject; this repetition is what enables a subject and constitutes the temporal condition for the subject' (Butler, 1993: 95). Again, she reminds us of a lack of presence or essence, the 'paradox of referentiality', at the subject's tropological inauguration. Such a point raises issue with the so-called 'expressive organization' (Schultz, Hatch and Larsen, 2000), as one is compelled to ask what is this pre-existing 'organization' that 'expresses' and to which these 'expressions' refer? Work on brand and corporate identity that draws upon semiotic insights into the referent's disappearance – explicit in Butler's analysis of the performative – suggests that when we look for the organization behind the sign, the 'real' thing to which a sign refers, we find nothing there (Borgerson, Escudero-Magnusson and Magnusson, 2005).

If a structure, ideal, or subject identity must be iterated, Butler argues, then it is not absolute or ideal, as the existence is in the iteration. Re-signification, or iteration, is necessary. Butler takes her lead from Derrida, including his essays 'Structure, Sign and Play', 'Signature, Event, Context' and 'Before the Law' (see Derrida, 1978, 1982b and 1992, see also Butler, 2002; Salih, 2004: 4), arguing that iterability counters a structuralist essentialist ideal or moment: anticipation of a moment in fact creates the moment. In other words, lack of the moment creates the context for the moment's presence. Moreover, iteration of anticipation in the waiting is all the 'moment' that really exists. Lack of ideals, generally, functions similarly, including, specifically for Butler, the ideal of gender. The gestures and performance of gender must be repeated endlessly to maintain the illusion of a natural category of masculinity and/or femininity. The moment, ideal, or structure is constituted in its re-enactments – the doing in time in the social context (Butler, 2002).

The concept of iteration expresses a continued occurrence or pattern without assuming that there was at some point in time an original instance, natural state or ideal of which the continued instances are simply re-iterations. Thus, iteration calls attention to the lack of an original, 'natural,' or ideal category – such as femininity – that exists prior to an appearance, instantiation, or iteration. This might profitably be recalled to link to the process of subject identity formation. Identities via iteration form over time and through repeated performances of socially constructed characteristics and appropriate gestures and signs. Theories of gender arising from notions of iteration and performativity stand against essentialist understandings of the relationship between femininity and the female, masculinity and the male. Moreover, it is the iterability, repetition, and representation of characteristic traits and gestures that create and sustain these various categories of identity, yet provide openings for subversive emergences.

Iterations, in conjunction with foreclosure, undergird cultural categories of identity that operate within a variety of social arrangements. Foreclosure creates contexts that both manifest and hide what the subject is not, can never be or know. Certain kinds of foreclosure produce the subject as an 'I' that is not 'that'

– some designated 'other' identity – in a self versus other epistemology of difference (Borgerson, 2001); and 'certain things become impossible for it; certain
things become irrecoverable' (Butler, 2004d: 333). Thus, even granting possibility for subversive emergences, repeated and reiterated versions of gender, and
race, underlie and continually revitalize what is considered natural, typical and,
often, appropriate for specific groups (Borgerson and Schroeder, 2002).

Stereotyped, foreclosed and, often, damaging representations of iterations
derived from essentialist standpoints remain a crucial concern for organization
theory, as well as, for understanding and changing organizational environments.
Of course, theory from many disciplines struggles to understand how hierarchical dualisms in the arenas of gender and race – instantiating foreclosure
around masculine and feminine, or white and black – function ontologically
when contingent social and psychological constructions nevertheless define and
limit embodied human agents (Bourdieu, 2001; Borgerson, 2001; Borgerson
and Schroeder, 2002; Butler, 1990, 1993, 2000; Diprose, 1994; Gordon,
1995a, 1995b). Here, dualistic categories are the manifestation of iterations –
productions and substantiations of gestures and traits that define them as
natural and ideal.

Certain tableaux – repeated representations, imposed codes of behaviour, or
organizational cultures – endlessly re-create normative values and identities
which are made available to, constitute and exist in tandem with the subject in
contemporary culture. In this way, the iterative normativity of an environment
contributes to the subject's constitution. Such is Hancock and Tyler's concern.
However – and this crucial point for Butler should seem familiar by now –
iterations fall under the rule of contingency. Moreover, Butler writes, '[The self's]
action is always governed by aims that exceed its intentions' (Butler, 2004d: 332).
For Butler, the hope that emerges in this scenario is something like this: if typical
iterations elide, alter, shift, then change in the previously recognized definitive
category, the apparent ideal, may emerge as well, opening up possibility for
diverse gestures and characteristics, demonstrating contingency, allowing alteration over time (Butler, 1997).

According to Butler, time and related contingency produce a different version
of foreclosure than, for example, fellow phenomenologist Žižek employs. Žižek's
Lacanian psychoanalytic theory derives much theoretical form and direction
from shared Hegelian origins – vocabulary, dialectical inversions, and phenomenology's non-empiricist starting point. Yet, Butler argues that the Lacanian
notion of foreclosure appears in fixed timelessness, not socially situated as a
'temporally renewable structure . . . subject to the logic of iteration, which produced the possibility of its alteration' (2004d: 333). From Butler's perspective,
nearness to foreclosure 'threatens to undo' the subject, perhaps producing
anxiety, yet opening up possibilities 'to reinstate the subject on new and different ground' (2004d: 333). Thus, foreclosure serves a foundational role in Butler's
vision of organizing subjectivity.

She draws, for example, upon foreclosures of homosexuality and miscegena-
tion – or racial 'mixing' – calling these 'forms of segregation and phobic forms

of organizing social reality that keep the fiction of those subjects intact' (Butler, 2004d: 333). That is, heterosexual social forms organize against notions of homosexuality mobilizing the aforementioned 'self versus other epistemology of difference' (Borgerson, 2001). Expressions of 'racial' purity iterate race and organize conceptions of acceptable, or terrifying, racial similarity or difference. In her attempts to explore the underlying structure of arguments against homo-sexual parenting in France, Butler (2002) finds women – as structuralist objects of exchange – still at the base of a nationalist anthropological imagination. She warns that entering into the frame provided by public legitimation of hetero-sexual relationships risks abandoning excluded and unlegitimated ways of being, a loss 'in the wake of the ungrievable' (Butler, 2002) – and invoking other the-orized foreclosures. Butler suggests that if state legitimization and legibility grant visibility and designate what will be considered 'real,' then that which remains true to what cannot and will not be granted visibility, is lost, perhaps unrecoverably.

What does it mean, then, to understand and accept that the state has the power to grant the legitimacy, legibility and reality of relations? Can we, will we, continue to bear this loss? Butler articulates her argument and set of con-cerns in *Antigone's Claim* (2000a), revisiting and critically re-evaluating argu-ments around kinship and taboo as the basis for social intelligibility that have developed around this character of Greek tragedy. In the following section, I contextualize and develop further Butler's guiding phenomenological insights and explore their implications for core concepts in contemporary organizational theory.

Self and other in organization theory: Butler's phenomenological interventions

A basic underlying notion of the self's reliance on the other for identity forma-tion – elaborated earlier in this chapter's discussions of tropological inaugura-tion; the turning gesture; subjection; foreclosure; and so on – glimmers at the foundation of influential articulations within phenomenology. Specifically, this process requires the continued existence of the other *as different* for meaning-ful intersubjectivity (eg, Merleau-Ponty, 2002). Indeed, Merleau-Ponty argues that the not-self, the realm that limits, *must not be conceived of as available for incorporation* (2002; see also Plotnitsky, 1994: 28; Borgerson and Rehn, 2004: 464). This stringent requirement is often left behind in analyses that per-ceive unequal power relations and the privilege of the self to create the other in the self's desired – self-same – manner (Fuss, 1995: 145).

Fournier (2002), for example, in her ethnographic work with female Italian farmers, draws on Strathern (see Munro, in this volume) to argue that 'the "post-modern" celebration of differences and diversity. . . . ends up just producing more normalization, for the celebration of differences share[s] the modernist conceptualization of difference as something that has to be made present by being translated, compared, made to count' (Fournier, 2002: 81). By way of opposition to this position, Fournier writes that by marking not difference, but otherness, '[the Other] remains absent from, indifferent to, the categories of differences we may want to cast upon it to understand or recognize it,' as a kind of 'blank' (Fournier, 2002: 81). This attitude could apparently be adopted by the scientist in a kind of desired striving for manageable ignorance. Fournier's trope as a methodology expresses the desire to leave one's object of study unaltered, uncompromised, and one's data uncontaminated by cultural myopia and authorial domination, and, perhaps, offers more emergent roles for the farmers to embody. The 'blank' of the Other, however, apparently does not in the present case extend to authorial limitations regarding recognition of subjects as such. Nor does it regarding epistemological claims about their world and reactions to it – which surely require comparative notions that demand more than a 'blank.'

Still, could Butler, who draws upon notions of difference, be part of this homogenizing, subordinating movement, not recognizing the dangers of conjuring presence and contradiction, of evaluating and comparing in order to name difference? Or might Butler from a phenomenological perspective be likely to understand difference differently? Consider the following claim: 'Difference' does not unquestioningly mark that which is contradictory or reside in a person as a matter of traits to be studied or compared. Rather difference might be a valence that can be addressed in and against varying contexts. Here we can recall Derrida's words that 'this conflictuality of *différance* – which can be called contradiction only if one demarcates it by means of a long work on Hegel's concept of contradiction – can never be totally resolved' (1981: 44). So, what do researchers believe they are looking for or reporting when they observe 'difference'? Does a phenomenological notion of difference, as captured by Derrida's 'différance', suffer from the reduction to mere difference, much as performativity has been reduced to 'performance'? Would remaining aware of 'différance' alleviate Fournier's concern? Might we, perhaps, explore this concern as manifesting elements of a deeper conflict between empiricism and phenomenology?

Let me be clearer about this last question, turning to philosopher Richard Zaner's (1970) description of the distinction between empiricism and phenomenology. He writes, 'while phenomenological philosophy, as critical philosophy, shares empiricism's insistence that philosophy be attentive to things themselves as experienced, it differs from empiricism in its contention that experience is seen to be, when critically viewed, much wider, more articulated, and far more complicated than empiricism traditionally acknowledged it to be' (Zaner, 1970: 38). There are varied ways to experience the same thing, he writes, such as different modes of sense perception, remembering or expecting. Moreover, 'some things are not at all accessible or reducible to sensory perception – for example, one's own mind and mental processes . . . the minds of other persons and animate beings, numbers, logical forms, values . . . Also, *these differences themselves* can be grasped and studied, and 'difference' is not itself open to what the empiricist understood by sensory perception' (Zaner, 1970: 38; emphasis in original). If these 'differences themselves' in how we experience, differences from the empiricist's observation or the mode of 'being difference', are to be studied, not traits or characteristics that denote a 'difference from' – as in difference of a self from an other – and this accomplished in a mode 'not itself open to what the empiricist understood by sensory perception', how might such study take place?

But, let me ask first, how does Fournier's call for otherness, not difference, resound elsewhere? How are these concepts analytically related in theorists that exhibit related desire to avoid domination, exploitation, and appropriation, particularly those united in their attempts to address power differentials and attitudes of domination lurking in theory's stance? Emmanuel Levinas has argued for the absolute otherness of the Other. For Levinas, this is demanded by ethics, the foundational mode of intersubjectivity, a 'face-to-face' relation of responsibility for the Other in what Levinas calls the 'curvature of intersubjective space' (Levinas, 1969: 291). Derrida, as well, assents to these notions, stating that, if alterity remains, then questions are not about individualized entities, but the relation. He notes, however, that if designations of alterity were for purposes of subordination, then they must be disputed (Derrida, 2000, see also 1999). Whereas Derrida does not undermine considerations of alternatives to subordinating dialectics, he has argued compellingly that Levinas becomes politically conservative – in ways that echo Fournier's notions – in his insistence on the possibility of innocence in the face of the Other (Derrida, 2000) implying, for example, possibility of recognition without struggle, exclusion, or foreclosure. If Butler's notions of intersubjectivity invoke otherness, however, not as antagonistic demand for recognition, nor subordinated difference as presence but in the potentially suspect role as a limit, would a turn to a different model be preferable?

Apparently sharing Fournier's concern to a certain extent, philosopher Kelly Oliver expresses dissatisfaction with Hegelian models of recognition at the foundation of many critical social theories, even those that contest and reformulate understandings of this relation (Oliver, 2001). Subjectivity's relation to subjection in Butler is troubling to Oliver, and she follows Franz Fanon's analysis of desire for recognition as itself an outcome of colonialist oppression (Oliver, 2001: 23–32). Oliver works to create the foundations for a kind of 'witnessing beyond recognition' that can explicate lived experience, as well as provide a model of subjectivity formation without assuming struggle. Oliver writes,

> Whether these theories celebrate the presence of an autonomous subject produced through intersubjective relations or mourn the loss of that presence produced through absence inherent in intersubjective relations, the subject – as presence or absence – still dominates its others. . . . What of the subjectivity of this so-called other? What of the subject position of those othered by these discourses of subjectivity?' (Oliver, 2001: 6)

Resonating concerns exist regarding subordinating or colonialist dialectics; however, here at least, recognition of absolute otherness – that which is not available for incorporation – does not require dispensing with notions of difference, nor invoking the anonymity of absence, or a 'blank.'

Perhaps, for the purposes of organization theory this 'not' that appears non-subordinating through the utter separation of self and other, yet subordinating in an analysis of difference, demands a retheorizing of intersubjectivity – and not only between the researcher and subject. For example, an alternative understanding of intersubjectivity, with the self and other maintained as different and sovereign, emerges from phenomenological concepts at work in global economic theory, including devolution of the exclusive territoriality of the modern state, 'the absolute sovereignty of the state over its national territory' (Sassen, 1996: 3). Social theorist Saskia Sassen writes, 'having achieved absolute sovereignty, the new states found they could only communicate with each other 'by tolerating within themselves little islands of alien sovereignty' (Sassen, 1996: 4), giving rise to a right of embassy, then evolving into a 'form of exterritoriality through which to resolve the tension between exclusive territoriality and the need for transactions among states' (Sassen, 1996: 13). Thus, in order for self and other to have relations – after having inaugurated separation – the self must 'allow' untranslated, unadulterated 'islands' of the other to exist within. Here the self opens its boundaries to an other that is beyond its own making. The self and other in such a view are seen as acting intentionally and uncoerced for mutual benefit, choosing first separation, then the extraterritorial solution to separation. In contrast to this, for Levinas no choice exists in the originary relation; and for him, ethics arises directly from this.

Pushing the implications of dominating and appropriating processes of subjection further, theorist Diane Fuss marks the shared concerns discussed above: 'In a colonial dialectics, based on a radical asymmetry of power, symbolic alterity operates precisely as a privilege of the Self-Same' (Fuss, 1995: 145). To put this another way, any gestures toward mutual recognition fail in the context of the subordinating Self's power – to name, to encroach upon, to violate – the Other. Has Butler simply overlooked this crucial inequality and antagonism in her acceptance of the trope and the role of subjection?

Recall, the figure of the turning is not a subject turning, not a subject and its other asking for recognition. Failing to attend to the paradox of reflexivity elides levels of theory. Whereas Butler (see, for example, 1997: 31–62) draws upon Hegel's dialectic of Master and Slave, she is more interested in using this as a way to understand the psychic forms of forces and the inauguration of subjectivity than in attempting to pronounce effects on particular people. That is, for Butler, Hegel's Slave is not a subordinated person. Claims that power and subjection's theoretical psychic forms directly lead to, or map onto, subordinated human identities and subject positions need to be carefully considered – though this may make interesting, if not universalizing, and therefore, coherent, theory. Butler's theory can be used to shed light on particular people in particular contexts, of course, but then we are observing, witnessing, and creating concrete, lived experiences, not tropological inaugurations. In other words, implications for subjectivities formed in subjection may not translate directly into subordinated people – clearly not, as subjection and the trope operate for all identity formations, not only for subjugated and oppressed embodied human lives. We may not be able to draw a direct line of causation between models of subjectivity formation and appropriate ways of engaging research subjects or organizing in 'corporate culturalism', for example.

For Butler no force, no discourse rests beyond contingency. Though she seems to loosen the meaning of the 'struggle' for recognition precisely where Oliver recognizes violated people, for Butler there is not a subject that struggles in the moment of turning. Moreover, power resides no more securely in a subject position than a human subject does, hence theorizing must note that power, conceptualized often as inauguarating subjection, cannot *do* things. A limit does not make itself a limit. Contingency, performativity, iteration, foreclosure, and the tropological inauguration brought together – the limitings and openings of each reinforcing, diminishing, overlapping, and disconnecting from each other – produce complex visions of possibility.

Conclusion

Life in action seems more readily captured by Butler's theoretical insights – a culture in iteration; the apparent solidity 'behind' the performative; and melancholy exclusions from legitimacy and intelligibility mourning in the 'wake of the ungrieveable.' Perhaps, as researchers, we can never get Butler 'right,' attempts to 'apply' her concepts always failing to maintain theoretical levels, drifting toward mundane descriptions altered in the very act of making them theoretical. But this is a familiar quandary in which the empirical appears honest and, with some effort, undistorted; yet, as Butler, the phenomenologist, argues 'empirical analysis in general cannot offer a persuasive explanation of its own constitution as a field of enquiry' (Butler, 2000: 274). In this sense, a critical phenomenology, such as Butler's, raises questions outside empiricism's certainties, demonstrating the analytic power of 'differences in themselves', and the way in which the tropological inauguration plays at limits and boundaries of difference and otherness, witnessing these not in essential opposition but as constituting each other's intelligibility through performativity, iteration and foreclosure.

Butler assures us that the movement, the gesture of motion, the tropological inauguration spurs us into an experiential realm that offers and expands the world, and especially domains of possibility. Thus, her contextualizing background itself provides openings for recognizing questions in contemporary organization theory; and this includes clarifying and distinguishing between empiricist and phenomenological ambitions in theorizing and research. Now is a critical time for organization theory to recognize Judith Butler's contributions – beyond common notions of postmodernism and gender – and embrace this profoundly influential thinker.

References

Austin, J. L. (1962) *How to Do Things With Words*. Oxford: Oxford University Press.

Borgerson, J. (2001) 'Feminist ethical ontology: Contesting "the bare givenness of inter-subjectivity"' *Feminist Theory*, 2(2): 173–187.

Borgerson, J. and A. Rehn (2004) 'General economy and productive dualisms' *Gender, Work and Organization*, 11(4): 455–474.

Borgerson, J. and J. E. Schroeder (2002) 'Ethical issues of global marketing: Avoiding bad faith in visual representation' *European Journal of Marketing*, 36(5/6): 570–594.

Borgerson, J., M. Escudero-Magnusson and F. Magnusson (2005) 'Branding ethics: Negotiating Benetton's identity and image' in J. E. Schroeder and M. Salzter-Mörling (eds.) *Brand Culture*. London: Routledge.

Bourdieu, P. (2001) *Masculine Domination*, trans. R. Nice. Oxford: Polity Press.

Bowring, M. (2004) 'Resistance is *not* futile: Liberating Captain Janeway from the masculine-feminine dualism of leadership' *Gender, Work and Organization*, 11(4): 381–405.

Brewis, J. (2002) 'Kinship that Matters' *ephemera: critical dialogues on organization*, 2(4): 352–356.

Brewis, J. and S. Linstead (2000) *Sex, Work, and Sex Work: Eroticizing Organization*. London: Routledge.

Butler, J. (1987/1999) *Subjects of Desire*. New York: Columbia University Press.

Butler, J. (1990) *Gender Trouble: Feminism And The Subversion Of Identity*. New York: Routledge.

Butler, J. (1993) *Bodies that Matter: On the Discursive Limits of 'Sex'*. New York: Routledge.

Butler, J. (1997) *The Psychic Life of Power: Theories of Subjection*. Stanford, CA: Stanford University Press.

Butler, J. (2000a) *Antigone's Claim: Kinship Between Life and Death*. New York: Colombia University Press.

Butler, J. (2000b) 'Dynamic Conclusions' in J. Butler, E. Laclau and S. Žižek (eds.) *Contingency, Hegemony, Universality*. London: Verso.

Butler, J. (2002) 'Antigone's claim: Is kinship always already heterosexual?' Lecture at University of Southern Stockholm, Sweden, 27 April.

Butler, J. (2004a) *Precarious Life: The Powers of Mourning and Violence*. London: Verso.

Butler, J. (2004b) *Undoing Gender*. New York: Routledge.

Butler, J. (2004c) 'Desire, rhetoric, and recognition in Hegel' in Sara Salih (ed.) *The Judith Butler Reader*. Oxford: Blackwell.

Butler, J. (2004d) 'Changing the subject: Judith Butler's politics of radical resignification' in Sara Salih (ed.) *The Judith Butler Reader*. Oxford: Blackwell.

Butler, J., E. Laclau and S. Žižek (eds.) (2000) *Contingency, Hegemony, Universality*. London: Verso.

Czarniawska, B. and H. Höpfl (eds.) (2002) *Casting the Other: The Production and Maintenance of Inequalities in Work Organizations*. London: Routledge.

de Saussure, F. (1972) *Course in General Linguistics*, trans. R. Harris. London: Duckworth.

Deleuze, G. (1991) *Empiricism and Subjectivity: An Essay on Hume's Theory of Human Nature*, trans. Constantin Boundas. New York: Columbia University Press.

Derrida, J. (1978) 'Structure, sign, and play in the discourse of the human sciences' in *Writing and Difference*, trans A. Bass. Chicago: University of Chicago Press.

Derrida, J. (1981) *Positions,* trans. A. Bass. Chicago: University of Chicago Press.

Derrida, J. (1982a) 'The pit and the pyramid: Introduction to Hegel's semiology' in *Margins of Philosophy*, trans. A. Bass. Chicago: University of Chicago Press.

Derrida, J. (1982b) 'Signature, event, context' in *Margins of Philosophy*, trans. A. Bass. Chicago: University of Chicago Press.

Derrida, J. (1992) 'Before the law' in D. Attridge (ed.) *Acts of Literature*. London: Routledge.

Derrida, J. (1999) 'A word of welcome' in *Adieu to Emmanuel Levinas*, trans P.-A. Brault and M. Naas. Stanford: Stanford University Press.

Derrida, J. (2000) 'Ethics and the law' Lecture at University of Southern Stockholm, Sweden, 30 May.

Diprose, R. (1994) *The Bodies of Women: Ethics, Embodiment and Sexual Difference*. London: Routledge.

Ford, J. and N. Harding (2004) 'We went looking for an organization but could find only the metaphysics of its presence' *Sociology*, 38(4): 815–830.

Fournier, V. (2002) 'Keeping the veil of otherness: Practicing disconnection' in B. Czarniawska and H. Höpfl (eds.) *Casting the Other: The Production and Maintenance of Inequalities in Work Organizations*. London: Routledge.

Fuss, D. (1995) *Identification Papers*. New York: Routledge.

Gherardi, S. (1995) *Gender, Symbolism, and Organizational Cultures*. London: Sage.

Gordon, L. (1995a) *Bad Faith and Antiblack Racism*. Atlantic Highlands, NJ: Humanities Press.

Gordon, L. (1995b) *Fanon and the Crisis of European Man: An Essay on Philosophy and the Human Sciences*. London: Routledge.

Hancock, P. and M. Tyler (2001) 'Managing subjectivity and the dialectic of self-consciousness: Hegel and organization theory' *Organization*, 9(4): 565–585.

Hartmann, K. (1966) *Sartre's Ontology*. Evanston: Northwestern University Press.

Hassard, J. and M. Parker (eds.) (1993) *Postmodernism and Organizations*. London: Sage.

Hodgson, D. (2005) ' "Putting on a professional performance": Performativity, subversion and project management' *Organization*, 12(1): 51–68.

Jones, C. and A. Spicer (2005) 'The sublime object of entrepreneurship' *Organization*, 12(2): 223–246.

Kant, Immanuel (1951) *Critique of Judgment*, trans J. H. Bernard. New York: Hafner.

Knights, D. (1992) 'Changing spaces: The disruptive impact of a new epistemological location for the study of management' *Academy of Management Review*, 17(3): 514–536.

Knights, D. (1997) 'Organization theory in the age of deconstruction: Dualism, gender and post-modernism revisited' *Organization Studies*, 18(1): 1–19.

Levinas, E. (1969) *Totality and Infinity*, trans. A. Lingis. Pittsburgh, PA: Duquesne University Press.

Merleau-Ponty, M. (2002) *Phenomenology of Perception*, trans. C. Smith. London: Routledge.

Nancy, J.-L. (1993) 'The sublime offering' in J.-F. Cortine, M. Deguy, E. Escoubas, P. Lacoues-Labarthe, J.-F. Lyotard, L. Martin, J.-L. Nancy and J. Rogozinski (eds.) (1993) *Of the Sublime Presence in Question*, trans. Jeffrey Librett. Albany, NY: State University of New York Press.

Natanson, M. (1970) *The Journeying Self: A Study in Philosophy and the Social Role*. Reading, MA: Addison-Wesley.

Natanson, M. (1973) *Edmund Husserl: Philosopher of Infinite Tasks*. Evanston, IL: Northwestern UP.

Natanson, M. (1986) *Anonymity: A Study in the Philosophy of Alfred Schutz*. Bloomington: Indiana University Press.

Oliver, K. (2001) *Witnessing: Beyond Recognition*. Minneapolis, MN: University of Minnesota Press.

Parker, M. (2002) 'Queering management and organization' *Gender, Work and Organization*, 9(2): 146–166.

Plotnitsky, A. (1994) *Complementarity: Anti-Epistemology After Bohr and Derrida*. London: Duke University Press.

Salih, S. (ed.) (2004) *The Judith Butler Reader*. Oxford: Blackwell.

Sartre, J.-P. (1956) *Being and Nothingness: A Phenomenological Essay on Ontology*, trans. H. Barnes. New York: Washington Square Books.

Sassen, S. (1996) *Losing Control? Sovereignty in an Age of Globalization*. New York: Columbia University Press.

Schultz, M., M. J. Hatch and M. J. Larsen (eds.) (2000) *The Expressive Organization: Linking Identity, Reputation, and the Corporate Brand.* Oxford: Oxford University Press.

Wray-Bliss, E. (2003) 'Research subjects/research subjections: The politics and ethics of critical research' *Organization,* 10(2): 307–325.

Zaner, R. (1970) *The Way of Phenomenology: Criticism as a Philosophical Discipline.* Indianapolis, IN: Pegasus.

Othering Organization Theory:
Marta Calás and Linda Smircich

Joanna Brewis

Introduction

Marta Calás and Linda Smircich's collaborative work on leadership, culture, gender and their intersections is remarkable in many ways for the consistency of its central thematics. Indeed Calás and Smircich have been at the forefront of developing arguments forming the bedrock of poststructuralist/ postmodernist 'critical management studies'; and their review of the contributions of the 'postmodern conversation' (Calás and Smircich, 1999: 666) to organization theory seems to me to summarize the key insights of their own research:

1. revealing 'the inner workings and assumptive basis' (1999: 649) of existing organization theory, identifying the arbitrary discursive limitations within which it operates;
2. focusing on the fixing of meaning in organization theory and therefore on how our scholarship represents some phenomena, interests and groups and marginalizes others (while implicitly or explicitly making much more universalist claims);
3. seeking to make space for non-traditional voices in organization theory, whilst being aware of the difficulties in attempting to speak for these Others;
4. disavowing notions of enduring truths about organizations;
5. acknowledging the 'real-world' power of organization theory and considering how it might best be undertaken;
6. creating localized, temporary and subjective accounts of organizations which are sensitive to how they 'real-ize' their subject matter; and
7. acknowledging that writing on organizations exists to be read, and that the author is 'just one interpreter among other readers' (1999: 653).

My reading of co-authored Calás and Smircich texts dating back to 1987 – and other sole and jointly authored work where appropriate – focuses on surfacing these themes. This review is instructive because it reminds us that these ideas were once far from commonplace in *any* form of organization theory and also marks out the continuing disparity between 'critical' thinking and the 'orthodoxy' in this regard. Finally, in considering criticisms of Calás and Smircich, I start with what they themselves describe as their 'hysterical reading' (1990: 704) of orthodox organization theory. Henry Mintzberg (1991) for example, whose text *The Nature of Managerial Work* was deconstructed in a very well-known Calás and Smircich (1991) discussion of leadership, retorted that it was seemingly an instance of sexual obsession on the part of its authors. He also accuses them of writing in an impenetrable way. Another issue to be pursued here is the potential tension between Calás and Smircich's opposition to teleology in organization theory and points in their work where they nonetheless appear to value one form of analysis over another. Finally, more recent critiques (Weitzner, 2003; Jones, 2004) of their use of deconstruction will be discussed. While taking all these criticisms seriously, however, I will also suggest potential ripostes as regards the overall Calás and Smircich project.

Taking aim at the taken-for-granted

Much of Calás and Smircich's work seems to be a response to the intellectual mood of the last two decades or so; to what they identify as a sense in various debates that organization theory has failed to fulfil its '*modern promises of progress* – for example, more efficient organization, better education, better jobs, better income for all' (Smircich and Calás, 1995: xiv). Instead of attacking existing commentary in traditionally oppositional ways, however – for example, as 'bad science' or suggesting 'better' theories or methodologies – Calás and Smircich suggest that organization theory's problem is that it *repeats itself*. They argue that it works within unspoken discursive constraints which mean it is possible only to say certain things in certain ways, making it difficult ever *really* to say anything different, whilst also identifying what might appear to be profound shifts in such theorizing as surface level alterations alone (Smircich and Calás, 1987: especially 246–248; Calás and Smircich, 1991: 568, 1992a: 229–230, 1993: 72, 2003a, 2003b).

Nonetheless, Calás and Smircich also acknowledge that reflecting on these discursive constraints is not straightforward because they represent our taken-for-granted intellectual environment. Indeed at times they suggest that this environment is so well-embedded as to provide the only way of 'speaking' organization theory (Smircich, 1983: 355; Calás and Smircich, 1992a: 245, 247, 1992b: 233, 1996: 245; Mir *et al.*, 1999: 277). The task they set themselves is therefore a formidable one: they aim to reveal how organization theory closes off 'what can be said to be organizational knowledge' (Calás and Smircich, 1991: 567) *and* to open it up to a wider range of orientations and interpretations. Although more recently they acknowledge that the 'postmodern turn' in organization theory has allowed us 'to try and think the unthinkable, to move *as if we were outside the limits of our thoughts*' (Calás and Smircich, 2003a: 30 – also see Calás and Smircich, 1999: 657), one key motif in Calás and Smircich's work is therefore a focus on the usually unacknowledged ways in which this theory is itself organized.

Perhaps the most famous example is their 1991 unpacking of four classic leadership texts. Here Calás and Smircich argue that conventional organization theory values leadership as 'something different' from the negatively-connoted activity of seduction. Their deconstruction of Barnard's *The Functions of the Executive*, McGregor's *The Human Side of Enterprise*, Mintzberg's *The Nature of Managerial Work* and Peters and Waterman's *In Search of Excellence*, however, suggests a different interpretation. Calás and Smircich argue that leadership is used here as a *euphemism* for a particular type of homosocial seduction, where the leader can only seduce others of the same kind (the masculine, or masculine-identified). In revisiting Barnard's definition of leadership, for example, they point out the multiple meanings of his language by reference to the *Oxford English Dictionary*. Barnard's suggestion that effective leadership creates the '**DESIRE** for **ADHERENCE**' (cited in Calás and Smircich, 1991: 575) amongst followers is thus reinterpreted as the claim that 'Leadership is the absolutely necessary creation of desire, a longing, wishing, craving – the creation of sexual attraction that promises to be satisfied through faithful attachment.' (Calás and Smircich, 1991: 575). In their reworking of these texts, Calás and Smircich suggest that a host of other versions of leadership become possible in the spaces that result.

Two other influential pieces deploy similar tactics to critique organization theory more generally. These include a discussion of 'the absence of women's values and concerns in organizational discourses' (Calás and Smircich, 1992a: 248) such as those on motivation, culture and (unsurprisingly) leadership. In the second paper, Calás and Smircich (1992b) revisit existing work so as to address this aporia. One of their targets is Schwartz's assertion that apparently immoral actions by organizational members can be alternatively understood as the product of high levels of commitment and a consequent compulsion to see off any threat to the organization. Calás and Smircich's 'women's voices' feminist reading positions this as a masculine form of commitment; one which interprets the employment relationship as turning on impartial, universal conceptions of what is just. They also question how women commit to organizations, and whether commitment is possible without the 'immorality' which Schwartz identifies.

Their 1992a paper, however, goes on to note that doing 'feminist organization theory' would mean more than just adding feminism to the many existing approaches to the study of organizations. Instead it would surface the gendered characteristics of theorizing itself, so as to move beyond ''talking about' pluralism, while the [objectivist, rational, universalist, dualistic] knowledge-making enterprise remains untouched' (Calás and Smircich, 1992a: 240). Calás and Smircich then attempt such a 're-writing' of organization theory in their postmodernist analysis of a piece by Karl Weick. For example, they argue that the Weick paper, which ironically is about the construction of organization theory, retains classic dualisms such as (masculine) mind/ (feminine) body and privileges the former over the latter as far as the attainment of 'better' theory is concerned.

Elsewhere, Calás and Smircich (1999, 2003a) review Foucauldian genealogy and Derridian deconstruction in terms of how they historicize, politicize and denaturalize accepted wisdom, as well as highlighting the uncontrollability of textual meanings. They also discuss how these approaches have been taken up in organization theory and the productive amendments offered by poststructuralist feminism, postcolonial theory and actor-network theory. Again the focus here is on challenges to the orthodoxy. One concern of the 2003a paper is to foreground the modernist tenor of organization theory, its preservation of divisions between the social, the scientific and technological and the institutional realms and its consequent privileging of scientific and technological knowledge. Thus, events such as the Challenger disaster are represented by such theory as *extraordinary* which 'excludes the everydayness about the fallibility of our knowledge and, in particular, the fallibility of science and technology insofar as these have become the surrogate models for 'all that is to be known' in our society' (Calás and Smircich, 2003a: 34).

Anti-teleology

Calás and Smircich, then, insist that mainstream organization theory arbitrarily forecloses the possibilities available for apprehending organizations. Their querying of the seemingly self-evident explicitly attends to marginal positions – especially those of women and people of colour. They also call explicitly for a recognition in organization theory that ' "lay knowledge" is not ignorance', but instead is more likely to pose questions and identify relationships to which 'expert' analysis would not attend. In Latour's words, then, a more collaborative dialogue between 'expert' and 'lay' sectors of society would, they suggest, result in genuine commitment to the slogan 'no innovation without representation' (Calás and Smircich, 2003a: 52–53).

But in suggesting that the orthodoxy is only one way to understand organizations, however self-perpetuating, Calás and Smircich also reject the claim that *there is any sort of enduring truth to be had* about organizations. Instead knowledge is presented as irrevocably indeterminate: as they say, 'we don't believe in ahistorical, acultural, universals' (Calás and Smircich, 1996: 242). This rejection of teleology is especially visible in their 2003a discussion. Here, as implied above, Calás and Smircich explore how poststructuralist feminism, postcolonial theory and actor-network theory might assist organization theory in '*radically rethinking* the modern idea of 'progress' and its normative undertones, still pervading our field, and possibly *resituating* this idea in a less harmful space' (Calás and Smircich, 2003a: 31). They point here to the problems associated with claims such as Hofstede's that 'collectivist' countries become more 'individualistic' as they '*develop*' – ie, become richer and more industrialized (Calás and Smircich, 2003a: 46).

Another well-known but much earlier piece in this mould, which builds on Smircich's (1983) discussion of the organizational culture literature, marks out both orthodoxy (functionalist, culture as organizational variable, managerialist) and discontents (interpretivist, organizations *as* cultures, emphasis on oppressive aspects of the workplace). Smircich and Calás (1987) suggest that the first category has not departed very far from prevailing tendencies in organization theory whereas the discontents are *genuinely* oppositional understandings of organizations. Nonetheless, they aver that the failure of the discontents to win any ground from their orthodox counterparts creates 'the conditions of possibility for a postmodernism of resistance . . . [and t]he transformation of the organizational culture literature into the *cultured organizational literature*' (Smircich and Calás, 1987: 257). This project denies the possibility of better truths, and challenges its own and others' 'discursive strongholds' (Smircich and Calás, 1987: 256). In other words, it does not aim at the attainment of a 'better truth' – its *raison d'être* is to puncture the totalizing efforts of the mainstream.

Similarly, Calás and Smircich's 1996 analysis of how feminism can speak to organization theory does not end with the assertion that feminisms of varying hues might disrupt prevailing (and circumscribed) interpretations of what organizations are and should be. Instead they go to considerable lengths to lay out the potential shortcomings of each feminist position – pointing, for instance, to psychoanalytic feminism's preoccupation with what might be regarded as a very Western, middle-class set of family relations or the ways in which postcolonialist analyses may also imply relative inattention to gender. Here then Calás and Smircich critique forms of scholarship which they themselves have identified as more inclusive and socially aware than conventional organization theory.

The material impact of theory

To summarize the argument thus far, I have suggested that Calás and Smircich are concerned with organization theory's 'one-sidedness', and that they also claim we cannot attain any universal truth about organizations. These commitments are underpinned by a Foucauldian sense of the 'real-world' impact of organization theory:

> [Organization] theories – once they are presented as knowledge – guide organizational participants in their efforts to understand and control organizations. In this sense organizational scientists 'make' organizations as much as we study them . . . Thus having a socially conscious organizational practice may depend first on having a more socially conscious organizational scholarship. (Calás and Smircich, 1992b: 223, 234)

Our theorizing, then, is not a neutral mirror of the world: it shapes understandings of the world and behaviour within it such that 'there is no world independent of the analytical approach to which a commitment for analysis has been made' (Calás and Smircich, 2003a: 39). This is especially true given the attempts by organization theory to be 'relevant' and the fact that management books often become best-sellers (Smircich, 1985: 68). Calás and Smircich wish to fore-

© The Editorial Board of the Sociological Review 2005

ground all organization theorists' accountability for the effects of their conceptualizations on real-world practice – and to challenge the resultant constraints. One example is the ways in which our literature tends to identify leadership as fundamentally grounded in power differences and hierarchy (Calás and Smircich, 1988: especially 216–217). This has implications both for employees, constructed as dependent on their leaders, and leaders, depicted as ultimately responsible for the behaviour of their followers (also see Smircich and Morgan, 1982: 269–272).

Calás and Smircich particularly emphasize these material effects of knowledge in their 1993 analysis of two discourses which were prevalent at the time in the US; the 'feminine-in-management' (rhetoric: the 'turbulent contemporary US business environment' requires managerial skills which women 'typically' possess – inspiring others, encouraging participation etc.) and globalization (rhetoric: the 'turbulent contemporary US business environment' is growing more 'complex' as the world becomes 'smaller' and increasingly 'borderless'). They suggest that these discourses may work in tandem to produce certain problematic consequences – for example, that the feminizing of organizations as recommended by the feminine-in-management discourse is likely to extend only up to the borders of the US so that

> the private/public divide (women in the household, men out in the world) will not have disappeared. It will have been displaced and recreated on a larger scale . . . the national organization – as feminine as it might become – would be a powerless pawn in a globalized organizational world. (Calás and Smircich, 1993: 74)

The claim here is that feminine-in-management's putative effects would be to move women into *national* organizations – but at a time when the discourse of globalization was busily constructing the *international* arena as the place where the important economic decisions get made.

Intellectual activity's 'real-izing' of the world is also central to the 2003a discussion. Here, as suggested above, Calás and Smircich identify modernist scholarship's emphasis on progress as having a potentially dubious impact. They argue for the need to pay explicit attention to the 'social consequences' of organization theory, especially given that the origin or exacerbation of social problems such as homelessness, child poverty and corporate domination lies for them in 'policies espoused as "good management" and "good organization"' (Calás and Smircich, 2003a: 42). Elsewhere they suggest that organization theory has in fact contributed very little that is *innovative* to institutional practice, so that the 19th century emphasis on bureaucracy, rationality and efficiency effectively remains the global Gold Standard (Calás and Smircich, 2003b: 598).

Subjectivity, ownership and the reader-as-author

The above concerns coalesce in Calás and Smircich's insistence on 'owning' their work. They attempt to 'write with less author-ity . . . being very conscious of the connection between the writer and the story she tells' (Smircich, 1995: 236). In their various reviews of the organization theory canon, for example, there is an explicit acknowledgement of their profound implication in the presentation of their material and their focus on specific authors or theories. Calás and Smircich also draw attention to the time at which they are writing, their intellectual context (the US business school) and their gender. In addition, they explicitly confess to the standpoints they themselves prefer – somewhere between postmodernism and postcolonial theory – and suggest that they do not wish to depict their perspective as superior to others' (Calás and Smircich, 1996: 219, 242, 1999: 650, 655). Calás and Smircich's own reworkings of organization theory are similarly characterized by this epistemological modesty. Their deconstruction of four seminal leadership texts, for example, is intended to open up other ways of reading these texts (and therefore leadership *per se*) as opposed to using 'typical argumentative logic' and presenting *'assertive arguments'* (Calás and Smircich, 1991: 570 – also see 1988: 216, 1992a: 228, 2003a: 30).

Indeed it is Calás and Smircich's resounding acknowledgement of their own voices which subdues at least some potential criticisms. Their categorizations of different theoretical positions seem to me to be contestable – such as the argument that poststructuralist feminism, postcolonial theory and actor-network theory are more politically motivated than postmodernism/poststructuralism (Calás and Smircich, 1999, 2003a). But their modesty allows the reader to engage more thoroughly with the suggestions they do make, to think about the reasoning that *these authors* employ, and thereby to reflect on *their own* frameworks as equally arbitrary.

In asking us to take responsibility for the texts that we *produce*, Calás and Smircich also focus on how we *read* others' texts, suggesting that reading in itself is a form of authorship. Therefore, no matter what the intentions of the author are,

> reading is not only understanding but interpreting what we read. In this sense, reading allows not only for multiple interpretations but also for the 'authority' of the reader and the critic, which goes well beyond the 'authority' of the writer. (Calás and Smircich, 1988: 204)

Both here and elsewhere they take the Derridian line that texts have a life of their own because readers *actively interpret and make sense of them*. So Calás and Smircich do not hold authors *wholly* responsible for the ways in which their writings are understood and acted upon. They also acknowledge that organization theorists are caught in a web of intertextuality because they derive their understanding of how organization theory should look, what it should say, what about and where it should be published from existing texts – and it is hard to break free of this web, as suggested earlier, because it is our taken-for-granted currency of exchange and the basis of our livelihoods.

Thus Calás and Smircich's target is not individual organization *theorists* but rather how organization theory *texts* signify and reproduce the prevailing discourse. They do not wish to impugn the relevant authors as people, to state that they have sought to suppress particular standpoints or to accuse them of sloppy research (Calás and Smircich, 1991: 572, 1992a: 245, 247, 1992b: 227). Similarly, Calás and Smircich (1988: 224) emphasize that they do not view organizational scholars as consciously erecting boundaries around what can and cannot be said to 'preserve a stronghold of academic domination'. They also frequently acknowledge that they could (and perhaps should) have revisited some of their own work, because they too are part of the organization theory tradition which they are simultaneously trying to subvert.

Gender, gender everywhere

One criticism mounted against Calás and Smircich is their apparent preoccupation with gender and sexuality. Mintzberg's (1991) letter to the authors, which appeared immediately after their deconstruction of his and other leadership texts, suggests that one can find traces of masculine sexuality and domination everywhere *if that is what one is looking for*. He illustrates this by 'deconstructing' the first four words of the Calás and Smircich piece, and proposing that 'following', for example, connotes 'pursuit, pursuing, undressing with eyes, ie, intention to seduce, also reference to the tail, hence the penis' (Mintzberg, 1991: 602). Mintzberg's point is that Calás and Smircich go too far, that for them all the workings of the modern Western world seem to be predicated on gendered forms of oppression.

We could take issue with Mintzberg's riposte as regards his understanding of deconstruction. It is also scarcely original, as a reviewer of this chapter pointed out, to accuse feminist scholars of being gender-obsessed – indeed such a criticism could be seen as nothing more than a patriarchal defence mechanism. However, for me there is something here which is worth pursuing a little further. In (re-)reading texts such as the 1991 paper, I have myself struggled to accept specific Calás and Smircich claims about other, concealed meanings in the sources they discuss. For example, they reproduce Mintzberg's claim that the managerial role of liaison emphasizes 'the significance of **HORIZONTAL** relationships. While vertical or authority relationships have received much attention in the literature – specifically in terms of the *leader* role – **HORIZONTAL** relationships have been largely ignored' (Mintzberg, cited in Calás and Smircich, 1991: 586). Their alternative rendering, given the dictionary definitions of both 'liaison' and 'horizontal', is as follows: '[the leader] would not conceal any longer the illicit sexual relationships he carries on with those who are like him and with whom he lies down' (Calás and Smircich, 1991: 586). This to me is perhaps a bridge too far – it seems to impute meanings to the original text in a less than plausible way.

I also have some sympathy with Mintzberg's (1991: 602) suggestion that the 1991 paper is at times 'impregnable'. I have often found Calás and Smircich's deconstructive work difficult to decipher, even as a feminist academic who is (putatively at least) schooled in postmodernist and poststructuralist theory. This impenetrability is something they themselves note as an established criticism of poststructuralist analyses; that they are 'elitist, inaccessible and full of jargon . . . despite the[ir] democratizing impetus' (Calás and Smircich, 1996: 245 – also see 2003a: 245). I therefore suggest that the complexity of parts of Calás and Smircich's own argumentation potentially disenfranchises some of those to whom they want to give intellectual houseroom. Put another way, their writing at times comes across as 'clever wordplay aimed at people who have nothing better to do with their time than translate these academic riddles' (Weitzner, 2003: 11). This may run the risk of undermining the ethico-political sensibilities to which Calás and Smircich clearly subscribe, and which are writ large across the wider deconstructive project, at least as Derrida conceived it (Weitzner, 2003; Jones, 2004). This last is a theme to which I return below.

It may also be that the 'one-eyed' nature of some of Calás and Smircich's claims deters possible sympathizers. Indeed, as Grey avers with regard to the 'gendering' of organization theory more generally,

> it is conceivable that the gendering of organizational analysis could become a shibboleth which critical thinkers would wish to de-bunk. This is not somehow to claim that gender should *not* be a central concept and object of study for organizational analysis, but that, in constituting it as central, power is being exercised in ways which would repay further analysis, perhaps in the form of a genealogy of gender. (1995: 50)

Whilst I and others may quibble with aspects of the Calás and Smircich output, however, this does underline the nature of their project; their message that orthodox organization theory represents a discursive 'sea' in which scholars 'swim', and which is difficult to reflect upon and resist. Consequently, their own resistances to this orthodoxy could be seen as *necessarily* both complex and inflammatory to compel others to think differently about how organization theory is done and its material effects. Calás and Smircich's reactivation of marginal voices in the discipline, however idiosyncratic, challenging to read and in part unconvincing, *arguably has to be so* in order to unsettle, dissipate and subvert the familiar and taken-for-granted. Indeed, as they say themselves, ' "Analytical strategies" like the ones deployed in this paper, in their own experimental form and farfetchedness, are attempts to reflect upon the limits of the *normal* logic' (Calás and Smircich, 1991: 597).

Learmonth (2004) agrees. Like Weitzner and Jones, he suggests that Derrida's work has substantial utility for any emancipatory critique, the claims of many organization theorists notwithstanding. At one stage Learmonth acknowledges that Derrida is also challenging to read, and that this is a contributory factor in any subsequent misinterpretations. He goes on, however, to argue, following Howells (1998) and Robert Cooper (see Spoelstra, in this volume), that 'Derrida's difficult style is symptomatic of an ambition to make language say things that it has not previously said' (Learmonth, 2004: 9); that it is a deliberate attempt to illustrate that *all* texts are dense, complicated and harbour many competing meanings. In addition, Learmonth makes specific reference to Calás and Smircich (1991) in suggesting that they have adopted *precisely the same tactic*, and for *precisely the same reasons*.

The return of teleology

On a different tack, and to borrow a well-worked phrase from another reviewer of this chapter, it is also possible to identify 'logical aporias and unintentional contradictions' in the Calás and Smircich *oeuvre*. Certainly in Smircich's early work there is often a relatively pronounced teleology. For example, and despite the broadly pluralist sensibilities of a Morgan and Smircich analysis of differing ontological and epistemological assumptions in organization theory, in their concluding remarks they argue that 'The really important methodological issues revolve around the problems of testing the grounds of these rival views . . . [but] the more fundamental need to test the assumptions has passed almost unobserved' (1980: 499). The idea of 'testing' such philosophical orientations (quite apart from its attendant difficulties) seems to me to presume that some will turn out to be more robust than others. Similar arguments regarding the possibility of more rigorous (/ scientific) research being able to capture 'what is really going on' in organizations appear in Smircich and Chesser's (1981: especially 204) discussion of performance assessment and there is also a suggestion in the Smircich and Stubbart (1985: especially 731–735) argument that strategy making can be *most usefully* understood as enacted, as a process of sense making, both by theorists and practitioners.

We could of course dismiss these sorts of claims as evidence of an academic standpoint being gradually worked through, and any latent teleology as Smircich juvenilia. Nonetheless, such tendencies are also visible in the later collaborative work. For example, Calás and Smircich (1988: 221) suggest of their review of 23 articles about leadership that only one bore any resemblance to the complex realities of 'lived leadership', depicting the leader as a 'real person' with 'strengths and weaknesses'. Elsewhere, they seem to sketch out a teleological development of academic knowledge in their aforementioned suggestion that the failed 'modernist' project of critiquing the orthodoxy in analyses of organizational culture allows for the possibility of a 'postmodernism of resistance' because 'These discourses prompted us to learn more, to become more cultured, and to resist entanglements in disciplinary boundaries.' (Smircich and Calás, 1987: 257). This is seen to represent such discourses' 'major contributions' – ie, they have allowed the emergence of a more 'desirable' approach to organization theory (also see Smircich and Calás, 1995: xxvii–xxviii).

Nonetheless, the balance that Calás and Smircich are attempting is a delicate one: it is a call for organization theory to become more self-aware and inclusive *without* privileging any of the newly emergent positions. They seem to want to cleave to Foucault's (cited in Smart, 1986: 171) suggestion that listening to marginal voices does not have to mean applauding them for telling 'the ultimate truth'. Instead such a project is justified simply because it reveals that there *are* other ways of seeing, telling and understanding. Moreover, Calás and Smircich's writing is of course avowedly political – they want to make a difference with their academic work, to open up silences and expose oppressions. In this regard, what from one angle look like occasional teleological lapses might be re-interpreted by borrowing from Rouse's observation about Foucault, that he

> was perfectly prepared to offer reasons for *his* choices of struggles and sides . . . what [he] was not prepared to do was to see those choices, statements, and reasons as more than a situated response to a particular political and epistemic configuration. (Rouse, 1994: 112, emphasis added)

This returns us, I think, to Calás and Smircich's constant reminders that their work speaks of their own intellectual preferences, gender, sociohistorical context and so on, as discussed earlier. Moreover, and as both of my reviewers pointed out, this identification of teleological traces in their *oeuvre* is not a particularly novel criticism of those adopting postmodernist tactics. Nonetheless, it may remind us of some of the key challenges of postmodernist approaches, and so bid us attend anew to the care that needs to be taken in this regard to avoid inappropriate prescriptions.

Derrida, deconstruction and the political

Another strand of critique, offered by Weitzner (2003), claims that Calás and Smircich are premature in suggesting organization theory has possibly 'gone past the "post", with very few achievements' not least because of the 'lack of strong political engagement and . . . remoteness from "the real world"' in deconstructive and genealogical analyses (Calás and Smircich, 1999: 658, 659). As a result of this apparent neglect, Calás and Smircich look to the aforemen-tioned trio of poststructuralist feminism, postcolonial theory and actor-network theory to create stronger, more socially aware 'bridges between 'the text' and 'the world'' (1999: 659). Weitzner argues that Calás and Smircich consequently – and mistakenly – downplay Derrida's focus on ethics, democracy and acade-mic responsibility; and I have already signalled my agreement in implicitly contesting their suggestion that some 'post' approaches are necessarily more politically engaged than others. Relatedly, Weitzner (2003: 4) accuses Calás and Smircich of using something Derrida 'claims cannot exist: a deconstructive methodology' in the 1991 paper on leadership. So he has it that they both misinterpret and misappropriate deconstruction in parts of their *oeuvre*.

Jones (2004: 40–41) criticizes the Calás and Smircich project (amongst others) on similar grounds. In problematizing Calás's (1993: 310–311) claim that 'all deconstructive analyses' make certain moves in their textual interrogations – the identification of binary oppositions, the reversal of such binaries to privilege the 'submerged' term and the consequent demonstration of the text's 'undecid-ability' – he identifies several flaws in this kind of reductionism. Firstly, Jones suggests, as does Weitzner, that understanding deconstruction as method risks presenting it as an original or distinctive interpretive tactic *alone*, one lacking any sociopolitical dimensions. This rendering may also depict deconstruction as taking place 'beyond' the text, in some kind of safe place, as well as implying that it can be applied identically, step by step, across a range of texts. Jones (2004: 55, *n*5) does, however, acknowledge Calás's (1993: 307) recognition that 'deconstruction cannot be considered a methodology in the traditional sense of the word', and thus by implication her suggestion that the deconstructionist analyst adapts and 'invents' their approach 'in accordance with the text being analysed. No deconstruction would [therefore] end up being like any other.' (Calás, 1993: 325, *n*1).

But Jones (2004: 41) goes on to suggest that Calás's own apparent submerging or 'forgetting' of these important observations perhaps means that her rendering of deconstruction as method represents a *pharmakon*, the Platonic word for writing which, *pace* Derrida, 'means both poison *and* cure'. Readings of deconstruction as method have a certain value, then, in that they familiarize us with the 'contours' of one approach to deconstruction, but at the same time are risky because of their reductive nature. So Calás's argument should not be understood as *either* right or wrong, appropriate or inappropriate. Instead we '*cannot not* describe deconstruction as a method, at the same time as we grapple with the dangers of doing so' (Jones, 2004: 41). Indeed Calás (1993: 325, *n*1) herself seems to imply just this both/and problematic in her suggestion that she has used a 'certain straightforward language' in her analysis due to the fact that it appears in an 'organizational journal located outside of both philosophy and literary theory'.

It is also worth recording the extent to which Calás and Smircich seem to waver in their characterization of 'post' analyses. They certainly, as we have seen, celebrate the political contribution of such theorizing in assisting us to grasp the 'consequences of *apparently innocent* textualizations', and so 'to accept the possibility of 'other knowledges,' *which otherwise may be ignored or deemed illegitimate*' (Calás and Smircich, 1999: 658, emphasis added). Indeed in the 2003a paper Calás and Smircich suggest that what is often forgotten about Derrida is that 'deconstruction is always engaged with the institutional forms of modernity within which we are all expected to perform, and . . . there are very material consequences emerging from such performances' – such that, for example, the divide between 'the concerns of theoretical reason and the various fields of practice where reason is put to use, such as the legal, administrative and military systems' is a difficult one to maintain (Calás and Smircich, 2003a: 36–37 – also see Calás, 1993: 309–310). Perhaps then it is possible to speculate that Calás and Smircich's specific reservation about the politics of postmodernism/ poststructuralism can be located in the observation that postcolonial theory, say, is not just about listening to the voices of the silenced but also focuses on returning 'agency and imagination to those who have been represented in subjection to others in the world', through mechanisms such as what Spivak has referred to as 'strategic essentialism' (cited in Calás and Smircich, 2003a: 45). In other words, the assertion here may be that poststructuralist feminism, postcolonial theory and actor-network theory are less inclined to shy away from making concrete and ethically-informed *recommendations . . .*?

Concluding remarks

This chapter has argued that Marta Calás and Linda Smircich's contribution to organization theory over the last two decades or so has been manifold. Their work on leadership, culture and gender has suggested that organization theory as it stands is discursively repetitive and narrow in its horizons. It thus forecloses what can be said about organizations and organizing, making it important to examine how organization theory knowledge is 'done', and what is left unacknowledged as a result. The orthodoxy, they argue, is only one version of the workings of organizations – and, while there are no 'better' truths to be had in this regard, attending to other interpretations does at least alert us to its less-than-concrete foundations. Moreover, the world-making impact of organization theory also (re)produces hierarchy, inequality and privilege, which makes it incumbent on scholars to take responsibility for their work, especially as it is only ever *their* rendering of the organizational arena. Calás and Smircich also insist, however, that readers are at the same time authors, effectively 're-writing' organization theory texts in the process of deciding what these texts mean to them. There are also several criticisms of Calás and Smircich's work – their gender 'one-eyedness', the complexity of some of their argumentation, their occasional teleological lapses and their misappropriation/misinterpretation of deconstruction. Nonetheless, for me these criticisms can be tempered at least to some extent by in some cases a different reading of their work and in others remembering what it is that their academic endeavours aim to achieve.

Moreover, and as pointed out by one of my reviewers, what through an early 21st century European lens may seem like naïveté was often revolutionary in the context of a post-war American organization theory tradition characterized by managerialism, empiricism, positivism and functionalism. Indeed, in the US in particular, managerialist positivism is still very much the organization theory norm. The Calás and Smircich 'corrective' to the unreflexive excesses of such thinking is therefore still an extremely important – perhaps essential – alternative.

Acknowledgement

Grateful thanks to Roy Jacques, Edward Wray-Bliss, an anonymous reviewer and the editors for their constructive criticism of earlier versions of this chapter.

References

Calás, M. B. (1993) 'Deconstructing charismatic leadership: Re-reading Weber from the darker side' *Leadership Quarterly*, 4(3–4): 305–328.

Calás, M. B. and L. Smircich (1988) 'Reading leadership as a form of cultural analysis' in J. G. Hunt, R. D. Baliga, H. P. Dachler and C. A. Schriesheim (eds.) *Emerging Leadership Vistas*. Lexington, MA: Lexington Books.

Calás, M. B. and L. Smircich (1990) 'Thrusting towards more of the same with the Porter-McKibbin Report' *Academy of Management Review*, 15(4): 698–705.

Calás, M. B. and L. Smircich (1991) 'Voicing seduction to silence leadership' *Organization Studies*, 12(4): 567–602.

Calás, M. B. and L. Smircich (1992a) 'Re-writing gender into organizational theorizing: Directions from feminist perspectives' in M. Reed and M. Hughes (eds.) *Rethinking Organization: New Directions in Organization Theory and Analysis*. London: Sage.

Calás, M. B. and L. Smircich (1992b) 'Using the "F" word: Feminist theories and the social consequences of organizational research' in A. J. Mills and P. Tancred (eds.) *Gendering Organizational Analysis*. Newbury Park, CA: Sage.

Calás, M. B. and L. Smircich (1993) 'Dangerous liaisons: The "feminine-in-management" meets "globalization"' *Business Horizons*, 36(2): 71–81.

Calás, M. B. and L. Smircich (1996) 'From "the woman's" point of view: Feminist approaches to organization studies' in S. R. Clegg, C. Hardy and W. R. Nord (eds.) *Handbook of Organization Studies*. London: Sage.

Calás, M. B. and L. Smircich (1999) 'Past postmodernism? Reflections and tentative directions' *Academy of Management Review*, 24(4): 649–671.

Calás, M. B. and L. Smircich (2003a) 'To be done with progress and other heretical thoughts for organization and management studies' in E. A. Locke (ed.) *Postmodernism and Management: Pros, Cons and the Alternative*. Amsterdam: JAI Press.

Calás, M. B. and L. Smircich (2003b) 'At home from Mars to Somalia: Recounting organization studies' in H. Tsoukas and C. Knudsen (eds.) *The Oxford Handbook of Organization Theory*. Oxford: Oxford University Press.

Grey, C. (1995) 'Review article: Gender as a grid of intelligibility' *Gender, Work and Organization*, 2(1): 46–50.

Howells, C. (1998) *Derrida: Deconstruction from Phenomenology to Ethics*. Oxford: Polity.

Jones, C. (2004) 'Jacques Derrida' in S. Linstead (ed.) *Organization Theory and Postmodern Thought*. London: Sage.

Learmonth, M. (2004) 'Derrida reappraised: Deconstruction, critique and emancipation in management studies', Working Paper Series, Department of Management Studies, University of York. Online at: http://www.york.ac.uk/management/research/working_paper_series/working%20paper%201.pdf.

Mintzberg, H. (1991) 'A letter to Marta Calás and Linda Smircich' *Organization Studies*, 12(4): 602.

Mir, R. A., M. B. Calás and L. Smircich (1999) 'Global technoscapes and silent voices: Challenges to theorizing global cooperation' in D. L. Cooperrider and J. E. Dutton (eds.) *Organizational Dimensions of Global Change: No Limits to Cooperation*. Thousand Oaks, CA: Sage.

Morgan, G. and L. Smircich (1980) 'The case for qualitative research' *Academy of Management Review*, 5(4): 491–500.

Rouse, J. (1994) 'Power/knowledge' in G. Gutting (ed.) *The Cambridge Companion to Foucault*. Cambridge: Cambridge University Press.

Smart, B. (1986) 'The politics of truth and the problem of hegemony' in D. C. Hoy (ed.) *Foucault: A Critical Reader*. Oxford: Blackwell.

Smircich, L. (1983) 'Concepts of culture and organizational analysis' *Administrative Science Quarterly*, 28(3): 339–358.

Smircich, L. (1985) 'Is the concept of culture a paradigm for understanding organizations and ourselves?' in P. J. Frost, L. F. Moore, M. R. Louis, C. C. Lundberg and J. Martin (eds.) *Organizational Culture*. Beverley Hills, CA: Sage.

Smircich, L. (1995) 'Writing organizational tales: Reflections on three books on organizational culture' *Organization Science*, 6(2): 232–237.

Smircich, L. and C. Stubbart (1985) 'Strategic management in an enacted world' *Academy of Management Review*, 10(4): 724–736.

Smircich, L. and G. Morgan (1982) 'Leadership: The management of meaning' *Journal of Applied Behavioral Science*, 18(3): 257–273.

Smircich, L. and M. B. Calás (1987) 'Organizational culture: A critical assessment' in F. M. Jablin, L. L. Putnam, K. H. Roberts and L. W. Porter (eds.) *Handbook of Organizational Communication: An Interdisciplinary Perspective*. Thousand Oaks, CA: Sage.

Smircich, L. and M. B. Calás (1995) 'Introduction' in L. Smircich and M. B. Calás (eds.) *Critical Perspectives on Organization and Management Theory*. Aldershot, Hampshire: Dartmouth.

Smircich, L. and R. J. Chesser (1981) 'Superiors' and subordinates' perceptions of performance: Beyond disagreement' *Academy of Management Journal*, 24(1): 198–205.

Weitzner, D. (2003) 'Deconstruction revisited: Implications of philosophy over methodology', Paper presented at the Critical Management Studies Workshop, Academy of Management Annual Meeting, Seattle, US, August. Online at: http://www.aom.pace.edu/cms/Workshops/Seattle/PDF/10623.pdf.

Stewart Clegg: Towards a Machiavellian organization theory?

Peter Fleming and André Spicer

Introduction

One of the most notable contributors to the cannon we now call organization theory is the Anglo-Australian Stewart Clegg. Over the span of three decades Clegg has made a range of interventions in organization theory. Topics addressed include modernism/postmodernism, Marxist, Weberian and Foucauldian theories of organization, epistemology and reflexivity, and comparative studies of capitalism (particularly in East Asia). The most enduring concern that runs through his work is the issue of power, which will be the focus of this chapter.

In his work on power there is a sustained attempt to debunk assumptions that it ultimately rests in the hands of the powerful. These assumptions are rooted in the political philosophy of Thomas Hobbes (1651/1985) and his idea that all power in society finally rests in the body of the sovereign (see also Kaulingfreks, in this volume). In place of this 'sovereign theory of power', we will argue that Clegg has made significant efforts to advance what we might call a Machiavellian theory of power. This involves conceptualizing power as a network of relations in which actors are embedded. While this more diffuse understanding of power remains an abiding strand throughout Clegg's work, the way he builds a Machiavellian theory of organizational power changes significantly. In this chapter we will trace out these shifting configurations of Clegg's Machiavellian approach. We will demonstrate how his early work focussed on interpretive action by examining how power involved the interplay of rule and domination (Clegg, 1975). In later writings, Clegg maintains that power is the product of concrete social structures such as bureaucracy, capitalism and class (Clegg, 1979; Clegg and Dunkerley, 1980; Clegg, Boreham and Dow, 1986). Then, during the late 1980s and 1990s, Clegg's theory of power undergoes some 'radical revisions' resulting in the rather baroque 'circuits of power' model (Clegg, 1989a). In what follows we shall trace this Machiavellianism through his three successive iterations of a theory of power. We will conclude by critically assessing some difficult issues that emerge from his *oeuvre*.

Power, rule and domination

Clegg's *Power, Rule and Domination* appeared in an intellectual scene dominated by functionalist approaches (eg, Thompson, 1967) which saw power relations as a subsystem used by groups to preserve 'function within the system rather than destroy it' (Hickson *et al*, 1971: 217). Clegg's major contribution in this monograph was to show that power is not immediately given by a functional system but is practically achieved through relational action, rules of the game, and deeper 'iconic' systems of domination. By attending to these three factors we are able to move away from seeing power as a series of sterile operations between subsystems and begin to trace out the lived processes through which actors attempt to negotiate and re-negotiate the rules, yet willingly submit 'to the iconic domination of a form of life in which the ideal of profitability is King Harvest – it must be reaped' (Clegg, 1975: 155–156).

Clegg launched his efforts to develop a theory of power by drawing on the later philosophy of Ludwig Wittgenstein (1953, 1958). Instead of seeking truth in a perfect match between words and reality, Wittgenstein suggests that truth lies in the conventions that mark something out as true. Truth about what power is can only be found in a '*conventional* agreement, with no necessity residing in the world' (Clegg, 1975: 7). Therefore 'the "reality" of power may be no more than our ways of speech' (Clegg, 1975: 8). This approach to power underlines the various conventions or language games that determine how power may be talked about. These conventions can be found in academic dialogue (like the community power debate) or in practices of 'doing' power in the office or workshop. What Clegg seems to be suggesting is a move away from the assumption that power is a single body which can be viewed from an external point. In its place we find a more Machiavellian engagement with power as a situation-dependent practical activity in which the theorist is already implicated.

Clegg situates his work in the community power debate. This consisted of a group of North American political scientists concerned with the question of who holds power in a community. C. Wright Mills (1957) sparked off this debate by arguing that a small power elite ruled American cities whose influence crossed politics, public institutions and business. Robert Dahl (1957, 1961) responded by arguing that power tends to be diffused among a range of largely independent individuals. For Dahl, power was observable in individual decision-making. Bachrach and Baratz (1962, 1971) subsequently responded to Dahl's behaviourist theory by arguing power was not only exercised through concrete acts of decision-making, but also through more insidious forms of agenda setting. By setting the agenda, powerful groups were able to define the issues that could be discussed, consequently rendering some issues non-decisions. Clegg locates himself in this debate because it moves away from the question of how power ought to be managed to that defining Machiavellian concern of how it is actually exercised.

The community power debate provides the building blocks for the way he studies power in *Power, Rule and Domination* (1975). He too identifies *power* as the everyday decision and non-decision making. Clegg supplements this approach with Wittgenstein's notions of 'language games' and 'forms of life'. These are the shared criteria of rationality actors use to assess a given situation. For instance, various bureaucrats and architects on a construction site share a deep-seated criterion of profitability that serves as the reference point for all decision-making. This deeper level, which was ignored by the community power debate, is what Clegg calls *domination*. A mediating process is then identified between the deep structure of domination and the surface play of power. He calls this mediating factor *rule*, which involves the 'perceived order' or 'the interpretive work that people engage in, when they make sense of the world' (Clegg, 1975: 60, 59). To understand a rule it is necessary to study how actors employ it 'to make sense of otherwise meaningless phenomena' (Clegg, 1975: 67). Clegg provides a number of examples of workers on a construction site negotiating and adjusting these rules to their own advantage. For instance, he reports on an episode when a contractor bored a hole deeper than the two metres rule specified on the architectural drawings (Clegg, 1975: 132–151). When asked by the site architect why he had done this, the contractor responded that he was following another rule specified on the drawings that suggested the bore needed to reach past 'normal clay' and into 'sandy stony clay'. The ensuing conflict between the contractor and the architect was largely around which rule should be mobilised.

Bringing the three elements of power, rule and domination together, Clegg provided a comprehensive definition of power as being 'about the outcome issues enabled by the rule of a substantive rationality which is temporally and institutionally located. Underlying this rule is a specific form of domination' (Clegg, 1975: 78). And each component is connected: 'The progression is from domination → rules → power' (Clegg, 1975: 78). This early phase of Clegg's work highlights the everyday pragmatics of power relations in organizations. These relations are conceptualized in a Machiavellian register, as tactical mobilizations of interpretive procedures, rather than formal structures. Clegg, however, provides an unelaborated and somewhat universal theory of domination. All on the construction site are dominated by the 'king harvest' (Clegg, 1975: 156) of profit, downplaying consideration of the asymmetrical distribution of life-chances between different social groups.

Social structure

Following the completion of *Power, Rule and Domination* (1975), Clegg set out to shift his analytical focus from language games to social structure, which he approached as ingrained 'forms of life'. To do this he evoked the radical Weberian and Marxist traditions in *The Theory of Power and Organization* (1979), *Organization, Class and Control* (Clegg and Dunkerley, 1980), and *Class,*

Politics and the Economy (Clegg, Boreham and Dow, 1986). These works attempted to explain how domination is produced through the structures of capitalist society and the function of law and rule.

To develop an explicit account of social structure, Clegg turns to 1970s European structuralism. Social structure is typically defined as an objective pattern of social relationships. In contrast, Clegg approaches it as the basic and unquestioned ground rules that actors invoke when they make decisions (Clegg and Dunkerley, 1980). Examples might include 'the profit motive' assumed by managers or 'truth' and 'progress' appealed to by scientists to garner the necessary resources to continue their obtuse experiments. A central feature of social structure is what Clegg calls 'hegemonic domination'. Following Gramsci (1971), Clegg (1979; Clegg and Dunkerley, 1980) argues that a cadre of intellectuals organize the background ethico-political commitments of certain social forms in civil society this group includes 'specific intellectuals' such as academics and writers as well as 'organic intellectuals' like union leaders, advertising and public relations officers, lobbyists and all others who seek to manipulate public assumptions. In the workplace, they are the vast group of rationalizers such as managers and consultants who systematically apply instrumental reason (Clegg, 1979). In this revised conceptualization of social structure, we notice that Clegg brings a significantly Machiavellian analytic to bear. Akin to Gramsci's (1971) 'Modern Prince', it is argued that systems of domination are created by intellectuals who carefully manipulate and organize the ground rules of social praxis. This alerts us to how social structure involves an ongoing process of cunning social reproduction.

Weberian themes of rationalization and a Gramscian emphasis on hegemony set the agenda for much of Clegg's subsequent scholarship. Ultimately, what is achieved is a modified structuralist account of organizational power relations. This understanding of power relations involves a move away from earlier concerns with the mobilization and negotiation of rules in the workplace. A broad thread in this research appears to be an explanation of how hegemonic relations of domination are linked to a constellation of capitalist structures. These include the world system, the nation state and the labour process. For example, the concept of 'organizational environment' is revised using neo-Marxist world systems theory (Clegg, 1979), the labour process is examined via the hegemony of rationalized selection rules (Clegg, 1979) and organizational conflict is explained with reference to the underlying class structure of society (Clegg, 1981). This leads him to sketch a 'political economy of organizations' (Clegg and Dunkerley, 1980; Clegg, Boreham and Dow, 1986).

It is possible to argue that the emphasis on structural concepts like hegemonic domination leads Clegg away from a Machiavellian analysis of how power is achieved and maintained. However, throughout his explication of hegemonic domination, Clegg consistently returns to the fact that this is something that must be actively produced and organized. The role that human labour plays in producing and reproducing these modes of domination is where the practical activities of power come into play.

Radical revisions

In the late 1980s and early 1990s Clegg's theoretical approach and method of analysis changed in a manner that was labelled 'radical' by even himself (Clegg, 1989a). Following his radical revision the focus transformed: class control and hegemonic relations of power, the rationalization of domination and world-systems were repudiated and in its place appeared putative post-modernism. In *Modern Organizations* (1990) post-modernism is treated as both a *scholarly* framework that is non-essentialist, non-reductive and sensitive to contingency and a *period* in which the organizing mechanisms of modernity (standardized industrial production and consumption) become obsolete. According to Clegg (1989a, 1990, 1994a) times have changed: 'the illuminative powers of the modernist representation of bureaucracy fade into dusk in our increasingly post-modern organizational times' (Clegg, 1994a: 151, also see Clarke and Clegg, 2002). And in terms of his erstwhile favoured critical theories of work, 'the grand-narratives of the past, licensed by Marx, by Science, by Reason, have now become discredited as icons of emancipation and enlightenment . . .' (Clegg, 1990: 12).

A key aspect of Clegg's revision in the 1990s was the championing of Foucault (eg, 1980) and his description of power as a disciplinary and micro-spatial process. *Frameworks of Power* (1989b) represents one of the clearest explications of his revised understanding of power. In it Clegg returns to the community power debate, paying particular attention to the radical Marxist approach developed by Lukes (1973). Lukes argued that while previous participants in the community power debate had identified significant dimensions of power in decision-making (Dahl, 1957) and non-decision-making (Bachrach and Baratz, 1962), they had inadvertently presumed that power was something behavioural and resource-based. Lukes famously counter-argued, 'is it not the supreme exercise of power to get another or others to have the desires you want them to have – that is to secure their compliance by controlling their thoughts and desires?' (Lukes, 1974: 23). The striking facet of Lukes' argument is that power may operate not only on what we do and do not do, but also on our subjective desires and beliefs, so much so that we act contrary to what may otherwise have been our objective interests.

Clegg locates Lukes in an analytical tradition that has its origin in the 17th century political theorist Thomas Hobbes. In his book, *Leviathan*, power is portrayed as the state-body of the Monarch, which is simultaneously a composite of the people (as the original frontispiece of *Leviathan* revealed). Central for Hobbes was the notion of sovereignty, understood as the expression of power in which a public good was achieved through the reproduction of the body politic – usually in the form of covenants and pacts via divine fiat (Clegg, 1989b). The Leviathan represents a structured, centralized and sovereign order that holds in abeyance the continuous threat of disorder or what Hobbes called the intransigent 'state of nature'. At the heart of the Hobbesian tradition, according to Clegg, is the idea that power operates in terms of a sovereign source, be that the state, the ruling class, capital, or a board of directors. Clegg has a number of objections. Power is automatically assumed to be something that the elite exclusively holds (and is thus reified), is concentrated in a zero-sum fashion (and thus deemed a quantifiable property), is intentionally exercised or revoked (and thus imputing rational intent), negates the ever-present threat of a 'state of nature' (and thus prohibits, denies and refrains action) and follows a simple cause and effect trajectory (and thus operates in a way analogous to New-tonian mechanics). Perhaps the greatest criticism that Clegg has of Lukes' evo-cation of this tradition is the idea of objective interests. He states here and elsewhere repeatedly that interests are not objectively structured by class or gender but are the products of powerful representations: 'it is a mistake to assume that interests get fixed by relations of production' or any other structure (Clegg, 1994a: 156).

Clegg approvingly cites Foucault's (1977, 1980) argument that this picture of power misses much of the complex processes of force found in disciplinary societies: 'Such theories still continue today to busy themselves with the problem of sovereignty. What we need, however, is a political philosophy that isn't erected around the problem of sovereignty, nor therefore the problems of law prohibition. We need to cut off the King's head: in political theory this is still to be done' (Foucault, 1980: 121). Following others (such as Gramsci, 1971; Foucault, 1979a; Wolin, 1960), Clegg brings Machiavelli to the fore. Rather than being a state-sponsored 'legislator' like Hobbes, Machiavelli is more a disenfranchised 'interpreter' of how power is used to gain desired effects (see Bauman, 1987). In his *Discourses* and *The Prince*, Machiavelli takes a very strategic and amoral stance towards power: it does not reside in anyone's hands but is the effect of strategic manoeuvrings and cunning. Power is a game of illu-sion and allusion, which was so prevalent in Medici politics. *The Prince* offers highly contextual and non-generalizing advice to the prince regarding the best way to attain and retain dominance. Clegg argues that Machiavelli provides a more useful view of power because it is sensitive to unstable alliances and has a 'disinclination to believe in any single originating and decisive centre . . .' (Clegg, 1989b: 6–7).

To flesh out a Machiavellian theory of power, Clegg turns to the Foucauldian themes of disciplinary power, subjectification and discourse (Foucault, 1977, 1980, 1984). The rise of disciplinary power saw intermittent state violence (in the form of spectacles such as public execution and torture) replaced by a con-stant, micro-spatial training of the body through power/knowledge routines linked to the school, prison, factory and other dominant institutions. Under dis-ciplinary power, both the mind and body are regulated by a force that is extremely quotidian (rather than spectacular) and becomes so pervasive that subjects come to apply it to themselves via a corporeal internalization (Clegg, 1989b; Clegg and Hardy, 1996; Clegg and Palmer, 1996). While Clegg has not provided the most persuasive application of this perspective to contemporary workplaces (for that see Knights and Willmott, 1989; Deetz, 1992; Sewell and Wilkinson, 1992), he does much to theoretically clarify the details of this form of power, which may then be used to shed light on organizational relations of domination and rule.

In defining this new kind of power, informed as it is by a more Machiavellian tradition than a Hobbesian one, Clegg argues in a rather convoluted way that:

> Power becomes conceived as a set of techniques disciplining practices, as well as the more or less stable or shifting networks of alliances that such disciplinary practices make possible through their elective affinities between wholly contingent forms of identity, extended over a shifting terrain of practice and discursively constituted interests. (1994a: 157)

There are a number of important points that are being made in this statement. Not only do we have Foucault's notion of disciplinary power and its focus on the technical and trained nature of the political field, but an interesting kind of *pluralism* now emerges in which power is thoroughly de-centred into a montage of floating alliances and temporary projects. This is not that far from the pluralism of Dahl (1961), despite the latter's episodic inclinations, which Clegg does not share. Moreover, power is taken to be something that produces identities and interests rather than simply repress them. Echoing Laclau and Mouffe (1985), Clegg argues this approach to power bypasses both an over-structuralized version of subjectivity (as a product of structure) and an under-structuralized notion of the subject (whereby people are the authors of their own identities). Accordingly, a more embedded approach would be one that 'sought to ask what makes possible specific words, actions and their patterned assemblies as rationalities' (Clegg, 1994a: 161) and views power as 'more or less complex organized agents engaged in more or less organized games' (Clegg, 1989b: 20). Analysing power identifies 'how relations of agency and structure have been constituted discursively, how agency is denied to some and given to others . . .' (Clegg, 1989b: 158). Here power is increasingly reduced to a discursive or even subjective process. We are told that an analysis of power is 'neither ethical nor micro-political; above all it is textual, semiotic, and inherent in the very possibility of textuality, meaning and signification in the social world' (Clegg, 1994a: 149) and that 'there is only representation; there is no fixed, real, hidden or excluded term or dimension . . . Power is the apparent order of taken-for-granted categories of existence as they are fixed and represented in a myriad of discursive forms and practices' (Clegg, 1989b: 183–184).

Clegg consolidates these insights in his 'circuits of power' model, developed in the closing chapters of *Frameworks of Power* (1989b) and is the fountainhead for subsequent research (eg, Clegg, 1990; Clegg et al., 2002; Stokes and Clegg, 2002; Clegg and Courpasson, 2004). The model is baroque, to say the least, and it is sometimes unclear how the conceptions of power discussed above apply to it, given its obvious debt to the system integration approaches proposed by

Lockwood (1964) and Giddens (1979). The basic argument Clegg makes is that power has different levels that involve dynamics that are not dissimilar to his early tripartite of power (now episodic power), rule (now rules of practice) and domination. On the level of episodic power relations A decides what B will do. On the rules of practice level, A will attempt to set the rules by which the activities of A and B are judged. And on the level of domination the taken-for-granted forms of life for A and B are set. A circuit of power (the modern nation-state is offered as an example) activates these levels by connecting to social relations, agencies, standing conditions, outcomes, rules, environmental contingencies, and obligatory passage points (see Clegg, 1989b: 214). The importance of acknowledging the multidimensional nature of power is explained in the following manner: 'In the circuits framework, power is multifarious: it is episodic; it is also the circuit of power through which rules and domination, as well as the overall empirical articulation which configures the theoretical circuits in any application of the model' (Clegg, 1989b: 215).

Critical assessment

The theory of power found in the circuits model is the apotheosis of his thinking on the subject. Indeed by his own admission:

> My views of power – the central concept that laces together just about everything I have ever written – have hardly shifted [since the publication of *Frameworks of Power* and *Modern Organizations*]. Indeed, in some essentials they were already in place in *Power, Rule and Domination*. Discourse is central; power is not a thing but a relation of flows; we are all practical ethnomethodologists seeking to enrol, translate, and otherwise socially construct the people, places, things and situations which matter to us – but they are doing it too. (Clegg, 2005: 300)

Clegg nicely summarizes some of his enduring concerns regarding power and organizations. While he contributes a Machiavellian analytic of power rule and domination, certain problems are evident that require further comment.

We have seen that central to Clegg's conception of power is the assertion that 'there are only representations' (Clegg, 1989b: 183) and that power works primarily by constituting subjectivity. But does power *only* do its work when it passes through representation or conscious discourse? The unconscious and 'material' dimensions of the labour process are not really dealt with here and could be usefully explored in relation to discursive mechanisms (see Collinson, 1992). Also, how does one decide which representations are related to power and which are not – are all representations an expression of power and would this not simply be claiming that power is everywhere? What Eagleton (1991) called discursive idealism is also a danger here because power is seen to be a purely discursive process – who I am, what I do, the global economy, the international division of labour are all seen to be brought about by talk. Such a move inflates discourse to a transcendental–causative principle. Indeed, it is not certain where these powerful discourses or representations come from. As Eagleton (1991) argues, because there are no interests or political forces before the operation of discursive practices, discourses 'thus become purely self-constituting, tautological practices. It is impossible to say where they derive from; they simply drop from the skies . . .' (Eagleton, 1991: 214).

Throughout Clegg's work there seems to be a strange tension between suggesting it is necessary to look at the concrete, contextually specific mobilization of power and the desire to build highly abstract models of how power functions. Given that Machiavelli eschewed generalities and focused only on the ethnographic and empirical context of power (something that Gramsci did too), there is something ironically abstract in Clegg's depiction of power. Whereas Machiavelli identified concrete tactics (examples abound of the Prince gaining the upper hand), Clegg tends to present or even legislate a universal definition of what power is and is not. Moreover, there is something very distant and cold in his rendition of Machiavelli, whose tales are vivid and rich with exemplary social practices. The amoralism thought to be at the heart of Machiavelli's analysis is translated by Clegg into an analysis of power (and resistance) that reads more like something we would find in a physics text-book. For example, Clegg maintains that after Machiavelli and then Foucault, 'instead of concentrating on the sovereignty of power [Foucault] argues that, on the contrary, we should study the myriad of bodies constituted as peripheral subjects as an effect of power' (Clegg, 1994a: 158). All of this seems to be a very aloof and sterile way of explaining something as hot and contested as power relations.

In each of Clegg's major explications of his approach to power, we find increasingly intricate models. The initial iteration found in *Power, Rule and Domination* is a relatively parsimonious attempt to bring a complex theoretical vocabulary to understand organizational power relations. However, as Clegg's work develops, he adds a bewildering range of variables and processes. The end result is the Byzantine 'circuits of power' system. This attempt to bring all possible variables into one conceptual grid reflects the grand theory tendency of mainstream 1970s sociology. When conceptual systems become all embracing the inevitable abstraction can leave one overwhelmed by its sheer scope and under-whelmed by its applicability to specific workplaces.

The final problem with Clegg's theory of power is his unwillingness to go beyond formalist description and develop a more normative political theory. As Clegg himself says, 'one does not tell people what they should do – there are churches and pulpits aplenty, as well as consultants, to fulfil that function' (Clegg, 2000: 78, also see Clegg and Courpasson, 2004). To put this another way, while Clegg provides an analysis of how power works in organizations and the possible problems associated with regimes of domination, we are not offered any statement of how he would like power relations to be. The only indication of a normative view is expressed in his work on postmodernism (Clegg, 1990). The political utopia we find here is one of liberal small-scale networked production. To develop a consistent normative political philosophy would require going beyond a Machiavellian approach of merely describing power relations.

We would be pushed to ask the broader questions about which political order we actually want in organizations. The resources we would draw upon would be found in political theories of justice. We would have to be clear whether we want a conservative order, a liberal order, a libertarian order, a socialist order, an anarchist order or perhaps something else altogether. We would also have to ask about the ethical criteria we use to assess organizations, and thus fully reclaim the language of politics.

References

Bachrach, P. and M. S. Baratz (1962) 'Two faces of power' *American Political Science Review*, 56: 947–952.

Bachrach, P. and M. S. Baratz (1971) *Power and Poverty*. Oxford: Oxford University Press.

Bauman, Z. (1987) *Legislators and Interpreters*. Cambridge: Polity.

Clarke, T. and S. Clegg (2002) *Changing Paradigms: The Transformation of Management Knowledge for the 21st Century*. London: HarperCollins Business.

Clegg, S. (1975) *Power, Rule and Domination: A Critical and Empirical Understanding of Power in Sociological Theory and Organization Life*. London: Routledge and Kegan Paul.

Clegg, S. (1979) *The Theory of Power and Organization*. London: Routledge and Kegan Paul.

Clegg, S. (1981) 'Organization and control' *Administrative Science Quarterly*, 26(4): 545–562.

Clegg, S. (1989a) 'Radical revisions: Power, discipline and organizations' *Organization Studies*, 10(1): 97–115.

Clegg, S. (1989b) *Frameworks of Power*. London: Sage.

Clegg, S. (1990) *Modern Organizations: Organization Studies in the Postmodern World*. London: Sage.

Clegg, S. (1994a) 'Social theory for the study of organization: Weber and Foucault' *Organization*, 1(1): 149–178.

Clegg, S. (2000) 'Globalizing the intelligent organization' in J. Garrick and C. Rhodes (eds.) *Research and Knowledge at Work*. London: Routledge.

Clegg, S. (2005) 'Vita Contemplativa: A life in part' *Organization Studies*, 26(2): 291–309.

Clegg, S. and C. Hardy (1996). 'Some dare call it power' in S. Clegg, C. Hardy and W. Nord (eds.) *Handbook of Organization Studies*. London: Sage.

Clegg, S. and D. Courpasson (2004) 'Political hybrids: Tocquevillean views on project organizations' *Journal of Management Studies*, 41(4): 525–547.

Clegg, S. and D. Dunkerley (1980) *Organization, Class and Control*. London: Routledge and Kegan Paul.

Clegg, S. and G. Palmer (eds.) (1996) *Politics of Management Knowledge*. London: Sage.

Clegg, S., M. Kornberger and C. Rhodes (2004) 'Noise, parasites and translation: Theory and practice in management consulting' *Management Learning*, 35(1): 31–44.

Clegg, S., P. Boreham and G. Dow (1986) *Class, Politics and the Economy*. London: Routledge and Kegan Paul.

Collinson, D. (1992). *Managing the Shopfloor: Subjectivity, Masculinity and Workplace Culture*. Berlin: Walter de Gruyter.

Dahl, R. (1957) 'The concept of power' *Behaviorial Science*, 2: 201–215.

Dahl, R. (1961) *Who Governs? Democracy and Power in an American City*. New Haven: Yale University Press.

Deetz, S. (1992). 'Disciplinary power in the modern corporation' in M. Alvesson and H. Willmott (eds.) *Critical Management Studies*. London: Sage.

Eagleton, T. (1991) *Ideology: an Introduction*. London: Verso.

Foucault, M. (1977) *Discipline and Punish: The Birth of the Prison*, trans. A. Sheridan. Harmondsworth: Penguin.

Foucault, M. (1979a) 'Govermentality' *Ideology and Consciousness*, 6: 5–21.

Foucault, M. (1979b) *The History of Sexuality, Vol 1: An Introduction*, trans. R. Hurley. London: Penguin.

Foucault, M. (1980) *Power/Knowledge: Selected Interviews and Other Writings 1972–1977*, ed. C. Gordon. Brighton: Harvester.

Giddens, A. (1979) *Central Problems in Social Theory*. London: Macmillan.

Gramsci, A. (1971) *Selections from the Prison Notebooks*, ed. and trans. Q. Hoare and G. N. Smith. New York: International Publishers.

Hickson, D. J., C. R. Hinings, C. A. Lee, R. E. Schneck and J. M. Pennings (1971) 'A strategic contingencies theory of intra-organizational power' *Administrative Science Quarterly*, 16(2): 327–344.

Hobbes, T. (1651/1985) *Leviathan*. London: Penguin.

Knights, D. and H. Willmott (1989) 'Power and subjectivity at work: From degradation to subjugation in social relations' *Sociology*, 23(3): 534–558.

Laclau, E. and C. Mouffe (1985). *Hegemony and Socialist Strategy*. London: Verso.

Lockwood, D. (1964) 'Social integration and system integration' In G. K. Zollschan and W. Hirsch (eds.) *Explorations in Social Change*. London: Routledge and Kegan Paul.

Lukes, S. (1974) *Power: A Radical View*. London: Macmillan.

Machiavelli, N. (1515/1997) *The Prince*, trans. A. M. Codevilla. New Haven: Yale University Press.

Machiavelli, N. (1517/1983) *The Discourses*, trans. L. J. Walker. London: Penguin.

Mills, C. W. (1957) *The Power Elite*. Oxford: Oxford University Press.

Pitsis, T., S. Clegg, M. Marosszeky and T. Rura-Polley (2003). 'Constructing the olympic dream: A future perfect strategy of project management' *Organization Science*, 14(5): 574–590.

Sewell, G. and B. Wilkinson (1992) 'Someone to watch over me: Surveillance, discipline and the Just-In-Time labour process' *Sociology*, 26(2): 270–289.

Stokes, J. and S. Clegg (2002) 'Once upon a time in the bureaucracy' *Organization*, 9(2): 225–248.

Thompson, J. D. (1967) *Organizations in Action*. New York: McGraw-Hill.

Westwood, R. and S. Clegg (eds.) (2003). *Debating Organization: Point-Counterpoint in Organization Studies*. Malden, MA: Blackwell.

Wittgenstein, L. (1953) *Philosophical Investigations*, trans. G. E. M. Anscombe. Oxford: Blackwell.

Wittgenstein, L. (1958) *The Blue and Brown Books: Preliminary Studies for 'Philosophical Investigations'*. Oxford: Blackwell.

Wolin, S. (1960) *Politics and Vision*. Boston: Brown.

Robert Cooper: Beyond organization

Sverre Spoelstra

Introduction

Apart from one short book on work design, Robert Cooper has exclusively written articles and book chapters. This early book (Cooper, 1974) and other works from the early 1970s (eg, Cooper, 1972; 1973) were part of a programme at the Tavistock Institute of Human Relations, London, whose object was to translate some of the theoretical ideas from sociotechnical systems thinking into practical language. Although interesting in its own right, it is Cooper's later work, roughly starting with his 1976 essay 'The Open Field', which is of greater interest for the study of organization, primarily because it raises profound theoretical questions concerning the ontological underpinnings of organization. In this chapter I am concerned with these later works, in which Cooper turns away from the core concerns of the Tavistock programme to address more general philosophical and sociological questions concerning the nature of organization.

From the mid-1970s until 1995, when he went to Keele University, Cooper worked in the Department of Behaviour in Organizations at Lancaster University. The 'Lancaster group', which in the late 1970s and early 1980s included Gibson Burrell and Gareth Morgan among others, questioned the status quo of organization theory by investigating its roots in sociology and philosophy. One of the key publications of these years is Burrell and Morgan's *Sociological Paradigms and Organizational Analysis*, first published in 1979 (see Hancock and Tyler, in this volume). Cooper and Burrell's introduction of postmodernism and poststructuralism to the study of organizations in the late 1980s (Cooper and Burrell, 1988; Burrell, 1988; 1994; Cooper, 1987; 1989b) was also strongly connected to the research performed by the Lancaster group. At Keele University, Cooper became the director of the interdisciplinary Centre for Social Theory and Technology, which was one of the largest groups of poststructuralists in the United Kingdom at that time. In his years at Keele Cooper further developed poststructuralist-inspired ideas (eg, 1998a; 2001a), in collaboration with the sociologist John Law among others. At the time of writing, Cooper is a visiting professor at Keele University.

It would, however, be a mistake to limit a discussion of Cooper's work to these 'contributions' to organization theory, since his treatment of organization is part of wider theoretical concerns. In spite of Cooper's well-documented importance for organization theory (eg, Böhm and Jones, 2001; Chia 1998a; 1998b), Cooper – as he repeatedly insists – has never been an organization theorist in the strict sense. His work does address questions about organization – the distinction organization/disorganization (Cooper, 1986) being a notable example – but his articles have never been directly concerned with 'real' organizations. In fact, much of his work, as I will explain in the next section, is directed against the idea of a 'real' organization (or organization*s*) and, consequently, questions the tradition in the social sciences that has made the individual organization its object of study.

Apart from organization, conceived as a social practice rather than a bounded thing in the world (Cooper, 1986; 1987; Cooper and Law, 1995), important themes in Cooper's writings are culture (Cooper, 2001a), cyborganization (Cooper and Law, 1995; Parker and Cooper, 1998), information (Cooper 1976; 1986; 1987), mass society (Cooper, 2001b; 2003), Otherness (Cooper, 1983; 1998a), representation (Cooper, 1992; 1993) and visibility (Cooper, 1989a). His theoretical inspirations are equally diverse: from contemporary French and Italian philosophy to anthropology, sociology, psychoanalysis, pragmatism, systems theory, chaos theory, cybernetics and art theory – to name only a few primary sources. What is remarkable is the lightness with which Cooper crosses these boundaries, or perhaps we should say in which he *un-forms* boundaries. Cooper moves almost effortlessly from one discipline to another as if there were no boundaries between them.

This style of thinking and writing, in which authors from different backgrounds are connected to each other, can be confusing. What is confusing is precisely the 'everybody knows' which Cooper often seems to disregard. This, however, is a conscious strategy, for it is precisely the 'everybody knows' (or simply 'knowledge') which Cooper seeks to unmask. Cooper is not interested in the knowledge embedded in the separate disciplines. What interests him is what moves through disciplines (or systems, organizations), what keeps them together and what allows them to fall apart. What is important for Cooper is the question of the *beyond*: What is *beyond* discipline? What is *beyond* knowledge? What is *beyond* subjectivity? What is *beyond* organization? The question of the beyond is primarily an ontological question, an investigation into the formation and — simultaneously— displacement of order, as well as its relation to the human condition. From these questions of the beyond other questions follow: technical questions (What techniques in organizing can be distinguished? What do they establish?); sociological questions (Do people follow orders? How can we, humans, participate in organizing processes?); and epistemological questions (How to know the beyond? Is there a method to reach out to the beyond?).

My reading of Cooper in this chapter, despite my attempts to find running threads in his work, is a partial reading. Indeed, it is *necessarily* partial as Cooper himself explains (Cooper, 1998a; 2001). That is to say: realizing that Cooper's writings, by definition, do not form one closed system, also means that any representation of his writings will be equally partial. Representation, says

Cooper, is never plain paraphrasing. It will always consist of displacement (Cooper, 1992). I have chosen to focus on Cooper's ontology of organization – in my view his most important displacement of organization theory. This is where Cooper takes organization theory beyond organization theory.

Against simple location

If there is one common theme in all of Cooper's later writings, then it is a negative theme. This is, at times passionate, a not *that* kind of thinking, a not *that* type of knowledge. Cooper has used various labels to designate this adversary to his thought. The clearest expression, perhaps, is one he borrowed from Whitehead: the logic of simple location (Cooper, 1998a; 1998b; see also Chia, 1998c). Whitehead defines simple location as the idea which says that 'material can be said to be *here* in space and *here* in time, or *here* in space-time, in a perfectly definite sense which does not require for its explanation any reference to other regions of space-time' (Whitehead: 1985: 62). For Whitehead, the logic of simple location is intimately related to the concept of Euclidean space: the idea that clearly distinguishable things, defined by their locations, move from one place to another by the force of universal laws (such as gravity). Once we know these laws the world becomes entirely predictable. For Whitehead this idea is based on simplification, missing primary forces not *in* time and space, but from which time and space effectuate. For Whitehead, true movement is a distortion of nature as a whole, simultaneously redefining time-space relations as well as the identity of 'things'. Whitehead was thus concerned with what we miss out when we present things as complete in universal time and space. To Bertrand Russell, who defended the idea that the world is formed of independent and complete entities, Whitehead once said: 'You think the world is what it looks like in fine weather at noon day; I think it is what it seems like in the early morning when one first wakes from deep sleep' (Russell, 1956: 41). Whitehead was interested in the point where the clear evaporates into the unclear. This is exactly what interests Cooper as well.

The logic of simple location, as Cooper understands it, attempts to translate raw matter into 'things' (Cooper, 1998b: 137). It is based on the idea that the conditions which define what a thing is capable of are located in the thing itself. According to Cooper, entities (and identities) do not have natural locations, and 'things' do not have an essence that keeps them together: 'Social terms are not bounded by "walls" – there are no containers and no contained in the social world' (Cooper and Law, 1995: 243). Identities, subjects, and organizations are generated, and continuously require regeneration, from a groundless mass or abstract field (Cooper, 1976). This groundless mass, which I will discuss in more detail shortly, is a field of possibilities. Forms derive their existence from this mass. In the idea of simple location this mass is denied: the cloud of possibilities that surround any being, always present through its absence, is excluded from analysis and excluded from knowing. Thus Cooper, drawing on Derrida and Serres, argues that the purity of an inside 'can only be attained . . . if the outside is branded as a supplement, something inessential, even parasitical' (Cooper, 1989b: 487). Every idea of the fixed is based on the flawed idea of simple location, the idea that there is no beyond: 'What you see is all there is', 'What you know is all there is'.

As with Whitehead, Cooper's dismissal of simple location is equally directed against the idea of the universal in general: the idea that nature consists of a fixed set of laws which determine the 'simple movement' of 'clear-cut, definite things' (Cooper, 1998a: 108). The social and technical world we inhabit, says Cooper, cannot be understood on the basis of universal laws. The idea of the universal, again, is an example of simple location – an abstraction in thinking of the concrete – resulting in the representation of partiality as wholeness. A universal law, even if infinite in its power, is finite in being forever closed: its formula remains forever the same. We find the same idea in Deleuze and Guattari. They say, 'We think the universal explains, whereas it is what must be explained' (Deleuze and Guattari, 1994: 49). So, for Cooper, as well as for Deleuze and Guattari, the moment we have established a bounded entity or a universal (Whitehead's noon), that is the moment when we need to start asking questions – that is when there is an opportunity and a need for thinking. Thinking for Cooper thus involves a displacement of established forms. It has the task to reach beyond the immediately visible and knowable.

The potential of the abstract field

Let us try to translate Cooper's dismissal of simple location in terms of potentiality. What does potentiality mean? What does it mean to be capable of something? In Book Theta of *Metaphysics*, where Aristotle developed his ontology of potentiality, one finds a critique of thinkers of the Megarian school, who argued that a being has potency only when this potency is active, when it is exercised. According to Aristotle, this is an absurd idea, leading to beliefs such as:

> that which is standing will always stand and that which is sitting will always sit; for that which sits will not get up, since it will be impossible for it to get up if it does not have the power to get up. (Aristotle, 1966: 149)

For Aristotle, a human being has the potentiality to stand when sitting, or to sit when standing. That is, human beings can be the moving cause of their own movement. This idea is safeguarded by the idea that being human is grounded in a substance in which the potentiality to sit and to get up find their natural location: as a human being I can talk, as a chair I can bear a human being. It is uncontested, says Aristotle, that to be able to do something is not the same as exercising this potentiality: the potential is different from its actual expression. To get up when one sits, one needs to possess the potentiality or the power to get up, and in getting up one's potentiality to get up is actualized.

As Agamben (1999) argues, however, in his brilliant essay 'On Potentiality' (see also ten Bos, in this volume), there is more to Aristotle's concept of potentiality than just this simple distinction between the potential and the actual. For Aristotle, he argues, potentiality is not simple non-being, it is the *existence* of non-being. It is not a what-could-have-been-but-simply-did-not-happen, not an *is not*. Potentiality is fully real, not disappearing in actuality but preserving itself in actuality. This is exactly how the relation of presence and absence in Cooper should be understood: possibilities surrounding the 'real' things we see are present in their absence. Cry and silence originate each other: silence is made possible through the cry, just as much as the cry is made possible through silence (Cooper, 2001a; see also Cooper, 2003). Similarly, the visible makes possible the experience of the invisible. In other words, to have the privation of light and sound enables us to experience darkness and silence (Agamben, 1999). The potential *exists*, precisely because it finds its moment of un-formation at the very same time as the actual finds its (temporary) formation.

Cooper would agree with Aristotle that a power to get up is needed to actually get up when one sits. He would also agree with Agamben's reading of Aristotle that this potentiality is an existing non-being. There is, however, also an important difference between Aristotle's idea of potentiality and Cooper's idea of potentiality. Contrary to Aristotle, potentiality for Cooper is never *located* within substance, genus or species (frames or boundaries which keep a set of potentialities together), or *defined* by function or law (the idea of the universal). The power is not a power from within, nor a power located in universal laws, but a power from the abstract field (Cooper, 1976). Actualization finds its origin in the abstract field, or ungrounding mass, from which life folds and unfolds. Heidegger's influence on Cooper can clearly be felt here: Heidegger's Nothing as the background out of which everything emerges resembles Cooper's concept of the abstract field.

For Cooper, the abstract field can never be touched directly. It can only be approached through the divisions we recognize as our world: 'The primary whole is always a lost whole, one which we can only see through the work of division' (Cooper, 1987: 402). We see a resemblance with Spinoza's thinking. In Spinoza's *Ethics* (2002) the finite and the infinite form one substance, Nature or God, where the finite beings (modes) express infinity through infinite attributes (thinking, extension). Cooper argues that the only key to the infinite (the abstract field) is through the finite: 'Unity or wholeness can emerge only through division or difference' (1983: 213). For this reason, one always needs to recognize that the infinite whole, or abstract field, is present in its absence. The abstract field is present in the incompleteness and mutability of actualities. Actualities are always unfinished, or partial, continuously moving through clouds of potentialities:

> Each object – chair, cup, spoon – can never be separate and self-contained; by definition, it is always partial, a *con-verse* in a dynamic network of *convertibilities*. The body, too, is necessarily partial, momentarily defining itself through assemblage with

another partial object. The understanding and definition of the human agent as essentially purposeful and self-directive now takes second place to agency as the general collection and dispersion of parts and fragments which co-define each other in a mutable and transient assemblage of possibilities and relations. (Cooper, 2001b: 25, emphasis in original)

Partiality, for Cooper, means that anything we conceive of as a bounded thing (the possessor of boundaries), is in fact generated from these boundaries, continually transforming itself through interaction with other partialities. The potentiality of a human body, for example, can only be understood through the interactions with other partialities. To sit on a chair means entering a relation with this chair: the human body and the chair temporarily co-define each other.

These interactions between partialities, which continuously reinvent our world, cannot be captured in knowledge because they resist abstraction. It is therefore important to realize that Cooper's abstract field is not abstract in itself. We think of it as abstract because we cannot define its essence or draw its borders. That is to say, we *abstract* from the abstract field. Cooper's abstract field is concrete just like abstract art is concrete. An abstract painting of, say, a human body reminds us of the complex *concreteness* of what it means to be human. As Sørensen put it, 'all abstractions are simple; everything that is concrete is complex' (2004: 12). Cooper's abstract field, as abstract art, thus reminds us of our forgetfulness of the concreteness of potentiality. We tend to make the concrete abstract through the logic of simple location.

Simple location and organization theory

Cooper's dismissal of simple location is primarily directed at dominant discourse in the social sciences. Social science has attributed social origins to complete structures, such as systems and organizations, which are in fact abstractions from far more complex processes of composition and decomposition. Establishing things or 'forevers in thought' has the purpose to stop thinking. It consists of building walls around the present, ie, locating that which is unlocatable, with the double purpose of creating certainty and advancing 'knowledge'. Simple presence, in its most extreme forms, becomes a collection of moments where one declares the infinite to be finite. This is how some versions of 'progress' (of knowledge) should be understood. Disciplines such as 'sociology' or 'organization theory' are thought to progress through abstraction upon abstraction. Sociology and organization theory, Cooper argues, all too often blind themselves from what goes beyond simple location. They tend to accept simple location as a given, as a natural fact of life, while the true task for thinking is to ask fundamental questions such as: Where does the logic of simple location lead us? Where would a generic (Cooper, 1998) or proximal (Cooper and Law, 1995) way of thinking, sensitive to the abstract field, take us? This, of course, is not to say that sociologists have only been preoccupied with simple location. The question of the beyond was at the heart of Max Weber's thinking and can also be felt in systems thinking of the 1960s and 1970s, both important sources of inspiration for Cooper. Nor would it be fair to say that organization theorists have only been preoccupied with simple location. There is a substantial body of literature within organization theory directed against the idea of simple location, to which this volume bears testimony.

An illuminating example of simple location in the social sciences, according to Cooper, is Herbert Simon's (1957) idea of bounded rationality. Simon critiques the idea of Economic Man, he who possesses all relevant information and who makes rational decisions based on this information. Simon corrected models of rational decision-making by arguing that (1) agents face uncertainty about the future, and (2) that there are costs and difficulties in acquiring the required information. In making decisions, Simon argues, decision-makers therefore have to rely on bounded rationality. Decision-making thus becomes a matter of satisficing rather than optimizing. Cooper, in his critique of Simon, says that rationality and prediction are not locatable potentialities in the first place: 'we recognize that it's not the rationality that is bounded but rather that the *boundedness* is *rationalized*' (Cooper, 1998b: 148; emphasis in original; see also Cooper, 1992). In the idea of bounded rationality the ideas of subjectivity and rationality remain unquestioned. That is, in bounded rationality, rationality is located within the minds of individual decision makers: rationality is bounded because boundedness is attributed to the form of the human mind. Mind, however, is something much more fundamental for Cooper since it directly links us with the undivided mass: the unconsciousness of mind touches the absent presence of potentiality. Forcing the mind to exclusively think in terms of bounded things loses sight of the formation and deformation processes of boundaries.

Another example is the idea of the division of labour. The division of labour, dividing labour into specific tasks or functions, is one of the key concepts in sociology and economics (classic studies are Braverman, 1974; Durkheim, 1984; Marx, 1992; Smith, 1979). While these studies certainly highlight important developments in the industrialization processes that characterize the past three centuries, what is usually forgotten, says Cooper, is what lies beyond the division of labour. This is what Cooper calls the *labour of division* (Cooper, 1989a; 1998a; forthcoming, a; see also Hetherington and Munro, 1997): the production of the visible in the stabilized forms of social knowledge, social objects or social objectives. Through labour of division human beings are able to give meaning and purpose to their lives. Vision, says Cooper, is intrinsically di-vision. That is, through acts of division are we able to see, are we able to create meaning and are we able to find purpose. Work or labour serves precisely this function. Hence what you see in the supermarket is not the unorganized or uninformed mass itself: you see products of the labour of division. Nor are what you hear and what you say rough data (as statisticians would have it): words are formed through division and are therefore meaningful to us.

For Cooper, for the socially and technically informed world at least, these variations on the idea of simple location are based upon an ontological error: the idea that difference is secondary to being. Thus,

> differentiation is not a process that occurs (naturally) in the world; rather, it is the world that occurs within the differentiation of dedifferentiation, displacement and uncertainty. (Cooper, 1997b: 12)

Cooper's point is not that organization theory, or the social sciences in general, focus too much on organization, and that, as 'poststructuralists', we should celebrate disorganization. The point is that the establishment of 'an organization' (in language) closes the door for thinking about organization (as a generic process). That is, precisely by being satisfied with 'an organization' as such, as a completed structure, we forget the beyond. Being occupied with organization*s* is thus a way to stop thinking about organization.

Organization as the transformation of boundary relationships

In saying that boundaries do not belong to the world, Cooper is not saying that boundaries do not exist. His point is that boundaries do not *belong*. As dividers, boundaries make up the world, ie, the world belongs to boundaries. To think of walls not as effect (of building, as in simple location) but as origin, is to move from atoms and laws as object for research to boundary-activity (Cooper, 1986), division (Cooper, 1989a), or the frame (1986; 1991b) as the origin of life and thought:

> Any 'I' is the transient and uncertain result of boundaries dynamically shared with 'you', 'he', 'she', 'it', and 'them'. This shared 'I' is therefore *common* and *communal* in the most radical sense of a boundary as that which *separates and joins at the same time.* (Cooper, 2003: 166, emphases in original)

Boundary-activity, division, or framing, is to divide and to connect at the same time; a condensing of time and space (unthinkable in Euclidean space where time and space are universal dimensions) where what comes after simultaneously comes before: the copy creates the original as much as the original creates the copy.

An event, or a reorganization of form, is what Cooper calls information. Information must be taken literally here: to in-form, that which goes into form (Cooper, 1976). As we noted earlier, the formed is only partial, looking for further connections that will change its identity. Thus, 'information is not a property of the individual message but of the set of possibilities which surround the message' (Cooper, 1991b: 3). Here we see a direct link to what Whitehead said to Russell: the moment when one wakes up from a deep sleep is the moment of information: 'in that imperceptible moment between the known and the unknown. [Information] lasts but an instant and is quickly gone' (Cooper, 2001a: 169).

To think about boundaries, frames, and divisions is to think of action (Cooper, 1976; Cooper and Law, 1995). Action does not take place inside or outside boundaries: action is always boundary-based, it takes place in the midst of things, continuously redefining the actual out of a cloud of potentialities. Actions or events make present what was absent, make visible what was invisible, possible what was impossible; they are innocent in the sense of being not-yet-formed, not-yet-defined: 'Action . . . occurs in a meaning vacuum, having become detached from clear purpose and outcome' (Cooper, 1976: 1002).

This is also precisely how Cooper understands organization: 'Organizing activity is the transformation of boundary relationships' (Cooper, 1992: 257). Organization or information is always reorganization, not in origin – it originates out of disorganization or unform – but in effect. 'Organizations' (what we in language refer to as organizations) do not organize. The earth organizes. What we commonly conceive as 'an organization' is the result of symbolic reproduction. The ontological moment of information or organization is not to be understood as a simplification of things (in translating matter into form); it is the moment when potentialities, or possibilities, come into being. It is the moment when space, or 'world' (as Heidegger would put it) is revealed.

One might object that if 'organizations' were in fact continually changing, or continually informing, it would be impossible actually to work in an organization, or to recognize an organization as such. Cooper has two answers. The first we have already seen: what we see is not sheer matter, or sheer potentiality. What we see is the symbolic order: we see the already divided, the already signified. This answer, however, is not enough in itself, for the question is: How do we act upon this symbolic order? This is Cooper's second answer: What we call an organization, in this regard, is no different from what we call an 'I', a 'we' or an 'it'. Just as 'we' continuously regenerate ourselves by speaking the already-formed concepts (affirming) and by inventing new concepts (informing), 'organizations' also continuously regenerate themselves. Newspapers, for example, recreate themselves on a daily basis through their reports (Cooper, forthcoming, b). On an ontological level there is no categorical distinction between human being and organizations: 'We' are equally part of 'organizations' as 'organizations' are part of 'us'. 'We', as well as 'organizations', produce what it means to be a 'we' or 'an organization' in taking part of the primary processes of formation and deformation – in short: in organizing.

Human production systems

Production, as Cooper understands it, is not simply the making of useful and desired objects. It is also the structuring of a world so that it endures into the future as a knowable creation in space and time (Cooper, 2001a). Production through acts of division is necessary for purposes of defence: 'production is transformation of information into systematized knowledge by means of prediction and control' (1987: 3). Here, again, we see the idea of simple location:

prediction is safeguarded by the universal, control by the stable boundaries belonging to an inside. That is, if we were only to experience the unformed or abstract field, consciousness would not be possible. As Schelling (1980) argues, we need objects in order to be reflexive because a thought can only turn back to itself (which, for Cooper, is no longer itself *because* of this return) after it has hit an object. Humans, by giving meaning and purpose to their lives, constitute themselves as objects: 'The subject has to posit itself as an object in order to know [or form] itself' (Cooper, 1987: 413). The formation of matter into graspable and controllable forms is what Cooper also calls institutionalization. Thus, to repeat the same point in different terms: institutionalization is not separate from human acts; we partly define ourselves by institutionalization, or by constituting ourselves as objects. Subjectivity is the product of institutionalization, not the origin.

To say that institutionalization is necessary for thinking is not the same as saying that institutionalization, in any form, is something that stimulates thinking. Even though one needs to encounter objects in order to think, these very same objects make thinking difficult. By definition, objects refuse thought since the thinking, of which objects are the result, has already been done. This is, as we have already seen, Cooper's problem with the idea of the organization as object: thinking in terms of organizations will refuse thinking of organization. Thus institutions:

> make it difficult for us to think of the 'nowness' or sublimity of the event, since they are continually structuring our thoughts and thinking processes for us. Universities, schools, political programmes, religious credos, academic theories are all 'infected' with the practical-useful'. (Cooper, 1991a: 11)

The danger inherent to any form of institutionalization is that we stop to think and question. In fact, the more powerful the institution is, and hence the more there is to think of, the less we are inclined to think – institutionalization, the production of 'subjects' and 'objects', makes us lazy. Through institutions we can undergo the structures of daily existence without acting upon these institutions. We affirm, hence regenerate, without thought – what Nietzsche (1967) has called the 'yes' (Y-A) of a donkey. This is how the human excludes him/herself from the 'human production systems' (Cooper, 2001c) – a process that, according to Cooper, is characteristic for our age. Indeed, some 'systems have lives of their own which make them fundamentally independent of human control' (Cooper and Burrell, 1988: 94).

This development, says Cooper, has to a large extent to do with the nature of post-industrial systems of production. Not only do modern corporations incorporate bodies into their production, the products (or objects) that these processes produce enter these very same bodies:

> The institutional product is also a social product in that we eat it, we wear it, we speak it; it enters our minds and bodies in such a way as to constitute us as a corporate body. (Cooper, 2001c: 326)

Human beings, or the 'innocent' human flesh, sheer matter and potentiality, is thus inscribed by institutionalization, which resists 'human' intervention: 'Without our realising it, we are in danger of becoming technical products of the technology we have produced' (Cooper, 2001a: 334). We have withdrawn ourselves from where the action is.

To think openly

How do we overcome the passivity that characterizes our (consumer) society? How do we re-engage in the human production systems to mould their processes into different forms? What forms should we strive for?

We have already seen versions of Cooper's answers: to think in terms of organization instead of organizations; to think about boundaries instead of within and between boundaries; to think the beyond (or the abstract field). Cooper's 'objects' of thinking are not objects, but that which goes beyond objects. It is not the objects that resist meaning (as we have seen they are full of meaning), but what goes beyond objects. In order to see what lies beyond objects, however, one paradoxically *needs* objects: only through the divided the undivided can be felt. One might therefore ask if scholars of organization theory continue to think if they no longer accept 'real' organizations as the objects of thinking. We are again reminded of Schelling's observation: without objects there is nothing to think, or better: our thoughts will never return to us, forever lost in the abstract field. Thus the further we reach to primary mind or ungrounding mass, the less we experience, and the more consciousness disappears. As such, the resulting 'thoughts' would be unable to emancipate or re-enlighten the bodies that are captured by un-human human production systems.

Cooper is well aware of this limit. We can never become one with the abstract field – we can only temporally approach it. The life of the mind, as well as of the body, is a continuous dialectic process of learning and unlearning (Cooper, 2003). In order to make room for the new, one must first negate that which is taken as positive. In other words, one must find the partiality in anything that is taken as a bounded whole in order to inform. While we are generally good at learning, ie, finding a simple location for 'real' things, what Cooper 'teaches' us is that renewal, and hence the possibility of ethics and politics, is grounded in unlearning. Unlearning, however, is not possible to zero degree. In approaching the abstract field one needs to be careful not to reach 'the point of no return'.

So the question becomes: how do you escape from a life that is dictated by the finished or the practical-useful without losing your mind or your body in the abstract field? Building on Anton Ehrenzweig's *The Hidden Order of Art* (2000), Cooper has used the concepts of 'scattered attention' and 'undifferentiation' in attempts to suggest theoretical answers to these questions (Cooper, 1998b; 2001c; 2003). Theory, however, will never provide final answers. Answers must always be demonstrated in action. One mode of action, for academics generally the most important mode, is writing. Writing can be a dislocation of seeing (see Foucault, 1987); testing the limit of what is possible, or seeking contact with the absent presence of potentialities. One can certainly find demonstrations of this power of writing in Cooper. Cooper is a master in displacing (or re-presenting) words and concepts, typically starting from their etymological roots in Heideggerian fashion. In this manner you control words and concepts as much as they control you. As a result, boundaries, including the boundaries that define your own being, become fluid and displace.

It is impossible to think without objects or live without objectives. It is therefore unavoidable that, in acting, one *selects* objects for displacement. Cooper does not go into the question on what basis we make this selection. We have nevertheless identified one important ethical or political moment in Cooper's writings: the idea that human production systems in which humans do not actively take part need to be resisted. This is another way of saying that there is a necessity for action in post-industrial times. How, exactly? Cooper does not answer this question in terms of a programme or in terms of techniques. What he does suggest, I believe, is that there is a need to think as concretely as we possibly can. We have a tendency to try to 'understand' the finished rather than to engage with the partial. This is particularly true for organization theory which, at least in some manifestations, seems to have *founded* itself on this tendency. In doing so, we lose sight of the potentialities through which we continually move and which continually move us. More importantly perhaps: we lose the potentiality to see new sights.

Acknowledgement

I am most grateful to Robert Cooper, Campbell Jones, Ruud Kaulingfreks, Martin Parker and two anonymous reviewers for their helpful comments on this chapter.

References

Agamben, G. (1999) 'On potentiality' in *Potentialities: Collected Essays in Philosophy*, trans. D. Heller-Roazen. Stanford, CA: Stanford University Press.
Aristotle (1966) *Metaphysics*, trans. H. G. Apostle. Bloomington: Indiana University Press.
Böhm, S. and C. Jones (eds.) (2001) 'Responding: To Cooper' *ephemera: critical dialogues on organization*, 1(4).
Braverman, H. (1974) *Labor and Monopoly Capital: The Degradation of Work in the Twentieth Century*. New York: Monthly Review.
Burrell, G. (1988) 'Modernism, postmodernism and organizational analysis 2: The contribution of Michel Foucault' *Organization Studies*, 9(2): 221–235.
Burrell, G. (1994) 'Modernism, postmodernism and organizational analysis 4: The contribution of Jürgen Habermas' *Organization Studies*, 15(1): 1–19.
Burrell, G. and G. Morgan (1979) *Sociological Paradigms and Organizational Analysis*. London: Heinemann.

Chia, R. (ed.) (1998a) *Organized Worlds: Explorations in Technology and Organization with Robert Cooper*. London: Routledge.

Chia, R. (ed.) (1998b) *In the Realm of Organization: Essays for Robert Cooper*. London: Routledge.

Chia, R. (1998c) 'From complexity science to complex thinking: Organization as simple location' *Organization*, 5(3): 341–369.

Cooper, R. (1972) 'Man, task and technology: Three variables in search of a future' *Human Relations*, 25(2): 131–157.

Cooper, R. (1973) 'Task characteristics and intrinsic motivation' *Human Relations*, 26(3): 387–413.

Cooper, R. (1974) *Job Motivation and Job Design*. London: Institute of Personnel Management.

Cooper, R. (1976) 'The open field' *Human Relations*, 29(11): 999–1017.

Cooper, R. (1983) 'The other: A model of human structuring' in G. Morgan (ed.) *Beyond Method: Strategies for Social Research*. Newbury Park, CA: Sage.

Cooper, R. (1986) 'Organization/disorganization' *Social Science Information*, 25(2): 299–335.

Cooper, R. (1987) 'Information, communication and organization: A post-structural revision' *The Journal of Mind and Behavior*, 8(3): 395–416.

Cooper, R. (1989a) 'The visibility of social systems' in M. C. Jackson, P. Keys and S.A. Cropper (eds.) *Operational Research and the Social Sciences*. New York: Plenum.

Cooper, R. (1989b) 'Modernism, postmodernism and organizational analysis 3: The contribution of Jacques Derrida' *Organization Studies*, 10(4): 479–502.

Cooper, R. (1991a) 'Institutional aesthetics: The case of "contestation" '. Paper presented at Utrecht University, The Netherlands, January.

Cooper, R. (1991b) 'Information theory and organizational analysis'. Paper presented to the Institute of Advanced Studies in Administration, Caracas, Venezuela, 12 March.

Cooper, R. (1992) 'Formal organization as representation: Remote control, displacement and abbreviation' in M. Reed and M. Hughes (eds.) *Rethinking Organization*. London: Sage.

Cooper, R. (1993) 'Technologies of representation' in P. Ahonen (ed.) *Tracing the Semiotic Boundaries of Politics*. Berlin: Mouton de Gruyter.

Cooper, R. (1996) 'Samuel Butler, cyborganization and the principle of symmetry'. Paper presented at Technology and Knowledge Conference, University of Crete, 17–18 October.

Cooper, R. (1997a) 'Millennium notes for social theory' *Sociological Review*, 45(4): 690–703.

Cooper, R. (1997b) 'Symmetry: Uncertainty as displacement'. Paper presented at Uncertainty, Knowledge and Skill conference, University of Limburg, Belgium, 6–9 November.

Cooper, R. (1998a) 'Assemblage notes' in R. C. H. Chia (ed.) *Organized Worlds: Explorations in Technology and Organization with Robert Cooper*. London: Routledge.

Cooper, R. (1998b) 'Interview with Robert Cooper' in R. C. H. Chia (ed.) *Organized Worlds: Explorations in Technology and Organization with Robert Cooper*. London: Routledge.

Cooper, R. (2001a) 'A Matter of Culture' *Cultural Values*, 5(2): 163–197.

Cooper, R. (2001b) 'Interpreting mass: Collection/dispersion' in N. Lee and R. Munro (eds.) *The Consumption of Mass*. Oxford: Blackwell.

Cooper, R. (2001c) 'Un-timely mediations: Questing thought' *ephemera: critical dialogues on organization*, 1(4): 321–347.

Cooper, R. (2003) 'Primary and secondary thinking in social theory: The case of mass society' *Journal of Classical Sociology*, 3(2): 145–172.

Cooper, R. (forthcoming, a) 'Making present: Autopoeisis as human production' *Organization*, 13(1).

Cooper, R. (forthcoming, b) 'Relationality' *Organization Studies*, 26(9).

Cooper, R. and G. Burrell (1988) 'Modernism, postmodernism and organizational analysis 1: An introduction' *Organization Studies*, 10(4): 479–502.

Cooper, R. and J. Law (1995) 'Organization: distal and proximal views' in S. B. Bacharach, P. Gagliardi and B. Mundell (eds.) *Research in the Sociology of Organization*. Greenwich, CT: JAI Press.

Deleuze, G. (1988) *Spinoza: Practical Philosophy*, trans. R. Hurley. San Francisco: City Lights Books.

Deleuze, G. and F. Guattari (1987) *A Thousand Plateaus: Capitalism and Schizophrenia*, trans. B. Massumi. Minneapolis: University of Minnesota Press.

Deleuze, G. and F. Guattari (1994) *What is Philosophy?*, trans. G. Burchell and H. Tomlinson. London: Verso.

Ehrenzweig, A. (2000) *The Hidden Order of Art*. London: Phoenix.

Foucault, M. (1987) *Death and the Labyrinth: The World of Raymond Roussel*, trans. C. Ruas. London: Athlone.

Hetherington, K. and R. Munro (eds.) (1997) *Ideas of Difference: Stability, Social Spaces and Labour of Division*. Oxford: Blackwell.

Marx, K. (1992) *Capital: A Critique of Political Economy Vol 1*, trans. B. Fowkes. London: Penguin.

Nietzsche, F. (1967) *Thus Spake Zarathustra: A Book for All and None*, trans. T. Common. London: Allen & Unwin.

Parker, M. and R. Cooper (1998) 'Cyborganization: Cinema as nervous system' in J. Hassard and R. Holliday (eds.) *Organization/Representation: Work and Organizations in Popular Culture*. London: Sage.

Russell, B. (1956) 'Beliefs: Discarded and retained' in *Portraits from Memory and Other Essays*. London: Allen & Unwin.

Schelling, F. W. J. (1980) 'Philosophical letters on dogmatism and criticism' in *The Unconditional in Human Knowledge: Four Early Essays: 1794–1796*, trans. F. Marti. Lewisburg: Bucknell University Press.

Simon, H. A. (1957) *Administrative Behavior: A Study of Decision-Making Processes in Administrative Organization* (second edition). New York: Macmillan.

Smith, A. (1979) *The Wealth of Nations: Books I-III*. Harmondsworth: Penguin.

Sørensen, B. (2004) *Making Events Work, or, How to Multiply Your Crisis*. Copenhagen: Samfundslitteratur.

Spinoza, B. (2002) *Complete Works*, trans. Samuel Shirley. Indianapolis: Hackett.

Whitehead, A. N. (1985) *Science and the Modern World*. London: Free Association Books.

Immaculate defecation: Gilles Deleuze and Félix Guattari in organization theory

Bent Meier Sørensen

Resumé

This chapter opens by situating the reception of Gilles Deleuze and Félix Guattari in organization theory, but does so by conceiving this reception as a instance of 'abstract machines' that territorialize 'reception' as a function that defines and confines a field of study to a territory, here a limited number of universities in the English-speaking world.

The chapter further expresses the (anti-)method of Deleuze and Guattari by trying to deploy the method itself: defocusing the problem in order to 'produce the problematic', straining to reach a language that stutters and breaks down, an affective writing, a 'line of flight' with infinite speed, and abstaining (perhaps specifically) from suicide by always experimenting not with the ultimate but with the '*pen*ultimate limit'. Despite rumours to the contrary, the writings of Deleuze and Guattari are most adequately characterized by the word *sobriety*. Language as such, however, is a slang, a machine that works by breaking down, moving intensely through dynamic states of crisis and equilibrium. This calls for a sober yet bloody style: 'Write with blood,' says Nietzsche, 'and thou wilt find that blood is spirit' (1969: 43).

Right into the heart of Organization Theory (and one wonders which *way* into the heart: the bowels, the veins? Through a taste for *camp* or really by way of an Outside?), Deleuze and Guattari release the dynamic double concept of the Plane of Organization and the Plane of Immanence. The organization – now construed as an 'assemblage' – is situated between these limits. As such, the assemblage is a multiplicity, but it is habitually botched or stratified, that is, reduced and simplified by the three great 'strata': the Organism, the Sign and the Subject. This brings the chapter to the concept itself, as it is composed as a multiplicity with the ability of counteractualizing our present, an often lamentable state of affairs. The concept also features the ability to produce the problematic of a given problem, instead of just solving it. The concept is, in particular, an event, and as such calls for an ethics by which one becomes worthy of the event. Becomes worthy of being present at the dawn of the world (Deleuze and Guattari, 1998: 280).

Reception-conception

Gilles Deleuze and Félix Guattari are advocates of philosophy, to be sure, but it is both a certain type of philosophy as well as it is a certain use of it. They call their philosophy, among other things, *geophilosophy* (Deleuze and Guattari, 1994: 85ff). In geophilosophy thinking takes place between the earth and a territory, thinking is a geographical matter-movement rather than a purely cognitive exercise. In fact, humans are only a smaller and historically conditioned part of this cosmic ecology, and via the concept of the assemblage Deleuze and Guattari manage to replace and reconfigure the staple sociological and philosophical concern, the relationship between the human and its world (Buchanan, 2000: 120). The assemblage consists of and relates bodies and signs. This makes organizations appear as *certain kinds* of assemblages, with certain kinds of problems and problematizations available to them. In any case, the assemblage is, as indicated, situated between the Plane of Organization and the Plane of Immanence (a.k.a. the Plane of Consistency or *the* body without organs).

When the assemblage comes more tied to the Plane of Organization, it becomes ordered to the limit of rigidification, much like a classroom of pupils is more ordered than a pack of hunters. This ordering is quite visible in what Deleuze and Guattari name the strata, comprised by man, language and the world as we know it (Deleuze and Guattari, 1988: 399ff). At the extreme limit of the Plane of Organization we should find, amongst other things, both fascism and anarchism, and psychosis. And, from time to time, we should find ourselves there. At the other extreme, on the Plane of Immanence, the assemblage returns to an intensively dynamic state of forming new connections everywhere and of transforming into completely new becomings: a state of cosmic revolution, 'oceanic differences, of nomadic distributions and crowned anarchy' (Deleuze, 1994: 265). Here Deleuze and Guattari find the nomads in the desert, and the organization is affirmed as a pure production of desire, the self is no longer a problem, and politics will equal nothing less than love: 'Every love is an exercise in depersonalization on a body without organs yet to be formed' (Deleuze and Guattari, 1988: 35). You certainly don't need to be in love to form a line of flight towards this plane, but that particularly insane state gives a good hint to what Deleuze and Guattari have in mind.

Thinking as a practice, then, always establishes territories or fields, and, more interestingly, thinking is also able to change these fields, able to 'deterritorialize' these territories and set the known connections free in order to let them form new connections (Deleuze and Guattari, 1988: 174ff). The new net of connections, the 're-territorialization', can either place things in an even worse situation, as when postmodernism returns only to haunt the social field with 'interesting lifestyles' and new commodities to long for. Or it can be 'absolute', as when Nelson Mandela's line of flight accelerated millions of bodies (of multiple colours) during the South African liberation, eventually bringing reconciliation to the haunted country.

Organization Theory (here capitalized in an attempt to call into being) proves to be a key example of the dynamic of de- and re-territorialization, whether the question is of 'traditional' or 'mainstream' theory, or the *avant garde* version of it, like the book you are currently reading, it makes no difference. In general, an obligatory passage point of introductory chapters like the present one is a paragraph depicting the reception of the *oeuvre* in question: how has, in this case, the work of Deleuze and Guattari been perceived in Organization Theory? This does appear as an opening gesture, thus signalling a possible process of absolute deterritorialization, that is, an opening to what is outside Organization Theory and what promises to change it. Yet what happens – and the reader is urged to test this claim in the present book – is that the referential regime so released immediately draws a definite territory, a negative reterritorialization: it singles out a series of indexed points situated almost exclusively at a certain number of universities in Great Britain, supplemented with a few, very few, points in North America, and including, sometimes, Australia and New Zealand. This practice connects, as it were, the assemblage of organization theory – let's dispense with the capitalization – understood as a heterogeneous multiplicity of thinking and writing, with a finite territory, an indexed network of already signified striations, coagulations, and sedimentations. On repeat, this procedure will create, says the geophilosopher, a *stratum* (see Deleuze and Guattari, 1988: 39ff).

'Splendid!' says the organization theorist: not only is organization theory being developed in a language that 'everybody speaks', but it has also, finally, established itself as a territory, that is, as a *field*, with all the associated opportunities to become stronger and to reach further with its messages of critique and deliberation (and the promises of permanent positions). 'No, not quite splendid,' say Deleuze and Guattari: as a language becomes *major* (English, white, rich, male), it loses its transformative power and becomes pure 'order word': 'Language is made not to be believed but to be obeyed, and to compel obedience' (Deleuze and Guattari, 1988: 76). This goes, *mutatis mutandis*, also for organization theory: organization theory is not made to convey messages, neither about organizations nor about theory. It is made to give orders regarding the organization of bodies, and the diagrammatization of signs. It concerns the sayable and the visible, and prescribes this with a sense of prefigured order: slogans, passwords, and instructions. The very order of reception of French and German poststructuralism 'into' organization theory has, on the whole, not followed some evolutionary, let alone revolutionary, path, nor any discernable logic of reason: the logic of, first, Foucault, then Derrida and, finally, Deleuze and Guattari is nothing but the chronological order of their translation into English (stay tuned: Gabriel Tarde, Michel Serres and Peter Sloterdijk are on their way).

Organization theory is ordered, all right, be it only on a highly contingent ground. Behind the smooth wrapping of every theory of organization there is indeed a teacher, just as there is a priest behind every betrayal of desire: the teacher does not so much instruct as give orders, and the compulsory education machine does not communicate information, but imposes on the student a set of semiotic coordinates (Deleuze and Guattari, 1988: 75). Overall, academics comprise the lowest part of this education machine, its rectum, where the last fluids of nutrition are extracted from the body material. This is the reason why most academics struggle with anal retentive character traits and a fear of youth, and why they enforce examinations in order to judge 'go' or 'no go' – and never 'go with us' (Deleuze and Guattari, 1988: 177).

Language is non-discursive, and on the whole subjected to circumstances: the seemingly important words 'yes' and 'no' work only as a function of the setting (an exam, a wedding, a courtroom). Every utterance becomes double binding: 'The principal says "Here's your diploma" (read: get a job, sucker)' (Massumi, 1992: 31). So, the much celebrated 'linguistic turn' that has run through organization theory like a shot of oxygen these last thirty years might be just that: an overdose of a poisonous gas injected into a dying organism, causing it to flare up in a sudden, fatal spasm. 'Language is not life; it gives life orders. Life does not speak; it listens and waits' (Deleuze and Guattari, 1988: 76). This doesn't save the great Other(s) of poststructural organization theory like transaction cost economy and similar functionalistic interventions from critique: what these abstract machines confirm is not how organizations and their inhabitants in fact *work*, but why, on the contrary, mathematics, too, must be understood as a slang, a *patois*, and how, historically, the social sciences have made a lasting contribution to the most profound betrayal of desire: by turning it into *interests*.

Organization Theory between interests and desire

The concept of 'interest' is the centre around which most motivation theory and HRM is build. Seen from the point of view of Deleuze and Guattari, interest is in itself a strategic and manageable reduction of desire, as it couples needs (stemming from a presumed ontological lack) with preferences (derived from a transcendent, stratified and organized hierarchy of being). The subject, who, of course, in capitalism is the consumer, who 'needs' this or that object, has been organized to suffer from this lack. Expressed in the form of wanting this and that as in the transaction cost calculus of preferences, desire has *already* been repressed and turned into interests (see Holland, 1999). But desire is not, in Deleuze and Guattari's Spinozist variant of it, characterized by a lack or a need, but simply by what *connects*: desire is connections, to desire is to produce connections.

Stratification, the construction of the strata, is obtained exactly by turning desire into interests, by making the Oedipal, nuclear family the model of *all* social organization: the *Vaterland* becomes the territory of the enterprise, its 'culture' becomes the mother tongue of the subject, the ingenious R&D boys become the preferred and well paid sons, the HR squad becomes the nursing sisters, compassionate but powerless in front of the grand signifier. Also HRM and motivation theory is currently being deterritorialized, and Alexander Styhre has, for instance, performed a well-wrought Deleuzoguattarian attack on this motivation discourse from the point of view of immanence and desire (Styhre, 2005).

As it goes, critical management studies should be a natural vista for an adequate 'reception' of Deleuze and Guattari in organization theory, but the latter's tenor *is* very different from Foucault's more tempered literary style, and only very slowly do Foucauldians find themselves sufficiently empowered to enter the Deleuzoguattarian bestiarium of grotesque neologisms and hyper-complex analytical constructions. Moreover, while Deleuze and Guattari never ceased to be Marxists (Manuel Delanda shamelessly claims Marx to be Deleuze and Guattari's Oedipus![1]) they reject the central Marxian orthodox legacy, that a society is defined by its contradictions. Also contradictions must be conceived as multiplicities, as manifolds, and Deleuze and Guattari point to a third and decisive component: 'from the viewpoint of micropolitics, a society is defined by its lines of flight, which are molecular' (1988: 216). These lines of flight – asignifying ruptures, not signifying breaks – concern that surplus value of desiring production that is *not* captured by the market axiomatic, the corporate logic, or the well-fare State politics. Just as Foucault (1979), their great forerunner in social analysis, Deleuze and Guattari have a fetish for the fringes and the margins, which might explain that organizational studies on control (Rose, 2000; Power, 2004), fraud (Bayou and Reinstein, 2001), crime (Jones, 2000; Ronnie, 2001) and gangster rap (Rehn and Sköld, 2005) seem to thrive under the infectious appeal of their bestiarium.[2]

Scholars dealing with gender first hesitated when faced with the seemingly conservative idea that women – and everyone else – should engage in 'becoming-woman' as a part of a micro-political strategy (as prescribed in Deleuze and Guattari, 1988: 291ff). However, as Rosi Braidotti acknowledges, the point is 'to by-pass the parameters of phallocentric representation in order to create a new, more intensive image of the thinking subject' (2003: 48; see also Buchanan and Colebrook, 2000). Furthermore, as technology gets plugged in everywhere in our bodies, Dianne Currier (2003) experiments with letting the assemblage replace the charged notion of *the* body, just as Stephen Linstead replaces the no less charged notion of *the* organization with the Organization without Organs (Linstead, 2000, see also Kornberger, Rhodes and ten Bos, forthcoming).

Neither is the social body itself, the *socius* as Deleuze and Guattari name it in *Anti-Oedipus*, a nice, compartmentalised landscape of ordered citizens under a sovereign, led by a social contract for mutual benefit. There might be organizations everywhere, but the world is not an organization. It doesn't work that way: rather, it is *at* work everywhere:

> It breathes, it heats, it eats. It shits and fucks . . . Everywhere *it* is machines – real ones, not figurative ones: machines driving other machines, machines being driven by other machines, with all the necessary couplings and connections. (Deleuze and Guattari, 1984: 1)

The book you are trying to read just now is also a machine: it cuts up sentences, it sprouts with fits of desire that keep running through it and escaping it, and it is probably also strapped down by a somewhat pretentious academic style. Maybe you Xeroxed it through another machine[3] in order to save money, trying to bypass your subsumption as consumer under the giant capitalist machine which, on its side, constantly exchanges more and more of your labour time, of your desiring production, with more and more commodities.

While the assemblage is situated between the Plane of Organization and the Plane of Immanence, it is concretely operated by machines: it is the configuration of these machines that either stratifies it more harshly, or furthers its connections to the Plane of Immanence (Deleuze and Guattari, 1988: 510ff). On the one hand there are textbooks with stupid test questions and on the other hand books that painfully force you to think. Most generally, a machine is able to connect very diverse elements in flat, rhizome-like structures. Analytically, the abstract machines can be grouped under three aspects (see Bonta and Protevi, 2004: 47ff): singular and immanent machines that direct concrete assemblages, like a national transportation system or a teacher-student interaction, to mention two somewhat different machines. Secondly, there is *the* abstract machine that draws the Plane of Immanence itself: pure desire, pure anorganic life, love.

Thirdly, the abstract machines can be judged according to the extent to which they create new connections and deterritorializations: this is, specifically, the function of the *war machine*. An example of this is the release of the Gutenberg Bible, an event that suddenly emancipated knowledge and spiritual desire out of the Catholic mega machine. The abstract machines can also, naturally, be judged according to which degree they further stratifications by way of coding and territorializations. Finally, there are the apparatuses of capture, obeying and enforcing the Organic, the Signifying and the Subjectifying. This happens, for instance, when the knowledge and the spiritual desire set free by Gutenberg is reterritorialized under the Protestant ethic and the spirit of capitalism (see Weber, 1985). Also this can be counteractualized, as demonstrated in both Martin Wood's and Silvia Gherardi's Deleuzoguattarian analyses of organizational knowledge as practices of 'folding' and 'desire' respectively (Wood, 2002; Gherardi, 2003).

But take a look around: all you see are actualized beings, the actual world is on the whole stratified and rigidly organized, the mission of the war machines we struggle to invent is to counteractualize this *actual* state of affairs into an intense, *virtual* sphere where everything again becomes possible, where thinking and living again becomes possible.

A scent of method: The problematic breakdown

Indeed, what in common sense theory appear to be quite concrete and pertinent problems, are as a rule squeezed and multiplied in the Deleuzoguattarian roundabout. Not only is the problem apparently left to its own devices, it reappears multiplied and intensified. The problem reappears as a real multiplicity by being produced as a *problematic*: the problem becomes an event. It is not just a suspicion. It is a method.

The notion of the problematic is already a central concern in Deleuze's own main works, *Difference and Repetition* and *Logic of Sense* (see also Buchanan, 2000). The problematic, argues Deleuze, must always be regarded as prior to the 'solution', which is a category of the already closed case. Solutions belong to the categories of being, truth and the real, in themselves markers of a certain history of philosophy and, we can safely add, the history of organization theory. These categories are, in Nietzsche's words, avatars of nihilism, mutilators of life, opposing life to life (see Nietzsche, 1969). This, says Deleuze, forces the solution to always have:

> the truth it deserves according to the problem to which it is a response, and the problem always to have the solution it deserves in proportion to *its own* truth or falsity – in other words, in proportion to its sense. (1994: 159)

The solution is confined to the empirical, historical determinations of its actualization in concrete bodies and collective statements, and in a certain sense the solution is not interesting; it is not *inter-esse*, between being, but is already essence. The category one should, with Søren Kierkegaard, like to examine, the relevant category, 'is that of the *interesting*, a category that especially today (just because we live in *discrimine rerum* [at a turning-point in human affairs]) has acquired great importance, for really it is the category of crisis' (Kierkegaard, 1983: 109–110).

The crisis is the process of virtualization offered by the problematic: indeed, the problem of the reception of Deleuze and Guattari in organization theory calls for a virtualization of both the notion of reception as well as the notion of organization theory. So, at the same time as the solution is inscribed in the actual event of the problem, the relevant problem to which it 'is a solution', must be counteractualized into its *virtual* phase, in a perpetual state of becoming, that is, becoming *actualized*. In this construction, Deleuze and Guattari go in the reverse direction, from the given solution (surgical warfare, downsizing corporations, upgrading competencies), to the painful problems that gave rise to these solutions. The notion of crisis found in Kierkegaard – with whom Deleuze felt a striking familiarity – also features such a reversal of the common sense denigration of crisis and death, and it finds an adequate framing in the dynamic processes of actualization and virtualization. In the actual world, any crisis is a problem and will make you, for instance, cancel an interesting date. At the virtual Plane of Immanence, however, the crisis draws a line of flight that enables you to leave your neurotic Self (which, to be honest, even *you* didn't want to date). The crisis is the passage from the virtual to the actual and vice versa, and it produces the problematic.

Henri Bergson is the prime problematizer of the problem, and the inspiration for the method: 'stating the problem is not simply uncovering, it is invention' (Bergson, cited in Deleuze, 1988: 15). The sense of the problem, then, is the expression of the problem as event. The problematic thus conceived is something like a kick in the teeth of organization theory, just to see how it works, to see for yourself (on the practice of kicking teeth and losing face, see Sørensen, forthcoming; for more on method, see Yu, 2004). It is a rage against the abstract machines, a rage that pits the problem against the problem:

> Not willing what happens, with that false will that complains, defends itself and looses itself in gesticulations, but taking the complaint and *rage to the point that they are turned against what happens* so as to set up the event, to isolate it, to extract in it the living concept. (Deleuze and Guattari, 1994: 160, emphasis added)

The world is a mixture. The assemblage of being (which has a multiple and coexisting assemblage of *becoming*) is situated between the stratifications and the body without organs, or, cosmologically, between the Plane of Organization and the plane of all bodies without organs, the Plane of Immanence (for more on the body without organs in organizational analysis, see Thanem, 2004). A mixture between an actual state of affairs and a virtual multiplicity, which is a becoming. Organizations are not *per se* situated at the Plane of Organization, although this is where we find them actualized: the organization as a practice is in a perpetual becoming which moves between the planes, 'a bureaucratic perversion, a permanent inventiveness or creativity practiced even against administrative regulations' (Deleuze and Guattari, 1988: 214). Consequently, creativity is rapidly becoming a theme in Deleuzoguattarian organization theory: Styhre and Sundgren (2003) perform an affirmative case study on rhizomatic innovation phases within the medical industry. Thomas Osborne (2003), reversely, opposes the idea that creativity 'as such' can be extracted from Deleuze's work and applied 'everywhere': this will only stratify creativity and create an 'image of thought'. In any case, the very notion of *the* Organization, as we know it from organization theory, is indeed an 'image of thought': that is Deleuze's expression for a common sense notion turned into a universal Truth (see Deleuze, 1994, especially Chapter 3). From an aesthetic point of view, Weiskopf attacks the iron-cage seen as another image of thought (Weiskopf, 2002). In reality, the organization is itself a mixture, despite the efforts organization theorists like Henry Mintzberg make in order to secure that all organizations resemble the human Organism, as they strikingly do in *Structures in Five* (Mintzberg, 1983).

Thinking itself is a practice that is able to produce the plane of immanence, just as art and science are (according, at least, to Deleuze and Guattari, 1994). The infinite movement of thought makes it capable of traversing vast distances and multiple flows in a single flash, and as a practice thinking draws a plane that maps these distances and these flows. In this way thinking draws the Plane of Immanence, which is composed of concepts. A practice of life is also able to produce the plane. So are you: moreover, you have now to follow that line of flight that will draw *your* body without organs. If you don't, you will be completely engulfed in the strata on the Plane of Organization, onto which organisms, signs and subjects are crafted. The Plane of Organization is folded and thickened into more stable layers; the Plane of Organization is stratified: Deleuze and Guattari erect a social ontology, which is finally a geology. They are geophilosophers.

Organizational research, then, if it aims to be non-transcendent and immanent and hostile to any image of thought, must be a diagonal or transversal movement between an actualized history and the virtual problem-event, an event that is 'immaterial, incorporeal, unlivable: pure *reserve*' (Deleuze and Guattari, 1994: 156). It is the concept itself that is able to bring the problem through its critical thresholds towards the problematic, where it will revolt. That is why the intuitive, critical method of creating concepts is so vital to Deleuze and Guattari (1994, Chapter 1). The problematic is realized in a milieu as a revolutionary becoming, implying that the crisis therefore designates a conjunction of philosophy, or of the concept, with the present milieu, in short, designates a *political philosophy* (Deleuze and Guattari, 1994: 100). Social analysis seen from the point of view of the problematic is the analysis of the event as a multiplicity, or the analysis of the expressible and the visible and their interrelation.

This is a social analysis of perpetual breakdown, instantiating series of measured collapses by turning the problem into the problematic. 'Certainly it is valuable to a trained writer to crash in an aircraft which burns,' said Hemingway. 'He learns several important things very quickly' (Hemingway, 1986: 127). Since each and every single machine works by breaking down (see Deleuze and Guattari, 1984: 151, or think of thesis writing or sex), our breakdown must become isomorphic with the machines the analysis tries to express and map, we must ourselves produce small machines that can be put at work everywhere: 'Hence we are all handymen: each with his little machines' (Deleuze and Guattari, 1984: 1). These machines are of diverse kinds: critical machines, literary machines, bachelor machines, fucking machines, micro-organizing machines, conservation machines, killing machines, creative machines of metamorphosis, affective machines that deterritorialize, decode, and transform. In one word: war machines.

> Willing the war against past and future wars, the pangs of death against all deaths, and the wound against all scars, in the name of a becoming and not of the eternal: it is only in this sense that the concepts gather together. (Deleuze and Guattari, 1994: 160)

As it turned out, postmodernism did not, in the final analysis, provide us with sufficiently strong weapons for dealing with the present situation: high capitalism with its global conjunctions of decoded and deterritorialized flows of labour and capital (Deleuze and Guattari, 1994: 33). Where postmodern organization theory excelled in the attack on signifiers and logocentrism, Deleuze and Guattari circumvent this very enterprise, thus reframing the problem of social analysis: it is precisely the global capitalist machine's *lack* of transcendent signifiers that makes it so strong and dangerous (Deleuze and Guattari, 1994: 97ff). Capitalism works through immanence (albeit a false one), and can readily accept 'ethnicity', 'gender', and 'faith', since these are instantly turned into commodities and life styles. The focus of the analysis should therefore be the practice by which our current conditions are preconfigured by the Market with the State as only an auxiliary apparatus: the latter captures our desires, and the former turns them into interests and cravings. Such analysis should recognise desire as a productive force, rather than as a Freudian/Lacanian lack, and should not just 'liberate' us as collectives of desiring machines, but should also draw a plane of consistency able to call forth a 'new earth' and a 'a people yet to come'. For sure a utopian thought for most contemporary organization theory, making precisely organization theory a suitable point of departure for a renewed theory of social change (see Bogard, 1998; Albertsen and Diken, forthcoming; Thanem and Linstead, forthcoming). This is a revolutionary utopia, but since historical revolutions as a rule only have supplanted one dominant discourse with another, the call is for another kind of revolution: 'The revolution that is needed is one of *thinking*' (Carter and Jackson, 2004: 121). It is a revolution that implies method as *style*: writing to the n'th power. The uninhibited excretion of pigshit, ie, immaculate defecation: 'speaking will be fashioned out of eating and shitting, language and its univocity will be sculpted out of shit . . .' (Deleuze, 1990: 193). Dystopian as it is, organization theory suffers from the same disease as did Kant: an inability to write affectively, to turn the wound against all scars, to write in blood. Maybe we should all leave behind the fetish for organizing theory and 'go on to write some extraordinary pages. Entirely practical pages' (Deleuze and Guattari, 1988: 27).

From organization towards the organizing refrain

While the assemblage and the territory are the two main components in the Deleuzoguattarian 'social ontology' (see Delanda, 2002; Sørensen, 2003), and while they criticize the noun organization for being an image of thought, they also offer 'positive' concepts for the process of organizing: the rhythm and the refrain. The assemblage becomes territorial on account of a mixture of chaos, organization and change, and 'these are not three successive moments in an evolution. They are three aspects of a single thing, the Refrain (*ritournelle*)' (Deleuze and Guattari, 1988: 312).

The refrain orders the social world as well as it orders other systems like birds establishing territoriality in the forest by singing, or geological strata that slowly create sediments through a long span of years. In the long and rather complicated 11. plateau 'On the Refrain' in *A Thousand Plateaus*, the refrain is considered under three aspects: injection (indicating scattered attempts to organize), inscription (the actualization of the organization) and interception (the deterritorialization of the organization, a possible line of flight).

To make the refrain work, let us, finally, consider the organization of warfare. It is well documented that organization theory is a child of war, and had it *only* been a question of organization, Germany could very well have won WWII. The following example sketches the rise of the Nazi Party in pre-war Europe, and points to a possible counteractualization, two organizing processes that *both* work by way of the refrain, if only in very different ways.

For our benefit, the German novelist and Nobel Laureate Günther Grass' novel *The Tin Drum* (trans. 1961) delivers convincing material in regard to this matter. In *The Tin Drum*, Oskar Matzarath, who was born when the Nazis were establishing the party in pre-WWII Germany and parts of Poland, decides at the age of three that he will not grow any more. Apart from being a sort of dwarf (a physical becoming-minor, see Deleuze and Guattari, 1986), you would recognize his extreme voice, with which he is able to break both windows and his teachers' glasses. Also, he carries a tin drum which he plays rhythmically almost without halt: against all demonic threats in a world going mad, Oskar plays his autonomous rhythms, which slowly develop into elaborated refrains. As a preliminary organizing force, this 'injection' is the initiation of a quasi-stable situation that connects Oskar's fragile assemblage (a dwarf among giants) temporarily to a territory following a local tactic of survival, just like a kid alone in the night starts chanting a little refrain, to get through the forest, to make it less uncanny.

But the refrain's capacity for injection is only its first characteristic. Its second characteristic is its capability of inscription. The inscription creates a more established territory as a geomorphic reality: folding the social stratum so as to create an inside and an outside, so as to create an organization. The inscription process is moving towards the stratified and the signified: it takes a more systematic effort and time to inscribe rather than just to inject. The Nazi rallies, as performed in Nuremberg, show the inscribing forces of a repetitive refrain when the Nazis built their frightening organization, the Party: the marches, the uniforms, the architecture. Here the refrain has become pure orderword. Organization as a noun is realized when the territorialization of a territory is taken to its limit, when the factor of territorialization is raised towards infinity, and in the end it will lose its creative movement. Via territorialization, inscription creates a home, *Heimat*, by drawing a circle and organizing a space with a firm inside/outside distinction: Arian/Jew, or, in more frequent or at least more mundane settings, member and non-member of the organization and the rhythm of the pay-check/the unemployment benefit.

But the refrain can *also* draw a line of flight, when it 'intercepts' and creates a way out. This happens when the territorial refrain (the organization) is deterritorialized by creative forces: music, art, philosophy, creative critique or simply *the outside*. The default situation, however, is the refrain's tendency to segmentize and rigidify, to become a habit, morphing into what is known as organizational culture.

In an early scene in *The Tin Drum*, the refrain as injection and as inscription is superseded by the creation of an interception, a complete and absolute deterritorialization. In Danzig,[4] where Oskar lives, a great rally is to take place. Half of the city attends, and every citizen is in line and order in the German way, the military orchestra is playing marches, everybody goes *Heil Hitler!* The refrain proves, here in Danzig, to be an exceptionally strong uniting force, drawing the desires and the bodies of the masses into a unified Organization. Unexpectedly, the tiny ten-year old Oskar hides under the grand, elevated scene, just beneath the microphones: here he starts drumming. Slowly, almost unconsciously, another rhythm spreads to the thousands of party members, and they begin moving around, leaving their lines and dropping down their hailing arms: *Oskar is drumming a waltz*. As the Nazi guest of honour arrives, everybody is dancing, smiling happily, the orderword has transformed into a love song and the Nazi rally has cancelled itself. The Germans have a word for such an event: *Mitfreude*, the joy, *Freude*, you have *mit einander*, together. In a proto-Deleuzian way, however, Oskar rejects to be a resistance fighter, as resistance is quite an exploited term. He is rather an eccentric, a singular event of difference that does not need an Other in order to produce difference.

To render the Nazi rally problematic and find the love inherent in the gathered crowd is to push the problem towards a liminal crisis between a deterritorialization and possible reterritorializations, that is, to push it into a critical passage. Organization theory should be exactly that: an elaborately developed question, rather than a resolution to a problem, an elaboration, *to the very end*, of the necessary implications of a formulated question (see Deleuze, 1991: 116).

We have all the time in the world, but we only have it *now*. It is time for you to enter into *your* crisis and find a problem worth problematizing. Usually, one starts off with a small thing. Realize that we are in a social formation. First see how it is stratified for us and in us and at the place where we are; then descend from the strata to the deeper assemblage. From here, you (and, perhaps, your pack of friends or wolves or colleagues) shall make the assemblage *pass over to the side of the Plane of Immanence*. You gently tip it; you don't use a sledgehammer, but a very fine file. Count the connections in the assemblage, find its rhythm, listen to its refrain, look for the detail where the refrain might become deterritorialized and connect anew with an outside. It is here, when you see the plane in the horizon that the body without organs reveals itself for what it is: connection of desires, conjunction of flows, continuum of intensities (Deleuze and Guattari, 1988: 161). It is here that you enter your becoming *together with the problem that you are problematizing*. It is a pure process or a movement with infinite speed, a molecular transmutation that goes from the subject towards a line of flight. Towards the crack in everything, which is where the light comes in (L. Cohen). This becoming goes from the established subject of enunciation to the infant; it is a becoming-speechless in the midst of a silent tremor. It is a becoming imperceptible: it questions the relation between the (anorganic) imperceptible, the (asignifying) indiscernible, and the (asubjective) impersonal (Deleuze and Guattari, 1988: 279). To become imperceptible means to be present at the dawn of the world.

Notes

1 Personal communication, 2004.
2 Gibson Burrell also takes interest in control and death from the point of view of Deleuze and Guattari, but he reads too many dichotomies out of Deleuze and Guattari to be convinced, in

the final analysis, that a nomadology will suffice in getting us beyond death, and he skips, finally, to the world of punk (Burrell, 1998: 150).

3 Xeroxing is also productive, as some sentences become cut off, some become unreadable, and some will end up signifying something completely different from the author's 'intentions'.

4 Danzig is the Polish city Gdansk, where 60% of the voters welcomed Nazism as a liberation in 1935. In 1927, Günter Grass was born in the city.

References

Albertsen, N., and B. Diken (forthcoming) 'What is the social?' in M. Fuglsang and B. M. Sørensen (eds.) *Deleuze and the Social*. Edinburgh: Edinburgh University Press.

Bayou, M. E., and A. Reinstein (2001) 'A Systemic view of fraud explaining its strategies, anatomy and process' *Critical Perspectives on Accounting*, 12: 383–403.

Bogard, W. (1998) 'Sense and segmentarity: Some markers of a Deleuzian-Guattarian sociology' *Sociological Theory*, 16: 52–74.

Bonta, M. and J. Protevi (2004) *Deleuze and Geophilosophy: A Guide and Glossary*. Edinburgh: Edinburgh University Press.

Braidotti, R. (2003) 'Becoming woman: Or sexual difference revisited' *Theory, Culture & Society*, 20: 43–64.

Buchanan, I. (2000) *Deleuzism: A Metacommentary*. Edinburgh: Edinburgh University Press.

Buchanan, I. and C. Colebrook (2000) *Deleuze and Feminist Theory*. Edinburgh: Edinburgh University Press.

Burrell, G. (1998) 'Linearity, control and death' in D. Grant, T. Keenoy, and C. Oswick (eds.) *Discourse and Organization*. London: Sage.

Carter, P. and Jackson, N. (2004) 'Gilles Deleuze and Felix Guattari' in S. Linstead (ed.) *Organization Theory and Postmodern Thought*. London: Sage.

Currier, D. (2003) 'Feminist technological futures: Deleuze and body/technology assemblages' *Feminist Theory*, 4: 321–338.

Delanda, M. (2002) *Intensive Science and Virtual Philosophy*. London: Continuum.

Deleuze, G. (1988) *Bergsonism*, trans. H. Tomlinson and B. Habberjam. New York: Zone Books.

Deleuze, G. (1990. *The Logic of Sense*, trans. C. V. Boundas. New York: Columbia University Press.

Deleuze, G. (1991) *Empiricism and Subjectivity: An Essay on Hume's Theory of Human Nature*, trans. C. V. Boundas. New York: Columbia University Press.

Deleuze, G. (1994) *Difference and Repetition*, trans. P. Patton. New York: Columbia University Press.

Deleuze, G. and F. Guattari (1984). *Anti-Oedipus*, trans. R. Hurley, M. Seem and H. Lane. New York: Viking.

Deleuze, G. and F. Guattari (1986). *Kafka: Toward a Minor Literature*, trans. D. Polan. Minneapolis: University of Minnesota Press.

Deleuze, G. and F. Guattari (1988). *A Thousand Plateaus*, trans. B. Massumi. Minneapolis: University of Minnesota Press.

Deleuze, G. and Guattari, F. (1994). *What is Philosophy?* trans. G. Burchell and H. Tomlinson. New York: Columbia University Press.

Foucault, M. (1979) 'The life of infamous men' in M. Morris and P. Patton (eds.) *Michel Foucault: Power, Truth, Strategy*. Sydney: Feral Publications.

Gherardi, S. (2003) 'Knowing as desiring: Mythic knowledge and the knowledge journey in communities of practitioners' *Journal of Workplace Learning: Employee Counselling Today*, 15: 352–358.

Grass, G. (1961) *The Tin Drum*, trans. R. Manheim. New York: Pantheon.

Hemingway, E. (1986) *Conversations with Ernest Hemingway*. Mississippi: University of Mississippi Press.

Holland, E. W. (1999) *Deleuze and Guattari's Anti-Oedipus: Introduction to Schizoanalysis*. New York: Routledge.

Jones, R. (2000) 'Digital rule: Punishment, control and technology' *Punishment & Society*, 2: 5–22.

Kierkegaard, S. (1983) *Fear and Trembling, Repetition*. Princeton, N.J: Princeton University Press.

Kornberger, M., C. Rhodes and R. ten Bos (forthcoming) 'The others of hierarchy: Rhizomatics of organizing' in M. Fuglsang and B. M. Sørensen (eds.) *Deleuze and the Social*. Edinburgh: Edinburgh University Press.

Linstead, S. (2000) 'Dangerous fluids and the organization-without-organs' in J. Hassard, R. Holliday and H. Willmott (eds.) *Body and Organization*. London: Sage.

Massumi, B. (1992) *A User's Guide to Capitalism and Schizophrenia*. Cambridge, MA: MIT Press.

Mintzberg, H. (1983) *Structure in Fives: Designing Effective Organizations*. Englewood Cliffs, NJ: Prentice-Hall.

Nietzsche, F. W. (1969) *Thus Spoke Zarathustra: A Book for Everyone and No One*, trans. R. J. Hollingdale. Harmondsworth: Penguin.

Osborne, T. (2003) 'Against "creativity": A philistine rant' *Economy and Society*, 32: 507–525.

Power, M. (2004) 'Counting, control and calculation: Reflections on measuring and management' *Human Relations*, 57: 765–783.

Rehn, A. and D. Sköld (2005) ' "I love the dough": Rap music as a minor economic literature' *Culture and Organization*, 11: 17–31.

Ronnie, L. (2001) 'Rethinking organizational crime and organizational criminology' *Crime, Law and Social Change*, 35: 319–331.

Rose, N. (2000) 'Government and control' *The British Journal of Criminology*, 40: 321–339.

Sørensen, B. M. (2003) 'Gilles Deleuze and the intensification of social theory' *ephemera: theory and politics in organization*, 3: 50–58.

Sørensen, B. M. (2005) 'Defacing the corporate body, or, why HRM needs a kick in the teeth' *Tamara: Journal of Critical Postmodern Organization Science*.

Styhre, A. (2005) 'Deleuze, desire and motivation theory' in J. Brewis, S. Linstead, A. O'Shea and D. M. Boje (eds.) *The Passion of Organizing*. Oslo: Abstrakt.

Styhre, A. and M. Sundgren (2003) 'Creativity as connectivity: A rhizome model of creativity' *International Journal of Internet and Enterprise Management*, 1: 421–436.

Thanem, T. (2004) 'The body without organs: Nonorganizational desire in organizational life' *Culture and Organization*, 10: 203–217.

Thanem, T. and S. Linstead (forthcoming) 'The trembling organization: Order, change and the philosophy of the virtual' in M. Fuglsang and B. M. Sørensen (eds.) *Deleuze and the Social*. Edinburgh: Edinburgh University Press.

Weber, M. (1985) *The Protestant Ethic and the Spirit of Capitalism*. London: Unwin.

Weiskopf, R. (2002) 'Deconstructing "The Iron Cage": Towards an aesthetic of folding' *Consumption, Markets and Culture*, 5: 79–96.

Wood, M. (2002) 'Mind the gap? A processual reconsideration of organizational knowledge' *Organization*, 9: 151–171.

Yu, J. E. (2004) 'Reconsidering participatory action research for organizational transformation and social change' *Organizational Transformation and Social Change*, 1: 111–141.

André Gorz: Autonomy and equity in the post-industrial age

Finn Bowring

Introduction

The social theorist known to his public as André Gorz was born in Vienna in 1923. His strong-minded and socially aspiring mother was the dominant figure in his childhood. A secretary in a local barrel-making business, she had married her Jewish boss, and later persuaded him to be baptised a Catholic and to change the family name to a more Germanic one. Viewing the marriage as something of a concession on her part, she hoped to transcend the limitations of her modest Jewish husband by raising her son to be, as Gorz later described it, 'a virile aristocratic super-Aryan whose handsome bearing would satisfy her own social ambitions and relieve her of the compromise she had had to accept' (1989a: 118). As Gorz would document in his acclaimed autobiography, *The Traitor*, the impossible expectations of his mother, combined with the contradictory identities of his parents, induced in the child a 'terror of identification' and a lasting sense of nullity and exile.

After the German *Anschluss*, or 'union', which Hitler prosecuted, in defiance of the Treaty of Versailles, with a swift military invasion of Austria in March 1938, the safety of both the family and the business was in jeopardy. In response, Gorz's mother sent him to a Swiss-German boarding school, saving him, at the very least, from conscription into the German army. After graduating with a degree in chemical engineering from Lausanne in 1945, he found work translating American novels for a Swiss publisher, and then began writing political articles for the Swiss co-operative movement. Drawn to the optimism and openness of newly liberated France, he moved to Paris in 1949 and married his English girlfriend. For the next 30 years Gorz's living would be earned as a journalist, working for a succession of French newspapers, beginning with *Paris-Presse* and ending with *Le Nouvel Observateur*, from which he retired in 1983. In between, he was recruited to the editorial board of *Les Temps Modernes*, where he was an important intellectual ally and friend to Sartre.

Given his self-confessed 'project of non-identification', it is little wonder that Gorz's public identity has been constructed with the help of pseudonyms. All his journalistic work was written under the name of Michel Bosquet, which he chose to adopt when the editor at *Paris-Presse* told him his 'real' name (itself a maternal contrivance) was too Germanic for the post-war French readership. A collection of his articles, published under the pseudonym of Bosquet, was also translated into English in 1977, under the title *Capitalism in Crisis and Everyday Life*.

Concerned that his more radical theoretical publications might endanger his application for French citizenship, and also worried at the effect his first book – a revealing autobiographical study – might have on his mother if she discovered it, he sought a second pseudonym for his books. Examining the factory origin of a pair of Imperial Austrian Army binoculars he had inherited from his father, he found they were imprinted with the word *Görz*. This was the German name of a town (called *Gorizia* in Italian, and *Gorica* in Slovenian) which straddles the Italian-Slovenian border. With a history of contested national identity, and a mixed community of Italian, German and Slovenian inhabitants, the town's name was a logical magnet for his inveterate desire 'to be nothing, invisible and indefinable' (1989a: 202).

Autonomy

Autonomy and equity are central ethical principles of modernity that are never wholly in tune with one another, and the tension between the two is a permanent feature of Gorz's work. For Gorz (1982: Ch. 8), the conflict between the social organization of society and the moral *cogito* is the ultimate foundation of modernity's dynamism and openness. Gorz attributes ethical primacy to the autonomy of the individual, for it constitutes a subjective imperative which, unlike social norms, rules and identities, can never be suspended or revoked. The personal roots of this philosophical position lie in Gorz's childhood relationship with his mother, his subsequent experience as a refugee from Nazi-occupied Austria, the complications of his mixed national and religious identity, and the weak sense of social belonging which these factors combined to produce. A 'half-Jew in anti-Semitic Austria,' he wrote in *The Traitor*, 'then Austrian half-Jew in the Pan-German Reich, then Austrian half-Jew with a German passport in a Switzerland favouring the Reich, he was neither Jew nor Aryan, nor Austrian, nor German, nor Swiss – nothing, in short, except the nothing that he was' (1989a: 42).

This personal experience of nothingness primed the young émigré for a life-changing encounter with Sartre's existentialism. After meeting Sartre in 1946, Gorz set out to develop and refine the principal insights of *Being and Nothingness*, producing, in 1955, an epic philosophical manuscript that was belatedly published in 1977 as *Fondements pour une morale*. The book is a rich phenomenological description of human values, and an important refutation of the argument that Sartre's ontology, because the 'for-itself' is the founding source of all values, commits us to regarding all actions and engagements as equivalent. Instead Gorz outlines a hierarchy of levels of value – a model which bears some interesting similarities to the three components of the *vita activa* defined by Hannah Arendt in *The Human Condition* – ranking these values (namely, the vital, the aesthetic, and the moral-practical) according to the intensity of freedom required to apprehend them. The book also offers a method of self-analysis designed to liberate the individual from forms of bad faith, and to facilitate a moral conversion through mastery of the highest level of valorisation: 'action'.

In *The Traitor* (first published in French in 1958), Gorz applied this method to himself, producing a fluid and intimate portrait of his family experiences, his relationships, dispositions and neuroses, and charting his own difficult journey in search of the conviction that existence is worthwhile. 'This book is organized like a feedback machine: the present ceaselessly metamorphosises the past from which it issues', Sartre wrote in a lavish foreword to the book. '*The Traitor* does not claim to *tell us* a convert's story: it *is* the conversion itself' (Sartre, 1989: 18). In *La morale de l'histoire* (1959), Gorz carried the principle of autonomy into the field of social and political relations. Arguing for a kind of existential Marxism, he challenged deterministic and scientistic versions of historical materialism, insisting on a definition of alienation – much as Sartre did in *Critique of Dialectical Reason* – as 'degraded praxis', as freedom turned against itself rather than as a static condition of powerlessness.

Although *Strategy for Labor* (1967), and *Socialism and Revolution* (1975), saw Gorz engaging directly with the strategy and goals of the European labour movement, in *Ecology as Politics* (1980), *Farewell to the Working Class* (1982), and *Paths to Paradise* (1985), Gorz broke with left-wing orthodoxy and began to defend a conception of personal sovereignty incompatible with the depersonalizing character of large-scale institutions and productive units. Showing the influence of Ivan Illich's radical critique of anti-convivial technologies, and driven by a desire to adapt Marxism to the insights and values of the ecology movement, Gorz described a working class being transformed into passive functionaries of a system-driven accumulation regime. Radical and progressive currents in capitalist society, he argued, would have to question the dominant norms and the established political vocabulary of that society, including the hegemonic status of 'labour'.

As all outcasts and outsiders are prone to do, Gorz looked to the margins and the interstices of the social structure for signs of a revolutionary challenge to a decadent capitalism. In doing so he registered a growing disenchantment with work-based society, and with the Fordist sacrifice of a meaningful life in exchange for a rising wage. Ignoring the traditional organs of working class mobilization, Gorz instead made a romantic appeal to the 'free subjectivity' of a 'non-class of non-workers' – an appeal whose logical target was the new social movements. The break with the logic of productivism, he insisted, could only be made by those 'recalcitrant to the sacralization of work', whose interests represent 'a negation and rejection of law and order, power and authority, in the name of the inalienable right to control one's own life' (1982: 74, 10–11).

In Gorz's more recent works, such as *Critique of Economic Reason* (1989) *Capitalism, Socialism, Ecology* (1994), *Reclaiming Work* (1999), and the as yet

136

untranslated *L'immatériel* (2003), Gorz deals more directly with the consequences of the information revolution and the emergence of a globalized, neo-
liberal, post-fordist system of 'cognitive capitalism'. The theme of existential
autonomy here appears in three noteworthy guises. First of all, there is a critique of the spread of economic rationality to activities whose use-value resides
in the giving of self and the transmission of meaning. When they are incorporated into the exchange economy, these activities – such as caring, educating,
and healing – are at best devalued, and at worst corrupted, so that autonomous
ethical motivations and personal commitments are replaced by egoistic calculation and the pursuit of private reward.

In an interesting digression on prostitution in *Critique of Economic Reason*,
Gorz argues that the purchasing of sexual services is the purest form of a
master-servant relationship which is becoming ubiquitous in work-scarce capitalist societies. Gorz notes how prostitution is distinguishable from professional
forms of personal service, such as medical therapies, where the worker performs
codified procedures following a disinterested interpretation of the client's needs.
In 'sex work', the purpose of the transaction is the pleasure of the client, and
the vehicle for this pleasure cannot be separated from the pleasure itself: the
prostitute (the servant) is *paid to please*, not simply to produce an agreeable
object or result. Pleasing another person in this manner means giving oneself,
one's freedom, to that other. Although prostitutes are skilled at *simulating* this
giving of self, drawing on a repertoire of gestures, roles and techniques, Gorz
argues that the physical nature of the sexual service always makes this simulation of personal involvement, this withdrawing of personal engagement, an act
of bad faith.

> Over and above offering of herself the gestures and words which she is able to *perform*
> without involving herself in them, she offers of herself what she *is* beyond all simu-
> lation: her body, that is, that through which the subject is given to itself, and which,
> without any possible dissociation, constitutes the ground of all its lived experiences.
> You cannot surrender your body without surrendering *yourself* or let it be used by
> other people without being humiliated . . . There is an inalienable dimension of our
> existence, the enjoyment of which we cannot sell to anyone else without *giving of our-
> selves* into the bargain, and the sale of which devalues the act of giving without reliev-
> ing us of the obligation to perform it as a gift. (1989b: 148–149, emphasis in original)

Hence the conventional argument that prostitution is 'exploitative' misses the
point, which is not that prostitutes are paid less than the value of what they give,
but that they give something which, as Simmel (1971) already observed, cannot
be paid for. Payment, no matter how important an incentive for the selling of
sexual services, cannot 'settle the account'; it can only cheapen and mystify what
is already a unilateral relationship of servility.

The concept of autonomy also features in a second way in Gorz's later work,
which is the relationship of the individual to the cultural lifeworld at a time
when aggressive value-fundamentalism is rife. Gorz champions the modernist
ideal of the autonomous subject in preference to the communitarian notion of

the 'constitutive self'. Against the belief, which he specifically detects in the work of the French right-wing Gramscian, Alain de Benoist, that rival cultures should protect their members' authentic identities by resisting interpenetration with and dilution by outsiders, Gorz argues that the peaceful co-existence of different cultures and societies presupposes a shared political space for dialogue and negotiation. Rational participation in this space – indeed, the very establishment of the space itself – requires autonomous subjects capable of transcending the constitutive community of their birth. In a shifting and complex world, Gorz points out, the passive reproduction of traditional values is in any case impossible, and society cannot help but create those 'dissidents, rebels, oppositionists – in a word, *subjects* who claim the capacity to judge and choose for themselves' (1999: 125, emphasis in original).

Gorz's anti-sociologistic perspective thus stresses, in what may be viewed as a third line of argument, that it is the incomplete bonds which bind individuals to the social order – and thus our sense of alienation from that order – which enable us to exercise autonomous action and judgement. These bonds are necessarily incomplete because society can effectively reproduce itself only by transmitting its impersonal norms through personal relations of trust, commitment and love, the most important of which is the relation between parent and child. As Gorz puts it: 'no one can *feel* they belong to a social group if that belonging is not rooted in an affective attachment to persons within that group' (1989b: 175). The paradox is that these same elements of affect and feeling, since they are always richer and more immediate than our second-hand culture and language can convey, refract the very norms and expectations they are meant to transmit. The socialization of individuals into society thus 'has its roots in an attachment that is not socialisable' (*ibid*).

Gorz goes on from this to argue that, in a post-fordist society where innovation, improvization and change is increasingly a requirement of social life and occupational culture, our imperfect socialisation is an indispensable resource. Contrary to the opinions of cultural conservatives, it is the 'excess of socialization, not the lack of it, which puts a block on individual autonomy', Gorz argues. And it is 'oversocialized parents', who yearn for their children to be integrated, via the formal acquisition of social and occupational skills, into a stable society – the 'employment society' – which no longer exists, who perpetuate this misunderstanding and increase the pressure on schools to prioritize the socialiszation of children over their genuine education (1999: 69).

Equity

In *The Human Condition*, Hannah Arendt attacks a long tradition of liberal political thought which has insisted on defining freedom as a withdrawal from the realm of public affairs and an assertion of private and self-sufficient sovereignty. Is this same theoretical deficiency, this neglect of the social and material conditions for autonomous action, evident in André Gorz's work? Gorz's existentialism certainly does not preclude him from a constructive evaluation of institutional arrangements, nor from an attempt to identify equitable forms of social organization and distribution. Nor does it commit him to a privatistic or consumerist conception of autonomy. Much of the discussion of consumption and need in *Strategy for Labor*, for example, focuses on the way the private satisfaction of needs denies the social nature of production and the collective needs which arise from it, thus resulting in 'public squalor within private affluence' (1967: Ch. 4). Here, and in *Socialism and Revolution*, Gorz outlined the path for a radical unionism, which is centred less on mitigating the effects of capitalism and protecting members' wages, than on articulating needs and desires whose satisfaction is incompatible with the existing social order.

Farewell to the Working Class, moreover, often reads like a tribute to Weber's analysis of bureaucracy in *Economy and Society* (1978: Ch. XI). Large-scale commercial and administrative organizations on which, Gorz concedes, the stable and efficient reproduction of society depends, impose functional hierarchy, soulless specialization and meticulous rule-following as a condition of their very existence. Consequently, Gorz argues, the collective appropriation and democratic self-management of society's productive and administrative apparatuses is a futile task, since it would achieve nothing more than a new 'permutation of office-holders'. What is required, instead, is the steady expansion of the time and space for genuinely self-governing activity, combined with a proliferation of convivial tools and other public resources which enhance the attractiveness of self-organized forms of production. Not the liberation of work, but its abolition, is the true emancipatory ideal.

A political programme to reduce work and expand disposable time must be accompanied by an incomes policy which divorces the right and capacity to consume from the performance of a specific quantity of work. Reflecting, in *Paths to Paradise*, on the consequences of the microchip revolution and the emergence of 'jobless growth', Gorz predicted that the steady decline in the need for work by the advanced economies would have profoundly destabilising effects unless an alternative means of distributing purchasing power in an era of vanishing jobs were established. Gorz's commitment to the idea of a 'guaranteed income' has taken several forms over the subsequent period. Initially he argued that the link between work and income should not be broken altogether, since without fulfilling a universal social obligation to work, people would be denied the status of abstract, interchangeable citizens, while their personal lives would cease to be the obverse – a sphere of sovereign choice and voluntary reciprocity (1989b: 205–208; 1992). In his more recent writings, however, Gorz has revised his position. Now he argues that a guaranteed income should be sufficient to enable people to refuse work which doesn't appeal to them, and that the purpose of this income should be to encourage its recipients to engage in productive activities which do not have profitability or exchange-value as their driving logic. The goal of the guaranteed income is not to promote inactivity, but rather, in the words of Frithjof Bergmann, to 'liberate work from the tyranny of the job' (Gorz, 1999: 163).

Gorz argues that an unconditional income is most appropriate for the post-industrial 'knowledge society', where 'direct working time is becoming negligible by comparison with the time required for the production, reproduction and extended reproduction of the capacities and skills of the workforce in the so-called "immaterial" economy' (1999: 87–88). In other words, we spend far more time creating, nurturing and enriching the intellectual, emotional and communicative capacities necessary for post-fordist organizational regimes than we do directly applying those faculties in productive labour. Drawing extensively on the famous 'Fragment on Machines' from the *Grundrisse*, Gorz insists that high-tech knowledge economies will only prosper if the preparation of workers for those economies – the development of their capacities for free invention, imagination and communicative collaboration – becomes an end in itself, liberated from the specific functional and economic imperatives of organizations and firms. This, ultimately, is the political aim of the unconditional income: to make the free and full development of the individual the immanent goal – not the servant – of economic development.

The purpose of the guaranteed income is thus more than distributive. Its real value is *tranformative*. It is meant to catalyse the contradictory relationship between the knowledge society and the logic of capitalism and, by forcing a break between the two, to bring historical development back within the horizon of human agency. According to Gorz, the knowledge economy represents a fundamental crisis of capitalism, of its systems of measurement and exchange, its relations of equivalence and its process of valorisation. In *L'immatériel* (2003: 105–112), Gorz distinguishes between two forms of knowledge: tacit know-how (*savoir*), which is acquired through practice, is exemplified by artistic virtuosity, and which is a living, pre-cognitive, culturally embellished apprehension of the world as we experience it; and technical and scientific knowledge (*connaisance*), which is a logical understanding of laws and relations, an understanding that can be formalized and transmitted independently of specific individuals, as well as converted into mechanical operations, such as software programmes, which can function without human intervention.

Both forms of knowledge play critical roles in modern, cognitive capitalism, Gorz argues, and both these roles are ripe with contradictions. The principal consequence of the growth of technical and scientific knowledge, and its crystalization in ever more powerful means of production, is that the labour value of commodities is drastically shrinking, and with it the surplus that can be extracted from workers. The shrinking value of manufacturing labour, combined with the saturation of demand for utility goods in the wealthy world, helps explain why major corporations are relinquishing the material operations of production and concentrating instead on the symbolic, immaterial value of commodities, as well as on cultivating service-centred relationships with their customers.

By exploiting human *savoir*, by drawing on the artistry, imagination and creativity of a culturally rich class of knowledge workers, companies are able to endow common, mass produced commodities with unique symbolic qualities which enable them, for a limited period, to win what is in effect a monopoly 'rent' for their products. The purpose here is to raise the appearance of those products above the level of vulgar merchandise, to brand them with a veneer of incomparability which, functioning like the artist's signature, authenticates the product as a rare and singular item worthy of its inflated price. In the service sector the same logic prevails: the economic value of the service depends on making the client feel unique, and on making the transaction appear not as a commercial exchange but as an authentic personal relationship devoid of economic rationality and motivation (Gorz, 2003: 61–63).

These economic trends are riddled with problems, of course. First of all, the profits yielded from these temporary monopolies are precarious and short-lived, so the symbolic identity of the product has to be continually modified and reinvented, forcing successful companies to devote more and more of their resources – in some cases over 40 per cent of expenditure – on publicity and marketing. Secondly, when the drive to produce unique, non-interchangeable commodities extends to labour power itself, the whole logic of equivalence, of the neutrality of the marketplace and the objective measurement and remuneration of interchangeable units of labour time, begins to look ideological. Workers who sell their distinctive imaginations and personalities cannot be paid the 'market rate', since what each individual offers is, by definition, beyond comparison. The value of labour is thus exposed as a political rather than mathematical construct. As Negri (1991: 172) puts it, the Law of Value dies and is replaced by the Law of Command.

Thirdly, the cultural resources which are exploited by capital in these kinds of enterprises are notable for being inherently social assets. The most valued forms of knowledge in the new economy cannot be systematically taught but are the product of a rich lifestyle and culture which extend far beyond the temporal and spatial parameters of the workplace. Here is where Gorz's analysis knowingly converges with the theories of 'mass intellectuality' and 'immaterial labour' developed by Negri and other like-minded Marxists (see Bowring, 2004; Mandarini, in this volume). It is also reflected in the well-documented preference of many successful employers for psychological and emotional skills, combined with a generic capacity for continual learning, over specialized technical qualifications: 'the manager told me they never recruited someone for their technical skills', Bunting reports from a call centre in North Shields. 'What they were looking for was a particular personality: cheerful, outgoing, flexible, goodnatured, adaptable – because these were the characteristics which they couldn't train' (Bunting, 2004: 68).

The contradictions raised by this situation revolve around the social and cultural leavening of immaterial labour. Capital's greatest economic asset now seems to be a form of labour power – imaginative, self-motivated, communicative and empathic – which capital itself cannot produce in a deliberate or formal way, and which therefore carries within itself both the possibility of dispensing with capital and a latent political critique of the alienation and use of that labour to yield a private profit. This critique is drawn forth by Jeremy Rifkin

(2000), who sees the centrepiece of the new economy as the privatisation and leasing of cultural symbols, experiences and relationships. Social and communicative networks are now both sold as commodities and utilised as productive assets, and their exploitation reaches well beyond the boundaries of paid labour, as when major social, sporting and civic events, which have high public participation and a prominent media profile, are used by private sponsors to advertise their commodities.

Another example is the use of 'viral marketing', where companies slip endorsements of new products into conversations in internet chat rooms, then allow interest to spread among a pre-existing community of consumers – primarily trend-setting children and adolescents – who have become jaded with and insensitive to conventional mass marketing campaigns (Lawrence, 2004). And with the growth of service-centred capitalism comes another exacting demand, that of the 'managed heart' (Hochschild, 1983), as more and more workers are required to *perform* that which they *are* (their feelings and emotions), and thus to suffer the commodification and servitude of the self or, at best, its simulation and superficialization.

In companies where workplace hierarchies are flattened to exploit the imaginative and communicative resources of the labour force, Gorz suggests that the parameters of corporate power have begun to dilate. Here Gorz's account of the structure and workings of modern corporations has something in common with mainstream organization theory. Although he offers a description of flexible, co-operative, learning-based labour which bears obvious similarities to those found, for example, in the work of Handy (1996), Senge (1990), Zuboff (1988), Kanter (1989), and Bartlett and Ghoshal (1989), Gorz has drawn more readily from the industrial sociology and labour process theory of Kern and Schumann (1984), Piore and Sabel (1984), and Womack *et al.* (1990), as well as from the cultural and political analyses of the contributors to the radical Franco-Italian journals *Futur Antérieur* and *Multitudes*.

From the perspective of contemporary organization theory, what is distinctive in Gorz's own approach is his political interrogation of the vanguard corporation and his attempt to identify the class tensions and power struggles it gives rise to. Gorz suggests that, instead of exercising detailed control over the worker's behaviour, the managers of the post-fordist company will typically seek to mobilize the whole of the worker's life and personality in the service of the firm. It pursues this task both by dissolving the boundaries between work and non-work (providing leisure and recreational facilities, for example, that make the workplace an attractive rival to the home), and by deepening its control over the appetites and loyalties of the consumer. This is why Gorz believes (1999: 39–46) that the key social conflict today is no longer primarily fought over the autonomy of work – an achievement which has, for the most privileged occupational groups, already been won – but over the *autonomy of that autonomy*. This effectively means the right to use one's autonomy for socially desirable ends, rather than allowing that autonomy to be the price paid by capital to enable the fragmentation of the labour movement, the extension of generalised insecurity and Taylorist work practices to the remaining sectors of the economy, and the transformation of civil society into a realm of unprecedented media manipulation and consumerism.

The other form of knowledge – *connaissance* – is subject to similar contradictions. A characteristic feature of this form of knowledge, Gorz points out, is that it can be reproduced in unlimited quantities at little cost and utilised without an intimate understanding of its origins. Knowledge of this sort is also cumulative – it expands through exposure to the minds and expertise of others. This form of knowledge is also inherently transmittable, and its sharing and dispersal can be accomplished at no loss to the distributor. Making this knowledge function as 'fixed capital' – as companies aim to do by drawing on intellectual property law – is thus both technically difficult and ethically problematic. If the 'knowledge society' is to deliver what it promises, attempts to render that knowledge scarce by privatising it will have to be resisted.

According to Gorz, this resistance must not only defy the logic of capital, but must also address the dangerous complicity between capitalism and science. Through the mathematical language of calculation, and the material accomplishments that have arisen from this, science has fostered the conviction that questions of meaning and sensibility have limited, if not irrelevant, value in the modern world, and that mathematical insights into the functioning of laws that are inaccessible to sensory experience are more real than the tangible but non-formalisable world of bodily life. The ascendance of scientific *connaissance* over corporeal *savoir* has been accelerated and exploited by an economic system determined to emancipate social relations and practices from the fetters of everyday life, and thus to make the 'fictitious commodities' (as Karl Polanyi called them) of the capitalist economy assume a reality greater than the world of human experience and the tacit arts of living. In Gorz's view, the end result of this process, as I too have argued (Bowring, 2003: Ch. 11), is the creation of a world in which embodied human beings are ill-equipped to live, and it is this that explains the passion and dedication of those artificial intelligence theorists and enthusiasts of human genetic engineering, who believe the human species can and should be upgraded to permit mastery of this hostile new world.

Assessment

Are there significant weaknesses or limitations in Gorz's analysis? Common criticism of Gorz during the 1980s came from committed socialists, many of whom accused him, as Marxists did of Sartre's existentialism (eg, Marcuse, 1983), of pandering to a romantic bourgeois individualism which obscured the continuing importance of class as a cultural, economic and organizational category (for a review, and rebuttal, of this literature see Bowring, 1996).

Sceptics may also argue, as again they have of Sartre (eg, Leak, 1989), that Gorz's existential-Marxism is best regarded not as political philosophy, but as a psychological by-product of his (class-specific) childhood experiences. Yet

Gorz's own explanation (1989a: 87, 264–265) seems more compelling to me: each of us, by the accidents of our background and upbringing, comes to live a particular facet of the human condition in a particularly intense way; the challenge of a meaningful existence is to find the link which articulates our individual condition with the universal, to discover a recognizable place to start from and a practicable goal to aim at, and thus to find a way of belonging, however incompletely, to a common social world.

Gorz's critical treatment of Marxist productivism and the glorification of the proletariat may also prove more revolutionary than his socialist critics gave him credit. In a detailed and scholarly re-reading of Marx's political economy, Moishe Postone has argued that Marx himself aspired towards a critique of capitalism that was not conducted from the standpoint of labour, because 'proletarian labour does not fundamentally contradict capital', representing 'capital-constituting, rather than capital-transcending, forms of action and consciousness'. The issue, Postone continues, is

> that capital rests ultimately on proletarian labour – hence, overcoming capital cannot be based on the self-assertion of the working class. Even the 'radical' notion that the workers produce the surplus and, therefore, are its 'rightful' owners, for example, points to the abolition of the capitalist class – but not to the overcoming of capital. That would require overcoming the value form of the surplus and the capital-determined form of the labour process. (1996: 371)

One could also argue that the stress Gorz places on individual autonomy is a reflection of the privileged society which he has lived in and commentated on, and that in the less developed world, where most of the human population live, it is a redistribution of wealth, not a change in the mode of producing it, which is the most pressing need. Gorz's focus on immaterial labour and post-fordist forms of work organization, and his belief that job-scarcity is an irreversible, and ultimately fatal, stage in the development of capitalism, is also often seen as a parochial, Eurocentric view, which fails to register the experience of hundreds of millions of peasant farmers as well as the appalling working conditions of millions of impoverished factory workers whose products are exported to the West.

Yet Gorz himself seems keenly aware of the interdependent development of post-Fordism and neo-Taylorism, and his insistence that the crisis of employment society is not simply a symptom of Western decadence is also born out by global trends. There are today over a billion unemployed and underemployed workers in the world, with few countries being exempt from the scourge of jobless growth. Despite being the fastest expanding economy in the world, for example, export-oriented China lost 15 per cent of its manufacturing workforce – 15 million jobs – between 1995 and 2002 (Rifkin, 2004).

Rifkin's account of the 'age of access' is also perfectly in tune with Gorz's own analysis. Rifkin notes the growing disparity between the dwindling exchange value of companies' fixed assets and their rising stock market value – a trend indicative of the way the knowledge, creativity and imagination of workers, combined with the currency of that knowledge in the wider consumer culture, has become a more profitable corporate resource than material property. The major players in the international economy are now divesting themselves of physical assets, with companies like Nike transforming themselves into parasitic branding licensers, owning little in the way of factories, machines and real estate, and even outsourcing their advertising and marketing operations (Rifkin, 2000: 30–55; Klein 2000: 195–229). The declining economic importance of physical property is also illustrated by the growth of franchises, which today account for over a third of all retail sales in the US, as well as the spread of leasing contracts, which are so popular in the transport sector that a third of all cars and trucks on the road in the US are leased rather than owned by their drivers (Rifkin, 2000: 59, 74). The dominant trend, according to Rifkin, is towards a form of service capitalism, where material commodities are simply the vehicles for the establishment of a long-lasting service relationship between company and client.

Gorz's analysis is by no means faultless, however, and it doesn't always provide a satisfactory answer to a range of questions which the growing literature on post-industrial capitalism has raised. Common to this literature is the tendency for terms such as 'immaterial labour', the 'network economy', 'information capitalism', to be deployed with a lack of precision, so that, for example, the physical and emotional content of service work is typically parcelled up with indiscriminate treatments of 'abstract labour' and 'knowledge work'. Perhaps more troubling is the extent to which the knowledge economy is founded on the sale of wasteful, trivial and culturally impoverishing products – ten per cent of global music sales, to give one recent example, are now accounted for by the purchasing of mobile ring tones (Petridis, 2004). Given the centrality of the marketing and advertising industry to knowledge-intensive capitalism, one has to ask whether this kind of economy is really ripe for democratic reappropriation by the networks which comprise it – an argument advanced most forcefully, via the concept of 'self-valorization', by Toni Negri and his collaborators – or whether we should be emphasizing the critique of work and consumerism which Gorz advanced in the late 1970s and '80s, and which thankfully reappears in *L'immatériel* with a lengthy attack on 'the production of the consumer' (Gorz, 2003: 64–71).

Some readers of Gorz, particularly those seeking to position him clearly in the field of organization theory, will remain unsatisfied by his failure to explicitly and consistently align himself with a distinctive academic discipline or established school of thought – a tendency that may simply reflect the fact that he has never worked in a university, and has always written for a wider public of intellectuals and activists. Yet Gorz's distance from the institution of academia, and from its often honorific and self-referential concerns, is also what gives his work its originality.

In assessing the value of Gorz's work to organization theory I would conclude with two commendations. First of all, it delivers an analysis of contemporary organizations, and of the wider structural environment they operate in, which is unflinchingly political in character. This analysis accepts, rather than dogmatically dismisses, the novelty of the modern economic landscape, whilst continuing to interrogate that landscape to uncover its enduring contradictions, hidden faultlines, and latent social conflicts.

Secondly, Gorz offers an account of social, cultural and economic relationships which never ceases to ask what *meaning* those relationships, and the activities that comprise them, have, or could have, to their participants. The most welcome effect of this phenomenological approach is to refresh our perception of social organization by inviting us to claim authorship of a world which, as organization theory has so often described, continually defies our intentions.

References

Arendt, H. (1958) *The Human Condition*. Chicago: University of Chicago Press.

Bartlett, C. A. and S. Ghoshal (1989) *Managing Across Borders: The Transnational Solution*. London: Business Books.

Bosquet, M. (1977) *Capitalism in Crisis and Everyday Life*. Hassocks: Harvester.

Bowring, F. (1996) 'Misreading Gorz', *New Left Review*, 217: 102–122.

Bowring, F. (2003) *Science, Seeds and Cyborgs: Biotechnology and the Appropriation of Life*. London: Verso.

Bowring, F. (2004) 'From the mass worker to the multitude: A theoretical contextualisation of Hardt and Negri's *Empire*', *Capital and Class*, 83: 101–132.

Bunting, M. (2004) *Willing Slaves: How the Overwork Culture is Ruling Our Lives*. London: Harper-Collins.

Gorz, A. (1959) *La morale de l'histoire*. Paris: Le Seuil.

Gorz, A. (1967) *Strategy for Labor: A Radical Proposal*. Boston: Beacon.

Gorz, A. (1975) *Socialism and Revolution*, trans. N. Denny. London: Allen Lane.

Gorz, A. (ed.) (1976) *The Division of Labour: The Labour Process and Class Struggle in Modern Capitalism*. Hassocks: Harvester.

Gorz, A. (1977) *Fondements pour une morale*. Paris: Galilée.

Gorz, A. (1980) *Ecology as Politics*, trans. P. Vigderman and J. Cloud. Boston: South End.

Gorz, A. (1982) *Farewell to the Working Class: An Essay on Post-Industrial Socialism*, trans. M. Sonenscher. London: Pluto.

Gorz, A. (1985) *Paths to Paradise: On the Liberation from Work*, trans. M. Imrie. London: Pluto.

Gorz, A. (1989a) *The Traitor*, trans. R. Howard. London: Verso.

Gorz, A. (1989b) *Critique of Economic Reason*, trans. G. Handyside and C. Turner. London: Verso.

Gorz, A. (1992) 'On the difference between society and community and why basic income cannot by itself confer full membership of either' in P. van Parijs (ed.) *Arguing for Basic Income*. London: Verso.

Gorz, A. (1994) *Capitalism, Socialism, Ecology*, trans. C. Turner. London: Verso.

Gorz, A. (1999) *Reclaiming Work: Beyond the Wage-Based Society*, trans. C. Turner. Cambridge: Polity.

Gorz, A. (2003) *L'immatériel: Connaissance, valeur et capital*. Paris: Galilée.

Handy, C. (1996) *Beyond Certainty*. London: Arrow.

Hochschild, A. R. (1983) *The Managed Heart: The Commercialisation of Human Feeling*. Berkeley: University of California Press.

Illich, I. (1975) *Tools for Conviviality*. Glasgow: Fontana.

Kanter, R. M. (1989) *When Giants Learn to Dance*. New York: Simon and Schuster.

Kern, H. and M. Schumann (1984) *Das Ende der Arbeitsteilung?* Munich: Beck.

Klein, N. (2000) *No Logo*. London: Flamingo.

Lawrence, F. (2004) 'Revealed: How food firms target children' *The Guardian*, 27 May.

Leak, A. N. (1989) *The Perverted Consciousness: Sexuality and Sartre*. London: Macmillan.

Marcuse, H. (1983) 'Sartre's existentialism' in *From Luther to Popper*. London: Pluto.

Marx, K. (1973) *Grundrisse*, trans. M. Nicolaus. Harmondsworth: Penguin.

Negri, A. (1991) *Marx Beyond Marx: Lessons on the Grundrisse*, trans. H. Cleaver, M. Ryan and M. Viano. London: Pluto.

Petridis, A. (2004) 'Lord of the rings' *The Guardian*, 21 May.

Piore, M. J. and C. F. Sabel (1984) *The Second Industrial Divide: Possibilities for Prosperity*. New York: Basic Books.

Polanyi, K. (1957) *The Great Transformation: The Political and Economic Origins of Our Time*. Boston: Beacon.

Postone, M. (1996) *Time, Labor, and Social Domination: A Reinterpretation of Marx's Critical Theory*. Cambridge: Cambridge University Press.

Rifkin, J. (2000) *The Age of Access*. New York: Tarcher/Putnam.

Rifkin, J. (2004) 'Return of a conundrum' *The Guardian*, 2 March.

Sartre, J.-P. (1956) *Being and Nothingness: An Essay on Phenomenological Ontology*, trans. H. E. Barnes. New York: Philosophical Library.

Sartre, J.-P. (1989) 'Of rats and men' in A. Gorz, *The Traitor*, trans. R. Howard. London: Verso.

Sartre, J.-P. (1991) *Critique of Dialectical Reason: vol. 1.*, trans. A. S. Smith. London: Verso.

Senge, P. N. (1990) *The Fifth Discipline: the Art and Practice of the Learning Organization*. London: Century Business.

Simmel, G. (1971) 'On prostitution' in D. Levine (ed.). *On Individuality and Social Forms*. Chicago: University of Chicago Press.

Weber, M. (1978) *Economy and Society*, ed. G. Roth and C. Wittich. Berkeley: University of California Press.

Womack, J. P., D. T. Jones and D. Roos (1990) *The Machine that Changed the World*. New York: Rawson Association.

Zuboff, S. (1988) *In the Age of the Smart Machine: The Future of Work and Power*. Oxford: Heinemann.

David Knights and Hugh Willmott: The subjugation of identity and . . . and . . . and organization-to-come . . .

Damian O'Doherty

Introduction

There will have been a time when 'Knights and Willmott' require no introduction, at least for that introduction which serves to respond and do justice to their work in organization. Our introduction is only going to work to the extent to which this will have been read (at least) more than once: *there will have been a time*. Read slowly, read quickly, there will have been a time when *contemporary* organization theory makes sense. We are, perhaps, going to have to learn to read differently in this wake that is coming after 'Knights and Willmott' – on the shores of contemporary organization theory. For now, we must remain with preliminaries.

1. Con-temporary: meaning, *with the times*. 2. Organ-ization: a ceaseless ex-static activity bordering reason and absurdity in a space(ing) that beats to the time of a heart rate recovered from seizure and attack. 3. Theory: of all these components theory offers some reassurance and orientation; it seems to be the most preliminary in the work of Knights and Willmott. It is what strikes the casual reader first. Their writings seem to demand an exercise of Herculean scholarship simply to surmount the preparatory building blocks that form the constituent parts of what is synthesized as 'Theory' in their mature studies of organization, management, and work. It still remains for us to ask, however, 'what' is 'their theory', or, what theoretical contribution do they make?

This will be our test: introductions, responsibilities, justice. In organization and out of time, we will have risen and then fallen to this challenge to introduce and comprehend the importance of 'Knights and Willmott' in organization theory. For, you see, there really is no theory in 'Knights and Willmott'. It is simply a double-barrel nomenclature, and as this chapter makes clear there is even no such thing as 'Knights and Willmott'. To the extent that we can realize this insight we will have served the ethical demand and implication of their writings and in so doing helped introduce their work to the challenges of contemporary organization theory. On the other hand, there will be some who argue that there has been nothing but theory; at least, nothing much has changed for the managers and workers they have been studying over the past 30 years or so. In this sense their writing is in the realm of pure theory – abstract, difficult, and discursively rarefied, working to promote ideas, possibilities, and dreams for its readers, rather than to stimulate any practical action in the mundane world of capital and wage-labour.

In another sense, however, there is no *theorizing* (see O'Doherty, 2004). There is selection, derivation, presentation, and application of continental philosophy and critical theory, but there is, strictly speaking, no *theorizing*. God or Truth, as *Theo*, does not arise out of a reading of their work and nor do Knights and Willmott put the light of *Theo* to work in their writing (see Derrida, 1982a). Instead, there is a darkening that recalls the writings of Maurice Blanchot (1955), the dark 'knights', if you will, against which a certain will of the word cries out, that 'mot' (derived from the Latin *mutt(um)*, meaning utterance) which the Webster's defines as 'a pithy or witty remark'. Knights and Willmott. We are here beginning to exercise organization in the realm of catachrestic theory/invention through what Derrida calls the work of 'signature effects', and it is all we are going to be left with in/after introducing Knights and Willmott. There will have been a time when nothing so profound as the superficial is once again restored to the practice of organization/theory. It is a con-trick, a temporary one at that: call it con-temporary theory.

Agency, subjectivity, reflexivity

It would be folly to attempt to identify seminal papers that lay out the groundwork or theoretical project of Knights and Willmott. Not only is the question of a constant and consistent *project* highly dubious in the context of how we know knowledge develops (Foucault, 1972, 1980; Feyarabend, 1975; see also Latour, 1987), and particularly given the commitment to this implicit in their own research and pedagogy (see Knights and Willmott, 1999), but the sheer volume of their publication itself would condemn any effort at summary and synthesis to a partial and contingent impression. The idea that there is a deliberate or purposeful, unified project guiding and informing the work of Knights and Willmott would certainly be an irony given the efforts they have made to reflexively question and circumscribe the simplistic models of agency and causality in social relations.

Bearing this is mind we might, nonetheless, usefully recover the traces of this apprenticeship in four joint authored papers published in the 1980s: their 1982 and 1989 papers published in *Sociology*; the *Praxis International* essay on the work of Erich Fromm and the problem of freedom; and their *Sociological Review* paper of 1985, which addressed the question of 'power and identity in theory and practice'. Knights and Willmott are, for many of their readers, associated with a form of theory in organization studies that emphasises the 'subjective' side of organization – that dimension of organization where social agents are busy interpreting, practically working, and reproducing the processes and content of organizational life. They will also be identified as 'radical humanists' in Burrell and Morgan's 1979 schema. In other words they interpret organization as a socially constructed and maintained dynamo of conflict and struggle that tends towards radical change, composing forces that periodically manifest as violent disruption in social relations. Their research is sensitive to the play of power and inequality in work organizations, forces that generate tension and conflict as inherent and chronic features of economic competition and capitalist work organization. This routine production of inequality finds expression across class, gender, age, racial and ethnic divisions. Indeed the capitalist mode of production tends to provide opportunities for those with inherited power and resource at the expense of those who find themselves with little economic or political capital. It rewards certain values and attributes at the expense of others and can be seen, therefore, as a mode of discipline that reduces the potentiality and richness of its 'human' labourers to a narrow and restricted set of qualities and skills. Creating further disparity out of inequality and inheritance, capitalist forms of economic competition are unfair and injust stoking up frustration and discontent amongst individuals and collectives who look towards emancipation and radical change as solutions to their problems.

The groundwork for this orientation to organization is prepared in these four papers under consideration where the key analytical and theoretical contribution made by Knights and Willmott is in the treatment they provide of how control and order is secured through an organizing of social relations characterized by such unfairness and inequality. Their explanation hinges on a radical and innovative reworking of the concept of 'agency' deployed in sociology and applied sociological studies of work and organization. Underpinning all four papers is the basic insight that human nature cannot be satisfactorily reduced to a biological or social determination. The predominant understanding in organization behaviour is one that still believes that individual and group action can be explained by inherent, mechanistic motivations. Identity, when it is considered at all, is assumed to remain fixed and enduring over time. As an explanatory variable it is predictable and determinate, and its isolation in categories or types is pursued in an effort to generate greater precision for the purposes of managerial prediction and control. Identity, itself, is often explained by relatively simple genetic and filiative heredity, or in more sophisticated sociopsychological analyses as a determinate outcome of some combination of nature and nurture. The influence of identity on behaviour at work is similarly delineated and defined in ways that assume it can be rendered consistent and predictable (see Huczynksi and Buchanan, 2001: 141–143).

Knights and Willmott help us to understand that whilst there is always a degree of determination, limit, and restriction, identity is more fluid and unstable, a medium and outcome of wider political-economic and social forces and deep 'interior' existential processes. Identity does not exist as some deterministic *fait-accompli*, but has to be actively worked at, created, and maintained by knowing, self-conscious social agents. For Knights and Willmott, agents are neither structurally determined nor abstract from the constraint of historically contingent patterns of social relations in an idealistic or voluntaristic realm of freedom and choice. To avoid this dualism of subject and agent Knights and Willmott tend to mobilise the term 'subject' and thereby index and reference a tradition of thinking in continental philosophy that helps students of organization work towards a *delimitation* of sociological dualisms. The 'subject' can easily be re-inscribed back into a dualism with a putative object, and, moreover, interpreted in ways that reify identity work. Many seeking to accommodate and incorporate the work of Knights and Willmott have, unfortunately, done precisely this, particularly where identity and its preoccupations are seen to form part of the pragmatic, rational and cognitive exercise of effort-reward bargaining (see Thompson and McHugh, 1995: 327–358; Ackroyd and Thompson, 1999; Thompson and McHugh, 2002: 334–354).

To delimit and circumvent the dualistic restrictions of sociological thinking Knights and Willmott develop an existential appreciation of identity and its struggles drawing on the work of Fromm, Freire, and Laing – whose roots go back to Nietzsche, Heidegger, and Sartre. In their writings our relationship to the world is understood to be one that is problematic but 'open'. Through exploration and interaction with others we are able to form and produce relatively stable but still essentially *contingent* meaning and identity out of this openness. In a basic ethnomethodology-inspired move we are made aware that as researchers of organization we share this routine practice with those members of organization we are studying. This insight also forms part of their challenge to the persistence of dualistic separation in management and organization studies, in this case between the object and subject in research. Their writings help us to see the ubiquity of these existential dimensions of being and to find ways of exploring those questions and struggles that form around this condition of being-in-the-world.

Although there is this basic openness to Being, Knights and Willmott develop their theoretical writings to show how man routinely flees from this openness because of what Fromm (1942) calls a 'fear of freedom'. The experience of openness arises in part because of the unique and dual relation between our species-being and nature: we are both 'in' and 'out' of nature, partly its product, but also its producer. Nature can be shaped and adapted to serve human needs, it is not simply a brute external, necessary fact to which we are subordinated and habituated by instinct and routine. At the same time, this separation from nature and the lack of instinctual programming – that makes us more like an architect than a bee, provokes massive insecurity. We find ourselves thrown into this world without having been asked, and, being of nature, we can only ever be a transient phenomenon, ultimately subject to decay and death for which we can do nothing (Novak, 1970). In the wider scheme of things we remain a rather insignificant and irrelevant feature of the universe confronted as we are by its impenetrable and infinite expanse. Given this contingency and irrelevance we inevitably encounter a whole series of questions: what should we do with our freedom? How can meaning be found so that we might create purpose for our existence? To what ends do our productive efforts in labour serve?

Compounding this basic existential anxiety are those insecurities that arise from the condition of wage-labour under a capitalist mode of production whose contradictions and dynamics amplify the individualization and isolation of self-consciousness. Willmott (1990: 339) was later to summarize this analytical focus as an effort to 'appreciate the intertwining and interdependence of the 'historical' and 'existential' dimensions of the dialectics of praxis'. Drawing on Fromm (1978), Knights and Willmott show how man is constituted historically: our goals, our values and ambitions, and, by extension, even our sense of what is a spontaneous, authentic, and free expression of self, are all historically relative. Human potentiality is protean and elastic and responds to historical conditions of possibility. The forces of capitalist production release man from his feudal fetters and mobilize tremendous energies, but in so doing remove the collective security and stability provided by the more inclusive and overarching pattern of social regulation that functioned in what E.P. Thompson (1968) called the 'moral economy', the premodern agricultural economy based on custom and practice. Here we encounter those familiar sociological motifs of suicide, anomie, and disenchantment, in the shift from the *Gemeinschaft* to the *Gesellschaft* of modernity (see also ten Bos, and Kaulingfreks, in this volume). At the risk of cliché, capital dissolves all that is solid into air. As subjects we are shaped and framed out of these historical discontinuities through a basic 'social character structure', which is an *intermedium* or historical blending of the socio-economic structure and the individual psychical structure (Willmott and Knights, 1982: 206).

In opening up this interjacent and dialectical space, Knights and Willmott begin to extricate their analysis from the dangers of an over-rigid, mechanistic dualism. Both the 'socio-economic structure' and the 'individual psychical structure' are in danger of producing artificial but reified heuristics, essentialist and timeless categories that purport to represent some inner essence of economy or the individual. Their reading of Marx, in combination with the reading of Fromm developed here, helps us to see the processual and dynamic force of capital in which structure and agency are inter-dependent and mutually imbricated forming something that Giddens (1976) would call the forces of 'structuration'. There is no simple cause-effect in operation here; the agent is not the product of social conditions and nor are social conditions the solipsistic product of individuals or a collective distillation of social relations in action. As a medium and outcome of existential and historical conditions the social character structure is what motivates our every activity in the world. It provides that sense of self which appears to us to be the most intimate and inner core of our being, to which we seek always to return and by which we inevitably become captivated. Indeed it conditions and makes available our very reality and helps explain the virulence of ego and egoism as motivating forces in social action and behaviour. This is one of the basic but paradoxical 'foundations' in the development of a non-essentialist theorization of subjectivity and identity.

The key to understanding how Knights and Willmott develop their conception of subjectivity and identity, which prepares and leads onto their reflexive critique of theoretical reification, is to be found in this critique of the ego. Unlike Freud, both Knights and Willmott commit to the idea that there is something beyond the compromises achieved by ego strengthening through which frustration and disappointment will inevitably persist as normal features of modern life (Willmott and Knights, 1982: 217). The ego is understood to arise in response to the primordial awareness, or 'shock' of being, to which the most primitive reaction is an understanding of disjunction and separation between (what becomes split and stabilized into) 'self' and 'others'. 'Other' is nature and fellow beings against which one recoils as they are made objects projected out into the horizon of perception – the first sensorial faculty that reinforces this distance and separation. One literally stands up and takes one's measure against this objectification and in so doing makes one-self subject, opening up the space of subjectivity (see Heidegger, 1977). Object and subject, then, mutually arise. The ego compensates and consolidates for this sense of isolation and abandonment by promoting self-consciousness in ways that compel man continually to seek gratification and reassurance that its being-subject is solid, real, and sustainable. Paradoxically, when individuals remain in the service of the ego through efforts to appease its anxiety/desire for confirmation, either by seeking reassurance from others, or domesticating the 'outside' (nature, earth, the chthonic), insecurity is increasingly aggravated by intimations or threats that the outside is not fully submissive or subdued. As individuals erect structures of order, routine, and control, and minister to the ego's appetite for a sense of solidity and durability, the slightest threat to this elaborate exo-skeletal defence is experienced as potentially catastrophic. The greater one's dependence on predictability and order, the more anxiety-raising becomes potential disturbance from the outside (Knights and Willmott, 1985: 26; 1989: 42–3, 49; Willmott, 1998). It is out of this basic existential experience that Knights and Willmott develop their four key concepts for the theoretical analysis of organization – power, inequality, insecurity and identity.

Power, identity, insecurity, inequality:
beyond structuration – the outside

Power, inequality, identity and insecurity are all dialectically inter-related in their analysis (see Knights and Willmott, 1999), and are used as temporary, heuristic devices in order to invite and cultivate a greater degree of attentiveness to a wider and deeper ontology of Being characterised by process and flux. They are all media and outcome of one another. In this sense there is an effort to avoid reductive or deterministic explanation which, for Knights and Willmott, would only preserve a mechanistic framework or 'grand narrative' that tells us more about the insecurity and identity project of the academic writer or researcher.

The analytical move that is always made in their work is to track the contradictions and paradoxes that surface out of those basic dualisms constructed and projected by theoretical and lay-practitioner agents in social relations, dualisms that emerge in tandem with their efforts to consolidate ego. This interplay of construction, projection and ego-confirmation finds expression in organization and social relations through that interplay of power, inequality, identity and insecurity experienced by managers and employees of work organization. Organization becomes a complex web of tension and paradox mobilized by the contradictory movements of order and disorder, collection and dispersal, routinization and innovation/change. Every effort to routinize and consolidate work practices in order to express and/or secure the subject's desire for control (re)creates the conditions and the fear of its opposite – the break in routine, the re-emergence of the surprising or unforeseen, and the arrival of the new or the unknown. Driven by ego, subjects are vulnerable to the self-reinforcing paradoxes of their own ceaseless suffering: the greater one seeks to maintain and hold on to a firm identity the more acute becomes the fear and likelihood of its opposite – insecurity and confusion.

We cannot really then privilege subjectivity or identity as the analytical signature of their work, nor locate this interest in the micro-dimensions of social relations, a mistake that is often made in casual treatments of their writing. One cannot really understand identity without seeing it as media and outcome of insecurity which is heightened by capitalist competition and the inequalities it produces. Insecurity is related to power and inequality in ways that intensify the competitive desire for symbols of power and success, helping to reinforce and reproduce the workings of the 'macro' or political-economic systemic levels of organization. The macro is related to the micro, structure with agent (in the traditional language of sociology), existentialism with the historical, and the personal with the political. It would therefore be wrong to classify their research as an example of a form of 'humanist' organization theory, one that is preoccupied with agency, subjectivity or the interpretative, but which ignores the objective, the structural, and the 'concrete reality' of material struggle (see Edwards, 1990). This critique admits the dualism of subjectivity-objectivity or structure-agency, the transcendence or deconstruction of which is precisely the underlying motivation and target of their theoretical endeavour.

What they tend to privilege is the subjective 'moment' in this dialectical structuration of organization with its attendant reproduction of enduring patterns of power and inequality. We might best understand this privileging as a practical and political compromise designed to spotlight those spaces and times in organization where we can identify how structure and agent are mutually and inextricably intertwined – and, therefore, where change or intervention might be best targeted. Hence their continued interest in 'labour process' theory and analysis (Knights and Willmott, 1990). Organization does not pre-exist its practical accomplishment, nor does it have dynamics or laws that operate independent of the embodied practice and consciousness of subjects at work. Furthermore, power is relational and cannot be satisfactorily analysed as a 'property' in which it makes sense to think that some people are congenitally or structurally endowed with more power than others (Knights, 1983). Those routinely deemed to be in positions of power and autonomy are as dependent on 'subordinates' as subordinates are dependent upon their super-ordinates. Both are dialectically co-dependent, in contradiction and antagonism (Edwards, 1986), and both can be deemed to mutually conspire to perpetuate routines and addictions and the suffering this entails. Power is created and sustained through the on-going practical accomplishment of social actors operating inter- and intra-collectively, interacting in ways that maintain the 'paramount' version of social reality (see Berger and Luckmann, 1967) through which individuals are reified and pitted against one another for what is perceived to be scarce material resources.

It is vital to make these points if analysis is to avoid the mistake of reification and crude reductionism. The critique of ego clearly distinguishes their work from that of Giddens (see Knights, 1983: 56ff; Willmott, 1986; Knights and Willmott, 1985: 30–32), and in following this move we are forced to acknowledge the limitations of adopting 'power, identity, insecurity and inequality' as an alternative theoretical framework for organizational analysis. To understand the on-going reproduction of work organization, theoretical analyses need to appreciate how this structuration plays itself out somewhere *between* or *outside* of the conventional terms of sociological dualism. This is the 'hidden' and implicit logic, but nonetheless the more promising legacy of the work developed by Knights and Willmott and in its pursuit we will eventually be taken into realms of organization where ontology distorts and dissolves opening up a volatile and vertiginous 'workspace'. Arriving at this dimension of organization we discover that the concepts of power, identity, insecurity and inequality are best understood as heuristics that *adumbrate* the basic processes of structuration in organization. They work by recalling and retaining the shadow of an absent-present that accompanies this analytical delineation of the ontological and operate like conceptual ladders needing to be thrown away once their steps have been mastered. This begins to take us to the root of their difference with Giddens and also most other 'synthetic' theoretical conceptualizations of work and organization, whether actor-network theory, Eliasian 'figuration' sociology (Layder, 1994: 114–124; see also Newton, 2001), or 'morphogenesis' (Archer, 1988).

This allows us to understand structuration as a process that is produced and reproduced through the illusions of identity and its attachments which form part of a wider meaning system and a social construction of reality. It is not so much that capital gets reproduced 'behind the backs' of its agents but rather that the surface of what they do perceive and value is mistakenly taken to be real. Our conventional categories of understanding and the dualisms of sociological method form one part of a complex *maya* of illusion, to which the scholar and the researcher are in danger of becoming similarly attached. Conceptual and theoretical apparatuses act to dim down the world of being (becoming) that is in processual flux *between* and *outside* object and subject (or structure and agent), a space of becoming for which moments of non-dualistic awareness temporarily give access and insight (see Willmott, 1994). With patience and practice, forms of research in organization can transgress the repressions and denials that exclude phenomena which do not fit within the categories and representational bias of a researcher's identity project and existential condition, a condition that is routinely sublimated as theory and methodology (O'Doherty, 2003). The awareness of the fragility and contingency of ego and identity permits some shift out of their tenacious hold as work organization and its paramount-reality spills out across our mundane categories and definitions. A certain phenomenal 'vagrancy' is then experienced as managers – with their retinue of everyday furnishings and artefacts, for example – seem to dissolve into a fluid flux of formation, to reappear, perhaps, as paranoid agents of capital, hirsute wild-men, or lascivious satyrs (see Burrell, 1997). Equally, working in or *out* of this space casts one into a highly volatile mode of being in research where organizational reality will begin to seem as if it *responds* to the 'will' of the researcher. If reality is reflexively maintained though a social construction of reality that reproduces the mediocrity of a lowest common denominator ego, then as one loses hold of 'self' – to drift in a region that Heidegger (1962) calls the *tarrying alongside* of everyday circumspective concern that is Dasein's everyday practical being-in-the-world of the ready-to-hand – we might expect that phenomena begin to fragment, split and dissolve into an *unready-to-hand*.

Re-embodying theory: spectral organization and metamorphosis

Interestingly, the impact of their teaching is to *heighten* the self-consciousness of the organization theorist, at least in the short term. The very quest for knowledge and theory is itself a reflection of a wider and deeper alienation, and in its analytical pursuit one exaggerates and soaks up some of the most extreme 'pathologies' of the modern condition. Driven by the potentially infinite regress that characterizes the search for the conditions of knowing and its conditions of possibility, their writing throws self back upon self, stimulating an awareness of how much of self is being projected into the putative object of study – namely management, work organization, or the labour process. In more familiar terms we know that every way of seeing is also a way of not seeing. This has become a standard methodological move for many working in organization theory *post* Burrell and Morgan (1979). What Knights and Willmott make available for reflection is the existential dialectics of this projection.

It will be recalled that Knights and Willmott treat the aggrandisement of self-consciousness in modernity as a problematic media and outcome of the *Gesellschaft*. It lies at the heart of their critical impetus and explains the illusory nature of ego-self and the tenacious hold it maintains on being. It is therefore possible to suggest that theoretical work in organization analysis which draws upon Knights and Willmott, or indeed even seeks to study and explain 'Knights and Willmott', invites and then exaggerates the symptoms of modern alienation. Certainly if our ambition is to 'bank' a package of conceptual tools or to abstract and elaborate some complex and integrated theoretical architecture, we are likely to experience frustration and a certain subjugation of our capacity for praxis and organization-to-come. Worked out most fully in Willmott's (1977) doctoral thesis, this alienation – the product of which is an attachment to ego – serves to maintain a separation between self and others in ways that deny progressive and engaged 'direct action'. The possibilities for creative organization are only made available as one comes to recognize the interdependency of social relations and the importance, and indeed inevitability (short of suicide or 'madness'), of participation.

Knights and Willmott invite people to share this highly problematic space and in so doing make available the question whether ego-self is necessary. As long as we find ourselves still able to ask the question, of course, we have to say yes: the ego self is necessary. If part of what is 'good' involves connecting with people in ways that do not antagonise or confuse, then in a world, particularly the academic world, which values methodology and the 'confession' of the grounds for one's interpretation and analysis (see Foucault, 1981), one must learn to use existing conventions. Play the game, in other words. Hence, why irony, satire, pastiche, or cynicism, are so tempting and perhaps *necessary*, offering some respite of identification to navigate what Klossowski calls 'the *mute intensity* of the tonality of the soul' in confrontation with the '*authorities of identity and reality*' (1997: xix, emphases in original). On the cusp of an hitherto un-thought and therefore inarticulable teaching, organization is all but lost as we stutter to explain . . . and . . . and . . . and . . . there (is) still organization-to-come. Organization theory, or theoretical construction and its endeavour, become little more than expediential exercises as a consequence of this experience but we have little else to explain or induct students into this realm of organization. Some might be tempted to say that they are then merely *tools*, an instrumental-technical practice that both Knights and Willmott have been so critical of in their analysis of management thinking and mainstream management studies. Yet, there is perhaps no contradiction here. The question is pedagogic and perhaps Socratic in nature.

In our modern period we can trace the suspicion about *theory* back to Nietzsche where it is seen as a form of existential displacement and sublimation based on a metaphorization of the most objectifying senses: sight and hearing. From the Greek *theoria*, from where we also derive the word *theatre*, theory is based on a viewing or seeing and connects back to the function and role of the official state ambassadors of the Greek city states, those *theorists* who report back from their foreign travels, who, in other words, bring back the *other* to the *same* (see O'Doherty, 2004). *Theo*, meaning God, also discloses the orthodox model of truth and *eidos* that governs theoretical initiative and which anchors discourse in the metaphysics of light, unveiling, the essential Platonic forms, the sun and revelation. Theo-rising, then, is literally the raising of a God. In its practice we participate in a certain unfolding of the *physis* that is, for Nietzsche, will-to-power. To see the guiding principles of our metaphysics, however, as *metaphors*, and if they are metaphors without a 'proper', or a literal referent, they are better thought as *catachrestic* – 'the imposition of a sign on a sense not yet having a proper sign in the language' (Derrida, 1982b: 270) – then theory is, at its 'origin', ordering and invention. It is typically, however, a quest for disembodied ordering and invention, one that is restricted and inhibited in proportion to the degree to which there is an ignorance or lack of awareness of its embodied origin.

By ignoring and abstracting from the rich and complex, shifting human sensorium, in deference to the reification of the cognitive and its dualistic logic, the 'violence' of its ordering is more extreme and exclusionary. Hence, the body is not allowed to 'speak' in theory – and it is deferred, as theory becomes a prosthetic displacement. Theory is a distillation or symptom of the body, a *rationalization* and form of organization or control that recoils back on our treatment of work organization understood in its wider, more empirical sense. It excludes what we might call the 'chemical senses', for example, offering a form of sensibility that would permit some kind of access (theory modelled on forms of thinking informed by taste, or smell; and 'why not?' asks Derrida, 1982b) back into the media and flux of a pre-dualistic awareness of organization. It is this space or time in/of organization (or better, the différance of space-becoming-time and time-becoming-space) in which Knights and Willmott discovered thinking *begins*, a 'thinking' that is spontaneous and open, intimately in tune with practice and compassion for suffering as it *opens* organization to the penumbra of disorganization. The self-concealment that reigns at the heart of disclosure, the shadow of ferment and restrained metamorphoses that is the condition of possibility and impossibility of organization and order (Cooper, 1986), arises in awareness at the same time that one realizes their inevitable complicity in the shaping and construction of organization. It is the opening from where our values and commitments are forged.

There is a tendency in Knights and Willmott, particularly in their formative groundwork to understand this space as an ontological transcendence that recovers a systemic-whole (Bateson, 1972), or an ontological fullness that places self (and) organization, subject (and) object, into a more universal cycle of birth, death and life, giving us a smooth, processual integration of parts and wholes. It is, in other words, dialectical, and what Derrida would call a 'positive infinity', which he mobilizes in his critique of Levinas (Derrida, 1978). Our departure, here, from Knights and Willmott, is in the attempt to uncover that space(ing) in organization that gives the condition of possibility *and impossibility* of the dialectic and permits the play of the 'negative' infinite. It is 'here' where we uncover the energy that gets the hermeneutic circle going. This is a more dangerous, heteroclite space, a Leibnizian space of interfolding and *incompossible realities* (Deleuze, 1993; chapter 5), a domain of agitated, fissile part-objects that flutter and disseminate from points of singularity in a space of molecular becoming.

Knights and Willmott, however, do encourage us to understand theory as metaphor, which is in effect a partial and evanescent *objectile* itself, a temporary *vehicle* (metaphor is literally transport, that which *bears* or carries translation) that invites research into the politics and praxis of organization, but which must be ultimately abandoned. In the process, self is also transformed and comes close to its own abandonment as 'theory' extends into and out of an expanded sensorial domain that is itself released into the wider currents of chthonic and telluric energy. We will call this the space/time of the 'trickster' (see Crapanzano, 1992), a space that is more space-ing than static. It is a vital and protean becoming, ex-static and out of time, a disquieting prospect for ego-centric theorists, but one through which organization theory might just find its survival and future(s). Extending, unfolding, and becoming, the elaboration of the senses forms part of our contemporary post-human transformation (see Serres, 1998), which is perhaps an urgent and inevitable task given the proliferation of new prosthetics of techno-science and the digital convergence that is threatening to make us merely 'eyewash' in the autopoietic loops of media networks (Kittler, 1999).

Disconnected from the *arché* and the controlling apparatus of presence, origin, and teleology, of Truth, signifier, and signified – that marks out what some call the 'metaphysics of being' (Chia, 1996) – *catachrestic-theory* becomes an originary production that gives licence to the idea that theory is not impoverished or at an end (contra Eagleton, 2003), nor inevitably repressive or disciplinary when rendered as a tool. The *ends* which theory serve become the site of contention and academic dispute. We then find some justification that theory needs to be artfully crafted and even disguised if it is going to perform as a pedagogic resource. If theory is to do its work the reader has to believe in these models and constructions. So there needs to be a degree of seduction in order to hold the tension that is the opening of learning, at least for a while. Betrayal, as we all know, forms an essential rite-of-passage in learning and apprenticeship.

Conclusion: arrival

We began this chapter by trying to exposit the difficulty of expositing the work of Knights and Willmott as there will have been a time when we lose sight of *organization, theory*, and even, perhaps, the very sense of *contribution*. If there is a legacy to organization theory it will be the bequest of this double bind: and we cannot help but to betray their work in any treatise or attempted explanation. And this gives chance (again) to organization. To find ways into their work incites a reflex that opens up and exposes self and its biography to the existential condition of being. In exploring their work readers (*ad*)*venture* themselves, to the point at which the dualisms of organization as an object of research, for a subject, dissolve into a wider, more general economy of organization. Here we not only begin to *think* organization is dangerous and volatile, disorganized by complex and fractious social relations at work and invested with the unpredictable energy of existential anxiety that compels ongoing management reparation to form complex cycles of order/disorder. Rather, we experience this as a more profound fragility at work in organization, one that emerges out of a 'zero' degree *before* ontology-epistemology that ignites and generates the social construction of reality. We *become* this phenomenon of organization, or we are returned to our inevitable participation – at least if we still want to understand organization (or if we remember to recall this objective, or still value it as an objective) – such that we can only understand organization to the extent to which we participate. There is no pure, disinterested, accurate rendition of organization. The way in which we participate, however, does become a 'choice', at least to a certain extent. In choosing we participate in changing the world of organization, although this choosing will condemn us to limits and compromise. We forsake understanding as a perfected, complete, or totalizing ambition, but in order to *give up organization for the sake of organization (to-come)*. For here, their here-and-now, there is no-thing upon which to stand other than that which we invent or accept as a useful fiction.

We take leave of their writing suspended on the question of identity, that 'identity' which is claimed in the 'and' of Knights and Willmott, because there is in fact no 'Knights *and* Willmott'. There will have been a time when we can ask – to what extent have they produced *a theory* of organization? How far is it even possible to say '*the approach* of Knights and Willmott'? Is it meaningful to seek to exposit or 'represent' 'Knights and Willmott? And what kind of organization is there – or what is the *degree* of organization – in the authority of their joint authorship? What we are dealing with in 'Knights and Willmott' is *our* denial of the death of the author, that we still hang onto the idea that it makes sense to think (of) theory as an authored project, the product of which then takes its place amongst the pantheon of heroic theoretical inventors. Any genealogy of Knights and Willmott will clearly show that they *do not exist*. What we have are just the names, or ghosts, revenants of a two-fold adumbration of disappearance/appearance that comes from the limits of an existential quest that allows them to *know* identity is a self-defeating motor and preoccupation of those working in organization: for who could they be to know this, from where do they speak, with what author-ity or identity? It is this shared exile and dif-férance that marks out a disjunctive tension, but it is a tension that we have dis-covered acts as a *constitutive* division, forming a generator of difference and repetition. Together *and* apart their writings proliferate, perhaps itself a sign of a desperate effort to flee this difference or to fill its mortal void. In this sense they trick time, they have managed to con-time . . . as all good theorists do – contemporary organization theory.

References

Ackroyd, S. and P. Thompson (1999) *Organizational* Mis*behaviour*. London: Sage.
Archer, M. (1988) *Culture and Agency*. Cambridge: Cambridge University Press.
Bateson, G. (1972) *Steps to an Ecology of Mind*. New York: Ballantine.
Berger, P. and T. Luckmann (1967) *The Social Construction of Reality: A Treatise on Knowledge*. Harmondsworth: Penguin.
Blanchot, M. (1955/1982) *The Space of Literature*, trans. A. Smock. Lincoln: University of Nebraska Press.

Burrell, G. (1997) *Pandemonium: Towards a Retro-Organization Theory*. London: Sage.

Burrell, G. and G. Morgan (1979) *Sociological Paradigms and Organizational Analysis*. London: Heinemann.

Chia, R. (1996) *Organizational Analysis as Deconstructive Practice*. Berlin: Walter de Gruyter.

Crampanzano, V. (1992) *Hermes' Dilemma & Hamlet's Desire: On the Epistemology of Interpretation*. Cambridge, MA: Harvard University Press.

Deleuze, G. (1993) *The Fold: Leibniz and the Baroque*, trans. T. Conley. London: Athlone.

Derrida, J. (1978) 'Violence and metaphysics: An essay on the thought of Emmanuel Levinas' in *Writing and Difference*, trans. A. Bass. London: Routledge.

Derrida, J. (1982a) *Margins of Philosophy*, trans. A. Bass. London: Athlone.

Derrida, J. (1982b) 'White mythology' in *Margins of Philosophy*, trans. A. Bass. London: Athlone.

Eagleton, T. (2003) *After Theory*. London: Allen Lane.

Edwards, P. (1986) *Conflict at Work: A Materialist Analysis*. Oxford: Blackwell.

Edwards, P. (1990) 'Understanding conflict in the labour process: The logic and autonomy of struggle' in D. Knights and H. Willmott (eds.) *Labour Process Theory*. London: Macmillan

Feyarabend, P. (1975) *Against Method*. London: New Left Books.

Foucault, M. (1972) *The Archaeology of Knowledge*, trans. A. S. Smith. London: Tavistock.

Foucault, M. (1980) *Power/Knowledge: Selected Interviews and other writings 1972–1977*. ed. C. Gordon. Hemel Hempstead: Harvester Wheatsheaf.

Foucault, M. (1981) *The History of Sexuality Volume 1: An Introduction*, trans. R. Hurley. London: Pelican.

Fromm, E. (1942) *The Fear of Freedom*. London: Routledge and Kegan Paul.

Fromm, E. (1978) *To Have or To Be*. London: Jonathon Cape

Giddens, A. (1976) *New Rules of Sociological Method*. London: Hutchinson.

Heidegger, M. (1962) *Being and Time*, trans. J. Macquarrie and E. Robinson. Oxford: Blackwell.

Heidegger, M. (1977) 'The age of the world picture' in *The Question Concerning Technology and Other Essays*, trans. W. Lovitt. New York: Harper & Row.

Huczynski, A. and D. Buchanan (2001) *Organizational Behaviour: An Introductory Text* (third edn.). London: Pearson Education.

Hughes, R. (1991) *The Shock of the New: Art and the Century of Change*. London: Thames and Hudson.

Kittler, F. (1999) *Gramophone, Film, Typewriter*, trans. G. Winthrop-Young and M. Wutz. Stanford, CA: Stanford University Press.

Klossowski, P. (1997) *Nietzsche and the Vicious Circle*. trans. D. Smith. London: Athlone.

Knights, D. (1983) *Organizations and Industrial Relations: Towards a Reconciliation of Their Theory and Practice*. Unpublished PhD Thesis. University of Manchester.

Knights, D. and H. Willmott (1982) 'Power, values and relations: A comment on Benton', *Sociology*, 16(4): 578–585.

Knights, D. and H. Willmott (1983) 'Dualism and domination: A critical examination of Marx, Weber and the existentialists' *Australia and New Zealand Journal of Sociology*, 19(1): 33–49.

Knights, D. and H. Willmott (1985) 'Power and identity in theory and practice' *Sociological Review*, 33(1): 22–46.

Knights, D. and H. Willmott (1989) 'Power and subjectivity at work: From degradation to subjugation in social relations' *Sociology*, 23(4): 975–995.

Knights, D. and H. Willmott (eds.) (1990) *Labour Process Theory*. London: Macmillan.

Knights, D. and H. Willmott (1999) *Management Lives*. London: Sage.

Latour, B. (1987) *Science in Action*. Milton Keynes: Open University Press.

Layder, D. (1994) *Understanding Social Theory*. London: Sage.

Newton, T. (2001) 'Organization: The relevance and limitations of Elias' *Organization* 8(3): 467–495.

Novak, M. (1970) *The Experience of Nothingness*. New York: Harper and Row

O'Doherty, D. (2003) *Subjugation and Labour Process Deconstruction: The Problematic Status of Order/Disorder in the Labour Process*. Unpublished PhD Thesis. University of Manchester.

O'Doherty, D. (2004) 'Organization after theory'. Working Paper. Manchester School of Management: UMIST.

Serres, M. (1998) *Les Cinq Sens*. Paris: Hachette.

Thompson, E.P. (1968) *The Making of the English Working Class*. London: Pelican.

Thompson, P. and D. McHugh (1995) *Work Organizations: A Critical Introduction* (second edn.) London: Macmillan.

Thompson, P. and D. McHugh (2001) *Work Organizations: A Critical Introduction* (third edn.). London: Macmillan.

Willmott, H. (1977) *The Commitment of Sociology: Research into Welfare Provision that Provided for an Investigation of the Epistemological and Ontological Grounds of Research*. Unpublished PhD Thesis. University of Manchester.

Willmott, H. (1986) 'Unconscious sources of motivation in the theory of the subject: An exploration and critique of Giddens' dualistic models of action and personality' *Journal for the Theory of Social Behaviour*, 16(1): 105–122.

Willmott, H. (1990) 'Subjectivity and the dialectics of praxis: Opening up the core of labour process analysis', in D. Knights and H. Willmott (eds.) (1990) *Labour Process Theory*. London: Macmillan.

Willmott, H. (1994) 'Bringing agency (back) into organizational analysis: Responding to the crisis of (post) modernity' in J. Hassard and M. Parker (eds.) *Towards a New Theory of Organization*. London: Routledge.

Willmott, H. (1998) 'Re-cognizing "the other": Reflections on a new sensibility in social and organizational studies' in R. Chia (ed.) *In The Realm of Organization: Essays for Robert Cooper*. London: Routledge.

Willmott, H. and D. Knights (1982) 'The problem of freedom: Fromm's contribution to a critical theory of work organization' *Praxis International*, 2(2): 204–225.

The ordering of things: Organization in Bruno Latour

Jan Harris

Introduction: From science in action to actor networks

Bruno Latour has become an obligatory point of reference for many working in the social sciences. This situation can be attributed to a unique combination of theoretical and methodological novelty – an engagement with the 'real' has inspired Latour's theory, and in turn this theory has transformed what we understand as the 'real'. Latour has not been afraid to get his hands dirty, to enter into the ignoble world of things and the human networks that surround them and in so doing call this very distinction into question. Arising directly from the kind of challenges encountered in the study of human organizations, we do not (as with so many theorists) have to engage in a procrustean struggle with Latour's thought in order to render it applicable to concerns of this field.

The evolution of this project might be seen in terms of a passage from ethnographic studies of the working practices of scientists and technicians to an increasingly wide ranging meta-theorization that has addressed itself to issues as varied as ontology, ecology, technology, epistemology and ethics. This chapter will seek to demonstrate the irreducible centrality of the problematic of organization and organizations in Latour's project. In addition this reading will explore the attendant problematic of the status of objects in organizations, which although not entirely outside the purview of organization studies have only recently begun to receive the attention they warrant. In identifying and illuminating the ontological blind spot that is the constitutive role of objects, Latour's thought holds out the possibility of revolutionizing our understanding of organizations and their components.

Of course Latour's project and its extension in the hands of a range of authors (eg, Callon, Law and Akrich) has not taken place within a vacuum. Both Latour's thought and Actor Network Theory (ANT) in general, explicitly and implicitly draw upon a range of influences as varied as the strong program in sociology of scientific knowledge of the Edinburgh school, the quasi-Bergsonian accounts of the technical object's genesis of Gilbert Simondon and Andre Leroi-Gourhan, the semiotics of the Prague School, ethnomethodolgy and American microsociology, and last but not least, continental philosophy, in particular Deleuze, Foucault and Serres (see Sørensen, Brown, in this volume).

While it will not be possible here to address the full import of these influences in the detail they deserve, we will have occasion to consider the use to which Latour has put a number of them when we consider the various critiques that ANT has provoked.

The inception of Latour's project was apparently innocent; to study, quasi-anthropologically, the relationship between the daily activities of scientists and the results they produced. But in doing this he discovered a disjunction between science's account of its own praxis and the ethnographic data he collected. The 'laboratory life' that Latour and Woolgar recorded was at once the essence of scientific endeavour and at the same time largely excluded from the heroic narrative of invention and discovery that characterizes the received view of science's labours. Thus what Latour's early work did was to challenge a certain vision of science's *being* (ie, the unmediated expression of objective facts) by offering an account of its *becoming* (the daily activities of working scientists). Hence Latour's insistence on science *in action*, that is its genesis or its processuality.

In Latour and Woolgar's initial study (Latour and Woolgar, 1979) this emphasis on processuality or action was seen in terms of a social constructivism, as if facts and things referred not to an objective nature but to the organizations in which they were realized. In this regard, Latour's work appeared to be allied to that of the Bath and Edinburgh schools of the sociology of science, which proposed a principle of 'symmetry' with respect to the production of scientific facts (Bloor, 1976). That is to say, that while the doxa of science might admit of a failed hypothesis or theory that it is social in origin; a 'correct' scientific theory is *ipso facto* outside the realm of the social, the sociology of scientific knowledge (SSK) argued for a fully symmetrical reading of science. Thus SSK's strong programme maintained that:

> sociologists of scientific knowledge should treat correct science and false science equally; they should analyse what are taken by most scientists to be true claims about the natural world and what are treated by most as mistaken claims in the same way. (Collins and Yearley 1992: 302)

In the second edition (1986) of *Laboratory Life*, Latour and Woolgar controversially excised the term social from the text's subtitle (substituting the 'the construction of scientific facts' for 'the social construction of scientific facts'). This signalled a break with the 'strong' programme in the sociology of scientific knowledge, since it rejected the explanatory power of the social and posited in its place a radical constructivism in which the social and techno-scientific were both equally constructed and within which the former could never hold the secret of the latter (see Bloor 1999, Latour 1998). The significance of this gesture should not be underestimated as the wider implications of Latour's work arise directly from this disavowal of the 'social'.

In this respect Latour's science studies accessed its subject through 'the back door of science in the making, not through the more grandiose entrance of ready made science' (Latour, 1987: 20), uncovering a challenging palimpsest of inscriptions, transactions, translations and recruitments which collectively combine to generate scientific facts. It is here, at the very outset of Latour's project, that we encounter the question of organization. In offering a genetic account of scientific discovery, Latour brought into focus the organizational nature of scientific work, organization here understood both in the restricted sense of the operations of a given social institution, and in the more general sense of an ordering or classification of the material world (see Böhm and Jones, 2002: 278). In Latour's account of science's action these two aspects are inextricably entangled; the organization of the material world cannot be dissevered from the institutional ensembles that carry out this ordering, nor can such institutions be understood without reference to their immanent acts of organization.

Translation

Having adumbrated the basic occasion of Latour's thought, ie, a desire to explore science's action or genesis, we will turn to the crucial operators through which Latour traces this action. Given that Latour engages in a prodigious invention with respect to his terminology we will concentrate on a few terms (translation, the quasi-object, and his so-called pragmatogony), whose selection is determined not so much by their direct utility in the study of organizations, but because they reveal most clearly the ineluctable elision that occurs between a social or institutional conception of organizations and a processual or operational understanding uncovered by Latour's theory. As we've indicated, from a Latourian perspective, institutions are loci of methods of ordering, whose essential operation resides in the recurrent patterns by which the relations between humans (subjects) and nonhumans (objects) are generated and maintained. These patterns are not architectonic, they do not precede or exceed the site of their operation: organizations (noun) are sustained by organization (verb). But what are these modes of ordering, how are these immanent acts of organization that yield institutions, facts, and artefacts to be described?

Latour's answer can encapsulated in a single term: *translation*: 'like Michel Serres, I use *translation* to mean displacement, drift, invention, mediation, the creation of a link that didn't exist before, [that] . . . modifies two elements or agents' (Latour, 1994: 31). Translations are what scientific facts and technical artefacts consist of, they are the means by which they are constructed and maintained (see also Brown, in this volume). To build a technical object or scientific fact requires: '. . . the simplest means of transforming the juxtaposed set of allies into a whole that acts as one, to tie the assembled forces *to one another*, that is, to build a **machine**' (Latour, 1987a: 128, emphases in original). A specific 'social' machine must be assembled in order to construct a technical machine, a 'machine' is here to be understood in terms of a machination, a 'Machiavellian' alliance between differing parties possessed of differing interests 'where borrowed forces keep one another in check so that none can fly apart from the group' (1987: 129). For this reason actor network theory rejects any separation between the genesis of scientific facts and technologies 'the problem of the builder of "fact" is the same as the builder of "objects" namely how to ally components so that they can resist controversies' (Latour, 1987: 131).

Latour (1994, see also Latour, 1999a: 175–225) has provided a cogent summary of this theory of translation within the context of the evolution of technical objects arguing that technical objects are intermediaries, or translations, that enable human 'actants' to achieve definite goals. Translation, however, is not a simple act of transposition in which a predetermined goal is realized through a neutral intermediary. Thus mediation begins with a *Goal Translation*: technical means involve a certain displacement or detour of the original actor and aim in order to accomplish their goal. Technological mediation is always an instance of 'shifting'; a task or goal that would initially be performed in a certain fashion, is shifted into an ensemble of alternate materials that can carry out this task and as a result it is subject to a certain 'function creep'.

Consider one of the most rudimentary technical operations, the production of a cutting edge to skin game or cut vegetable matter. The ancestors of early man would have used the cutting edges provided by the body (for instance the teeth) but in time this cutting edge is shifted or delegated to a separate matter that can accommodate this function (for instance flint). But for Latour 'translation is wholly symmetrical' (Latour, 1999a: 179) thus this matter is itself recruited, prepared, or in Latour's terms translated into a cutting edge, just as the cutting edge of the human is translated into a matter.

This is a very basic example but within Latour's thought, all techniques materially, conceptually, and in the case of more complex technologies, socially, involve these symmetrical translations. The production of more developed techniques involves the recruitment not only of technical means (themselves the products of earlier translations) but also of a range of individuals with differing competencies and aims, all of whom must be allied if the technology in question is to be successfully realised. The original goal will be displaced or 'detoured' as a result of the elements necessary for its realization and the technological act in question is itself altered. It is no longer an individual or group with a single goal that acts but rather a composite entity, made up of the aims and properties of all the enlisted actants and the strategies and negations involved in making them behave as one.

This represents another dimension of Latour's theory of translation which lies behind his substitution of *actant* for actor, namely *composition*. Actor implies a fully present human agent that realizes its aim through a technical intermediary. Actant, on the other hand, is indicative of a symmetry between human and nonhuman agents; since both are subject to translation; both are actants within the context of techniques. Moreover, given that any technical translation involves earlier detours or techniques as subprograms to fulfil the original task, we move further and further from a position from which we might speak of the aims of an original actor (Latour, 1994: 36). If we apply Latour's vision of translation to a relatively sophisticated piece of technology, we have not only the detours carried out to realize the technical object before us, but also, in a virtual sense, a whole range of earlier translations that were carried out with respect to the individual components gathered together in this object. All of these components or 'sub-programmes' imply previous couplings of actants, such that 'the prime mover of an action becomes a new, distributed, and nested series of practices whose sum might be made only if we respect the mediating role of all the actants mobilized' (Latour, 1994: 46). From this perspective a given technical object begins to reveal an almost fractaline aspect, an apparently infinite folding of actants.

Through these translations aims and functions are subcontracted to technical objects, which can be seen as encoding gestures and acts. For instance, Marx (1976: 492ff) observed how industrial machinery began by replicating the actions of an individual worker, then later embodies the operations of an entire system of human workers, and it is in a similar manner that Latour speaks of the delegation of actions to technology (Latour, 1999a: 182). Technologies abstract formerly human functions, but for Latour this represents a transgression of the common sense dichotomy between words and things. It is not only physical acts but semiotic acts that are delegated to objects. Rather than language as a description of a state of affairs or distribution of 'things', matter in the composite form of technical objects is said to 'signify'. Technical objects and systems are 'articulations', meaningful arrangements of actants and instead of a one-way translation of meaning into matter, we witness the meaningful articulation of actants through the simultaneous translation of humans and non-humans.

Yet by virtue of a process of *folding*, we are seldom cognizant of these multiple translations and only apprehend unified objects, facts or systems. In Latour's early exploration of the working practices of scientists, this folding took the form of 'black-boxing', in which the processes that made up science's action were collapsed into the apparent self-sufficiency of the fact; the consolidated fact or result was substituted for the process that allowed its realization. From this perspective a scientific fact is a successfully constructed black-box, and science's action that of passing from translations and unallied actants to the solidity of facts. When this process is successful, science claims that 'nature' has spoken; it is not the networks of reference that have produced the result, but nature itself as uncovered by science. But for Latour the 'nature' to which science appeals is merely the sum total of its repository of successfully consolidated facts, each of which could be decomposed into the kinds of transactions between actants that we have outlined (Latour, 1987).

It is only when technologies break down or when scientific facts fail to take on consistency that we see the processes they enfold. When controversy surrounds a scientific fact then the data, methods, and appeals to other consolidated facts or black-boxes are brought into question and so to light, since the trail that leads from the claim to the field must be traced so that the weak link in the chain can be identified and consensus restored. In the case of the technical object, Latour gives the example of an overhead projector, which when it is working manifests to our awareness as a single object. If it breaks down, however, then a host of humans gather round it, testing its subroutines in an attempt to locate the problem. In this manner the black box of the artefact unfolds before our eyes and is revealed as 'composed of steps in sequence that integrate several human gestures' (Latour, 1999a: 183).

Circulating reference

A useful illustration of the relation between the processes of translation that occur in the construction of scientific facts and the wider translational processes that occur in organizations can be found in Latour's account of a group of pedologists carrying out fieldwork in the Amazon (Latour 1999a: 24–79). The aim of the soil specialists' research was to establish the precise nature of the transition from rain forest to savannah through the collection and analysis of soil samples. Latour's ethnographic analysis of their project details the translatory acts that occur in the transposition of an inchoate piece of nature into a set of ordered and apparently concrete facts or statements. This is achieved by the creation of what is in effect a virtual laboratory, assembled through the ordering of the field of enquiry, as Latour dissembles ' I thought I was deep in the forest, [but] we are in a laboratory, albeit a minimalist one, traced by the grid of coordinates' (1999a: 32). This series of translations begins with the subdivision of the area to be studied through the imposition of a Cartesian grid. The grid is then measured by a 'clinometer' which records its gradient, after this the subdivisions of the grid are sampled and the soil to be examined is indexed against the grid and in relation to the depth from which it is taken. In turn these samples are indexed by colour (assessed according to the Munsell Code by comparing the sample with coloured card) and by their consistency.

To allow the results of this ordering to be seen simultaneously, a draw-like device called a 'pedocomparator' is used, which provides an indexed overview of the rainforest/savannah interface as it is represented by the soil samples. Returned to the laboratory these samples are further analysed to determine their chemical composition, and the results of these various translations condensed into the form of a diagram that maps the transition from rainforest to savannah. What Latour stresses is the 'chain of transformation' that enfolds one ordering into the other, implicit in the acts that order the forest as a data set is the organizational space of the laboratory proper, in which the objects of that ordering will be assembled (through a range of other tactics) so as to yield up their 'facts' – the substantive conclusion of the research team regarding the transition from forest to savannah.

The final graphic presentation of the 'facts' dictates all of the operations carried out in the field, and the value of these facts is determined by the ability to trace their reference to the field, ie, to reverse-engineer the facts and follow the network of translation through their various stages and so arrive at the original field of enquiry. In this process of translation or 'circulating reference' the original sample is at once *reduced*, in that various facets of its particularity are removed in favour of those that contribute to the solution of the initial problem, and also *amplified* or extended in that they become interwoven with a range of prior knowledges. This amplification points to the virtual presence of a range of other acts of translation, and also to the manner in which this circulation of reference is both organized by institutions and organizes institutions (eg, the laboratory whose structure and function is an index of translatory processes in which it is involved).

Thus rather than a polarity of a subject and object in which the former, via the methodology of natural science, attains knowledge of the latter, we have a network of 'circulating' references or translations. The objects of the field imply the facts of the laboratory, likewise these facts return us to the field. What is important then, is neither brute objects nor the incorporeal facts that express them, but the processes that lead us from one to the other. These processes are a variety of acts of organization, in this manner the order of things revealed by science emerges as the result of an ordering of things.

It is the extension of this insight that constitutes one of the major contributions of Latour's work to the study of organizations. It is in the work of Law (1994) that this potential finds its most lucid exposition. Law argues that organizations are not stable structures subject to occasional perturbation, but systems of dynamic equilibrium borne of overlapping ordering processes. These process overlap because they are each semi-autonomous; organizations do not operate from a central point of survey or command, but exist as a *moiré* of organizational narratives or procedures 'recursively told, embodied, and performed in a series of different materials' (Law, 1994: 259).

Law is not alone in exploring the implications of Latour's flat ontology for organizational analysis, for instance Brown (2001) explores the digitisation of time-sheets at *Narajo*, an oil company, arguing that this apparently minor reconfiguration of an administrative procedure reveals a whole series of translations that extend from the hours of individual workers to the financial flows that link organization to organization in an era of outsourced labour. Brown argues that the tracking of this chain demonstrates that there is not a point at which there is a move from the micro to macro, but only translations that enfold different levels of organization, and that these translations are materially heterogeneous. Similarly Doolin (2003) explores changes in New Zealand's health services through the various 'narratives of ordering' that enable a public institution to reconfigure its practices in accordance with the putative benefits of privatisation. Indeed Lee and Hassard (1999) suggest that ANT is particularly suited to anatomize the kinds of heteroclite formations that result from the deregulation of various organizational forms.

Pragmatogony

It would appear then that the chain of translation involved in an given technical object can be extended indefinitely, rendering the identification of an inaugural translation impossible. The activity of even the most primitive human is technically mediated, and given this, the processes that later technologies abstract are never purely human actions but composite articulations of humans and nonhumans – the tools of which Marx's workers were dispossessed were already abstract embodiments of gestures and acts. Thus Latour posits a continual exchange of properties between humans and non-humans that renders us collectively an 'object-institution' endlessly 'brewing' hybrids (Latour, 1994: 47). We never encounter a pure human or artefact but only these composites that imply endless networks of translation:

> we are faced with chains which are associations of humans (H) and nonhumans (NH). No-one has ever seen a social relation by itself . . . nor a technical relation . . . Instead we are always faced with chains which look like this H-NH-H-NH-H-NH. (Latour, 1991: 110)

Given these anastomotic chains, there can be no human action or labour that precedes the technical, no original delegation:

> Our delegation of action to other actants that now share our human existence has developed so far that a program of anti-fetishism could only lead us to a nonhuman world, a lost, phantasmagoric, world *before* the mediation of artefacts. (Latour, 1999a: 190)

Latour here approaches the thesis of *originary technicity* (Stiegler, 1998). The pre-technical human is a fantasy; our world, ourselves, are born of the mediation of artefacts. Technology is not an extension or assertion of a prior and inviolate will, we cannot subscribe to the hylomorphic fantasy of 'an all powerful human agent imposing his will on shapeless matter' (1994: 38), but must recognize a historically mediated matter whose descent is our own. There is never an unorganized field that is subject to ordering, the orderings that maintain organizations are always orderings of prior orderings.

From this position, we have always been impure, but our current techno-social condition is such that this hybridity can no longer be denied. The human, from its very origin, is characterized by impurity (that is, its relation to objects), and by way of illustration Latour offers his 'pragmatogony' – a genealogy of the 'hybridisations that make us humans'(Latour, 1999a: 202). Its significance in the present context resides in its exposure of interplay between human organizations and the organization of nonhumans or matter, and its demonstration that this reciprocity is neither modern nor confined to the techno-scientific. Latour's pragmatogony offers a quasi-dialectical, co-evolution of the human or social and the technical or material, in which properties are exchanged between these differing actants, such that 'whenever we learn something about the management of humans, we shift that knowledge to nonhumans and endow them with more and more organizational properties' while in turn 'what has been learned from nonhumans is reimported so as to reconfigure people' (1999a: 207–208, emphasis in original).

Thus, Latour avers that human collectives have always exchanged their characteristics with nonhumans, that the organization of inorganic matter (as

Stiegler describes the production of tools), a process that begins with the earliest forms of hominoid tool use, determines the organization of humans. The tool is the 'extension of social skills to nonhumans', the impartation of the organizational tendencies of the human to material artefacts (Bergson, 1911: 138). In turn these objects permit the preservation and transmission of a sequence of acts of ordering through a durable form that outlasts their originators. Techniques here function as mnemotechniques, and as forms of epigenetic storage represent a 'socialization' of matter. In turn they facilitate the socialization of the human animal, to the extent that society is recognized as being predicated upon a cultural memory that exceeds the individual or somatic memory (Leroi-Gourhan, 1993).

The preservation of operational sequences in the production of tools provides a strategy that can be applied to humans, demonstrating how they may 'accept a role and discharge a function' through the 'ability to nest several subroutines' (Latour, 1999a: 209). Humans thus disciplined are ready to become components in the creation of 'megamachines' (Mumford, 1967), that is the organization of humans and tools as vast working assemblages. These megamachines predated and prefigured the machines of the industrial revolution, in which

> non-humans enter an organization that is already in place and take on a role already rehearsed for centuries by obedient human servants. . . . Management . . . precedes the expansion of material techniques. (Latour, 1999: 207)

Industrial technology, understood as the socialization of non-humans, itself necessitates new forms of human organization and Latour cites T.P. Hughes' study of the electrification of the West in which an organizational technique (the corporation) and a material technology (the electric grid) are presented as two dimensions of a single innovation (Hughes, 1983). Within the context of these new forms of organization nonhuman actants come to develop and exhibit new properties (Latour, 1999: 203), in other words become the kinds of hybrids that characterize contemporary culture.

In view of this history of transaction between human and nonhuman, Latour envisages a society that is technically determined by a technology that is socially determined, in other words he shatters the either/or logic that has dominated debates in the social sciences regarding the relation between society and technoscience. Indeed, rather than society Latour talks of *collectives* which from the outset involve techniques and evolve through interplay of humans and nonhumans.

The quasi-object

The genetic account of science and technology and the processes of translation and black-boxing they imply are not ruptures or breaks in a historical field, but rather the heirs of this long pragmatogony. It is this position that lies behind

Latour's insistence that 'we have never been modern'. Latour maintains that our modernity (whose inception was the Enlightenment) is marked by two contradictory practices (Latour, 1993: 10–12). The first he terms 'purification' – the division of the phenomenal world into two categories, those of society and nature, respectively understood as the world of humans and nonhumans. Science and technology are the instigators and beneficiaries of this division, they define what exists in the world of human culture and what by contrast belongs to the realm of nature. The second set of practices are the processes of translation explored above, which fabricate novel entities; hybrids or chimera born of the intermixture of nature and culture, society and matter. Thus these contrary tendencies (ie, purification and translation) exist in mutual presupposition: the modern settlement (as Latour terms this division) produces the hybrids its purification precludes. Science in theory exists outside society, the repository of apparently objective facts, but in practice science breeds hybrids, mixing society and nature in complex networks or assemblages.

In place of this dichotomous constitution Latour offers the category of the quasi-object (a term adopted from Michel Serres). For Serres the quasi-object reveals a mobile realm in which object and subject are moments in an originary aporia:

> in which the transcendental constitution of the object by the subject would be nourished, as in return, by the symmetrical constitution of the subject by the object . . . of [this] direct constitutive condition on the basis of the object we have witnesses that are tangible, visible . . . however far back we go in talkative or silent prehistory, they are still there. (Serres, in Latour, 1993: 84)

As we have seen this quasi-object is what determines humanity through the long history of exchanges between objects and subjects. Its role is not only historical but extant: our social relations continually revolve around quasi-objects. The description, exchange, creation and consumption of objects define our individual actions and collective transactions. Given this we can never grant sovereignty to either the subject or the object, what is important is the transaction or swapping, the role that the quasi-object plays in constructing and maintaining relations. Thus the quasi-object is to be seen as a generator of intersubjectivity constructing the 'we' and the 'I', the collective and the individual, which both emerge as the result of its exchange or 'passing'.

If this is the case then the collective cannot be figured as the sum total of individuals. Rather the 'I' of the individual and the 'we' of the collective must be understood solely in terms of the network of transactions that is the quasi-object: 'the "we" is less a set of "I" 's than the set of the sets of its transmissions'. It is this decomposition into a set of transmissions that lies at the heart of the quasi-object, since it establishes an ontology of pure relations: 'it is . . . the transubstantiation of being into pure relation. Being is abolished for the relation' (Serres, 1982: 228).

In recognition of these arguments Latour calls for a new constitution that honours the specificity of quasi-objects. This constitution will, of necessity, be characterized by an anti-humanism. From the perspective of the quasi-object 'it is impossible to define the human by an essence', the human is rather the focus of a historical succession of contingent networks, the product of particular ways of 'passing' the quasi-object. The human is the nexus of relations, the site where properties are exchanged. In keeping with a commitment to symmetry, this perspective also alters the status of matter or objects which can no longer be regarded as outside or prior to history or society, for Latour 'matter is not a given but a recent historical creation'.

The discovery of the quasi-objects brings to an end the era of systematic and global totalities, science and society; the social and natural can no longer be held apart or wield their former explanatory force. Instead of a natural science that could explain society or vice versa, we arrive at a 'flat' ontology or sociology in which there is neither the global or local, but only networks of translation that extend and multiply without hierarchy. There is only the organization of the 'glocal' as a single plane of endlessly entangled translations 'the intermediary arrangements that we are calling networks' (Latour, 1993: 122). Humanity is made by the objects it makes; the human emerges as that which is 'delegated, distributed, mediated'. It is not a thing, since there are no things but only exchanges: 'the human is in the delegation itself, in the pass in the sending . . .' (Latour, 1993: 138), an insight Latour believes has its origin the work of Gabriel Tarde, who argued for small acts of differentiation and imitation as the basis for social form (as opposed to the social facts of Durkheim) (see Latour, 2002). In this manner the quasi-object casts a new light on organizational structures – which are perhaps too often reduced to abstract systems of interpersonal relations. ANT would seek to locate the construction and transmission of quasi-objects at the heart of organizations, not merely as products but as the loci of a range of organizational activities. In this respect Latour is seen to break with the structure/agency problematic that has exercised much organizational theory, although critics have suggested that this is done at the expense of a recognition of the determinate impact of macro-structures on individual conduct (see Reed, 2003).

Discussion

Having addressed some of the major themes of Latour's enquiries, let us now briefly consider a number of the critiques it has inspired, both generally and more specifically in the field of organizational analysis. The first and perhaps most easily dismissed is that Latour's theory is essentially reactionary. This charge issues (in perfect illustration of the symmetry of the modern settlement) from both within the humanities and from those representatives of the natural sciences that have seen it fit to engage with science studies. In the case of the first camp (Collins and Yearley, 1992; Bloor, 1999), Latour is accused of abandoning the fundamental insights of the sociology of science and thus returning to the hard sciences the mantle of objectivity that SSK struggled to overturn.

For the second, Latour's alleged reaction resides precisely in this infusion of the social into science, here read as a return to a pre-modern constitution, ie, a disavowal of enlightenment reason and its scientific and social legacy (Sokal and Bricmont, 1998). As we have seen, both perspectives arise from a failure to recognize the existence of Latour's modern constitution and so critique his work from either side of the great divide of the two cultures. Latour's constructivism is more subtle than these critiques allow and requires, in Serres' words, an acknowledgment that 'science is conditioned by postulates or by decisions that are generally social, cultural, or historical in nature; nevertheless science is universal' (Serres, 2000: 115).

The second constellation of possible critique revolves around the question of the symmetry of humans and nonhumans and in particular the granting of agency to the latter. For instance it has been said that Latour's 'flat society' deflates its terms:

> installing a great indifference between the countless things of the world, an indifference which arises when they end up being portrayed as potentially all the same . . . Thus humans can be treated as if they are nonhuman things, while nonhuman things can be treated as if they are humans. (Laurier and Philo, 1999: 1060)

Here, actor network theory appears to posit an indiscriminate monism, in which the agency of objects or matter is equal to that of human subjects – a difficult position for many so-called 'realists' to swallow. In part this situation can be traced back to a circumspection or ambivalence on Latour's part with respect to his own ontology. For instance, he has declared that 'Actor Network Theory should be called actant/rhizome ontology . . . because it is an ontology and it is about rhizomes' (Latour in interview in Crawford, 1993: 263) and avowed his fidelity to Serres. But, in contrast to the immanent multiplicities of these thinkers, and in particular the univocal political ontology developed by Deleuze-Guattari – whose material vitalism attempts to account for all forms on either side of the subject/object dichotomy, Latour is often content to replicate the traditional categories of subject and object. And while their relation in highly vascularized in his work, this basic dichotomy is never truly abandoned. One suspects that this is not the result of an oversight but rather out of deference for his audience who, of an empirical disposition, are unlikely to tolerate the more extreme ontological speculation of Deleuze and others. This critique of Latour has found its inflection in the problem of 'cutting the network', in other words at what point do we bracket or discount actants (McLean and Hassard, 2004: 499)? If translations are potentially innumerable, at what point does their influence drop to zero, how is a researcher to determine which actants to follow and which to discount?

The third class of objection is that Latour is indifferent to questions of power, gender, culture and ecology. As Ellam puts it:

> the key actants in Latour's hybrid networks of science and technology are all too often men and machines, with other humans and other non-humans remaining largely invis-

ible. Consequently, there remain many sides and many interfaces to the non-modern world that Latour is distinctly unwilling to either recognize or address . . . [Latour] largely ignores the interfaces between machines and other nonhumans and between humans and non-machine non-humans. (Ellam, 1999: 4)

In organization theory this problem has found its echo in suggestions that empirical studies drawing on Latour and ANT have a tendency to concentrate on the determinate influences of the 'big' actors, the managerial translation engines who enrol or recruit actants to their vision (McLean and Hassard, 2004: 501). Indeed the whole discourse of enrolment can be seen as implicitly gendered, in that it depicts a world of struggle and contention in which male actants (understood as 'Machiavellian princes') attempt to overpower each other in pursuit of their particular vision (Latour 1988).

The problem of the political in Latour is taken up by Langdon Winner who argues that Latour's 'excessive concern with origins' results in a total disregard for technological consequences and 'the broader distribution of power in society'. Latour's reluctance to couple his analysis of techno-science with a politics of difference might be seen to be at one with an apparent disregard for the socio-economic systems that drive the innovations and lubricate the alliances actor network theory explores: capital is not a term in Latour's vocabulary. As a result of these lacunas Latour's work can be 'sanitized of any critical standpoint that might contribute to substantive debates about the . . . environmental consequences of technology' (Winner, 1993: 431).

However, there is a political dimension to Latour's thought; as he is fond of reminding his readers, the term thing has its origin in *Ding*, an old German world that is etymologically related to a notion of a meeting (see Latour, 2004). In other words, politics and objects are not as far apart as the modern constitution would have us believe, indeed now more than ever our politics is that of 'a parliament of things', bound up with the effects of our quasi objects. Nevertheless, this remains the most serious of challenges to Latour's theory and what politics there is, more often than not seems eclipsed by the centrality that Latour grants to problems of science and technology. Networks however are networks of power, in the Foucauldian sense, and network analysis, particularly of organizations, should be attentive to these problems. There is no fundamental reason why a sociology of translation should not embrace the kind of micropolitical analysis found in Deleuze-Guattari and Foucault, indeed as Munro has observed:

Contrary to imagining power . . . as running through structures . . . power is theorized as exercised in the networks that cut transversally across structures. The point is that structures like gender and class continue to have their effects . . . Indeed a principle of Actor-Network analysis is to explain the durability of structures, while stressing the underlying mobility of actor's interests. (1999: 431)

Nevertheless, within Latour's own work these problems remain largely unexamined.

Conclusion

Latour's theory has often been reduced to ready acronyms and the unproblematic application of set terms or processes to a given field of study. This approach is not without its success, and in this form Latour, and ANT more generally, has proved of heuristic value, enabling researchers to view their subjects in a new light. Nevertheless, Latour has been keen to distance his own thought from the consolidated methodologies that it has inspired (see Latour, 1999b), stressing instead its status as a set of open problems. In many ways the problematic of Latour's thought is its most interesting dimension and it is this aspect that perhaps needs to be extended through a fidelity to implicit tensions in Latour's work (such as those discussed above). There are a number of ways in which this could be achieved, for instance Latour's work can be mapped back on to its influences, and the divergences traced in the hope of better understanding the tensions that produce them. Similarly, Latour's work should be juxtaposed against that of others concerned with the analysis of the techno-scientific (for instance Haraway, Stengers, Stiegler and Kittler), here again points of convergence and disjunction are likely to provide impetus for further theoretical production. But it is not only through theory that Latour's thought can be developed, its confrontation with specific fields of inquiry is likely to cast as much, if not more, light upon its subject. It is here that organizational analysis can make its greatest contribution, since it is here that the sociology of translation is subjected to the acid test of the real. This may serve both to confirm Latour's insights and reveal its limits and in this fashion organizational analysis and actor network theory can enjoy a fruitful relationship, in which neither would hold the secret of the other.

References

Bergson, H. (1911) *Creative Evolution*, trans. A. Mitchell, New York: Henry Holt & Co.

Bloor, D. (1976) *Knowledge and Social Imagery*. Chicago: University of Chicago Press.

Bloor, D. (1999) 'Anti Latour' *Studies in History and Philosophy of Science*, 30(1): 81–112.

Brown, B. (2001) 'Representing time: The humble timesheet as a representation and some details of its completion and use' *Ethnographic Studies* (6), online at: www.equator.ac.uk/PublicationStore/ representingtime.pdf (accessed 24/2/05).

Collins, H. and S. Yearley (1992) 'Epistemological chicken' in A. Pickering (ed.) *Science as Practice and Culture*. Chicago: University of Chicago Press.

Crawford, T. (1993) 'An interview with Bruno Latour', *Configurations*, 1(2): 247–268.

Doolin, B. (2003) 'Narratives of change: Discourse, technology and organization' *Organization*, 10(4): 751–770.

Ellam, M. (1999) 'Living dangerously with Bruno Latour in a hybrid world' *Theory, Culture & Society*, 6(4): 1–24.

Hughes, T. P. (1983) *Networks of Power: Electrification in Western Society, 1880–1930*. Baltimore, MD: John Hopkins University Press.

Jones, C. and S. Böhm (2002) 'Hors d'oeuvre' *ephemera: critical dialogues on organization*, 2(4): 277–280.

Latour, B. (1979) *Laboratory Life: The Social Construction of Scientific Facts*. London: Sage.

Latour, B. (1987) *Science in Action: How to Follow Scientists and Engineers Through Society*. Cambridge, MA: Harvard University Press.

Latour, B. (1988) 'How to write The Prince for machines as well as for machinations' in E. Brian (ed.) *Technology and Social Change*. Edinburgh: Edinburgh University Press.

Latour, B. (1992) *We have Never Been Modern*. London: Harvester Wheatsheaf.

Latour, B. (1994) 'On technical mediation: Philosophy, sociology, genealogy' *Common Knowledge*, 3(2): 29–64.

Latour, B. (1999a) *Pandora's Hope: An Essay on the Reality of Science Studies*. Cambridge, MA: Harvard University Press.

Latour, B. (1999b) 'On recalling ANT' in J. Law and J. Hassard (eds.) *Actor Network Theory and After*. Oxford: Blackwell.

Latour, B. (2002) 'Gabriel Tarde and the end of the social' in P. Joyce (ed.) *The Social and Its Problems*. London: Routledge.

Latour, B. (2004) *Politics of Nature: How to Bring the Sciences into Democracy*. Cambridge, MA: Harvard University Press.

Laurier, E. and C. Philo (1999) 'X-morphising: A review essay of Bruno Latour's *Aramis or the Love of Technology*' *Environment and Planning A*, 31: 1043–1071.

Law, J. (1994) *Organizing Modernity: Social Order and Social Theory*. Oxford: Blackwell.

Law, J. and J. Hassard (eds.) (1999) *Actor Network Theory and After*. Oxford: Blackwell.

Lee, N. and J. Hassard (1999) 'Organization unbound: Actor-Network Theory, research strategy and institutional flexibility, *Organization*, 6(3): 391–404.

Leroi-Gourhan, A. (1993) *Gesture and Speech,* trans. A. B. Berger. Cambridge, MA: MIT Press.

Marx, K. (1976) *Capital* (vol 1), trans. B. Fowkes. Harmondsworth: Penguin.

Mclean, C. and J. Hassard (2004) 'Symmetrical absence/symmetrical absurdity: Critical notes on the production of Actor Network accounts' *Journal of Management Studies*, 14(3): 493–519.

Mumford, L. (1967) *The Myth of the Machine (1): Technics and Human Development*. New York: Harcourt, Brace and Co.

Munro, R. (1999) 'Power and discretion: Membership work in the time of technology' *Organization*, 6(3): 429–450.

Reed, M. (2003) 'The agency/structure dilemma in organization theory: Open doors and brick walls' in H. Tsoukas and C. Knudsen (eds.) *The Oxford Handbook of Organization Theory*. Oxford: Oxford University Press.

Serres, M. (1982) *The Parasite*, trans. L. R. Schehr. Baltimore, MD: John Hopkins University Press.

Serres, M. (2002) *The Birth of Physics,* trans. J. Webb. Manchester: Clinamen.

Sokal, A. and J. Bricmont (1998) *Intellectual Impostures*. London: Profile Books.

Stiegler, B. (1998) *Technics and Time, 1: The Fault of Epimetheus*, trans. R. Beardsworth and G. Collins. Stanford, CA: Stanford University Press.

Winner, L. (1993) 'Upon opening the black box and finding it empty: Social constructivism and the philosophy of technology' *Science as Culture*, 16: 427–452.

Organizations as decision machines: Niklas Luhmann's theory of organized social systems

Armin Nassehi

Introduction

Rationality, efficiency, collective goals, and objectives – these are the keywords of the organizational narrative. This is true both for the self-descriptions of organizations that try to concern themselves with a reality they can deal with as well as for the traditional sociological perspective on organizations. Rationality stands for the idea of repeatable, controllable, and goal-oriented practices. Efficiency symbolizes a practice which is able to relate several forms and practices to each other, achieving an outcome that is more than the sum of its parts. Organizations bundle their members into different positions, duties, and responsibilities within different levels of a hierarchic structure in order to pursue a single, collective set of goals and objectives.

Until recently much of the sociology of organizations was content to repeat this narrative and so is able to supply organizations with key words for self-description, change and further development. In addition, the basic notions of organization research yield a special semantics of thinking about organizations with their unique kind of rationality, efficiency, and collectivity, with the aim of detecting dysfunctional or insufficient practices that inhibit rational decisions, efficient problem solving, and collective orientations amongst the members of an organization. Beginning with Max Weber's esteem of efficient and rational bureaucracies and leading to James Coleman's description of organizations as devices for bundling and strengthening individual interests, the sociology of organizations always had an ambivalent feeling about organizations. So in regard to my examples, Weber also bemoaned the depersonalizing practices of organizations, whereas Coleman diagnoses an asymmetric society in which individuals lose their potential for self-determination.

Why begin with these examples in a chapter in which I want to introduce Niklas Luhmann's sociology of organizations? The mentioned keywords and examples show that Luhmann begins at a different starting point. For him, rationality, efficiency, collectivity, and the ambivalent appreciation of the relationship of organizations and the individual scope of action are not theoretical figures in the stricter sense. He begins with the question how and why organizations describe themselves as they do. He is not interested in asking whether organizations are really rational entities or if they are really efficient. Rather he emphasizes that these forms of self-description as rational and efficient, and their self-binding by purposes and objectives, are themselves part of the *practice* of organizations (Luhmann, 1973). Thus Luhmann neither believes in those self-descriptions nor rejects them. Instead, he questions the function of such self-descriptions for the constancy or the continuity of organizations. Luhmann's sociology is a sociology that does not acknowledge any external position or any external observer. He emphasizes that any operation, including, for example, self-descriptions of organizations, are operations of a system.

From its inception, the sociology of Luhmann was looking for counter-intuitive solutions and descriptions. But the purpose of this perspective never was motivated by an unmasking attitude. His perspective does not criticize ideologies. What Luhmann offers is the basic premise that all (self-) descriptions of systems are internally generated and, further, that no evidence about what is going on in social systems results from an external point of observation. All (self-) descriptions for Luhmann are parts of the described systems. Thus, his query centres on the function of such descriptions for the operations of systems. This perspective then becomes counter-intuitive per se *because* it keeps its distance from the self-evidence of such descriptions. Luhmann's sociology of organizations uses this distance from the self-made stories of organizations (and their traditional sociology) to achieve off-key observations.

Luhmann's sociology does not only consist of organization theory. The main topic of his works is a general theory of social systems on the one hand and a theory of society on the other. But his scientific starting point in the 1960s combined empirical research with theorizing of organizations as social systems (Luhmann, 1964; 1973). One of his last works was a book on organizations which can be regarded as the encompassing conclusion of his organization theory. The result was the fruit of 30 years of research on organized social systems (Luhmann, 2000). Unfortunately, none of Luhmann's books on organizations have been translated into English.

I shall present this sociology of organizations in the context of and in relation to his broader sociological project, beginning first with some remarks on his systems theoretical approach. Then follows a characterization of organizations as a special type of social system, situated between systems of interactions and society. The third section attends to Luhmann's theory of decisions as basic elements of organizations. In the final section, I focus on the place of organizations within a modern, functionally differentiated society.

General theory of social systems

The notion of systems often gets associated with the adage that a particular phenomenon can only be understood as a part of a whole. In this tradition, the term system refers to a holistic structure that controls all constituent phenomena, with each and every particular in subordination to the general structure of the encompassing system. Thus, in sociology too, the notion of systems or of a systemic approach stands for the enforcement of a general reason rather than for the actor or the actor's freedom to do something. One who speaks about systems supposedly emphasizes a top-down hierarchy of control. This understanding of systems, however, even though it is part of the collective memory of sociological nomenclature, has nothing to do with the basic idea of the contemporary systemic approach deriving from cybernetic and systems theoretical research, closely connected with the names C.E. Shannon, W. Weaver, L.v. Bertalanffy, W.R. Ashby, and H.v. Foerster. The basic idea of the contemporary systemic approach is to reject a worldview in which any particular phenomenon can only be understood as the result of a deduction from general principles, as the effect of one-way-causalities, or as an outcome of control by a higher level of order. Systemic approaches do not begin with causalities but with interrelations, with feed-back-processes, and with self-steering; practical processes that let systems' own structures emerge through their own practices. Bertalanffy speaks of 'organized complexity' (Bertalanffy, 1956: 2), emphasizing the idea that systems are units in which the interaction between parts or individuals brings forth the structure which afterwards is the starting point for new interactions. A system, then, is the result of interactions of its parts, not the other way round. Furthermore this implies that systemic operations are operations in real-time; that is, they build up 'organized complexity' in present-based practice. Due to the operational closure of their own practice, the relation between a system and its environment is asymmetric. This implies that changes in the environment do not cause linear effects inside of a system, but rather adapting effects, which appear in conjunction with the system itself. On the one hand, this means that a system reduces the possibilities of its future operations. On the other hand, the closing down of possibilities is precisely what enhances the system's ability to develop a special kind of complexity.

The appearance of systems theory can be regarded as a reaction to experiences with modernity, if modernity stands for the idea that order is the result of practice, not its precondition. Thus one of the basic concepts shared by systems theoretical approaches is a criticism of the Newtonian worldview which emphasizes linear relationships and one-to-one causations as the basic principles of the world. Nonetheless, systems theory does not explicitly assert the world as a system. In the end, the world as a wholeness gets deconstructed as *noise*; that is, a space in which order is both possible and improbable. Thus, all areas of order are spaces with limited possibilities and degrees of lower improbability. The functional meaning of systems, therefore, is the appropriation of reduced degrees of freedom which cannot be controlled by the world but only by themselves. As they refer to themselves, the order of systems is the order of recursive processes, based on the present state of a system.

The theoretical figure of self-referential processes resolves the problem of absent external control and one-to-one causal and hierarchical relations.

Systems theory does not begin on the level of systems, i.e., on a general level as the fundament of possible deductions. On the contrary, systems theory begins with practice, with operations, with the dynamics of self-enforcing and self-energizing processes which bring about order from and against the noise of the world. In the end, a system is anything but an algorithm of practice – it is the practice itself. A system is not a mechanical device that controls everything which happens inside of it. In short: it *is* what happens inside of it. Systems theory rejects the notion of a system in its traditional denotation as a top-down-controlling device. As a theoretical outcome of experiencing modernity, the nature of structures, problems, and their solutions can no longer be described as self-evident. In this sense, the term system deconstructs itself by analysing the instability and improbability of all stabilities and probabilities that successfully come into being (Baecker, 2001: 69f.).

In sociology, systems theory reached its first climax with Talcott Parsons, who was interested in cybernetic control-processes and homeostatic mechanisms, i.e., interactions among different subsystems on behalf of integrating the entire system. But although sociology owes to Parsons the insight into the self-stabilization of systems – and their ability to cope with dysfunction and anomaly by self-adapting processes – his theory was all too focused on the problem of stability and continuance. This was explicitly symbolized by his basic assumption to presuppose a general four-function scheme, consisting of functions which have to be fulfilled to maintain the system's structure.

This is the starting point of Luhmann's sociology. Like Parsons, he refers to general systems theory, but he makes a shift of emphasis from the conditions of stable systems to the dynamics of an emerging order. Furthermore, social systems for Luhmann are not analytical categories to rearrange the miscellaneous sociological observations by presupposing a set of pre-operational and prerequisite functions. In this sense Luhmann's sociology is much simpler than Parsons' – simple in terms of disclaiming categories, specific functions, or problems in the sense of pre-empirical conditions of the possibility of systems. Luhmann conceptualizes social systems as operating units which themselves produce the relation between problems and solutions with which a system must cope (Luhmann, 1995: 53). Whereas older systems theories regard the frame of problem-references as an external frame, Luhmann emphasizes that social systems produce both their problems and the compatible functional solutions using their own resources. For him, social systems consist of a network of communications which emerge in time; that is, from event to event. Social systems therefore are *autopoietic* systems because they are operationally closed. Closure, in this context, does not mean that such systems are not able to experience contact with their environments but that the only mode to get in contact is based on their own operations. It is a significant difference to former theories of social systems that Luhmann focuses on the dynamic and operational aspects of the system's reproduction, instead of on functionally presumed structures.

The only mode of operating for social systems is communication, or rather the connectivity of communicative events in time. Thus the only basis of the autopoiesis of social systems is communication. Communication for Luhmann is not only the utterance of information. The condition of success for communication has to be found in the next utterance of information. The dynamics of communication are hidden in-between communicative events. 'Only in the process of connecting can one tell whether one has been understood' (Luhmann, 1995: 143). And understanding for Luhmann is not a psychic reality but a part of the three-selection-process of communication, in which communication itself has understood if and how the next communication connects. This does not foreclose psychic understanding, but only communication can understand what has been communicated. Social systems are operationally different from psychic systems, which does not mean that communication could occur without psychic complexity.

If one conceptualizes communication as a present-based, operationally closed, and insurmountably self-referential process, then there occurs a paradox: for self-referential systems the only basis for their own events is their own reality. That means that anything that happens is its own condition, because there cannot be assumed another condition for communications other than that it happens. Finally, communicative systems become surprised by themselves because there is no place where the communication can be communicated unless in communication. This does not bar psychic realities in which communicative events get planned or expected, but the communicative reality begins at the earliest when communication has started or continued. Luhmann's systems theory is admittedly not a theory which rejects or refuses the participation of human beings – actors or psychic systems – in the process of communication. Whereas this seems to be the basic and often repeated criticism against Luhmann (concerning organizations see Mingers, 2003), his theory may not be understood as a theory that emphasizes a system level in opposition to a level of acting individuals. Luhmann's theory is interested in understanding how events that can be attributed to individual actors become meaningful within a process that itself cannot be attributed to individual actors – neither to one actor, nor to a number of actors. Systems theory in that sense is not a macro theory, and it is not a micro theory either. It rejects the distinction between micro and macro phenomena. Thus Luhmann does not look at organizations as entities that can be described as transindividual or that can be evaluated as more or less compatible with individual needs for individual freedom – not because he would not be interested in such semantics, but only as semantics; not as theoretical figures. He does not appreciate 'the actor' as a theoretical concept.

That actors act, or that human beings communicate from this point of view, are not theoretical statements which have to be accepted or rejected. For Luhmann such perspectives are empirical solutions of social systems that make their own permanently threatening paradox invisible. Actors and human beings, routines and structures, expectations and experiences – not least language – are mechanisms which release social systems from the danger of losing themselves in their own self-reference. Social systems – by the way, this is true also for psychic systems – let structures emerge in which their operative circularity becomes invisible. The most important mechanism for this is *time*. It is always the next communication which makes the former real and which stabilizes the *as-if-structure* of self-referential processes. Time lets structures emerge in which social systems can be embedded in themselves.

One of the myths perpetuated about systems theory is its fixation towards stability and constancy. It should have become evident that Luhmann's systems theory is not a theory which proposes a stable structure or which begins with complex theoretical presuppositions. Although Luhmann's theory often gets characterized as a very abstract and over theorized sociology, it is in fact a remarkably empirical theory because it is interested in the basic processes in which social systems occur and in which structures come into being.

Interaction, organization and society

According to another myth, systems theory suffers from a macro-bias. Customarily the problem of micro and macro is considered as a problem of alternative levels of social order. The macro-level then is the more general and collective level, whereas micro-phenomena are regarded as phenomena which can be observed as individual action. There exists a broad debate in sociology about how macrosocial structures can be derived from micro-behaviour (so for example Weintraub, 1979; Coleman, 1987; Hechter, 1983). The differentiation between micro and macro is a consequence of methodological individualism, which has to deal with the problem that, although only individual behaviour is observable, individual behaviour cannot be explained by itself. Organizations – neither mere face-to-face orders nor abstract collectivities – customarily seem to be observable social units comprising a meso-level of society.

Luhmann rejects this commonsensical nomenclature. Although Luhmann's systems theory does not begin with individual action, it is not a macro-theory. Systems theory has to take into account how and where the connectivity of communication lets systemic orders emerge. Therefore, Luhmann does not make a distinction between different levels of generality, or between different levels of aggregation. He writes:

> The distinction of micro and macro is formulated as a distinction of *levels*. The concept of system has *empirical* references; the concept of level has *logical* references. The concept of system can be used to *include* self-references as empirical phenomena. The concept of level has been invented to *exclude* self-references insofar as they amount to tautologies or paradoxes. (Luhmann, 1987: 126f)

What Luhmann emphasizes here is that the idea of levels does not take into account that the conditions of order can be different on different levels.

Shifting to the concept of systems, these different conditions become visible above all in the different forms of coping with the basic paradox of self-reference. Luhmann rearranges the hierarchy of levels by the differentiation of types of social systems. The first differentiation he makes is the differentiation of interaction and society, which he calls an 'evolutionary differentiation'. Interactions for Luhmann are social systems which use the co-presence of persons as the delimiting criteria of such systems. The autopoiesis of interactions depends on the mutual perception of persons who are able to respond to each other in real-time. Interaction systems are social systems with strong coupling to local and personal references, therefore 'they must recognize that their environment contains communications that cannot be controlled by the system' (Luhmann, 1987: 114).

In comparison societies are 'encompassing systems' (ibid.). No accessible communication occurs in the environment outside their boundaries. In modern times there only exists one society, what Luhmann calls 'world-society'. The forms of connectivity of these two types of social systems are rather different. Whereas interactions control themselves by limiting themselves to local, personal, and temporal selectivity, a society is an encompassing system that includes anything which appears as communication. The connectivity of such systems is ruled by mechanisms that are not dependent on co-presence and mutual perception of persons.

The mechanism of structuring societies is differentiation, which unfolds systems that emerge within a system. So Luhmann describes pre-modern societies as societies differentiated through stratification, in which an encompassing order follows the restriction of more or less stable social strata. All other forms of selectivity get subordinated under this strata-scheme. In contrast, in modern societies societal order is associated with functional differentiation (Luhmann, 1982; Luhmann, 1999; Nassehi, 2004). The logic of connectivity follows generalized symbolic media; such as money in economics, power in politics, belief in religion, truth in science or justice in the legal system. It is important to emphasize that these notions do not mean strong criteria for authentic belief, justice or truth. As communication media they are only semantic media used to make possible forms of belief, truth, justice and so on. These communication media are able both to make improbable forms of connectivity less improbable and to facilitate the emergence of function systems. Furthermore, in contrast to Parsons, Luhmann does not presuppose an analytical set of functions with respect to communication media; he is interested in an empirical reconstruction of the historical genesis of such mediatization of communication (Chernilo, 2002).

What should have become evident is that the relation between interactions and societies is not a relation between different levels, but a relation between different types of social systems. Societies may be regarded not as emergent entities of cumulating interactions but as completely different social systems with their own conditions of reproduction and self-structuring. If it is right that social systems have to cope with their own self-referential and paradoxical structure by structuring their connectivity, then the conditions of this connectivity are categorically different in interactions, societies, and in function systems.

Luhmann subsequently characterizes organizations as a third type of social systems (Luhmann, 1975: 13). Organizations are neither systems that depend on the co-presence of actors, nor are they systems without a social environment. What is characteristic for them is not the quality of occupying some alleged socially in-between level. Organizations for Luhmann are social systems which are able to stabilize forms of action and behaviour by *deciding* about more or less strong conditions of membership and about their practices and procedures.

Organizations are able to emerge as a special form of languid stability by institutionalizing transparent roles and positions, redundant procedures, and repeatable practices. Whereas the form of connectivity in interactions depends on mutuality of persons and the form of connectivity in societies gets structured by differentiation, in the modern case by functional differentiation, organization systems continue themselves by connecting decision to decision. Therefore organizations can be designated as *decision machines*.

It is important to notice that the theoretical differentiation of interaction, organization, and society/function system serves to make empirical criteria available for the system's own (self-) referencing of empirical situations. Thus, it makes a difference if a sociologist observes a situation only from the point of view of interactions, or if he or she takes into account that the situation may be structured by an organization or by the special conditions of a societal function system. The empirical meaning of this threefold typology is to reconstruct the different systemic conditions of reproduction. Beyond that it makes visible the special kinds of invisibilization strategies of the respective form of paradoxical self-application.

Decision machinery

To propose decisions as basic elements of organizations refers to a long tradition in organization research. Already Max Weber's theory of bureaucracy was fascinated with the efficient application of means to achieve objectives of rational power. The central horizon of this kind of organization theory is the condition of rational decision making within organizational practice. This tradition leads from the scientific management approach (Taylor, 1911), to the human relations movement (Roethlisberger and Dickson, 1939), and onward to the principal-agent-theory (Pratt and Zeckhauser, 1985). Different as all these theories are, they are all fixated on the question of how the potentials of rational decision making can be enhanced. Ironically, there is also a long tradition of scepticism towards the potentials of rational decisions in organizations.

Weber has already emphasized the irrational effects of organizational structures for individuals, and Herbert Simon's concept of *bounded rationality* (Simon, 1997; March and Simon, 1958) has become a proverbial term in organization theory. This sceptical perspective focuses on structural restrictions of decision rationality from the perspective of the individual decider. To cope with anarchic ambiguity, however, this approach presumes rationality of the entire organization on the structural level (March and Olsen, 1976), which leads to mutually non-transparent local rationalities (Cyert and March, 1963) and to a battle of rationalities (Crozier and Friedberg, 1977). The best known diagnosis about this problem is the 'garbage can model of choice' (Cohen, March and Olsen, 1972). The frame of reference of the entire debate about the rationality of decisions in organizations is the relationship between rational reasons for a decision and non-rational outcomes of such decisions.

In Luhmann's sociology of organizations, the problem of decisions also plays a prominent role, but Luhmann locates rationality at another point of the decision making process. As Karl Weick (1969, see Czarniawska, in this volume), who emphasizes that rationality is an ex-post account, Luhmann comes to the conclusion that rationality is a retrospective scheme of observation, dealing with the contingency and the paradox of decision making processes. For Luhmann organizations consist of decisions, and they have to cope with their self-made form of decision practice. Different from decision theory, Luhmann emphasizes that the notion of choice does not explain anything, but that choice assigns the point that has to be explained (Luhmann 2000: 135). The idea of choice does not entail that any choice suffers under the menace of deconstruction. That a decision is a choice means that the choosing could have preferred the other possibility. If there were any secure knowledge about how to decide, there would not be a choice. To have the choice means *not to know what to do*.

This is the main problem of organizations as social systems, consisting of the communication of decisions to perform strategies to make this problem invisible. As emphasized above, the autopoiesis of communication must make the problem invisible: the only basis of the system's operation is the system itself. This permanently menacing problem of self-deconstruction has to be overcome by constructing accountable anchors or by stabilizing expectable connectivities in time.

The most common technique to do so in decision making processes is the construction of a decider as an accountable address – and thus organization theory copes with the problem of choice, customarily, by describing the limited resources of individual deciders in complex organizations. For Luhmann, however, the decider is only a construction of the system to overcome the menacing deconstruction of its own conditions. This has the consequence that with Luhmann one can disburden the decider as an actor, both in theory and in empirical organizational processes (see Luhmann 2000: 147).

Another technique is to make decision processes visible. This means to stage-manage them in meetings, in special rooms, at special times, with special rites, and on special documents. Part of this also is the communication of goals and objectives, which instruct the attention of internal and external observers of the organization and so are able to simulate a 'rational' type of order. Thus organization systems are not systems, which are based on the mutual and immediate recognition of persons, but systems which have to make visible their decision-making processes (Luhmann 2000: 149). That does not mean that decisions really are observable, but it means that organizations have to supply themselves with forms of visibility which cloak the basic problem of self-reference.

What the decider is on the personal level, the visibility of procedures, addresses, and objectives is on the level of matters and facts.

Although an organization system for Luhmann consists of decisions, the organization as a whole is not the result of a decision because this too would have to be the result of a decision. This strange formulation may show how Luhmann has dissociated himself from the rationalistic implications of decision theory. He emphasizes how organizations have to cope with their own problem to construct a secure and expectable world by their own decisions – developing a self-constructed view of the world and a self-constructed certainty about and confidence in the world. Luhmann recommends searching for the non-decided prerequisites for decision in concrete organizations. He calls this the *culture* of an organization in the sense of a structure which has emerged by the practice of the organization itself (Luhmann 2000: 145). The empirical challenge and provocation for the sociology of organizations then, is to give an answer to the question of how organizations are able to hide their self-referential conditionality and to simulate their own constructions of the 'real world' they find themselves in.

Organizations and modern society

It is a truism that modern society depends on the contribution of organizations for social order. Nevertheless, from the perspective of Luhmann's theory of functional differentiation, function systems such as the economy, politics, science, education, religion, etc., are categorically different from their organizations. Here we can repeat what has been said about the difference between a sociology that is only able to distinguish different levels of order and a sociology that emphasizes the difference between types of social systems, each with its own character of reproduction. Reconstructing Luhmann (2000: 380ff.), three functional aspects of organizations in modern, functionally differentiated society can be differentiated. I want to stress them under the titles *reflexivity*, *rationality* and *inclusion/exclusion* (Nassehi 2002a).

Reflexivity

From Luhmann we learn that function systems are only structured by the connectivity of specially coded communications, but that the empirical reality of such function systems is characterized by organizations. To give an answer to the question concerning the basic functions of organizations for modern societies, we can learn from an operative theory of society that organizations are neither based on purposes, which stem from basic societal requests and tasks, as, for example, Parsons would assert; nor are they social systems which tie individual interests into bundles to give such interests more power, as for example James Coleman would argue.

Luhmann can teach us that the frame of reference of organizations and organization-building is the structuration of function systems. For example in the economic system the logic of allocation, of payment, of distribution, and the formation of prizes and values can in principle be explained by the free accumulation of economic transactions in time. The economic system therefore is a recursive system, determined by its own prevailing state.

As even this description shows, the pure recursivity of a system cannot stabilize its own structure – it takes organizations to install forms of reflexivity into the function systems. This holds true for all of the specialized systems. As firms, companies, and banks make economic exchanges more reflexive (repeatable, structured, and expectable), modern forms of political decision-making processes would not be possible without governmental organizations. A legal order depends on a set of legal organizations. Education is possible in families or in pure interactions, but a reflexive and structured form of education in a society also depends on establishing kindergartens, schools, and universities. Although the code of religious belief is not directly dependent on churches, without churches and their 'organization' of beliefs, the modern system of religion would implode. The same applies to art, which in its modern form would not be possible without art galleries, museums, and art dealers.

Reflexivity in this sense does not mean that organizations are able to make more reflexive decisions than the free allocation and cumulation of communicative events in the function systems. Reflexivity implies that there is a special kind of density in organizations which allows them to localize decisions that are important for the function systems. In economics there is, in principal, an unstructured space of economic transactions, customarily called the 'market', where the economy reproduces itself. Organizations, however, are the locations where such forms of decisions get concentrated and where a special form of decision history and decision routine can arise.

Rationality

In this manner, and only in this manner, do organizations produce a special kind of rationality – and again I do not hint at the long debate about the rationality of organizations in the face of the bounded rationality of its actors. What has to be understood by the rationality of organizations is their accountability for decisions. The accountability of organizations makes the structure of function systems observable. It does not mean that function systems can become entirely observable, but only that observers of organizations can gather some accountable information about economy, politics, religion, art, or the legal order.

If we want to observe function systems, we usually observe organizations, states, and their organizations as the political system, decisions of courts as the legal system, decisions and strategies of firms and companies as the economic system, and so on. I repeat: this does not mean that function systems are really observable; but if we want to observe them we usually come upon organizations.

Already this routine of observations is a hint at the special function of organizations to install rational addresses of accountability into function systems.

The rationality of organizations is their ability to concentrate the allocation both of goods and of observable decisions. In that manner both *reflexivity* and *rationality* install special forms of asymmetries into the function systems, asymmetries of observations and asymmetries of accountabilities, which help to make the world less complex – not the unachievable 'real' world, but the world of our observations, and for observers there does not exist any other world.

Regarding a theory of society, according to Luhmann organizations play the same role as 'persons' for action theory. For Luhmann, action is nothing that exists as the result of what an actor does or has done. But the actor is a construction of communication processes, which make themselves observable by constructing actions which can be accounted to actors (see Luhmann, 1995: 137–75). Therefore I think that critics against Luhmann, who bemoan that this theory does not adequately thematize the level of individual actors within and outside of organizations (eg, Mingers 2003), misdirect their criticisms. They demand what Luhmann tried to avoid: to repeat the everyday accounting processes rather than to observe them.

Inclusion/exclusion

The basic narration of modernity uses the *basso continuo* of equality. The invention of human beings as equally born, or the promises of political freedom; at least the universal inclusion of entire populations into the function systems, is a narrative which cannot really be doubted, but at least empirically becomes limited by organizations. In the words of Luhmann: 'By means of organizations, society lets fail the principles of freedom and equality which society cannot negate' (Luhmann 2000: 394; my translation).

Organizations are able to suspend the form of equality on several levels. Whereas (modern) society is based on a universal inclusion of populations, organizations are able to exclude and to restrict access. Universal inclusion does not mean equal inclusion, but it means that nobody can be barred from participation in economical, political, or legal affairs, be it by having too little money, no political representation, or bad chances in achieving justice (Nassehi 2002b). Organizations are authorized to exclude by their own means, arranging the relation of included and excluded persons. Whereas the latter pertains to the external relationship of organizations, a second form of suspending principles of equality is the distribution of unequal and hierarchical positions within an organization.

One should not underestimate the cultural impact of this normalization of experienced inequality for the formation of 'modern' mentalities and the legitimation of social inequality. The cultural power of organizations is to utilize their structural internal and external asymmetries to produce the forms of will, motivation, and creativity, which are decisive productive powers of modern society. Here, inside organizations, we find the paradoxical source of that form of modern subjectivity we are accustomed to accepting as an anthropological constant. The provision of a free will and the ability to limit this free will voluntarily, that is: by one's own free will. Without organizations, the free and in principal equal form of universal inclusion in function systems would not be possible.

Luhmann's sociology of organizations is one of the most empirical parts of his sociology. Luhmann was interested in the question of how organizations let a special level of order emerge, one which is not characterized by something that can be called a meso-level of social order. The great achievement of this organization theory is to correct an image of organizations imparted by the experience of stability and redundancy one can make in organizations. A desideratum of Luhmann's organization theory is to describe in more detail how the special kind of order of organizations is related to interactional and societal levels. More than Luhmann's theoretical works imply, I think that especially his distinction between different kinds of system-building in interactions, society and organizations could have a strong impact on empirical research about how these different logics of order bring forth the special modern kind of contexts within and between organizational settings.

In closing I want to emphasize that this reconstruction of Luhmann's sociology has been written with a special concern to his organization theory. Some of my reconstruction, especially regarding to the relationship of function systems and organizations, as well as the impact of organizations on social asymmetries, are more implicit than explicit in Luhmann's books and papers. This suggests that this sociology is an open project which – after Luhmann – waits for its empirical use and application. For the moment, the approach I have outlined is able to supply sociology and the sociology of organizations in particular, with key descriptions and analytical insight.

Acknowledgement

I want to thank two anonymous reviewers and Daniel Lee for their helpful comments.

References

Baecker, D. (2001) 'Why systems?' *Theory, Culture & Society*, 18: 59–74.
Bertalanffy, L. (1956) 'General system theory' *General Systems: Yearbook of the Society for the Advancemtent of General Systems Theory*, 1: 1–10.
Chernilo, D. (2002) 'The theorization of social co-ordination in differentiated societies: The theory of generalized symbolic media in Parsons, Luhmann and Habermas' *British Journal of Sociology*, 53: 431–449.
Cohen, M. D., J. G. March and J. P. Olsen (1972) 'A garbage can model of organizational choice' *Administrative Science Quarterly*, 17: 1–25.

Coleman, J. (1987) 'Microfoundations and macrosocial behavior' in J. C. Alexander, B. Giesen, R. Münch and N. J. Smelser (eds.) *The Micro-Macro-Link*. Berkeley, CA: University of California Press.

Crozier, M. and E. Friedberg (1977) *L'acteur et le système: Les contraints de l'action collective*. Paris: Le Seuil.

Cyert, R. M. and J. G. March (1963) *A Behavioral Theory of the Firm*. Englewood Cliffs, CA: Prentice-Hall.

Hechter, M. (ed.) (1983) *The Microfoundations of Macrosociology*. Philadelphia: Temple University Press.

Luhmann, N. (1973) *Zweckbegriff und Systemrationalität*. Frankfurt: Suhrkamp

Luhmann, N. (1975) *Soziologische Aufklärung* (vol. 2, third edn.). Opladen: Westdeutscher Verlag.

Luhmann, N. (1982) *The Differentiation of Society*, trans. S. Holmes and C. Larmore. New York: Columbia University Press.

Luhmann, N. (1987) 'The evolutionary differentiation between society and interaction' in J. C. Alexander, B. Giesen, R. Münch and N. J. Smelser (eds.) *The Micro-Macro-Link*. Berkeley, CA: University of California Press.

Luhmann, N. (1995) *Social Systems*, trans. J. Bednarz and D. Baecker. Stanford: Stanford University Press.

Luhmann, N. (1999) 'The concept of society' in A. Elliott (ed.) *Contemporary Social Theory*. Oxford: Blackwell.

Luhmann, N. (2000) *Organization und Entscheidung*. Opladen: Westdeutscher Verlag.

Luhmann, N. (2001) 'Notes on the project "poetry and social theory" ' *Theory, Culture & Society*, 18: 15–27.

March, J. G. and H. A. Simon (1958) *Organizations*. New York: John Wiley.

March, J. G. and J. P. Olsen (1976) *Ambiguity and Choice in Organizations*. Bergen: Universitetsforlaget.

Mingers, J. (2003) 'Observing organizations: An evaluation of Luhmann's organization theory' in T. Bakken and T. Hernes (eds.). *Autopoietic Organization Theory: Drawing on Niklas Luhmann's Social Systems Perspective*. Copenhagen: Copenhagen Business School Press.

Nassehi, A. (2002a) 'Die Organisationen der Gesellschaft: Skizze einer Organisationssoziologie in gesellschaftstheoretischer Absicht' in J. Allmendinger and T. Hinz (eds.) Organisationssoziologie. Special Issue 42, *Kölner Zeitschrift für Soziologie und Sozialpsychologie*. Opladen: Westdeutscher Verlag.

Nassehi, A. (2002b) 'Exclusion individuality or individualization by inclusion?' *Soziale Systeme*, 8: 124–135.

Nassehi, A. (2004) 'Die Theorie funktionaler Differenzierung im Horizont ihrer Kritik' *Zeitschrift für Soziologie*, 33: 98–118.

Pratt, J. and R. Zeckhauser (eds.) (1985) *Principals and Agents: The Structure of Business*. Boston: Harvard Business School Press.

Roethlisberger, F. J. and W. J. Dickson (1939) *Management and the Worker: An Account of a Research Program Conducted by the Western Electric Company*. Cambridge, MA: Harvard University Press.

Simon, H. A. (1997) *Administrative Behavior: A Study of Decision-Making Processes in Administrative Organization* (fourth edn.). New York: Free Press.

Taylor, F. W. (1911) *The Principles of Scientific Management*. New York: Harper & Row.

Weick, K. (1969) *The Social Psychology of Organizing*. Reading, MA: Addison-Wesley.

Weintraub, E. R. (1979) *Microfoundations: The Compatibility of Microeconomics and Macroeconomics*. Cambridge: Cambridge University Press.

Antagonism, contradiction, time:
Conflict and organization in Antonio Negri

Matteo Mandarini

Introduction

Antonio Negri's militant conception of organization undergoes several shifts over almost half a century of commitment to the critique of capital and to the development of a communist politics. Notwithstanding these shifts, there persists, throughout his thinking, a forceful undercutting of all homologies, objectivisms and determinisms.

Building upon the notion of 'class composition' in order to analyse the (re-)production of capitalist relations, Negri reveals how this notion short-circuits the linear, deterministic understanding of 'base' and 'superstructure', 'forces' and 'relations of production' and – at the same time – breaks the homology between workers and capital that, all too often, has been characteristic of orthodox Marxism. Negri's notion of organization affirms the *discontinuities of development* and the *antagonism of the non-homologous* because it comprehends how production is always in the service of reproduction and that elements of the latter are caught up in the former; and because capitalist organization supervenes upon a working class that is both *within* and *against* capital, i.e., is non-homologous with capitalist logic.

The working class progressively asserts itself and its forms of organization against those of capital, blocking any simple cyclicality between production and reproduction. According to Negri, capital posits the working class subject and organizes it technically (at the level of production) and politically (at the level of reproduction). Since it is posited only insofar as it can be exploited, the working class is immediately antagonistic. Thus, it refuses the capitalist form of organization and develops its own forms by way of a subversive re-appropriation of capitalist organization and the progressive development of a dialectic of separation that shatters the recuperative dialectic of capital. What we uncover in Negri is the passage from an understanding of the proletarian subject as determined by dialectical conflict with capitalism to one in which this subject is constituted in its autonomy from capitalist organization.

It is impossible to discuss the question of organization in Negri's work without providing a general outline of his political theory. I will also try to show that, for all the theoretical and practical fractures in the development of his thinking, all attempts to separate a Marxist (or Marxist-Leninist) Negri from a postmodern or, more properly, a post-structuralist one (his very own 'epistemological break') fail to grasp either his Marxism or his post-structuralism.

Operaismo

> We too saw first capitalist development and then workers' struggles. This is an error. The problem must be overturned, its terms must be changed and one must start again: at the beginning is the class struggle. At the level of socially developed capitalism, capitalist development is subordinated to workers' struggles; it comes after them and it must make the political mechanism of its production correspond to them. (Tronti, 1971c: 89)

> The history of capitalist forms is always necessarily a *reactive* history: left to its own devices capital would never abandon a regime of profit . . . *The proletariat actually invents the social and productive forms that capital will be forced to adopt in future.* (Hardt and Negri, 2000: 268)

These two passages, written at a distance of almost forty years from one another, arguably represent the single most important methodological statements of the tradition of Italian Marxism called *operaismo*.[1] They also express the central dynamic of Negri's notion of organization under capitalism. Before turning to Negri's own thinking, I believe it will be useful to outline, briefly, the foundations of *operaismo* in the work of Mario Tronti.

In the 1960s, *operaismo* concerned itself with capital's capacity for adaptation; that is, with the fundamental Marxist question of the *(re)production* of capitalist organization. In two seminal papers, 'La fabbrica e la società' and 'Il piano del capitale', Mario Tronti (1971a, 1971b) argued that capital had increasingly subsumed society as a whole, reducing it to the model of factory organization: the 'factory-society'. In the first essay, Tronti showed how capital's extension of relative surplus value extraction in the struggle against labour socializes labour and its exploitation, thereby generalizing the more advanced productive processes so that 'labour is not only *exploited* by the capitalist but is *integrated* within capital' (Tronti, 1971a: 46) as society is further subsumed by capitalist relations.

The core of this unstable dynamic is the class struggle, and the non-homologous nature of the two subjects is represented by the struggle over necessary labour, the wage and, thus, over the basis of exploitation itself. These elements vary in accordance with the changing relations of force between the subjects in struggle. The stakes are highest for capitalist organization in the immediate process of production, where capitalist and worker confront one another directly and fight their decisive battles. The success of capitalist 'rationalization' stands or falls here. Capital's task, Tronti asserted, is to recuperate and neutralize its antagonist but it can only do so by perpetually renewing the conditions of the antagonism in ever-new regimes of exploitation; whereas the worker can only hope to escape subordination to capitalist organization by shattering capitalist relations themselves. The central problem, then, is that of the reproduction of a form of organization that is perpetually re-presented by the capitalist but that rests on a relation of force: exploitation.

Over a century prior to Tronti, classical political economy had established capital's dependence upon labour and Marx had described how its expansion is predicated on the possibility of reducing the value of labour-power through revolutionizing the means of relative surplus value extraction. Capital's '*vital* necessity' (Tronti, 1971a: 57) is to integrate the worker (to *subordinate* and *organize* the worker) but this opens up a space in which the working class can intervene. The working class is *within* and *against* capital, it is the immanent critical moment – at once an '*internal component* of development and, at the same time, its *internal contradiction*' (Tronti, 1971a: 57). The irreducible contradiction of capitalist development is the working class.

In the later essay, Tronti explores the question of the reproduction of the 'total social capital' as discussed by Marx (1978, part 3), i.e., not only capital's need to reproduce the world of commodities but the need to reproduce capitalist society itself, the capitalist class and the working class. The social organization of exploitation determines a specific level of capitalist development – in the case where capital subsumes society as a whole, the whole of society operates as a moment of production. The unintended consequence of this socialization of exploitation is the socialization of antagonism. When society itself becomes the basis of production and the class struggle is socialized, capital needs increasingly to achieve a rationalization of the process of integration across all sectors of society. The relationship of capitalist and worker is re-presented on an ever larger scale as the antagonism between two, massified subjects. The working class, once posited by capital, is always the dynamic element of capital but, increasingly, it is as a class, not as fragmented individuals that its dynamism is harnessed (through rationalization, planning) and placed in the service of the advance of capital. The working class cannot allow itself to be simply included, allocated a place within development, trying – perhaps – to attenuate some of capital's harsher aspects through mediation. Mediation always resolves conflict within the unity of the mediating system; i.e., it remains systemic. Rather, the working class must realize its centrality and its own antagonistic character, demonstrating both *initiative* and capacity for *anticipation* in its own organization.

The workers' movement must present itself as the 'irrational' moment within capitalist 'rationality', both a *part* of capital but *partisan* – i.e., *non-homologous*. Once capitalist society presents itself as the subject of production itself (as social capital), the enemy of the working class is society as a whole and itself as variable capital, i.e., as subordinated partiality (Tronti, 1971b: 82–85; Žižek, 1991: 23). The task of the working class is to shatter the totality that aims to render it homologous and so reduce it to a one-sided moment of the whole by converting antagonism into a contradictory moment mediated by the totality. The working class must take contradiction back to the point of antagonism, affirming its partiality against all recuperative strategies of capitalist organization. Somewhat schematically, there are, for *operaismo*, two dominant modes of organization within capitalism: the mediatory one of capital itself, which aims to dis-organize and re-compose working-class organization in accordance with its own totalizing exigencies; and that of the working class, which attempts to dis-organize the capitalist regimentation of the working class and advance its own dynamic, antagonistic and autonomous organizational forms.

The pivotal notion adopted by *operaismo* to draw together these two modes of (dis)organization is that of *class composition*. It is in the immediate process of production that capitalist integration and working class antagonism come together. What are the relations between the capitalist organization of exploitation and the working class organization of conflict and how are they to be understood? How is the working class subject to be grasped in its autonomy and as a moment in the development of capital? How can one hold together these apparently contrasting positions? The answer is in the notion of 'class composition'. There are two aspects to class composition: one 'technical', the other 'political'. Each aspect can be relatively easily defined but the nature of their interrelation is complex and always requires specific analysis since it is only determined in struggle. *Technical class composition* is best understood in relation to the organic composition of capital (Marx, 1990a: 762ff). It is determined by the differing, historically specific valorization regimes; the varying intensity of the rate of exploitation that corresponds to the different distributions of capital into means of production employed and mass of labour necessary for their employment; changes in variable capital dictated by the different historically determined needs of the production and valorization processes; changing ratios of constant to variable capital dependent upon the conditions necessary for their reproduction, and so on. Each of these elements – and their precise interrelation – is determined by the level of struggle at any one time. Conversely, the *political composition* of the class concerns the subjective sphere of the working class: the needs, desires and co-operative relations established within the working class and the degree of unity or consistency of the class:

> The composition of the working class is not only the result of a phase or a form of capitalist development, or of the trend of constant capital under these relations; it is also a reality that is continuously modified, not only by the needs but by the traditions of struggle, the modalities of existence, of culture, etc., in other words by all those political, social and moral facts that go to determine, along with the wage structure, the structure of the relations of production of this working class. (Negri, 1979: 59–60, see also Negri, 1988b: 209)

Separate discussion of the technical and political aspects of class composition is a theoretical convenience. It is only in their interrelation that the two aspects exist in practice. What must be carefully avoided is any simple economistic derivation of class composition from the organic composition of capital.[2] The importance of the notion of class composition for Negri's analysis cannot be underestimated. If 'at the beginning is the class struggle' (Tronti, 1971c: 89), i.e., subjects in struggle, and if 'the analysis of the subject must pass by way of class composition' (Negri, 1979: 60), then the analysis of class composition is the theoretical core of any understanding of the dynamics of organization of the working *class* and of capital. Whereas capitalist recomposition of the production process can serve to break up a particular form of political composition of the workers, it is up to the workers correctly to appropriate the forms of organization deployed by capital within the workplace, which serve as the material of working class antagonism and to turn them against their intended aims, thus converting them into material for working class organization.

Class composition and the state-form

International capital reacted to the Bolshevik revolution, and the German and Italian council movements with a combination of social repression and technological restructuring that shattered those organizational forms by 'destroying the key role of the professional worker' (Negri, 1988a: 109). The repression was particularly fierce in Germany and Italy but, from the standpoint of revolutionary organization, the capitalist intervention in the composition of the class through technological restructuring in the advanced economies (particularly in the U.S. and Britain) was more important. Capital's aim was to prevent the formation of a class vanguard, which – as in Russia – could appropriate the technical conditions of capitalist production, interlinking 'spontaneous' economic demands with political ones. As we have seen, the organization-subordination of the working class within the workplace, in the immediate process of production, provides the material, the *dispositif* for the organization of the class as antagonistic subject. In pre-revolutionary Russia, for instance, a small, elite group of highly skilled workers (the *professional worker*), who understood the production process as a whole, existed alongside a large mass of unskilled workers who laboured under them. The vanguard model translates this *dispositif* into a weapon. Taylorism and Fordism were innovations designed to block this interlinking of technical composition and subversive political organization, thus preventing the proliferation of the Bolshevik vanguard model and separating the revolutionary vanguard-model of organization from the movement of the class as a whole. It was Keynes, however, who noted that reconfiguring the technical class composition in increasingly socialized terms by revolutionizing the forces of production would extend the pivotal position of an ever more homogeneous working class within capital and merely delay the political recomposition, unless capital was able to intervene in that recomposition.

Keynes pointed out that the massification of production and the resulting overproduction that characterizes the Great Crash, where a mass of goods was produced without a corresponding increase in demand, was the dual result of the strategy of technological repression and the transposition of war time industrial production to peace time. According to Keynes, overproduction crises arise when a mass of commodities is produced without sufficient levels of consumption, as this provokes a crisis of realization (and so the devaluation of capital). Moreover, where a mass of investment money exists without possible productive investment opportunities, this leads to a preference for liquidity and to an excess of money in the market that reroutes cash to unstable short-term speculative opportunities and generates a monetary flow that varies independently of production and of the real economy. In such a situation, Keynes argued, the capitalist State would have to intervene directly in consumption through expansive wage policies and in liquidity preference by control of the monetary flow (e.g., linking interest rates to the marginal efficiency of capital). The Great Crash demonstrated that the steady rise in the organic composition of capital could not co-exist with the anarchy of capital characteristic of a liberal State. The ensuing hegemony of the *mass worker* was, in conditions of rising organic composition of capital, able to bring the entire industrial machine to a standstill through struggle in any number of core sectors. Thus, State intervention and planning (of investment and production) became a technical necessity to assure that imbalances did not damage the system. Equally, the socialisation of antagonism called for a unified capitalist response, setting the collective (capitalist) good against private (capitalist) interest.

The struggle, which no longer stopped at the factory door, would need to be absorbed at the level at which it was posed by the *mass worker*. To be able to truly disorganize-reorganize-subordinate the class enemy, preventing economic demands being taken up in a revolutionary political organization, capital would have to intervene directly at the level of needs, turning them into functional components of the system. In this way demand ceased to be a merely economic category and became a political one. Economic restructuring was followed by political and juridical re-organization, the properly recuperative dialectical moment of synthesis that follows upon the antagonism that shatters the previous regime. The ensuing changes in the US and British State-forms expanded the State functions beyond those of guarantor of bourgeois liberties. The coincidence of political and economic realms had to be registered so as to neutralise all subversive potential. This eminently political aim was realised by turning the antagonistic working class into a dynamic element of advance and by reducing new needs and demands arising from the struggle to a moment of the system, i.e., to consumption (by intervening in the wage and employment levels). What had emerged as an independent variable at the heart of capital, the working class, had to be recuperated on its own terms, as a political entity, if capitalist control was to be effectively organized. We can speak of this as the effective projection of a politically constituted equilibrium once the 'natural' equilibrium of free markets and the guarantor Liberal State had broken down or, in dialectical terms, as the need to turn antagonism into contradiction. The success of this strategy rested on the integration of politics and planning within capitalist organization, i.e., merging capital with the State, and on the activation of a general social interest that would operate a synthesis within a pacific totality. Keynes' answer, however, proved to be a mystification. The reactivation of the labour theory of value through the re-establishment of the connection between money and production, without the acknowledgement of the law of exploitation that subtends it, could not co-exist with the Keynesian notion of 'effective demand'. Whereas the former is designed to excise antagonism, the latter recognizes it. This latter notion is far more prescient politically and scientifically because it recognizes the antagonism at the heart of capital and provides capital with a set of tools to impose its own form of equilibrium. The mystification is a crucial moment in the newly emergent systematic account of capitalism. This dynamic tension – if not downright contradiction – brings together the foundations of the new reality of modern capitalism: (a) the 'general interest,' which serves to link the working class to the development of capital and (b) the working class as the class antagonist.

The situation described above leads us to pose a series of questions: with the advent of the mass worker, how does the State appropriate the mechanisms of political re-composition and subsume them to the expansion of social capital? What does it mean to turn antagonism into contradiction and how is it done? Given the antagonism at the heart of capitalist organization, what totality can act as mediator? What occurs to the State-form in order for this to occur? In answering these questions, we hope to clarify Negri's theorization of capitalist organization.

The constitutionalization of labour

Negri's critique of capitalism registers the changes in the State-form. The shift to a new accumulation regime, able to comprehend the new class antagonist, calls upon a transformation in the State-form itself. With the tendency towards the merger of State and capital, when science becomes a moment of the advance of capitalist accumulation through planning, comes the emergence of what Negri calls the 'Planner' or 'Social-State.' Central to this transformation in the State is the reconfiguration of juridical theory and practice, which goes hand in hand with the analysis of the transformations of capitalism discussed in the preceding sections. The fundamental mechanism explored is that of the transformation of the material relations of society into its legal framework, i.e., the form of appropriation and organization of the relations and dynamics that compose the materiality of society into the juridical sphere. This is the *reformism of capital*: i.e., the way capital appropriates and puts to work its class antagonist without altering the class nature of society. Once again, the question is that of the (re)production of capitalist organization.

The possibility of this succeeding depends upon a point of contact being found linking materiality and legality, fact and norm, in such a way that the State actually intervenes dynamically in the configuration of society. Negri finds a clue to what this element may be in Article One of the Italian Constitution: 'Italy is a Democratic Republic, founded on work.' But, before discussing Negri's conclusion, i.e., that abstract labour is the principle of unification, the basis of the capitalist ordering (material and juridical), let us take a brief digression to uncover the material relationships that subtend it. The increasing social-ization of labour that capital produces in its response to worker antagonism requires capital to be ever vigilant, to watch over and control its negation. The socialization of labour advances as capital subsumes society and labour becomes all the more antagonistic, the more the 'social accumulation of capital abstracts the value of labour and consolidates it in the dead substance of its own power' (Negri, 1994: 60). What this conflict opens upon is an uninterrupted struggle between the capitalist class, 'the managers of abstract labour' and the working class. The latter is defined negatively in contrast to capitalist development and positively in struggle.

> The double relationship between capitalist reformism and workers' struggles . . . is born within capital. It imposes on capital a continual process of restructuring, designed to contain its negation . . . Capital is constrained to reabsorb continually the determinate levels of the workers' refusal of alienation. Capital's internal restructur-ing is at once a demand of development and a mystification of the worker's response. (Negri, 1994: 60)

This dialectic is, and can only be, 'virtuous' for capital as long as the internal restructuring, the capitalist organizational dialectic, is able to bend antagonism to the specific requirements of development; i.e., working-class conflict must become a moment of the capitalist dynamic. As Althusser argued, it is only by presuming an internal essence, a *'unique internal principle*, which is *the truth* of all those concrete determinations' (Althusser, 1990: 102), i.e., the principle of totality, that contradiction can be turned into the dynamic moment. Working class conflict must be relegated to the rank of moment of the capitalist totality, *aufgehoben* in the totality of capitalist development. But the working class per-petually presses beyond the particular stage of development of capital and, thereby, forces capital to restructure so as to reabsorb the threat. The Social or Planner-State emerges as a means to manage the increasing socialization of conflict.

It is labour that assumes the role of internal principle, the *truth* of the or-ganization of capitalist accumulation (the source of dynamism, of accumula-tion and ordering).[3] With the socialization of exploitation in the factory-society, the distinction between political and economic realms begins to dissolve. Furthermore, the rule of accumulation and the *regulation of abstract labour* to-gether become the framework for the productive and normative organization of society. This means that command over the technical composition of the class is not enough; equally important is its political composition. More precisely, command can no longer operate through the attempted divorce of these two spheres. In the factory-society, subordination-organization extends across the whole of society. By turning labour into the exclusive element of valorization investing the social totality, the Italian Constitution is able to connect the 'juridi-cal organization of power with the social structuring of power' (Negri, 1994: 65). The Social State turns abstract labour into the 'exclusive criterion' (Negri, 1994: 80) unifying the social totality, i.e., society is immediately *capitalist society*,

199

society based on the exploitation of labour. In the Social State, the maintenance and production of right operates 'as norm and plan of development' (Negri, 1994: 94). The law loses its purely formal character in order to become subordinated to administration (direct intervention, planning and construction of the social order), turning class conflict into a moment of integration through the effective management of dissent (to capitalist subordination) and consent (submission to capitalist accumulation) and turning abstract labour into the source of the self-government (the 'democracy of labour') of capitalist development and the unifying foundation for the production of law. In this way, a series of normative values finds its origin in a set of real, social forces expressed in law while the constitutionalization of (abstract) labour ensures that the integration of labour no longer stops at the gates of the factory (Negri, 1994: 80–81).

Crisis and separation

Whereas the capitalist organizational dynamic should be quite clear by now, that of the working class remains indistinct. Indeed, the entire dynamic is said to stem from a subject whose consistency is anything but determined. There is an antagonism to which capital reacts but the negation to which it responds is an indeterminate, abstract one. The negative has been the dynamic principle but the determinacy of the negative appears, so far, to be afforded by that which it negates (i.e., capitalist organization), thereby making capitalist *aufheben* possible. With a Spinozist shift, Negri returns to the question of the negative and tries to think it in its autonomy, in the substantial consistency of its organizational forms (see Spinoza, *Ethics*, I, Pro: VIII, Sc. I,: 88). He does so by considering the positivity of working class composition or the '*negative power of the positive*' (Negri, 1997: 282) in the organizational dynamic of the working class. Central to this enterprise is Negri's adoption of a dialectic that – in contrast to the recuperative Hegelian one – appears as an 'articulation of separation' (Negri, 1980: 15). This is a crucial shift in Negri's development; one that signals a deficit in his early analyses but that could only have materialized with the advance of struggle, of capitalist development and through the recomposition of working-class organization.

To clarify this passage, let us briefly return to the Planner-State. It emerges as a result of the extension of working class demands by taking those demands and making them functional to the system. This strategy works until wage demands (but not only) outstrip the capacity of capitalist organization to recuperate them. The clarion call of the mass worker is 'the wage as independent variable'; i.e., that the wage should be detached from productivity. The mass worker's attack proceeds through a progressive autonomisation of its subjective composition resulting from the increasing mobility of labour. Abstract labour assumes a subjective aspect that refuses to be allocated a place according to the demands of capitalist organization but only according to workers' desires and workers' use of circulation, i.e., refusal of the capitalist organization of the working day into work-time and non-work-time. Thus, the equality at the heart of abstract labour is advanced to block the separation between production and reproduction, resulting in increased demands upon wage and Welfare structures (see Negri, 1988b: 210ff and 1980: chapter 2). The mass worker advances the socialization of antagonism. The capitalist response is 'developed along two complementary lines – the social diffusion, decentralization of production, and the political isolation of the mass worker in the factory' (Negri, 1988b: 208). These changes (extension of production outside the factory and breakdown of the distinction between productive, unproductive and reproductive labour, etc.) set the course for the new subject of fully socialized, increasingly autonomous antagonism: the *social worker*, in whom mobility – the generalized equivalence of abstract labour – becomes a 'global potentiality which has within it that generalized social knowledge which is now an essential condition of production' (*ibid.*: 223). From the standpoint of the technical composition of the class, this is the passage from the hegemony of immediately productive material labour exploited in the factory to that of abstract and intellectual labour distributed and exploited across the social space. From the standpoint of the political composition, this new figure of antagonism is no longer *within and against* capital but *autonomous and against*. Whereas the previous form of organization stemmed from the factory regime and could be appropriated and deployed in antagonistic fashion; that of the social worker is produced immanently, in the co-operative networks of the social. This fundamentally alters the balance of the organization-subordination coupling, in which the latter preceded and was the condition of the former. With the advent of the social worker, capitalism relies upon the immanent organization of cooperating productive subjects, whose productivity it must appropriate (subordinate) *post factum*. No longer is antagonism understood as a contradiction that can be recuperated through the 'virtuous' dialectic of capitalist restructuring and as a need to serve as dynamic element for the development of capitalist organization. The working class is immediately antagonistic. It breaks with all measures of proportionality and all possibility of being reduced to labour-power, to variable capital, to a moment of development.

With the *real subsumption* (Marx, 1990b) of labour by capital and the social diffusion and decentralization of production that inserts ever new subjects into the category of productive labour, dissolving the division between work time and non-work time and shattering the rationale of mediation by time-as-measure (of value) until it reappears in the form of command, the struggle ceases to be over the wage and takes the form of a struggle for appropriation of the social product. Struggles gain momentum, crisis strikes the Planner-State's recuperative mechanisms (i.e., capital's positive dialectic) and a new State-form steps in to manage crisis: the Crisis-State. At this stage, 'no longer the dialectic that leads difference (however it may have been produced) to unity but antagonistic difference, unity against unity' (Negri, 1988a: 104, translation modified). That is not to say that capitalism is able to do without the working class – that is mere capitalist utopia – it is simply that there are no longer any 'organic links' between production and development. In other words, the labour theory of value is no longer the intrinsic rationale of development but measure must be imposed from without, by capital, upon the increasing consistency of class autonomy. The emergence of the Crisis-State marks the end of capital's positive dialectic.

Time and subjectivity

The class composition of the social worker has yet to be illustrated. Around what does class composition and struggle coalesce? In the cases of the professional worker and the mass worker, the factory formed the organizational space in which class composition emerged and gained an organizational consistency, thanks both to the technical composition of the production process as well as to the workers' struggle against its dictates and the desires and needs emerging from within the dialectics of conflict. In the case of the social worker, capital has broken down the disciplinary spaces of the factory, shifting its regime of exploitation across the social itself. This same shift in the form of capitalist command forms has been described by Deleuze as the passage from 'disciplinary' to 'control societies' (Deleuze, 1995). What, now, gives consistency to class composition, to its antagonism and in what way does capital hope to organize its forms of exploitation? Within the factory space labour can be disciplined by the overseers of the production process and by the machinery itself. The factory provides the space for antagonism to be transmuted into contradiction in the service of production (mediated further through the State's planning mechanisms). But it is less clear how this can occur in a system of diffuse production where the positive dialectic comes to an end.

At this point, the question of the origin or source of resistance also rears its head. This issue is best understood in relation to the so-called *crisis of the labour theory of value*. The labour theory of value, the immanent rationale of capitalist development, is first formulated on the basis of an analysis of primitive accumulation. Individuals 'freed' from the land and their means of production are then (formally) subsumed into the process of production and put to work. Thus, there is a set of *relatively autonomous* (from capital) subjective elements – understood through the category of 'use value' – that are not shaped by capital and that can form the ground of antagonism outside capital. Money acts as mediator between capital and its (relative) 'outside', i.e., labour. This dialectic of inside/outside formed the very rationale of capitalist development as expressed in the classical labour theory of value. In order to calculate this value quantitatively, however, it was necessary to have a common temporal unit by which labour-power could be measured as well as a means of reducing the various concrete forms of labour to a simple unit of *abstract* labour.[4] Concrete or complex labour could thus become a multiplication of simple abstract social labour. 'The various proportions in which different kinds of labour are reduced to simple labour as their unit of measurement are established by a social process that goes on behind the backs of the producers' (Marx, 1990a: 135). These determinations were immediately social.

In 'The Constitution of Time' Negri identifies how time 'measures labour in so far as it reduces it to homogenous substance, but also determines its productive power in the same form: through the multiplication of average temporal units' (Negri, 2003a: 24). This central aporia, which affirms the immediacy of the temporal determination of value and its operation of mediation, is born of Marx's failure to reduce the complex, material, qualitative elements – of struggle, of new social subjectivities, of productive innovation – to the analytic, synchronic, reversible elements of the theory of value. By highlighting the aporia, Negri shows how Marx holds the key to moving beyond Marx. The aporia is resolved by displacing the terrain upon which it operates. As we have seen, the labour theory of value demanded that labour-power existed, in some sense, outside the disciplinary regime of capital and needed to be drawn in; its form of organization determined immediately by the productive regime. One could only think of measuring value by understanding the temporal unit of measure through which it would be calculated as being formed independently of exchange value (i.e., as dependent upon a relatively independent use-value). But capital increasingly draws labour-power under its rule. It does so, initially, through the de-skilling that fuelled the generation of the mass worker, whose labour is entirely abstract but, increasingly, by subsuming the whole of social life and extending its regime of exploitation socially in the attempt to remodel its accumulation regime across the co-operative networks of the social worker and to fully accomplish the redefinition of use-value (and the circuits of [re]production generally) in terms of exchange-value. The result of this is that there is no obvious place from which a dialectical recuperation can proceed (as in the Keynesian recuperation of workers' desires through control over consumption via the wage, linking the satisfaction of desire to productivity) since the notion of a rational measure to value ends with the demise of an external unit of measure and monetary command becomes increasingly abstract – i.e., unrelated to the exchange between capital and labour-power – and tautological.[5] Equally, there is no exteriority from which resistance can stem. Antagonism must, therefore, be discovered on the same plane as real subsumption. But the end of a positive dialectic of capitalist organization also means that antagonism cannot be determined in a dialectical relation with capital. The social worker signals the death of all forms of mediation. The question is one of identifying the mechanism capital employs to organize exploitation after the end of the (recuperative) dialectic. What does 'organization' mean once the subjective composition of the new antagonistic subject asserts itself in its autonomy and separation from capital? What does Negri mean when he speaks of a dialectic of separation? The key is to be found in the return to the question of time beyond the understanding of time-as-measure.

We have noted that the real subsumption of labour by social capital means that time ceases to be understood as *measure* and becomes *substance*. It becomes 'the fabric of the whole of being, because all being is implicated in the web of social life: being is equal to *product of labour: temporal being'* (Negri, 2003a: 34). Time gains a consistency and autonomy; 'it is life itself' (*ibid.*: 35), it 'becomes the exclusive material of the construction of life'. Equally, the end of time-as-measure in real subsumption gives us time as 'collective and structural' (*ibid.*: 49) even on its own terms: as collective capital, collective labour, etc. All too often, real subsumption is interpreted as the production of indifference and, hence, as the denial of the persistence of antagonism: the utopia of total control, the complete victory of capitalist organization. But what is forgotten is that real subsumption is, nevertheless, based upon exploitation and, so, upon a constitutive antagonism.

> If it is true that the terms of exploitation are now relocated on the social terrain, and if, within this social terrain, it is no longer possible to reduce quantity and quality of exploitation, absolute surplus value and relative surplus value, to the time-measure of a 'normal' working day – *then the proletarian subject is reborn in antagonistic terms, around a radical alternative, an alternative of life-time against the time-measure of capital.* (Negri, 1988b: 219)

These two polarities, which bring to mind the distinction between *Chronos* and *Aion* of which Deleuze (1995: 162–168) spoke, differentiate radically asymmetrical organizations of time or *practices* of time. On the one hand, a *'formal* schema of manifold time, a scientific centralisation of the combination of multiple times . . . in other words a new *space* of organization of time . . . an analytic of the combination of these modalities' (Negri, 2003a: 42–43). On the other hand, the 'multiple, antagonistic, productive, constitutive' (*ibid.*: 42) time of the collective proletarian subject. Capital aims to perpetually reorganize this collective subject on the basis of a 'functional schema' (*ibid.*: 49), perpetually reconstituting a dynamic equilibrium of organization 'within the recapitulative totality' (*ibid.*: 50). With the crisis of the law of value, *mediation* no longer characterizes capitalist organization. Instead, capital aims to occupy, in advance, 'the whole of social space' (*ibid.*: 51). The 'totality is presupposed' (*ibid.*: 52) in the shape of a formal schematism of organization by which unity is recomposed and difference is subsumed through an analytic of time that aims to segment, disassemble, render reversible the constitutive times of proletarian class composition.

Negrian real subsumption, ontologically substantial and constructed in struggle, concretizes the Deleuzian plane of immanence. A political ontology of time, a politics of immanence or a *biopolitics*[6] of endogenous antagonism emerges in which a 'political precept' (*ibid.*: 43) of the organization of command is counterpoised to a 'political precept' of multiple practices of time, a 'new proletarian practice of time' (*ibid.*: 21). Here, time is 'interior to class composition . . . the motor of its very existence and of its specific configuration' (*ibid.*: 35). We witness, here, the gradual transformation of social labour power from being a *relatively* independent variable to *'independence tout court'* (Negri, 1988b: 221), organized around the exacerbation of abstract labour's subjectification of *mobility* and understood as a practice of time. As social labour extends across the entire day, existing as '*flow and circulation within time*' (*ibid.*: 218) – and comprising '*the relation between production time and reproduction time, as a single whole*' (*ibid.*: 219) – capital aims to impose time-as-measure against '*the conception of working-class freedom over the temporal span of life*' (*ibid.*). In effect, the crisis – of the mechanisms of mediation, of measure, of the positive dialectic – that real subsumption reveals leaves us with two distinct subjects, each one subjectivised 'around its own conception of time, and a temporal constitution of its own' (*ibid.*: 220). This new class composition of the working class, no longer reducible to a variable part of capital, is able to act 'across the entire span of the working day' (*ibid.*: 224), which now comprises production time and reproduction time. We find ourselves with a labour-power that is entirely social and subjective. Its organization is no longer pre-determined by the composition of capital because there is no longer any 'natural rate' between capitalist profit and wage. It is truly *immeasurable* as the subjective consistency of needs and desires augments its autonomy. No longer do we have a positive dialectic of recuperation of antagonism, then, but an endogenous dialectic of separation.

Beyond the dialectic?

> In the 60s the fundamental problem, for those who operated within materialism and critically reinterpreted Marxism, was that of pitting historical materialism against the dialectic. The problem that is posed, now, in continuing this battle, is to oppose the prospective of absolute immanence to all transcendentalisms. (Negri, forthcoming)

The boldness of some of Negri's statements can sometimes be misleading. In this passage, Negri somewhat schematically situates the whole of his work squarely against 'the dialectic' and affirms, instead, 'historical materialism' or 'absolute immanence'. The analysis of his work until the early 1980s provided above problematises the categorical nature of this claim by uncovering the way in which he champions a variety of dialectics.

We can explain the schematic, if not the ambiguous nature of such statements, by noting that what Negri attacks is simply the commonly understood notion of the dialectic, which proceeds through the notion of *Aufheben*, 'supersession', 'sublation' or, more formally, 'synthesis' in which oppositions are 'integrated' into a 'reasonable totality' (Miller, 1977: x) or into 'the state of annulment [as] an absolute' (Lukács, 1975: 276). We have referred to this dialectic as the *recuperative* or *positive* (capitalist or bourgeois) dialectic, in which contradiction is always subsumed in an integrating totality. Against this, Negri advances two distinct notions of dialectics, both of which emphasize antagonism since the dynamic is all on the side of the negative and there is no possible moment – other than in mystified form – for rest in a pacific totality. These dialectics are resistant to all homologies, socialist or capitalist, which seek resolution to the antagonism either in the sublation of one or the other side by a common demand – profitability, productivity – that presupposes a fundamental rational unity (as exemplified in the notion of the worker as merely an aspect of capital or in Lenin's idea that Soviets and Fordism could co-exist under communism). The decisive importance of periodization should, now, be stressed. All attempts to make general, 'supra-historical' statements (to borrow Marx's phrase) concerning the efficacy or otherwise of 'the dialectic' or any other methodological criterion for that matter, fails to grasp the specificity, the materiality of the class struggle. The problem of dialectics is not (or is not only) an academic one. Not only should it be recognized that 'every metaphysic is in some way a political ontology' but also that the continuing validity of such a metaphysic 'is linked to the power of the *political dispositif implicit* in the ontology' (Negri, forthcoming), i.e., to the relations of force that structure reality. The validity or otherwise of dialectics and the form that a possible dialectics takes must always be measured against the concrete reality of subjects in struggle. As Negri puts it:

> when a new configuration of the social fabric appears, we will also have a change in the epistemological prospective . . . *Thus, every time the historical context changes the method also changes.* (Negri, 2003c: 67)

Nevertheless, Negri's notion of a *dialectic of separation* is highly paradoxical. Can one truly speak of dialectics when the two subjects in struggle are conceived of as absolutely separate? The *absoluteness* of this separation is especially problematic when it comes to defining capital, which, Negri argues, is increasingly parasitic on labour but no less so with reference to labour, as Negri notes in his comments on the escalating violence of capital's relation to labour. Also, can a *dialectic* exist with the demise of mediation? The problematic nature of Negri's position did not escape him (Negri, 2003a: 131–132) but formed an important part of his thought throughout the 1980s. Although it is beyond the scope of this chapter to consider the course this question took during those years, examination of Negri's latest works, including the collaborations with Michael Hardt, points to a reconfiguration of the notion of organization stemming directly from the answers to these questions developed through the engagement with thinkers such as Deleuze, Guattari and Foucault (see, for example, Hardt and Negri, 1994: 309).

In the later work, Negri's analysis advances the definition of immanent forms of control and resistance, which – in the collaborative work with Michael Hardt – come under the headings of Empire and Multitude.

Empire

Once again, at the heart of the analysis of this new transformation in the capitalist accumulation regime, we find the composition of the proletarian subject. Before turning to this question, we should note the subtle shift in Negri's terminology. This 'shift' is both a substantial marker of discontinuity and a return to some of his concerns of three decades ago. In the wake of the analyses of the relationship between legal and constitutional theory, the State and the economy (discussed above), Negri redefines 'sovereignty' in capitalist societies as: 'the control over the reproduction of capital, that is, the command over the proportions between the forces (workers and bosses, proletariat and bourgeoisie, multitudes and Imperial monarchy) that constitutes it' (Negri, 2003c: 36).

This clearly recalls the 1964 essay, 'Labour in the Constitution', in which Negri shows how the development of capitalist organization draws ever closer the notions of the State (sovereignty) and capital. This process of combination or unification intensifies with the development of capitalist relations. Indeed, 'in real subsumption, command is no longer something added from outside the process of exploitation but is something that organizes it directly' (Negri, 2003c: 51). As the nation state's ability to regulate the (re)production of capital diminished, sovereignty migrated to another level. In the period following 1968, capital was forced to restructure in order to break the workers' (and anti-colonial and anti-imperialist) struggles that had eroded its profit rate and threatened its regime of accumulation. This period was characterized by massive changes in the production process and, hence, in the technical composition of the class: downsizing of large-scale industry in the 'advanced' economies, delocalization (to countries with lower labour-costs), outsourcing, tertiarization, and *regulation along multinational lines*, deploying a whole set of apparatuses for capitalist accumulation across the entirety of an increasingly internationalized social and productive space. As we noted in the discussion of the social worker, capital was faced with a working class subjectivity that was no longer determined immediately by itself (unlike the mass worker within the confines of the factory) and whose organization was no longer something brought to labour from the outside, by capital, but was inherent in labour itself: today, '*co-operation is completely immanent to the labouring activity itself*' (Hardt and Negri, 2000: 294). Progressively, capital's operation of restructuring aimed to draw ever larger numbers of this new, socialized and co-operative labouring subject under its rule, extending exploitation across the social totality internationally. This process of erosion of the sovereignty of the nation state as the space of accumulation continued with the shift to dollar inconvertibility (1971), the first oil crisis (1973) and the Anti-Ballistic Missile treaty (1972). These changes attacked some of the central pillars of the modern conception of sovereignty; namely, the ability to coin money and the monopoly of force, which includes the right to go to war. Restructuring followed upon struggle. As we have seen, capital's response to such struggles was to decentralize production and to raise the mobility of capital and the (relative) mobility of workers. But the corollary of this was that the nation state could no longer regulate the flows by which it was now exceeded. The relative decline of the sovereign power of nation states does not mean that they have become redundant (political controls and regulations persist) but that sovereignty has changed its form. 'Empire' is the name that Hardt and Negri give to the political organization of global capital and global sovereignty.

Empire is understood on the model of the mixed constitution that Polybius provides in his discussion of the Roman Empire, where the three principal forms of government – Monarchy, Aristocracy and Democracy – are brought together. The modern-day successors to these forms are represented by the IMF, World Bank, WTO, NATO (Monarchy); trans-national capital (Aristocracy); and nation states and NGOs (Democracy). This model of global sovereignty allows for a modulated and non-univocal understanding of the lines and operations of capitalist organization and points to the underlying changes in the material organization discussed above. It presupposes that capitalist relations have expanded 'to subsume all aspects of social production and reproduction, the entire realm of life' (Hardt and Negri, 2000: 275). This *total subsumption* expresses the material conditions grounding the claim that, in Empire, there is no longer an outside. Capital subsumes the whole of social life and the emerging juridical constitution watches over the process, supervising and regulating the relations at a global level. The escalating subsumption of labour and society leaves us with no outside to capital, so that even nationally differentiated accumulation regimes are situated within a fully integrated, modulated and flexible space of reproduction.

This means that all borders are internal to real subsumption; thus, *the organization of control and of antagonism can only be conceived immanently*. 'Not only the political transcendental but also the transcendental as such has ceased to determine measure' (Hardt and Negri, 2000: 354–355). In fact, such a 'pure field of immanence' (Hardt and Negri, 2000: 354) can only be immeasurable – outside and beyond measure. For, as we have seen, with the end of all natural rates, measure can only be *enforced*. Consequently, Negri later describes Empire as a *'non-place'* (Negri, 2003c: 37), lacking both outside and centre, existing, as he writes with Hardt, 'outside of every preconstituted measure' (Hardt and Negri, 2000: 355). 'Empire constitutes the ontological fabric in which all relations of power are woven together' (Hardt and Negri, 2000: 354). Its operations are biopolitical. While Hardt and Negri borrow from Deleuze, Guattari and Foucault, they also reconfirm the fundamental theses of *operaismo*, arguing that the ontological fabric of the Imperial order is not *constitutive* but *constituted*; i.e., 'resistance is actually prior to power' (Hardt and Negri, 2000: 360). What Empire reveals is the absolute immanence of the *immeasurable* social relations of co-operation, of the subjective antagonist of the age of Empire, i.e., the multitude.

Talk of 'sovereignty' marks a discontinuity in Negri's thought as well. The genealogy of the multitude assumes the end of the nation state as *the* space of capitalist accumulation and the end of the transcendental function of the State as that point from which 'the people' is defined (as theorized in modern political thought from Hobbes to Hegel and beyond). The multitude is defined as that *'reality that remains* once the concept of the people is freed from transcendence' (Negri, 2003c: 129). Despite the fact that in 'the concept of the multitude, there is an incomplete, imperfect, superimposition of a legal-political concept and a political-economic concept' (Negri, 2003d: 98–99), the discontinuity marked by the shift to a concern with sovereignty (as defined in Negri, 2003c: 36) is one that allows for the comprehension of the 'universality of work as a constituent function of the social and the political' (Negri, 2003d: 99). From the standpoint of Empire, the definition of the multitude signals the point at which the integration of politics and economics has been completed, at which real subsumption is realized absolutely.

The multitude, or, the immanent organization of antagonism

A full-length account of the multitude would require detailed discussion of immaterial labour; that is, of the informationalisation or computerisation of labour practices in industrial production as well as the analytical, symbolic functions and affective forms of labour in the tertiary (or service) sectors of the economy. Suffice it to say, here, that when the computer becomes the central tool of production, whether of immaterial or material goods, it becomes the 'universal tool' that homogenizes labouring processes. In this way, 'labour tends toward the position of abstract labour' (Hardt and Negri, 2000: 292).[7] The need to comment on the political ontology of the multitude (i.e., on the notion of immanent organization of the immeasurable subject of Empire); on the question of the dialectic and on the question of Empire post-9/11 is also pressing.

As we have seen, the increasing autonomization, the independence *tout court* of the antagonistic subject, passes through a subjective appropriation of a time beyond measure, of the immeasurable as an alternative to the dead-time of capitalist measure. The problem was that of:

> dissolving objective temporality and drawing it into the subject, turning temporality into the stage within which the subject constructed the world . . . [that] disengages the conception of value-time from measure and its structures . . . *proposing a new way of living and enjoying time.* (Negri, 2003c: 147)

The question posed is that of the practical construction of an alternative organization of time that is able to re-appropriate, in subversive form, the subjectivation processes of control within Empire. The precondition for this lies in the quality of the subjective composition of the labouring subject, of the multitude, whose labour is increasingly immaterial, relational and collective. The extreme level of socialization of labour – the immanence of the collective itself to the productive labour of the multitude – means that production of goods is simultaneously production of (collective) subjectivity, of commonality itself. Certainly, Empire extends its forms of control over this immanent productivity – of goods, of subjectivity, of the common – and produces subjectivities but it does so from within a relation by which it is limited. The relations of power – capital/labour, Empire/multitude – can be tipped towards sovereign power if the relations of force are favourable. But the relation itself is fundamental. Imperial organization finds an *obstacle* in the multitude and a *limit* in the very relation of exploitation that subtends it. After all, what is capitalism without the relation of exploitation? What is Imperial sovereignty without a multitude to govern? In contrast, the multitude has no need of sovereign power that produces only control. Returning briefly to the question of dialectics, it is clear that there is no homology, no chance of a resolution from the standpoint of sovereign power. The antagonism cannot be removed if Empire is to persist, whereas the multitude has no need of a dialectical relation to Empire. The multitude produces; it constructs and organizes common-being across the immeasurable plane of immanence (Negri, 2003c: 137).

We cannot pretend that this is a wholly satisfying conclusion to the problem of dialectics. It is not. At least one niggling question remains: if the dynamic moves from the side of antagonism – that is, from the side of negation – can one do without a form of dialectics? Perhaps a more satisfactory resolution would move from a consideration of the question of the critique of the negative and the notion of positive – non-dialectical – differenc/tiation in the work of Deleuze (see Deleuze, 1994, especially chapters 4 and 5) and the question of multiplicities in Deleuze and Guattari (Deleuze and Guattari, 1988, especially chapter 10). Whether this can be combined with a concrete notion of antagonism remains to be seen. We can appreciate how this might work by considering Negri's call for resistance as a creative and constructive exodus from relations of sovereignty (Negri, 2003d: 96–97), which affirms the necessity for the multitude 'to take leave of domination, to take leave of the Power of the State and of every transcendental illusion' (Negri, 2003b: 259–260ff). Nevertheless, we are faced with the same problem. On the one hand, there is the positing of an absolute separation of the multitude, already independent *tout court* in the case of the social worker. On the other, Negri admits that he still does not feel able to speak of fully liberated labour. In fact, capital, in its Imperial form, remains parasitical upon the co-operative multitudes and its forms of control can be equally brutal and are even more totalizing than those deployed by the earlier, disciplinary accumulation regimes. The multitude is, thus, antagonistic to the order of reasons of Empire. The problem is to think the multitude as autonomous and antagonistic without thinking that antagonism as a *negation* of Imperial power but as one that undercuts the relation. As we have seen, sovereignty, capital, in contrast to the multitude, is dependent upon a structuring, antagonistic relation. By severing the relation through an alternative subjectivization, could capital, Empire be cut free? But have we not seen capital violently re-impose measure, control despite the end of natural rates? If so, if the multitude is not able to directly attack the structures of Imperial command, is there a risk that the relation is perpetually, violently re-established? Although these indications may serve towards a resolution, we, as yet, have to leave this problem open.

The need to re-examine the Imperial tendency post-9/11 is pertinent owing to claims that, on the one hand, in the wake of the attacks on the Twin Towers and the Pentagon, 'nothing will be the same again'. At the same time as, on the other hand, the US response to the attacks, in Afghanistan and, to an even greater extent, in Iraq, led many to argue that imperialism was not dead and that, therefore, one of the fundamental presuppositions for Empire, of *Empire*, had been disproved by the facts (see, for example, many of the articles in Balakrishnan, 2003). Of course, it is not enough to point out that these statements are in apparent contradiction to confirm the analysis made by Hardt and Negri. But surely, the US failure in Iraq and its return to the UN to legitimize its occupation indicates that not even the United States is capable of acting as a sovereign power ruling over the global order. Moreover, it should not be forgotten that Hardt and Negri's discourse on Empire aims to uncover certain tendencies. This does not exclude the possibility that counter-tendencies will block the full expression of Imperial tendencies; nor does it deny various intra-tendencies or attempts by different elements of the Imperial complex (Monarchical, Aristocratic and Democratic) to gain an ascendancy in the determination of Imperial command. For example, Negri has spoken of the Bush administration as carrying out a monarchical coup within Empire. But aside from questions that are – at least partly – empirical, that of war is central to a comprehension of the process of Imperial formation. Negri insists that 'it is through war that the material forces that constitute Empire, that determine the hierarchies and the internal circulation of powers, come to light' (Negri, 2003c: 154; see also Hardt & Negri, 2004, pt. 1).

Thus, the doctrine of pre-emptive war 'is not only a military doctrine but a constituent strategy of Empire' (Negri, 2003e: 127) and what we are experiencing is an '*ordering Imperial war*' (Negri, 2003c: 155). This interpretation sees war no longer as the extension of politics but as the foundation of Imperial politics, ordering new national spaces, hierarchies and new legal regulations. There is no space of mediation for the recuperation of the multitude, nor can it be defeated (without an Imperial implosion). War deploys strategies of control and legal tribunals completely unrelated to the old international legal order. It produces subjects, enemies, the structuring relation, perpetually. Negri reminds us: 'It is their war; we are left with resistance and exodus' (2003c: 156). But we are left with the question, given this new strategy of infinite war as a constituent strategy constantly re-establishing the antagonistic relation, if exodus, however creative and innovative it may be, is sufficient without an attack on Imperial command itself.

Acknowledgements

Thanks to Julian Reid, Timothy Murphy and Tariq Goddard for comments on early drafts of this chapter. Particular thanks to Alberto Toscano for making comments on several drafts of this chapter, to Campbell Jones for his support and for the final cuts to what was a far too lengthy chapter and to Juliet Rufford for her continuing efforts to tighten up my writing.

Notes

1 *Operaismo* or 'workerism' has its origin in the journal *Quaderni Rossi* (1961–1963), founded by Mario Tronti and Raniero Panzieri and including, amongst others, Antonio Negri, Romano Alquati and Alberto Asor Rosa. For more on *operaismo* see Balestrini and Moroni (1997), Borio, Pozzi and Roggero (2002), Boutang (1989) and Wright (2002).
2 Negri shows how it is precisely by grasping the notion of class composition that one avoids economism. Class composition highlights the fact that there is no pure terrain of capitalist action, no place where capital is fully able to determine labour-power and from which one could simply 'read off' working class behaviour, because antagonism traverses the entire system. Thus, the relation between technical and political class composition is not one between determining and determined elements. There is no linearity, no determinism here.
3 Recognition of this can be traced back to Hegel (1977: 117–119 and 1991: §189ff) and lies at the heart of the influential exegeses of Kojève (1980: 48ff), Hyppolite (1974: 174–77 and 1969: 165–7), Lukács (1975: 326ff) and Löwith (1991: 265–70).
4 That is, labour understood in terms of its 'abstract quality of being human labour' (Marx 1990a: 150), determined by the '*social configuration* in which the individual worker exists' (1990b: 1052).
5 Thus, money loses its rationale and the mediatory functions by which it advanced the socialisation of production. For at this level of development capitalist production can only advance on the basis of fully socialized labour. Money as rationale is redundant, which does not mean that its effects cease but that it returns in the form of command.
6 All too often, in Foucault the notion of 'biopolitics' is understood as an aspect of (capitalist) command rather than as a practice of subversion (Foucault, 1998, chapter V). However, it is precisely thanks to Foucault's heterogeneous conception of the nature of power and resistance, of the impossibility of a homogeneous continuum of command, that Negri can develop a more productive and antagonistic conception of biopolitics. For more on this concept post-Foucault, see Negri (2003b; 2003d: 78–85) and *Multitudes* (2000).
7 See also Hardt and Negri (2000, chapter 3.4), Negri (2003d: 67–87), Lazzarato (1996; 1997), Virno (1994; 1996; 2004) and Marazzi's groundbreaking explorations of what he terms the 'linguistic turn' in the economy (Marazzi, 1999; 2002).

References

Althusser, L. (1990) 'Contradiction and overdetermination' in *For Marx*, trans. B. Brewster. London: Verso.
Balakrishnan, G. (ed.) (2003) *Debating Empire*. London: Verso.
Balestrini, N. and P. Moroni (1997) *L'orda d'oro*. Milan: Uniervsale Economica Feltrinelli.
Berardi, F. (1998) *La nefasta utopia di Potere operaio*. Rome: DeriveApprodi.
Borio, G., F. Pozzi and G. Roggero (eds.) (2002) *Futuro Anteriore: Dai 'Quaderni Rossi' ai movimenti globali: Ricchezze e limiti dell'operaismo Italiano*. Rome: DeriveApprodi.
Deleuze, G. (1994) *Difference and Repetition*, trans. P. Patton. London: Athlone.
Deleuze, G. (1995) 'Postcript on the societies of control' in *Negotiations, 1972–1990*, trans. M. Joughin. New York: Columbia University Press.
Deleuze, G. and F. Guattari (1988) *A Thousand Plateaus*, trans. B. Massumi. London: Athlone.
Foucault, M. (1998) *The History of Sexuality 1: The Will to Knowledge*, trans. R. Hurley. London: Penguin.
Hardt, M. and A. Negri (1994) *The Labor of Dionysus*. Minneapolis: University of Minnesota Press.
Hardt, M. and A. Negri (2000) *Empire*. Cambridge, MA: Harvard University Press.
Hardt, M. and A. Negri (2004) *Multitude: War and Democracy in the Age of Empire*. New York: Penguin.

Hegel, G. W. F. (1977) *The Phenomenology of Spirit*, trans. A. V. Miller. Oxford: Oxford University Press.

Hegel, G. W. F. (1991) *Elements of the Philosophy of Right*. Cambridge: Cambridge University Press.

Hyppolite, J. (1969) 'The human situation in the Hegelian phenomenology' in *Studies on Marx and Hegel*, trans J. O'Neil. New York: Basic Books.

Hyppolite, J. (1974) *Genesis and Structure of Hegel's* Phenomenology of Spirit, trans. S. Cherniak and J. Heckman. Evanston, IL: Northwestern University Press.

Kojève, A. (1980) *Introduction to the Reading of Hegel*, trans. J. J. Nichols. New York: Cornell Paperbacks.

Lazzarato, M. (1996) 'Immaterial labour' in M. Hardt and P. Virno (eds.) *Radical Thought in Italy*. Minneapolis: University of Minnesota Press.

Lazzarato, M. (1997) *Lavoro Immateriale*. Verona: Ombre Corte.

Löwith, K. (1991) *From Hegel to Nietzsche*, trans. D. E. Green. New York: Colombia University Press.

Lukács, G. (1975) *The Young Hegel*, trans. R. Livingstone. London: Merlin.

Marazzi, C. (1999) *Il posto dei calzini: La svolta linguistica dell'economia e i suoi effetti sulla politica*. Torino: Bollati Boringhieri.

Marazzi, C. (2002) *Capitale e linguaggio*. Rome: DeriveApprodi.

Marx, K. (1978) *Capital Vol. II*, trans. D. Fernbach. London: Penguin.

Marx, K. (1990a) *Capital Vol. I*, trans. Ben Fowkes. London: Penguin.

Marx, K. (1990b) 'Results of the immediate process of production' in *Capital Vol. I*, trans. Ben Fowkes. London: Penguin.

Miller, A. V. (1977) 'Foreward' to G. W. F. Hegel *The Phenomenology of Spirit*, trans. A. V. Miller. Oxford: Oxford University Press.

Moulier Boutang, Y. (1989) 'Introduction' in A. Negri *The Politics of Subversion: A Manifesto for the Twenty-First Century*. Cambridge: Polity.

Multitudes (2000) 'Biopolitiques et biopouvoir', vol. 1.

Negri, A. (1979) *Dall'operaio massa all'operaio sociale*. Milan: Multhipla Edizioni.

Negri, A. (1980) *Il comunismo e la guerra*. Milan: Giangiacomo Feltrinelli Editore.

Negri, A. (1988a) 'Crisis of the planner-state' in *Revolution Retrieved*. London: Red Notes.

Negri, A. (1988b) 'Archaeology and project: The mass worker and the social worker' in *Revolution Retrieved*. London: Red Notes.

Negri, A. (1994) 'Labor in the constitution' in M. Hardt and A. Negri, *The Labor of Dionysus*. Minneapolis: University of Minnesota Press.

Negri, A. (1996) 'Twenty theses on Marx: Interpretation of the class situation today' in S. Makdisi, C. Casarino and R. E. Karl (eds.) *Marxism Beyond Marxism*. New York: Routledge.

Negri, A. (1997) 'Il dominio e il sabotaggio' in *I libri del rogo*. Rome: Castelvecchi Editoria & Comunicazione.

Negri, A. (2003a) 'The constitution of time' in *Time for Revolution*, trans. M. Mandarini. London: Continuum.

Negri, A. (2003b) 'Kairòs, alma venus, multitudo' in *Time for Revolution*, trans. M. Mandarini. London: Continuum.

Negri, A. (2003c) *Guide: Cinque lezioni su Impero e dintorni*. Milan: Raffaello Cortina Editore.

Negri, A. (2003d) 'Il contro-impero attacca' in *L'Europa e l'Impero*. Rome: Manifestolibri.

Negri, A. (2003e) 'L'ordine della guerra' in *L'Europa e l'Impero*. Rome: Manifestolibri.

Negri, A. (forthcoming) 'Postface to the English Edition' in *The Political Descartes: Concerning the Reasonable Ideology*, trans. M. Mandarini and A. Toscano. London: Verso.

Spinoza, B. (1994) 'The Ethics' in *A Spinoza Reader*, ed. and trans. E. Curley. Princeton, NJ: Princeton University Press.

Tronti, M. (1971a) 'La fabbrica e la società' in *Operai e capitale*. Torino: Giulio Einaudi Editore.

Tronti, M. (1971b) 'Il piano del capitale' in *Operai e capitale*. Torino: Giulio Einaudi Editore. English translation: http://geocities.com/cordobakaf/tronti_social_capital.html.

Tronti, M. (1971c) 'Lenin in Inghilterra' in *Operai e capitale*. Torino: Giulio Einaudi Editore. English translation: http://geocities.com/cordobakaf/tronti_england.html.

Virno, P. (1996) 'Notes on the "general intellect"' in S. Makdisi, C. Casarino and R. E. Karl (eds.) *Marxism Beyond Marxism*. New York: Routledge.
Virno, P. (2004) *A Grammar of the Multitude*. New York: Semiotext(e).
Wright, S. (2002) *Storming Heaven: Class Composition and Struggle in Italian Autonomist Marxism*. London: Pluto.
Žižek, S. (1991) *The Sublime Object of Ideology*. London: Verso.

Online resources

There are numerous online resources for material on Negri and *operaismo*. This is just a selection:

http://www.endpage.com/
http://geocities.com/cordobakaf/
http://www.emery.archive.mcmail.com/

The Theatre of Measurement: Michel Serres

Steven D. Brown

Introduction

The philosopher and historian of science, Michel Serres, has an established reputation within several fields. Across the humanities, Serres is known as the author of critical studies which situate authors such as Emile Zola, Jules Verne or La Fontaine in relation to a broader cultural and scientific field. His audacious claim that the arts prefigure science, or rather that the work of art may in some sense *translate* between cultural problematics and scientific formalizations has helped to renew an entire field of studies in 'Literature and Science' (see in particular the journal *Configurations*). Conversely, in Science and Technology Studies (STS), Serres' notion of *translation* is recognised as one of wellsprings of Actor-Network Theory (ANT). As such, his work has served as an essential resource for theorists looking to resituate science as part of the hybrid networks which cut across the division between politics and nature. Finally, within the heterogeneous literature on Information Systems, Serres is recognized as offering a distinctive account of *information* and *communication* and of the globalization of 'message bearing systems'. His beautifully illustrated text *Angels: A Modern Myth* stands alongside contemporary work by Pierre Levy and Geoffrey Bowker.

What then of organization theory? In recent years a steady stream of 'French thinkers' such as Foucault, Lyotard, Derrida and Deleuze have all been co-opted into the field, sometimes under the overly broad rubric of 'the postmodern', but more usually as touchstones which enable a speaking in the name of 'critique' (see the adroit summary by Jones, 2004 on the case of the reception of Derrida). According to Sørensen (in this volume), Serres is next in line. That remains to be seen. But what is clear is that the co-option of Serres presents particular challenges. Whilst the Foucauldian or Deleuzian *oeuvre* defies ready summary, there are at least clear points of division and routinely established categories in the work with which to engage, along with a burgeoning secondary literature. The Serresian *oeuvre*, by contrast, varies wildly in terms of project, technique, style, method and content. What to make of a writer who authorizes himself to veer between topics as diverse as the Diogenes' encounter with Alexander the Great, the Columbia space shuttle disaster, the origins of geometry, the operation of

Charles de Gaulle airport, rats meals, the foundation of Rome, and the work of Hergé (creator of Tin Tin)? A writer whose best known work in English resembles a coffee-table book and whose recent work in France includes starring in a series of television advertisements for a telecom company?

William Paulson, responsible for some of the English translations of Serres' work, and one of his most astute Anglophone commentators, sums up the difficulty of the reception of Serres in the following way (albeit within the English literature graduate school model):

> Michel Serres is no ticket to the Ph.D.-and-tenure express: if you don't know his work, no one will flunk you on general examinations or turn down your manuscript because you haven't 'situated yourself' with respect to his 'problematic', and if you study him, you won't find an applicable method that you can use in turning out your own dissertation and books on schedule. In the present state of the disciplines, Serres is *extracurricular*: you have to read him on your own time. (Paulson, 1997: 1)

A given text by Serres can appear to be endowed with such a radical specificity, a narrowed and focussed ambition, that it is difficult to see what – if anything – could be extracted and put into general circulation. *Detachment* (Serres, 1989), for example, consists of four meditative essays that read almost as mini-novellas, organized under the headings 'Farmer', 'Sailor', 'Wanderer', 'Friar', which encompass questions of history, epistemology, cartography and 'objectivity'. There is certainly nothing like a 'model' to be found here, as that term is usually understood. Nor is there anything that conforms especially to expected notions of 'method' (but note Serres' fierce rejection of such a charge in his conversations with Bruno Latour, 1995). Much as one might be carried away with the seductive power of the homologies, analogies and unexpected, almost fantastical juxtapositions that Serres works through (here, rats steal from the farmer's table, and over there, the receiver extracts a surplus from the sender's message), it is difficult to know *just what to do with Serres* when the cover closes back on the book.

My aim then in this chapter is not to construct preferred readings or strategies that make Serres 'relevant' for the thinking of organization, nor to provide a comprehensive overview of his work (see, however, attempts by Abbas, 2005; Assad, 1999; Brown, 2002, 2004; Latour, 1987; Serres and Latour, 1995). Rather I will demonstrate, through a reading of a single piece by Serres, how some of the lines of thought developed in that text are necessarily entangled with and refracted through some of Serres' major works.

General background

Before this, some brief background. Michel Serres is author of over thirty books, an erratic selection of which has been translated into English (I will make reference principally to translated work). He is nominally counted as a philosopher of science, but has worked for the major part of his career in departments

216

of history and of literature, in North America as well as France. Serres was trained under the great French epistemologist Gaston Bachelard, under whom he completed a doctorate on Leibniz. At first glance, Serres' early work, as represented in the *Hermes* series, might be mistaken as operating within orthodox history of ideas. *Hermes I: La Communication*, for instance, is built around linked essays on mathematics, communication theory and classical sources such as Descartes. In these texts, however, Serres demonstrates a complete disregard for existing epistemic demarcations. He refuses both established demarcations, notably that of 'scientificity' and 'non-science', and the infamous 'breaks' or 'ruptures' in the progress of knowledge that characterize the Bachelard approach. The Hermes texts are primarily explorations of a complex cartography of knowledge, where the formal and the informal, the scientific and the cultural become intertwined.

In subsequent work, Serres shifts away from critical interrogation of canonical texts towards a more open, and often highly stylized, exploration of problematics that subtend both the human and the exact sciences. *Rome* (Serres, 1991), for instance, interrogates the notion of 'foundation' as it appears in Livy's classical description of the founding of the Imperial City. Serres approach is to subject Livy's account to the experimental application of a series of concepts that are marked by biology and physics (notably complexity science). Thus Serres treats founding as an operation performed on a 'multiplicity' that exists between several threshold states ('white' and 'black'). He seeks the criterion which will denote passages between these states and, moreover, analyses the extent to which these transformations may be seen as reversible or not. Yet despite this apparent subjection of the historical to what appears to be an explanatory grid with aspirations of scientificity, Serres' espoused intention is to contribute to a distinctly anthropological question: what is social order and how is it rendered durable? His approach remains consistent with the earlier *Hermes* texts – read culture 'scientifically' and read science 'culturally'.

This formula, which amounts to a demand continuously to cross disciplinary and epistemic faultlines, has been pushed yet further in Serres' work of the past fifteen years. *Troubadour of Knowledge* (Serres, 1997), for instance, is loosely organized around the relationship of pedagogy to 'wisdom' in cultures where the latter is seen as the stakes in an increasingly polarised split between technology and myth. In a sparsely structured text which tends towards the aphoristic, Serres attempts to perform 'instruction' as a matter of taking direction from every point of the epistemic compass, with rather mixed results. More ambitious still is *Angels: A Modern Myth* (Serres, 1995a), which proposes to analyse the globalization of information communication technologies by pushing the metaphor of the angelic messenger to its very limits. Through a mixture of sumptuously presented visual images framed with gnomic statements, themselves interleaved with an invented dialogue between two characters working at Charles de Gaulle airport, Serres proposes a formative 'philosophy of prepositions' where mediation and connection rather than substantives dominate.

217

Serres is currently one of the forty 'les immortels' of the Academie Francaise. His writing – which now currently spans 1968 to 2004 – shows little sign of diminishing in output. It is perhaps fair to say that in France, despite coming from the tail end of the generation of thinkers that includes Derrida and Deleuze (Serres worked for a time with Foucault at Clermont-Ferrand), Serres has never really acquired the status of his peers, although a book of dialogues with Bruno Latour published in the early 1990s went some way towards a public explication of his work. Amongst the Anglophone world, both the delay and curiosity in choice of works in translation has not really helped to establish Serres as a name. And as Paulson succinctly puts it 'the real problem with the translations is that they are usually not reviewed in the most visible or influential publications, and they are not exactly flying out of the bookstores' (2000: 215).

A history of scientific thought

The piece which will serve as the basis of discussion is drawn from a collection edited by Serres in 1989 (Serres, 1995b). The publication is drawn from an ambitious project, aiming at nothing less than restoration of the history of science as a discipline to a general readership. The ambition is to 'restore depth' to the modern world, by demonstrating how the colossal power of modern technics is co-extensive with what it is that we think we know about the development of human society. In this respect, what is offered is a history of science *and* technology. The version of history that is performed, however, is one that is at odds with the usual historiography of the scientific. Typically, this offers a positive definition of 'scientificity' and then proceeds to show how this criterion has been progressively met through the gradual development and elaboration of science from its precursors in the ancient world to its full blossoming in the post-Enlightenment West. Serres and his collaborators, by contrast, wish to restore a provisional and contingent character to science:

> Far from tracing a linear development of continuous and cumulative knowledge or a sequence of sudden turning-points, discoveries, inventions and revolutions plunging a suddenly outmoded past instantly into oblivion, the history of science runs backwards and forwards over a complex network of paths which overlap and cross, forming nodes, peaks and crossroads, interchanges which bifurcate into two or several routes. A multiplicity of different times, diverse disciplines, conceptions of science, groups, institutions, capitals, people in agreement or in conflict, machines and objects, predictions and unforeseen dangers, form together a shifting fabric which represents faithfully the complex history of science. (Serres, 1995b: 6)

The difference in approach could not be starker from that of Bachelard. Science proceeds not by breaks or by wholesale revisions in its fundamental conceptual and phenomenological base (that is 'paradigm'), but rather through the contingent unravelling of a tangled weave of pathways and vectors that often turn back on themselves. Moreover, science is not thinkable outside of the collectives and the technologies that provide its proper milieu. But if this is so, then how is it possible to conceive of any continuity? Or, put more simply, what are the points that provide the necessary hooks for a history? In language that echoes the latter Foucault, Serres describes these 'hooks' as the problematics which afford choice and selection:

> [W]hile the sciences, separately or together, accumulate and fragment into hundreds of disciplines, while they are constantly changing and shifting, producing different times often unpredictable in their progress, what does remain relatively invariant in their dramatic and turbid history are the points of convergence and bifurcation where problems are posed and decision are or not taken. What problems? What decisions? These are the nodes or summits of the various networks, relatively stable intersections which are the chapters of this book. (Serres, 1995b: 7)

The chapters of the collection are then focussed on the points of intersection, or knots, where heterogeneous currents of thought are brought together and rendered fit for judgement. Sometimes these knots are precisely dated, at other times this dating is merely prototypical, and designed purely to establish a field of relative intensities (as is the case, notoriously, in Deleuze and Guattari's *Thousand Plateaus*). In either case, the work of analysis involves restoring the radical specificity and contingency to the problem that is effaced when science is considered merely as the progressive elaboration of concept and method.

Serres' principal contribution to the project is an exploration of the origins of geometry in Greece. This rather unpromising topic is actually one to which Serres has turned on numerous occasions, most notably in *Les origines de la géométrie* (Serres, 1993). Serres begins with a puzzle. The ancient Greek world exists for us only in the form of the fragments and contested versions that make up the modern historical method. But Greek geometry is seemingly preserved in an immediate and tangible way. Or as Serres puts it:

> Iranians, Spaniards, French, English and Tamils – we all speak Greek when we say parallelogram, logarithm or topology . . . Nothing remains of the cities of Cyrene or Perga, or of the Elean School or that of Croton, not a temple or weapon, no trade or workshop, but the list which runs from integers to conic sections has not aged one bit, even though sometimes we do not understand the terms number and diagonal in exactly the same way as the ancient Greeks. Who better triumphed over history and its fluctuations than that little collective which so quickly established this signal subject which has so resisted erosion by time? (1995c: 77)

The apparent durability of Greek geometry sets up several problems. If geometry is preserved in this fashion, does this not indicate that it stands outside of the historical, properly speaking? And if this is so, then what hope can there be for a history of science, if a given body of knowledge is taken to transcend the conditions of its own emergence? Serres' response is to invert the problem. If geometry overcomes history then this represents a 'triumph' by 'the Greeks' as a collective. We may then ask, in a properly historical fashion, what led this collective to appeal to the transcendent, and the social and conceptual apparatus which made such a strategy possible. To do so we must begin with the concrete, rather than the abstract.

Gnomon

In a classic early essay *Mathematics and Philosophy: What Thales Saw . . .* Serres (1982a) retells the fable of the philosopher who measured the height of the great pyramids. Thales, the fragile mortal, stands before the immortal and vast stone monuments. He is equipped solely with a peg sunk into the sand. As the sun sets, the shadows cast by pyramid and peg create two corresponding isosceles triangles, which can be measured and compared using basic geometric principles. Here truly is the 'Greek miracle' – one man dominates a mighty pyramid. In this 'theatre of measurement' invented through the simple act of placing a peg in the sand, it is as though everything changed place. The weak human overcomes ancient hewn stone, the mobile sun produces immobile geometric forms, a third space of knowledge emerges on the sand enveloping both philosopher and pyramid.

The Thales fable contains many of the elements that Serres denotes using the term *translation*. There is an interaction or communication between two diverse partners (Thales, Pyramid) which involves a switching or exchanging of properties (weak/strong, mortal/durable). This exchange occurs in a 'third space' that is opened up between the two where a new means of determination or of finding settlements is produced (the geometry of shadows cast). The space itself is opened up by something which mediates or interrupts the original relationship (in this case, the peg that 'borrows' the suns rays). This basic schema is repeated throughout nearly all of Serres' work (and was adopted by Michel Callon (1980) in one of the original formulations of Actor-Network Theory).

To study 'what Thales saw' in terms of translation means beginning from the seemingly least important element in the fable – the peg pinned in the ground. Serres similarly begins his questioning of Greek geometry by describing a mundane instrument inherited from the Babylonians known as 'Gnomon'. A gnomon is a stationary shaft mounted on a plinth, on which various inscriptions are made. The shaft casts shadows at varying angles and lengths according to the sun's position overhead. We would then assume that the mounted gnomon is a sundial, used for establishing a chronographic division of the day. Serres argues, however, that there is no need for such a device in a social order already highly sensitive to natural cycles against which human activities are coordinated. The gnomon was instead used, Serres claims, as a 'instrument of scientific research in its own right, demonstrating a model of the world, giving the length of shadows at midday on the longest and shortest days, and indicating the equinoxes, solstices and latitude of place, for example. It was more of an observatory than a clock' (1995c: 9).

If the gnomon really was an observatory, it functioned very differently from our modern conceptions of such a device. The telescope, Serres notes, clearly defines a space for the human observer at the eyepiece. The subject is afforded a space of 'contemplating, observing, calculating, arranging the planets' (1995c: 80), which simultaneously sets up the heavens as a space to be observed and on which order will be projected. But the gnomon functions differently. It does not define a space for the human subject in this clear way, since one can read the gnomon from various positions. Moreover, for the Greeks, it was the gnomon itself rather than the subject which 'knew, discerned, distinguished, intercepted the light from the Sun, left lines on the sand as if it were writing on a blank page and, yes, understood' (1995c: 80). The gnomon projects the heavens down onto the sand – it makes inscriptions. It is as though the constellations were 'writing themselves' through the mediation of the gnomon. This is a scene which is, Serres claims, entirely outside of the Cartesian space of representation, and hence, to us moderns, somewhat inexplicable.

The theme of nature 'writing itself' recurs through much of Serres' latter work (see Brown, 2003). In *The Natural Contract*, for instance, Serres (1995d) aims to recover a notion of the Earth as a 'global subject' that produces marks which deserve to be treated as responses to the innumerable 'contracts' that human affairs form with nature. We assume that the only contracts, and the only marks, which matter are those produced by humans as communicative social acts. But such contracts are, Serres notes, typically shored up by an appeal to nature as a grounding space outside of human collectivity, whose relevance is seen purely in terms of its utility as a resource in social governance. Yet when that external space becomes so encroached and exhausted by the 'weight' of the collective human mass upon it, we must, Serres argues, find other ways of reading those marks.

The analysis of the gnomon provides the start of the story that will culminate in *The Natural Contract*. The inscriptions which the gnomon makes on the sand remain the mysterious and inaccessible writing of a world where subject and object are not cleaved asunder:

> The world represents itself, is reflected in the face of the sundial and we take part in this event no more and no less than the post, for standing upright, we also cast shadows, or as seated scribes, stylus in hand, we too leave lines. Modernity begins when this real world space is taken as a scene and this scene, controlled by the director, turns inside out – like the finger of a glove or a simple optical diagram – and plunges into the utopia of a knowing, inner, intimate subject. (1995c: 80)

Human and gnomon are interchangeable. Either one may stand in such a way as to allow the world to write itself as cast shadows. It is the inversion of this scene, where the writing is seen as the merely the trailing edge of the projection of human knowing onto the world as observed and ordered, that characterises, for Serres, the 'modern attitude'. Greek geometry is then caught between these modalities of inscription.

Machine, intelligence, table

The notion that the gnomon itself 'knows', 'discerns' or 'judges' may sound an instance of pure anthropomorphism. Likewise, when Actor-Network Theorists such as Callon and Latour demand that 'things' (ie, artefacts, objects, natural kinds) be accorded a form of rights which recognises them as participating agents in human affairs (see in particular Latour, 1993; 2004, and the discussion by Harris, in this volume), it is difficult to see this claim as anything but entirely fanciful. By demonstrating, however, both the crucial role of mediators, such as gnomon, in the constitution of knowledge, and the fundamental instability of the positions of 'observer' and 'observed' (or 'sender'/'receiver'; 'subject'/'object'), Serres begins to make a sound case for suspending the traditional division between human and artefact.

The sort of judgement and discernment performed by the gnomon is automatic. That is to say that it produces inscriptions in a continuous and immediate fashion without need of any particular observer or user. In this sense the gnomon is a 'machine'. But it is nevertheless, Serres claims, endowed with a form of intelligence, albeit of a special sort: 'In the literal sense, the gnomon is intelligent because it puts together situations chosen amongst thousands of others, therefore it discerns and understands. A passive receiver, it sees the light and then actively traces the fringe of the shadow on the page while theoretically showing the model of the sky' (1995c: 86).

Conceptualized in this way, intelligence amounts to a twin process of selecting and redistributing. This formulation betrays Serres' surprising reliance on a classical form of information theory. With the exception perhaps of the work of Robert Cooper (see Spoelstra, in this volume), there are few contemporary theorists who would seek to draw much from the thoroughly debased edifice of knowledge that information theory represents. Yet Serres manages to find a rich stockpile of provocative allegories and tools for thinking within this edifice. For example, *The Parasite* (Serres, 1982b), takes up an implication, developed by Henri Atlan (1974), of the relative difference in the discernment of signal against noise that exists between sender and receiver. The sender transmits a 'signal' which differentiates itself against background 'noise'. But the receiver is not necessarily committed to this differentiation. It may be that some of what has been relegated to the position of noise has some informational value. The receiver then makes the cut (ie, discerns, distributes) between signal and noise in their own fashion. Serres then takes the basic premise, and extends it into a generalized model of relations, where each placeholder selects and discerns from the mix of signal and noise they receive, before transmitting onwards their own particular signal, fashioned against what they take to be noise. And so on. In the process doubtless there is something preserved through the successive communicative acts, but it is transformed as it is repeatedly 'cut' (ie, mixed, interspersed) with noise on each occasion.

The gnomon is then a selector, a distributor, a means of making cuts, in the sense of both divisions and mixtures. Serres refers to it as an artefact that does not depend on human intervention – the gnomon produces its cuts automatically. The inscriptions it produces might then be recorded in the form of tables, which render durable the patterns drawn on the sand. These tables then establish ratios and progressive series. The gnomon becomes the basis for a geometric arithmetic based on the repeated application of established procedures. The Greeks then also named 'gnomon' that device we now call a 'set square'. This tool enables progressive bands of squares formed at the right angle. For the Greeks, it also served as a tool for calculating the odd numbers required to construct a series of successive square numbers. In all three cases the gnomon functions automatically, as machine for generating inscriptions.

Serres summarizes this development of the gnomon as giving rise to a form of knowledge that is 'algorithmic'. The automatic knowledge of the gnomon is both given in advance of the deliberations of any subject (it is to be found already in the table, or given by the series) and moreover acts as a form of 'memory'. As Serres puts it – 'for us, knowing consists of putting ourselves into a form similar to what we know. The object we construct, we create in a fashion which is similar to certain things of the world, ultimately our guides' (1995c: 96). The gnomon is then an automatic generator of forms, which, through the repeated application of the machine, extend into infinite repeating series and patterns. The world orders itself through the gnomon, and that which we call 'knowledge' consists of ordering ourselves in line with what is granted in the process. Elsewhere Serres (1987) names these machines as 'statues' – the points around which a closed system of forms can be gathered up and restarted, that part of the system which seems to lend an impetus and direction, but does itself not move.

Meno

Thus far we have been following the development of one aspect of Greek geometry – the algorithmic calculation of ratio and series. But what of the other aspect of knowledge that the Greeks broadly called geometric – demonstration and deduction? Serres articulates the differences between these two forms of geometric knowledge through a reading of the Meno dialogue in Plato. Ostensibly, the Meno dialogue concerns Socrates' assertion that what is called 'learning' is reducible to the recollection of transcendental forms which are already given. Socrates makes his case by instructing a slave boy to draw a square on the sand, and then asks him to double the area of the square. The boy initially fails, but through structured reflection enacted in concert with Socrates eventually manages to approximate an answer.

For Serres, this dialogue is a clash between older and newly emerging versions of Greek geometry. The boy approaches the task using the older knowledge, that which is authorized by the gnomon – 'in those days people trusted the gnomon, whose job it was to know. The new school had lost that knowledge, which had become contemptible and only fit for slaves. And the young man knows it, says it and represents it' (1995c: 103). The older knowledge, based on ratios, suggests that multiplying the lengths of the square will be sufficient to double the area. Such would be the procedure of applying a set square. But this procedure proves fruitless – the boy overestimates, firstly wildly, then modestly. This is of course the point of the demonstration, since 'Socrates is cheating, he knows he will not find the exact length' (p. 105). He is cheating because the puzzle cannot be solved by drawing lines on the sand and applying the algorithmic principles of whole numbers. The puzzle can only be tackled through knowledge of the diagonal and a new arithmetic base in irrational numbers and integers. This new knowledge cannot be laid out in the sand, like the inscriptions of the gnomon, it can only be performed in an abstract third space that is beyond that of the immediate:

> The gnomon knows only perfect squares, the perfect science of the logos, unaware of the irrationals; the archaic and highly imperfect science of the perfect logos. Mathematics in its demonstrative authenticity is born, as a result, outside the logos, when it distances itself from the logos and can rigorously measure this distance. Science begins outside language. The gnomon therefore does not know at all. (1995c: 107)

The point then of the dialogue is, Serres claims, to establish that henceforth discernment and understanding, previously given over to the gnomon, can now only be performed through a relation to another space, that of ideal figures and pure geometric forms (such as the diagonal), to which access is limited and tightly controlled. Only he or she who is authorized to speak on behalf this space may be trusted to adequately exercise judgement. If the fable of Thales produces the third space of the peg, the gnomon, which thenceforth takes charge of knowledge in an automatic fashion, here we see a second form of translation, where the gnomon itself is placed in relation to a new 'third space', but this time one which is placed outside of the sensory realm, which constitutes a very definite space for the thinking subject. For unlike the gnomon, which requires no subject to inscribe the world on the sand, this new space requires the mediation of he or she who can enact formal demonstrative procedures to translate the abstract back into the concrete. It requires a Socrates who can subtly 'cheat' a boy who he demands make insoluble marks on the sand before them (and in this do we not see here the final humiliation of the gnomon before the 'new knowledge', since Socrates is now its avowed master).

The *Meno* dialogue also makes clear that choices between various geometric frameworks are not simply technical choices. They are also human choices, which are, in essence, matters related to the control and governance of social relations. Socrates does not merely cheat, he makes a power play. Serres then imagines a genealogy of Greek geometry, which, very roughly, takes the following form.

224

First, we have the fable of Thales, the realization that the single, fragile human can dominate the impersonal mass of the world. From the third space which arises as a result, we have the birth of arithmetic and of the use of whole numbers as a means of creating inscriptions on the natural world, which can then be projected back on the human collective (in *The Natural Contract* Serres offers the example of the *harpedonaptai* who were tasked with applying geometric principles to redistribute the Nile floodland to the populace). Second, we have the emergence of another set of geometric principles, which, whilst they promise to thematise 'equality', have the result of constructing a new third space of the ideal which is entirely outside of human relations, and which can only be made accessible through the demonstrative/deductive method.

But something happens as a consequence, something which is quite unforeseen. The creation of the ideal space means that human affairs can now only be realised in relation to something outside of themselves. This is something new. Unlike the gnomon, a device by means of which nature writes itself, this space demands a collective subject who may interrogate its properties. This, Serres claims, is the birth of science – the emergence of a community who take themselves as such by virtue of their relation to a space which is outside of their own collective bonds:

> The special – epistemological – conditions of science lie in the general – gnosiological – conditions of knowledge which in turn lie in the hitherto obscure and unrecognized anthropological relations between the collective and the objects of the world, culture and nature. Does the group as a group become a thing? If yes, how? (1995c: 117)

Yes, the group becomes a thing, in the sense that social divisions now reflect the extent to which access to this space outside of human affairs is granted. What we call science is now possible. And this happens through the shifting of a problematic which took as its object social relations to a new object of the relation between humans and this new space, which hitherto will be entangled with the question of 'nature' – 'scientists believe in the existence of the outside world as the monk believed in God: neither can prove it, but they cannot exercise their faith or their science without this fundamental belief' (1995c: 119).

Conclusion

To what extent then is Michel Serres a theorist of organizations? In the proper sense, not at all. Serres has no interest in how organizations are structured, in their emergence, nor in their broader place in the social order. In contrast to Foucault, he has resisted any desire to interrogate the specific forms in which governance is forged and performed. There is very little in his work that will interest a researcher who is seeking a ready made framework for performing either theoretical or empirical studies of organizational life. You have to read Serres on your own time. He is extracurricular.

So why bother? Because, I think, of his ability to display that the neat categories in which we place questions of organizing are often ill founded. His dictum of thinking science culturally and culture scientifically neatly problematizes what it means to do social science, which can so easily descend into a parody of both science and culture, desperately in search of its own auto-authorisation (which may seem to come, does it not, through uttering the proper name of the theorist).

The sorts of things that Serres worries about – the problem of founding social relations in something other than themselves; what happens when communication goes astray; the tension between those things that hold a system together and those things that crack open a system to its outside; what to do, and how to understand, power and violence – all these strike me as central to what the study of organizations ought to concern itself with. Following Serres' brilliant, if complex and tortuous, responses is certainly instructive.

One could, of course, if so minded, simply treat Serres as a field which may be mined for a set of concepts and ideas which can be put to work elsewhere. This is perfectly possible. No-one will tell you off, few will even find you out, if you sneak a concept such as 'translation', 'substitution', 'blankness' or 'quasi-object'. I have done so myself. But, what, ultimately, Serres offers is an exemplary model for how to think across borderlines, how to pursue a problem through the many inevitable transformations that it succumbs to. To read any text of Serres is to come away feeling the power of allusion, of the oblique, of the diagonal. Ultimately, Serres demonstrates what it means to do the work of translation, to accept the wildest of juxtapositions as the necessary conditions of academic labour. Are these texts gnomon? Or demonstration? Engage, translate, decide.

Acknowledgements

To the editors, for their tolerance. And to the doctoral students at University of Leicester Management Centre for their enthusiasm and critical engagement with two previous versions of this chapter.

References

Abbas, N. (ed) (2005) *Mapping Michel Serres*. Michigan: University of Michigan Press.
Assad, M. (1999) *Reading with Michel Serres: An Encounter with Time*. Albany: State University of New York Press.
Atlan, H. (1974) 'On a formal definition of organization' *Journal of Theoretical Biology*, 45: 295–304.
Brown, S. D. (2002) 'Michel Serres: Science, translation and the logic of the parasite' *Theory, Culture & Society*, 19: 1–27
Brown, S. D. (2003) 'Natural writing: The case of Serres' *Interdisciplinary Science Review*, 28(3): 184–192.

Brown, S. D. (2004) 'Parasite logic' *Journal of Organizational Change Management*, 17(4): 383–395.

Callon, M. (1980) 'Struggles to define what is problematic and what is not: The socio-logic of translation' in K. D. Knorr, R. Krohn and R. Whitley (eds.). *The Social Process of Scientific Investigation*. Dordrecht: D. Reidel.

Jones, C. (2004) 'Jacques Derrida' in S. Linstead (ed.) *Organization Theory and Postmodern Thought*. London: Sage.

Latour, B. (1987a) 'The Enlightenment without the critique: A word on Michel Serres' philosophy' in A. P. Griffiths (eds.). *Contemporary French Philosophy*. Cambridge: Cambridge University Press.

Latour, B. (1993) *We have Never been Modern*, trans. C. Porter. Cambridge, MA: Harvard University Press.

Latour, B. (2004) *The Politics of Nature*, trans. C. Porter. Cambridge, Mass: Harvard University Press.

Paulson, W. (1997) 'Writing that matters' *SubStance*, 83: 1–10.

Paulson, W. (2000) 'Michel Serres's utopia of language' *Configurations*, 8(2): 215–228.

Plato (1956) *Protagoras and Meno*, trans W. K. C Gutherie. London: Penguin.

Serres, M. (1968) *Hermes ou la communication*. Paris: Minuit.

Serres, M. (1982a) 'Mathematics and philosophy: What Thales saw . . .' in J. V. Harari and D. F. Bell (eds.) *Hermes: Literature, Science, Philosophy*. Baltimore, MD: Johns Hopkins University Press.

Serres, M. (1982b) *The Parasite*, trans. L. Schehr. Baltimore, MD: Johns Hopkins University Press.

Serres, M. (1987) *Statues: Second livre des foundations*. Paris: Flammarion.

Serres, M. (1989) *Detachment*, trans. G. James and R. Federman. Athens, Ohio: Ohio University Press.

Serres, M. (1991) *Rome: The Book of Foundations*, trans. F. McGarren. Stanford: Stanford University Press.

Serres, M. (1993) *Les origins de la geometrie: Tiers livre des foundations*. Paris: Flammarion.

Serres, M. (1995a) *Angels: A Modern Myth*, trans. F. Cowper. Paris: Flammarion.

Serres, M. (1995b) 'Introduction' In M. Serres (ed) *A History of Scientific Thought*. Oxford: Blackwell.

Serres, M. (1995c) 'Gnomon: The beginnings of geometry in Greece' In M. Serres (ed) *A History of Scientific Thought* (originally published 1989). Oxford: Blackwell.

Serres, M. (1995d) *The Natural Contract*, trans. E. MacArthur and W. Paulson. Ann Arbor: University of Michigan Press.

Serres, M. (1997) *The Troubadour of Knowledge*, trans. S. Faria Glaser and W. Paulson. Ann Arbor: University of Michigan Press.

Serres, M. and B. Latour (1995) *Conversations on Science, Culture and Time*, trans. R. Lapidus. Ann Arbor: University of Michigan Press.

Practical deconstructivist feminist Marxist organization theory: Gayatri Chakravorty Spivak

Campbell Jones

Introduction

In this chapter I attempt to give a sense of how one might read organization and organization theory in the light of the work of Gayatri Chakravorty Spivak. Taking up this task, and trying to take Spivak's work on its own terms, I have found it necessary to bracket a number of divisions that are often set up between, for example, inside and outside, theory and practice, conception and execution. These divisions are basic grounds for organization theory, even if, as will emerge, they are often groundless. Here I call into question these divisions in something of the spirit of Spivak and in the spirit of a certain organization theory, an organization theory that may already be with us, or may very soon arrive. In the name of organization theory, questions of theory will bleed into questions of ownership, and hence of property, propriety and the proper. Organization theory has, of course, always asked itself questions of what can be properly known, owned and done. Here I propose that we take these traditional tasks of organization theory quite seriously, and suggest that Spivak, who has always been concerned with these questions – these founding questions of organization theory – is a crucially important organization theorist.

Given these tasks, we will necessarily fall prey to a certain dislocation. With Spivak, I propose to call into question many received ideas about practicality, deconstruction, feminism, Marxism and organization theory, as well as received assumptions about the contents and form of Spivak's work. I am also concerned to not merely speak 'about' Spivak, but to put her thought into motion. A reader expecting an introduction to Spivak should look elsewhere, for example to the reductive and simplifying account provided by Stephen Morton (2003). But further, if Spivak's work and the work of deconstruction more generally are, as she insists and as I will argue, a practical matter, then there is little point in laying out critical principles in advance of their application (see Brannigan *et al.*, 1996). So rather than speaking 'about' Spivak I will follow her own injunctions regarding the setting to work of deconstruction (see, for example, Spivak,

1999: 423–431) and set her to work. Or better, I will show that she has already been at work, in a number of places that many, even herself, might not have expected.

If there is one thing that we learn from Spivak then it is how to deal with the experience of a reading that produces something other than was expected. For Spivak this discovery of the unexpected is something positive and represents possibility and an openness to the future. In doing so she sets the task of reading and rereading as a task of change and of affirmation of the possibilities produced by that rereading. So if Spivak can be described as a practical deconstructivist feminist Marxist organization theorist, then we should be aware of the risks of this combination. This combination almost immediately provokes consternation from the practitioners of any of these isolated elements. I propose that we think through that immediate reaction, and see what can be done with, and beyond it.

The chapter starts with deconstruction and with Derrida who is, for Spivak, 'The most important philosopher of the twentieth century' (2005a: 52), and is often the starting point of her writing. Having done this we consider the relation between Spivak and organization theory. As we shall see, even the question of Spivak being 'inside' or 'outside' of organization theory is called into question almost immediately by her work on the practices of division. As we progress, we find far less stability than is often assumed in a series of divisions, and set to work in dismantling them or, rather, showing how they are already in the process of dismantling themselves.

Crossing borders

Many readers familiar with Spivak will know her from the English translation that she prepared in the early 1970s and published in 1976 of Jacques Derrida's *Of Grammatology*. This book features a lengthy 'Translator's preface', which served both as an introduction to Derrida and also as an introduction to his translator. In several later interviews, Spivak speaks of the way that she found, in this book, a way of approaching texts that resonated with what she, and others, were trying to do in the early seventies. As she explains, 'When I first read *Of Grammatology*, I felt I had understood what it was saying, and that it was a better way of describing what I was already trying to do' (Spivak, 1990: 133). Of particular interest for our purposes, as we consider what is 'inside' organization theory, is the way that she describes her excitement in the way that, in this book, Derrida was involved in a project of 'dismantling the philosophical tradition from *inside* rather than from *outside*' (Spivak, 1990: 7, emphases in original).

Following the publication of her translation of *Of Grammatology*, Spivak has produced a considerable body of work, mainly in the form of essays, but also in interviews, lectures, and finally in her magnum opus, *A Critique of Postcolonial Reason*, which appeared in 1999. In these works she has set to work dismantling the Western academy from within. Initially this involved English literature, and Spivak often describes herself simply as a literary critic and a teacher of comparative literature. But this is too modest. It is too modest because of her detailed and extensive engagement with other disciplines – at one point describing herself as a 'wild anthropologist' (Spivak, 2002: 620) – and with developments in deconstruction, Marxism and feminism. She has intervened in postcolonial studies, and is probably not adequately described as a 'postcolonial theorist', but as someone who works from a certain inside of postcolonial theory. In the four chapters of *A Critique of Postcolonial Reason* she dismantles a great deal of philosophy, literature, history and culture, but in each case this involves engagement from inside each of the disciplines. Here she is operating deconstructively, to the extent that she is dismantling these disciplines from the inside, from a certain inside.

It is often thought that the goal of deconstruction is to cross borders. Challenging an earlier regime of signification, deconstruction destabilizes by proposing a movement across what was previously thought to be a stable division, producing the possibility for 'the irruptive emergence of a new 'concept', a concept that can no longer be, and never could be, included in the previous regime' (Derrida, 1981: 42). So, for example, a division had been presupposed between organization and disorganization and one was prioritized over the other. Deconstruction calls this division into question, introducing the latter term into the former. Which is not to simply reverse the opposition between organization and disorganization, but is to introduce the two terms into one another (see Cooper, 1986, see also Spoelstra, in this volume).

But this is to move too quickly. If we think of deconstruction as the introduction of an excluded element, then we are still thinking in terms of externality and of imposition from outside. We should remember that deconstruction is more a matter of negotiating that which is already on the inside. One of the first principles of deconstruction, if we can speak of such things, is that 'The movements of deconstruction do not destroy structures from the outside' (Derrida, 1976: 24). Deconstruction is not a matter of imposing something from outside, but of demonstrating that it was always already there. Deconstruction, we should recall, operates 'necessarily from the inside, borrowing all of the strategic and economic resources from the old structure' (Derrida, 1976: 24).

The task of this chapter, therefore, is not to introduce Spivak to organization theory. It is not a matter of introduction or addition. Rather, by way of introduction, we will suggest that Spivak is already at work within organization theory. The proper name 'Spivak' will be used, then, to designate this work that is already at work. If there is any introduction of Spivak, then, it will be of the proper name 'Spivak'. Spivak is, and has always been, a theorist of organization – which is also to say, of capital, of culture, of language, of history, of planetarity. And these matters have been, and remain, crucial to even the most narrowly conceived organization theory. Spivak here speaks, then, not 'to' an organization theory that is located somewhere else, but speaks as an organization theorist. So any prior division between Spivak and organization theory would itself need some explaining. To suggest that Spivak was not an organization theorist would rest on a version of proprietoriality about both Spivak and about organization theory that is, we will see, foreign to both Spivak and to any serious organization theory.

This attempt to dismantle disciplines from the inside also has significant outcomes for the practice of organization theory. In recent years it has been possible to observe, amongst many organization theorists, a sense of frustration and a pull that moves outside of organization theory. This is perhaps most notable amongst those who, in their frustration with the theoretical shallowness and political quietism of a great deal of organization theory, have been moved to present themselves from an outside. This manifests itself in a number of ways, but we can see this clearly in many who propose one or another critical position, or who sign up to a project of 'critical management studies'. Over the past few years examples of this tendency to look to the outside, or move to the outside, can be seen in the work of organization theorists such as Parker (2002), Alvesson and Willmott (2003), Linstead (2004) and Böhm (2005).

If we wanted immediate practical results from Spivak, then perhaps a starting point would be to indicate the limits of this move to the outside. This is not to suggest that these critics have nothing worthy to say, and is certainly not to deny the absolute necessity of a directly critical and oppositional stand in the face of the contemporary geopolitical regime. But from deconstruction we can learn to see how opposition is often deeply embedded in the thing that is resisted. We can learn from Spivak the possibility of another way of engaging with texts and with traditions. Rather than abandoning the past in the name of a critical bonfire that would destroy organization theory, might we not inhabit it, from a certain inside? This is not just because inhabitation is unavoidable, but further because organization theory is not a singular or united thing but is a complex tissue, a weave of fragments. Which needs to be patiently and painstakingly undone, acknowledging complicity. Rather than attempt, however well intentioned, to throw it on the fire.

This proposes a way of working with the tradition of organization theory, in a way that does not conserve any more than it opposes. If we were to search for a name to try to describe something of this way of approaching texts and traditions from a certain inside, then we could do worse than the word 'deconstruction', a word that is very important for Spivak. But if we are to use this word then we should remember that deconstruction is not a method, is not critique, and involves no relativism, as I have tried to show elsewhere (Jones, 2004). Following these precautions – and noting how often they have been ignored, in organization theory and elsewhere – it might then be useful in this chapter to outline in a little more detail Spivak's setting to work of deconstruction. This will take us from deconstruction and the political, to the subaltern, to supplementarity, to what might be done beyond Spivak.

Deconstruction and the political

I am moving quickly, condensing too many things, and perhaps worst of all refusing to respect the separation of deconstruction from the political. After all, doesn't deconstruction involve the very denial of politics? We have heard, so often, that deconstruction questions everything, and with this will only soften radicalism or hopefulness. In the hands of organization theorists such as Alvesson and Willmott (1992, 1996), for example, the lesson of deconstruction is that politics of a radically ambitious kind is no longer tenable.

Like many, when I first read Derrida I was concerned about the lack, in his work, of what presents itself as a recognizable politics. My sense is that many others have felt the same, which might explain the popularity of Foucault and Deleuze over Derrida in certain theoretical corners of organization theory. Of course, if this initial reaction to Derrida had any sense, it is certainly confounded by the increasing use of recognizably political language in Derrida's later work, at least from the 1990s on, with a continual return to politics, ethics, hospitality, justice and democracy. And in the case of Spivak we find her practicing deconstruction *and* a strong insistence, throughout her work, on the importance of an engaged politics. My own experience of reading Spivak sent me back to Derrida, and showed me what can be taken from Derrida while also remembering the need to 'be practical', to be engaged in change, which is to say, a reminder that we cannot not be involved in the political.

Having got this far, and sensing the political importance of deconstruction, there is little to be gained here by simply asserting catchphrases to the effect that 'deconstruction is political', or some such. As serious commentators have made clear, there is much more to the articulation of Derrida and the political that is at stake here (see Beardsworth, 1996, Bennington, 2000). As Spivak expresses this aporia, deconstruction is vital for any meaningful politics, but at the same time deconstruction cannot found a political programme (1990: 104). As she explains:

> It is not just that deconstruction cannot found a politics, while other ways of thinking can. It is that deconstruction can make founded political programs more useful by making their in-built problems more visible. To act is therefore not to ignore deconstruction, but actively to transgress it without giving it up. (Spivak, 1993: 121)

From here, we might be able to make more sense of the political relevance of deconstruction for organization theory. It is not that deconstruction will found another organization theory, or another politics of organization. But at the same time deconstruction – whether using the name or not – is crucial for organization theory and for the politics of organization. This politics does not arrive exposing errors or condemning pathologies, which would be to stand outside shouting. Rather, deconstruction takes us inside, to a certain inside, and in doing so gives us a certain way of renegotiating organization, theory and the political.

Commenting on the place of politics in deconstruction, Geoffrey Bennington writes:

> Deconstruction then, on the one hand generalizes the concept of politics so that it includes all conceptual dealings whatsoever, and on the other makes a precise use of *one* particular inherited politico-metaphysical concept, democracy, to make a pointed and more obviously political intervention in political thought. (2000: 32–33, emphasis in original)

We find something like this in Spivak. Her writing involves a dispersal of the political, demonstrating the operation of politics across a wide cultural text. But on the other hand, she has also engaged a more traditional politics – not always articulated around democracy, as might be suggested by Bennington – in relation to responsibility, justice, and what used to be called concrete political struggles. For those in organization theory, the utility of this should once again be immediately apparent. Spivak is concerned not only with 'high theory', but is also profoundly concerned with global capital and with gendered super-exploitation.

In her critique of contemporary capitalism, Spivak continues to act in dismantling the division that has often been assumed between theory and practical politics. This relates both to a way of being engaged in concrete struggles, and it also involves questions of the refiguration of theory. Spivak's exemplar here is Marx who, as she puts it 'could hold *The Science of Logic* and the Blue Books together' (1999: 421). And in the same way as Marx learned from Hegel and from the reports of the British parliament (see Hegel, 1961, Marx, 1976: 1113–1117, 1978: 607–608, 1981: 1061–1064), Spivak learns from Derrida and connects this with a practical politics. The image we might imagine, then, would be one of Spivak being the one who can hold together *Of Spirit* (Derrida, 1987) and a Flood Action Plan for Bangladesh prepared by the European Parliament (see Spivak, 1994).

It seems to me that organization theory today faces exactly the same demand. It is drawn towards both the most esoteric and demanding theoretical and philosophical questions, and at the same time is drawn to practice and politics, to registering the contemporary empirical situation and responding to it. I am not going to suggest that Spivak has an answer to this aporia. If you want satisfying answers then you should probably go elsewhere. But Spivak has done something important towards illustrating one way of negotiating this aporia between the theoretical and the political.

Given what we have said about the inside and the outside and about deconstruction and the political, we might be starting to see, then, why it is that Spivak might describe herself as a 'practical deconstructivist feminist Marxist' (1990: 133, cf. MacCabe, 1987: ix). This slightly comical mouthful points to the way that Spivak draws on various different strands of theory, many of which are often considered to be distinct. And this relation is thought in an interesting way, in which feminism, Marxism, deconstruction and practice are not folded into, or reduced to, one another. Their specificities and contradictions are maintained, so that we have to continue thinking the complexity of their relations. Avoiding easy and intellectually undemanding pluralisms, she stresses the discontinuities and disagreements between practicality, deconstruction, feminism and Marxism while also stressing the need to continue to negotiate between these.

These movements between positions, then, is quite different from eclecticism, which would involve jamming together theoretical and political positions in spite of the specific points of inconsistency between them. On this count, Terry Eagleton (1999) misses the mark when he accuses Spivak of wild eclecticism, although it does draw attention to the dangers of the breach of expectation that are produced by Spivak's movement between traditions that are normally kept apart. It is perhaps this movement that characterizes Spivak, which might be thought of in terms of what is known as interdisciplinarity, but still recalling her remark: 'I am not erudite enough to be interdisciplinary, but I can break rules' (Spivak, 1999: xiii). Continually struggling with the discrepancies between theoretical positions and between theory and practice, Spivak is rather hard to locate in recognizable positions. And then, when some had a sense that she could be located – even if located, as we have been trying, as a practical deconstructivist feminist Marxist – under the influence of a turn to ethics that is indicative of shifts in Derrida's later work (see Spivak, 1999: 426; 1994) she starts to describe herself as a 'paradisciplinary ethical philosopher'.

The subaltern

So far we have said very little about the contents of Spivak's work, and this level of abstraction from her texts runs the risk of breaching the closeness and practicality of deconstructive reading. So here we might turn our attention more closely to some of the substantive arguments that Spivak makes, if these can be distinguished from how she makes them. In an earlier design for this chapter, I had planned to write directly on Spivak's relation to Marx, and her reworking of what a critique of capital might look like today. This is a task that concerns her throughout her work, and that she has addressed directly in a series of essays (Spivak, 1984, 1987a, 1995a, 1995b, 1996a). Her work both with and on Marx offers important possibilities for understanding capital and for understanding Marx that are all but silent in what has, to date, been called organization theory.

But rather than turn directly to Marx, let us start instead with Spivak's work on the subaltern, even if a rereading of Marx is urgent in the context of contemporary capital and the particularities of the reading of Marx in certain corners of organization theory, such as labour process theory, which has turned the narrowness of a reading of Marx into something of a 'virtue'. As should be clear, Spivak's work on the subaltern is far from the only contribution of Spivak to organization theory. But to discuss the subaltern here reflects something about the systematic silences that have governed organization theory. Because,

234

given all of the talk about things such as international business, globalisation, and so forth, it is possible that right now we might have most to gain from a critique of the colonial grounds of both organization and organization theory.

To introduce these, we might consider Spivak's work with and around the subaltern studies collective (see Guha and Spivak, 1989). This group, rereading and transforming the word 'subaltern' from Gramsci's notes on Italian history (Gramsci, 1971: 52, *passim*), uses this word to designate the position of those subjected not only to class-based domination, which typifies certain critiques, but also to register other forms of marginalisation and exclusion, perhaps most obviously along the lines of gender and race. The subaltern is defined against the elite, and hence is used early on to describe 'the general attribute of subordination in South Asian society whether this is expressed in terms of class, caste, age, gender and office or in any other way' (Guha: 1982: vii). The subaltern studies collective, engaged in a politicization of historical and theoretical conceptions of change, focusing in particular on South Asia, but also elsewhere. Working deconstructively, at the edges of, or 'from a certain inside', Spivak both extends and questions subaltern studies.

In addition to her critical interventions in subaltern studies (Spivak, 1987b, 1996b, 2000a), we find Spivak's engagement with subaltern history in what is perhaps her best known essay, 'Can the Subaltern Speak?'. This essay, first appearing in 1985 then in an extended version in 1988, was subsequently revised for a version that appeared with the title 'History' in *A Critique of Postcolonial Reason* (Spivak, 1999). It is an enormously complex text, with many overlapping layers. It performs a great deal of what I have been saying so far about the movement between inside and outside, about deconstruction and the political and about interdisciplinarity. It might also be suggested as a starting point for an organization theorist coming to Spivak for the first time.

Little would be gained from a summary of this text, which in its 1999 version is more than 100 pages long with 174 footnotes. It moves between 'high theory' – introducing an account of the 'worlding of worlds' based on a reading of Heidegger's 'Origin of the Work of Art' essay, an account of overdetermination from Freud, and a critical intervention in Deleuze and Foucault's 'Intellectuals and Power' interview, to mention a few points of reference – together with discussions of historical minutiae around Indian colonial administration, the practice of widow sacrifice (*sati*), and contemporary global financialization. She moves between the level of the universal and the particular, the micro and the macro, the interpretive and the descriptive. In the revised version, she sets the scene with a description of the settlement of the Shimla hills in the first two decades of the 19th century.

This is the Highland scrub country of the lower Himalayas between Punjab proper on the West, Nepal and Sikkim on the East, and what was to be named the Northwest Provinces – today's Uttar Pradesh – in the south. The country lies between the two great rivers Sutlej and Yamuna, and there are thus two valleys tucked in between the scrub, the Kaadah and the Dehra valleys, or doons. The many kings of these hills had lived out a heterogeneous and precarious equilibrium surrounded by the militarily and political energetic Sikhs of the Punjab and Gurkahs of Nepal and by those relatively distant 'paramount powers', the Murghal Emperor and the Pathan King of Delhi, the latter through his proxy the Nazim of Sirhind. It is the centuries-old scene of the dispersal of the space of power, with representations of representation operating successfully though not taking anyone in as the representation of truth – and, above all, animated by no desire to compete with those four greater surrounding powers. (Spivak, 1999: 210–211)

Spivak uses this 'minimal account' to set the scene for one of her examples, which comes in the form of Captain Geoffrey Birch, a representative of the East India Company, which has come to settle this area, and to bring order to these 'uncivilized lands'. Birch is not an exceptional figure, and Spivak is at pains to show how the determination of colony takes place through the workaday activities of such characters. Birch was 'born in a petty merchant's family in Middlesex just before the French Revolution, he is twenty-nine at this point' (Spivak, 1999: 211). He is on a civilizing mission, in which he undertakes his journey 'to acquaint the people who they are subject to, for as I suspected they were not yet properly informed of it' (Birch, cited in Spivak, 1999: 213). Birch, despite the distance in time and his mode of transportation, provides an image redolent of the contemporary student of organization theory.

> Birch in the meantime is advancing his career, riding about in the hills with a single native escort – a slightly romantic figure if encountered in the pages of a novel or on the screen. He is actually engaged in consolidating the Self of Europe by obliging the native to cathect the space of the Other on his home ground. . . . He is worlding *their own world*, which is far from an uninscribed earth, anew, by obliging *them* to domesticate the alien as Master. (Spivak, 1999: 211, emphases in original)

Here Spivak picks up her earlier discussion of Heidegger's 'Origin of the Work of Art' (1978). In this important essay, Heidegger presents the work of art as a matter of unconcealment, of 'the work of disclosure of a particular being, disclosing what and how it is' (1978: 162). He shows how a work of art such as Van Gogh's painting of peasant shoes functions not merely to 'represent' an image, but to bring into being what he calls 'a world'.

It is this 'worlding a world' that concerns Spivak, and she uses this image to frame the operation of the writing of colony. Importantly, however, she stresses the need to depart from Heidegger, arguing, for example:

> If the Heideggerian concept-metaphor of the earth and world is used to describe the imperialist project, what emerges out of the violence of the rift (*Riss* in Heidegger has the violent implication of a fracture – 'fighting of the battle', the 'intimacy of opponents' – rather than the relatively 'cool' connotation of a gap) is the multifarious thingliness (*Dinglichkeit*) of a represented world on a map, not merely 'the materiality of the oil paint affirmed and foregrounded in its own right' as in some masterwork of European art, being endlessly commented on by philosopher and literary critic. (Spivak, 1999: 212, emphases in original)

236

She continues, shifting again in tone and style:

> The agents of this cartographic transformation in the narrow sense are not only great names like Vincent Van Gogh, but also small unimportant folk like Geoffrey Birch, as well as policy makers. (Spivak, 1999: 212)

From these passages by Spivak, we can see something of the stakes of her project and something of her arguments and writings style(s). In this chapter I do not have the space to do justice to the complexity of here arguments or her writing, which often require considerable work reading and rereading. Rather than seeking to summarize her arguments in this and other texts, perhaps more would be gained from here adding some cautions about the dangers of mis-reading or speed-reading, which is the typical strategy of so many in organiza-tion theory, and against which Spivak's project is directly opposed (cf. Derrida, 1999: 264n22). Spivak's writing can be frustrating, and sometimes one senses that things could be put more clearly. But this should not excuse the haste with which some critics have understood little more of it than can be gleaned by reading the title of 'Can the Subaltern Speak?', or from her polemical conclu-sion to the first version of that essay, where she claims, outright: 'The subaltern cannot speak' (1988: 308). Here we should recall that in the revised version of this paper, Spivak explains her frustration at the failure of communication between the colonial administration and women engaging in *sati*, and writes:

> I was so unnerved by this failure of communication that, in the first version of this text, I wrote, in the accents of passionate lament: the subaltern cannot speak! It was an inadvisable remark. (Spivak, 1999: 308)

Given the sophistication of her writing, and the continual reworking of ideas and rewriting of texts by Spivak, we should be alert to the danger of reducing Spivak to soundbites. This risk of the reduction of theorists to familiar categories is something that has, I have argued, typified so much of the reading of theorists in organization theory (Jones, 2003). The danger is that Spivak will, likewise, be reduced to little more than a liberal multiculturalist defence of 'voice', while the task of reading her text in all of its complexity is set a side. Because Spivak is constantly drawing attention to the need to negotiate with difficulty, which is a scholarly matter, but is also a matter that is crucially practical.

The postcolonial supplement

I started by arguing that there is no need to bring Spivak into organization theory, the suggestion being that Spivak is doing organization theory, whether or not she uses the name. But on the other hand, let us not forget that disci-plines persist, and some will keep talking of organization theory as a relatively stable, coherent and bounded discipline, no matter how implausible such an image appears to others. If we constructed a sharp dividing line between Spivak and organization theory, then we might embark on a critical project by introducing Spivak, the supplement, from the outside. Would this operate in the same way that organization theory, a bounded discipline, has encountered 'post-colonial theory' in recent years?

Here we might take pause to reflect on some of the moves that have been made in recent years to introduce postcolonial concerns into organization theory. Much has been done to disclose the colonial grounds of organization theory, ranging from drawing attention to the denial of slavery in the history of management (Cooke, 2003), the appropriation of the other in comparative management (Westwood, 2001) to discussion of the neocolonial grounds of globalization, multiculturalism and anthropology (Bannerjee and Linstead, 2001, 2004). Gibson Burrell (1997) has pointed to the importance of the peasantry for organization theory and Calás and Smircich (1999) have argued that postcolonial theory is one of the pathways 'past postmodernism' (see also Hancock and Tyler, in this volume, and Brewis, in this volume). Amongst all of these many and diverse arguments, which I will not attempt to survey here, we have seen streams at conferences, special issues of journals and a new journal *Critical Perspectives on International Business*, which propose to explore the postcolonial. Notable here also is the book *Postcolonial Theory and Organizational Analysis* edited by Anshuman Prasad (2003) and other volumes moving in a related direction (Jack and Westwood, forthcoming; Zein-Elabdin and Charusheela, 2004).

This postcolonial supplement might impose itself in one of two ways. On the one hand, we have what could be called 'the postcolonial in organization'. This is a drawing into organization theory of issues or empirical facts that reflect colonial domination, but have been hidden from view. Here we might think of Burrell's call on the peasantry, an issue that is also reflected in Spivak's reminder of the place, today, of the rural in contemporary globalisation. For Spivak, importantly, this is not just to call to see the rural today, but to show how it has always been there. Spivak stresses the centrality of the rural poor in what is described as globalisation, and reminds us that farming remains the principal economic activity for the statistical majority, that this activity is both gendered and racialised and that it is typically rendered invisible in discussions of work in organization theory. She notes the way accounts of the information age such as that propounded by Castells 'excludes not only the rural poor and the underclass of global North and South' and further that 'the movement of data is indistinguishable from the movement of finance capital' (Spivak, 2005b: 17).

> I point out the virtualization of the rural, the conversion of the rural into data through the patenting of indigenous knowledge and through pharmaceutical interests in seeds and population control. Indigenous peoples, for example, are fined by trade-related investment and intellectual property measures, because they obviously had not patented their knowledge over the last few thousand years and so that's retroactively seen as an illegal trade practice. Through the conversion of the phenomenon of the rural, not blue skies and green trees, into data, the rural front is the real front of globalization. (Spivak, 2002: 611)

But the postcolonial is about much more than reintroducing forgotten issues such as farming, the peasantry and the rural. The postcolonial supplement also offers itself in terms of a more general decolonization of organization theory. This is not just a matter of pointing to a particular issue or groups of people, such as 'the indigenous', but is a matter or rethinking relations with these issues and groups, and seeking to identify what occluded them in the first place. This is not just adding the postcolonial to organization theory, but the postcolonial as an unworking of organization theory, a broad and diverse strategy of decolonization. 'Postcolonializing organization theory' as opposed to 'the postcolonial in organization' involves not just adding the postcolonial to organization theory, but involves reworking the colonial heritage of organization theory.

One of the crucial things that Spivak teaches is how this process of decolonisation might work. Important for us here is the way that Spivak speaks of an 'unlearning of privilege' (Spivak, 1990: 30, 42, 121). The 'post-' in postcolonial then is seen not as a once-off operation, which leaves us safely on the other side of colonialism, imperialism and racism. Postcolonializing or decolonizing organization theory would involve, following Spivak, something of what she calls a 'practical politics of the open end'. This practical politics of the open end – and here we will see again the importance of deconstruction – 'is not like some kind of massive ideological act (the surgical operation) which brings about a drastic change' (Spivak 1990: 105). Rather, it is something persistent, and something you have to work at. And recall, this is not a purely theoretical operation, but a practical matter, and it is no surprise that Spivak offers everyday examples to illustrate this task. She speaks of acts such as cleaning your teeth, and notes 'You don't do these things once and for all' (1990: 41). This persistence, which is the undoing of colony, is not a massive immediate change, but is a work, a work of unlearning.

> For example, when we actually brush our teeth, or clean ourselves everyday, or take exercise, or whatever, we don't think that we are fighting a losing battle against mortality, but, in fact, all of these efforts are doomed to failure because we are going to die. On the other hand, we really think of it much more as upkeep and as maintenance rather than as an irreducibly doomed repeated effort. This kind of activity cannot be replaced by an operation. (Spivak, 1990: 105)

This is not to say that postcolonialising organization theory would not have significantly radical consequences. Quite the contrary. But it would involve thinking carefully about how such a radicalization might be achieved. It threatens to do far more than supplement organization theory with the postcolonial. It threatens to displace the very grounds of organization theory.

In her *Critique of Postcolonial Reason* Spivak discusses a conference that she attended in 1982 with the title 'Europe and its Others'. In response to the title, Spivak proposed to rewrite the title, so that it read as 'Europe as an Other'. This reversal involves a move that exceeds the mere addition of the Other to a stable centre, but makes an intervention that reverses priorities as a first step towards a displacement of the division itself. What would happen today, if we were to operate the same displacement on organization theory, after which we spoke of 'organization theory as an other'?

The first consequence would be the breach of a liberal consensus that dominates so much of academic organization theory. Even the Academy of Management has founded a 'special interest group' that can work on a critical management studies. This group is legitimated as holding a 'perspective' that operates according to the logic of the supplement. It is allowed 'inside' on the grounds that there are legitimate concerns to be heard, 'voices' to tell their stories, but at the same time is domesticated by this very inclusion, reduced to being just one story among many others. And because it is 'just a perspective', it can be one amongst many, as the march of rapacious corporate capital proceeds unhindered.

Spivak, unless we read her in such a way that totally trivialises her, does not offer this kind of supplementarity. Her postcolonial supplement is not something that could be written under the sign of the addition of colonialism to a stable world. Spivak does not supplement organization theory but opens a space of thinking supplementarity in general. Spivak transforms, both theoretically and politically, the grounds for an engagement with supplementarity. From here, there is no going back to some good old days in which the rest of the world didn't matter, or if neocolonialism is a 'special interest'. Following this transformation, there is no Other that might be added to a stable centre. The Other is always already on the inside, and the task of thought is to work on this inhabitation. If the other, as Other, is to be encountered, then this will call into question the very foundation of the centre.

Beyond Spivak

As is to be expected, Spivak has not escaped criticism. She breaks rules, and uses her rule-breaking as an opportunity to further interrogate the limits of specific academic conventions. This, along with the density of her writing, has been the subject of many polemics, but as we know, ill-informed polemics against critical scholars are not a new matter (on this matter see Spivak, 2000b, 2003d). And as she speaks today for global justice and against capitalist expansion and war (Spivak, 2003c, 2004a, 2004b), these polemics against her are almost certain to continue.

Although these polemics are to be expected, and are typically informed by motivations of which we can rightly be suspicious, we should not excuse Spivak from all criticism. To respect her text, we might recall exactly what she teaches us about alterity and about reading. Recall her emphasis on radical alterity, which she takes from Levinas, via Derrida: 'to be human is to be angled, that is to say, leaning toward another' (2003d: 193). And reading Spivak, with respect for her alterity, recall her repeated protocols for deconstructive reading. Deconstruction is 'unaccusing, unexcusing, attentive, situationally productive through dismantling' (1993: 146; 1999: 81). Taking Spivak with us in the decolonization of organization theory we can learn from her protocols, in terms of both how we read organization theory and how we read Spivak. The analogies are clear here with her proposals for a deconstructive postcolonializing reading of comparative literature:

> What I am suggesting may sound discouraging. I hate to use this word, but perhaps it gives us a certain kind of honesty. It should not paralyze us. We cannot not try to open up, from the inside, the colonialism of European national language-based Comparative Literature and the Cold War format of Area-Studies, and infect history and anthropology with the 'other' as producer of knowledge. From the inside, acknowledging complicity. No accusations. No excuses. Rather, learning the protocol of those disciplines, turning them around, laboriously. (Spivak, 2003a: 10–11)

In the same way that we are following Spivak in sensing the need for dismantling organization theory, from a certain inside and with an eye to the colonial, if we are to go beyond Spivak then we will need to both read her carefully and to go beyond her. These aporias no longer paralyse us, but come now as a relief. We also find a position from which we will be able, at a certain point, to do without Spivak. In fact, at a certain point we must. Because we no longer need to see some great figure – Derrida, Spivak, or anyone else – waiting out there to save organization theory from itself. Here a recognition of inhabitation and complicity becomes a space for action, a leaning towards the other of organization theory.

If we continue to read Spivak, we will read not only her work to date, but a persistently prolific and changing work. Not only does she continue to produce articles and interviews at an astonishing rate, we are promised a number of new books. We should soon see a collection of essays under the title *Other Asias*, and for some time have been told of the forthcoming books *Of Derrida* and *Red Thread: A Book of Essays on Identity*. Spivak is also involved in her activist work in West Bengal, and we should note the importance that she places on her role as a teacher of the humanities (see Spivak, 2003b). Her work continues to offer itself to us.

I must conclude, and I have the sense that this chapter has failed to do justice to the detail of Spivak's dense writings. I am also concerned that my discussion of the way that Spivak moves to keep both theory and politics moving may be too easily accommodated by some. I know that there are many, who work in spaces not too far from what I am calling organization theory, who are struggling to work in a way that is both theoretically sophisticated and also meaningful in terms of a more practical or engaged politics. Many who are emerging today as critics of organization take this as a vital prerequisite for the work we are doing. And while I cannot not commend such moves, Spivak can help remind us of the risk that we run of forgetting complicity, of thinking that our teeth are once and forever clean. One of the crucial ways in which she does this, in addition to her continuous mobilization of deconstructive moves, is to remind us of how much of even the most critical and apparently sophisticated writing on organization today (poststructuralist or otherwise), has yet to alert itself to the task of dismantling colony.

Acknowledgements

Thanks to participants in the seminar on theoretical management research at the University of Leicester, to Melanie Micir at Columbia for bibliographical assistance, and to Stefano Harney, Gavin Jack, Eleni Karamali, Rolland Munro, Wayne Pihema, Carl Rhodes and Bob Westwood for their comments on an earlier draft of this chapter.

References

Alvesson, M. and H. Willmott (1992) 'On the idea of emancipation in management and organization studies' *Academy of Management Review*, 17(3): 432–464.

Alvesson, M. and H. Willmott (1996) *Making Sense of Management: A Critical Introduction*. London: Sage.

Alvesson, M. and H. Willmott (eds.) (2003) *Studying Management Critically*. London: Sage.

Bannerjee, S. B. and S. Linstead (2001) 'Globalization, multiculturalism and other fictions: Colonialism for the new millennium?' *Organization*, 8(4): 683–722.

Bannerjee, S. B. and S. Linstead (2004) 'Masking subversion: Neocolonial embeddedness in anthropological accounts of indigenous management' *Human Relations*, 57(2): 221–247.

Beardsworth, R. (1996) *Derrida and the Political*. London: Routledge

Bennington, G. (2000) 'Derrida and politics' in *Interrupting Derrida*. London: Routledge.

Böhm, S. (2005) *Repositioning Organization Theory*. Basingstoke: Palgrave Macmillan.

Burrell, G. (1997) *Pandemonium: Towards a Retro-Organization Theory*. London: Sage.

Brannigan, J., R. Robbins and J. Wolfreys (eds.) (1996) *Applying: To Derrida*. Basingstoke: Macmillan.

Calás, M. and L. Smircich (1999) 'Past postmodernism? Reflections and tentative directions', *Academy of Management Review*, 24 (4): 649–71.

Cooke, B. (2003) 'The denial of slavery in management studies' *Journal of Management Studies*, 40(8): 1895–1918.

Cooper, R. (1986) 'Organization/disorganization' *Social Science Information*, 25(2): 299–335.

Deleuze, G. and M. Foucault (1977) 'Intellectuals and power: A conversation between Michel Foucault and Gilles Deleuze' in D. Bouchard (ed.) *Language, Counter-Memory, Practice: Selected Essays and Interviews by Michel Foucault*, trans. D. Bouchard and S. Simon. Ithaca, NY: Cornell University Press.

Derrida, J. (1976) *Of Grammatology*, tr. G. C. Spivak. Baltimore: John Hopkins University Press.

Derrida, J. (1981) *Positions*, trans. A. Bass. Chicago: University of Chicago Press.

Derrida, J. (1987) *Of Spirit: Heidegger and the Question*, trans. Geoffrey Bennington and Rachel Bowlby. Chicago: University of Chicago Press.

Derrida, J. (1999) 'Marx and sons' in M. Sprinker (ed.) *Ghostly Demarcations: A Symposium on Jacques Derrida's* Specters of Marx. London: Verso.

Eagleton, T. (1999) 'In the gaudy supermarket (review of *A Critique of Postcolonial Reason* by Gayatri Chakravorty Spivak)' *London Review of Books*, 13 May. Reprinted in T. Eagleton (2003) *Figures of Dissent: Critical Essays on Fish, Spivak, Žižek and Others*. London: Verso.

Gramsci, A. (1971) *Selections From the Prison Notebooks*, ed. and trans. Q. Hoare and G. Nowell Smith. New York: International Publishers.

Guha, R. (1982) 'Preface' in R. Guha (ed.) *Subaltern Studies 1: Writings on South Asian History and Society*. Oxford: Oxford University Press.

Guha, R. and G. C. Spivak (eds.) (1989) *Selected Subaltern Studies*. Oxford University Press.

Hegel, G. W. F. (1961) *Science of Logic*, trans. W. H. Johnston and L. G. Struthers. London: Allen and Unwin.

Heidegger, M. (1978) 'The origin of the work of art' in D. F. Krell (ed.) *Basic Writings.* London: Routledge.

Jack, G. and R. Westwood (forthcoming) *International and Cross-Cultural Management Studies: A Postcolonial Reading.* Basingstoke: Palgrave Macmillan.

Jones, C. (2003) 'Theory after the postmodern condition' *Organization,* 10(3): 503–525.

Jones, C. (2004) 'Jacques Derrida' in S. Linstead (ed.) *Organization Theory and Postmodern Thought.* London: Sage.

Linstead, S. (ed.) (2004) *Organization Theory and Postmodern Thought.* London: Sage.

MacCabe, C. (1987) 'Foreword' in G. C. Spivak *In Other Worlds: Essays in Cultural Politics.* London: Routledge.

Marx, K. (1976) *Capital: A Critique of Political Economy, Volume One,* trans. B. Fowkes. London: Penguin.

Marx, K. (1978) *Capital: A Critique of Political Economy, Volume Two,* trans. D. Fernbach. London: Penguin.

Marx, K. (1981) *Capital: A Critique of Political Economy, Volume Three,* trans. D. Fernbach. London: Penguin.

Morton, S. (2003) *Gayatri Chakravorty Spivak.* London: Routledge.

Parker, M. (2002) *Against Management: Organization in the Age of Managerialism.* Oxford: Polity.

Prasad, A. (ed.) (2003) *Postcolonial Theory and Organizational Analysis.* Basingstoke: Palgrave.

Spivak, G. C. (1976) 'Translator's preface' in J. Derrida, *Of Grammatology,* trans. G. C. Spivak. Baltimore, MD: John Hopkins University Press.

Spivak, G. C. (1984) 'Marx after Derrida' in William Cain (ed.) *Philosophical Approaches to Literature: New Essays on Nineteenth and Twentieth Century Texts.* Lewisburg: Bucknell University Pres.

Spivak, G. C. (1985) 'Can the subaltern speak? Speculations on widow-sacrifice' *Wedge* 7/8 (Winter/Spring): 120–130.

Spivak, G. C. (1987a) 'Speculations on reading Marx: After reading Derrida' in D. Attridge, G. Bennington and R. Young (eds.) *Post-Structuralism and the Question of History.* Cambridge: Cambridge University Press.

Spivak, G. C. (1987b) 'Subaltern studies: Deconstructing historiography' in *In Other Worlds: Essays in Cultural Politics.* London: Routledge.

Spivak, G. C. (1988) 'Can the subaltern speak?' in C. Nelson and L. Grossberg (eds.). *Marxism and the Interpretation of Culture.* Urbana, IL: University of Illinois Press.

Spivak, G. C. (1990) *The Postcolonial Critic: Interviews, Strategies, Dialogues.* New York: Routledge.

Spivak, G. C. (1993) *Outside in the Teaching Machine.* London: Routledge.

Spivak, G. C. (1994) 'Responsibility' *Boundary 2,* 21(3): 19–64.

Spivak, G. C. (1995a) 'Ghostwriting' *Diacritics,* 25(2): 65–84.

Spivak, G. C. (1995b) 'Supplementing Marxism' in B. Magnus and S. Cullenberg (eds.) *Whither Marxism? Global Crises in International Perspective.* London: Routledge.

Spivak, G. C. (1996a) 'Scattered speculations on the question of value' in D. Landry and G. Maclean (eds.) *The Spivak Reader.* London: Routledge.

Spivak, G. C. (1996b) 'Subaltern talk: Interview with the editors' in D. Landry and G. Maclean (eds.) *The Spivak Reader.* London: Routledge.

Spivak, G. C. (1999) *A Critique of Postcolonial Reason: Toward a History of the Vanishing Present.* Cambridge, MA: Harvard University Press.

Spivak, G. C. (2000a) 'Discussion: An afterword on the new subaltern' in P. Chaterjee and P. Jeganathan (eds.) *Community, Gender and Violence: Subaltern Studies XI.* New York: Columbia University Press.

Spivak, G. C. (2000b) 'From Haverstock Hill to the US Classroom, what's left of theory?' in J. Butler, J. Guillory and K. Thomas (eds.) *What's Left of Theory? New Work on the Politics of Literary Theory.* London: Routledge.

Spivak, G. C. (2002) 'A conversation with Gayatri Chakravorty Spivak: Politics and the imagination' *Signs: Journal of Women in Culture and Society,* 28(2): 609–624.

Spivak, G. C. (2003a) *Death of a Discipline.* New York: Columbia University Press.

Spivak, G. C. (2003b) 'Globalization, rights and poverty' Presentation at the 25th Anniversary Conference of the Centre for the Study of Human Rights. Available online at: http://www.columbia.edu/cu/news/vforum/03/globalization_rights_poverty/ (Accessed 19 February 2005)

Spivak, G. C. (2003c) 'Righting wrongs' in N. Owen (ed.) *Human Right, Human Wrongs: The Oxford Amnesty Lectures 2001*. Oxford: Oxford University Press.

Spivak, G. C. (2003d) 'The politics of the production of knowledge: An interview with Gayatri Chakravorty Spivak' in J. Culler and K. Lamb (eds.) *Just Being Difficult? Academic Writing in the Public Arena*. Stanford: Stanford University Press.

Spivak, G. C. (2004a) 'Globalicities: Terror and its consequences' *CR: The New Centennial Review*, 4(1): 73–94.

Spivak, G. C. (2004b) 'Terror: A speech after 9–11' *Boundary 2*, 31(2): 81–111.

Spivak, G. C. (2005a) 'Class individual: Gayatri Chakravorty Spivak on Jacques Derrida' *ArtForum International*, 43(7): 49–52.

Spivak, G. C. (2005b) 'Remembering Derrida' *Radical Philosophy*, 129: 15–21.

Spivak, G. C. (forthcoming) *Of Derrida*. Cambridge, MA: Blackwell.

Spivak, G. C. (forthcoming) *Other Asias*. Cambridge, MA: Blackwell.

Spivak, G. C. (forthcoming) *Red Thread: A Book of Essays on Identity*. Cambridge, MA: Harvard University Press.

Westwood, R. (2001) 'Appropriating the other in discourses of comparative management' in R. Westwood and S. Linstead (eds) *The Language of Organization*. London: Sage.

Zein-Elabdin, E. and S. Charusheela (eds.) (2004) *Postcolonialism Meets Economics*. London: Routledge.

Partial organization: Marilyn Strathern and the elicitation of relations

Rolland Munro

Introduction

A leading social theorist, whose work stands at the front of a reanimation of relations, Marilyn Strathern would hesitate to align herself with those who write directly about organization. Her commitment to the discipline of social anthropology is too strong to risk contamination with a concept that was, until the 1970s, a major colonising trope of sociology. Yet Strathern can hardly be said to have ignored questions of organization within anthropology.[1]

On the contrary, as part of her major contribution to the rethinking of both theory and the social, Strathern points directly to how the term 'society' often acts as a 'metaphor for organization' (1988: 11). 'It is a working tenet of the comparative method in anthropology that societies everywhere do similar jobs in terms of exploiting the environment, providing nurture, reproducing their internal organization' (Strathern, 1988: 31). Her profound disagreement with this gloss on societies as similar has proved a potent force. Following Edmund Leach, among others, much of Strathern's writing has been concerned to help unpick how the concept of society 'organizes so much of the way anthropologists think'.

Strathern's tactics of consumption (de Certeau, 1984) are to embrace this heritage. Rather than merely move analysis to 'new ground' (Derrida, 1982: 135), she deploys the comparative method to dismantle the very 'society' perspective it has spawned.[2] Moving on from early field studies in Melanesia in which she made an 'easy living' (1988: 11) out of showing critical 'absences' of Western constructs (like that of nature and culture), her work graduated from re-working the 'structures' of kinship (1985), through an analysis of the 'divisions' of gender (1988) to more direct scrutiny of the Western inheritance of seeing relations in terms of 'parts' and 'wholes' (1991). Like Heidegger, Strathern's form of deconstruction is to *recover* the ground extruded by previous analyses (see Munro, 2004a).

In taking up the method of comparison, Strathern does not try to de-reify Western thought directly. By always 'working backwards with our archaeologies' (Strathern, 1999: 6), I show below how her comparative method follows Heidegger's (1962) method of 'questioning the question'. Deftly she brings analysis to bear on what is being made visible: she ensures first that we can see the *issue*. She re-minds us of the questions we are, so to speak, being asked to 'reproduce'. But what, she then seems to add, could make us see *that*? So, instead of leaving us in thrall to the lines of flight, the 'dazzle' of her anthropological gaze, we find her always sounding out depths that lie masked and occluded beyond these disciplining beams of light.

In what follows I do not attempt to do justice to the immense field affected by Marilyn Strathern's multifarious, ingenious interventions. For the purposes of this chapter I focus instead on the implications of her work for organization theory and argue that the contribution here circulates around her radical rethinking of three critical issues: the 'reification' inherent in the production and consumption of *division*, 'reductionism' and the nature of *relations*, and the 'totalizing' effects of what she calls the *ethnographic moment*.

I

Antinomies of the whole

Strathern begins her re-working of social theory by approaching 'the artifacts and images – the cultures – of Melanesian societies through a particular displacement'. We must, she suggests, stop thinking that at the heart of these cultures is an antinomy between 'society' and 'the individual' (1988: 12).

The contrasting figures between individuals and society set up an all-too familiar comparison for Strathern to explore. As she argues, 'society' in the Western imagination is taken to be:

> what connects individuals to one another, the relationships between them. We thus conceive of society as an ordering and classifying, and in this sense *a unifying force* that gathers persons who present themselves as otherwise irreducibly unique. (1988: 12, emphasis added)

Caught within this figure of 'society' are persons as 'parts' who receive the 'imprint of society', with this 'unifying force' of society going on to change the character of their connections. Yet, confusingly, in the figure of 'the individual', as Strathern points out, persons are then 'imagined as conceptually distinct from the relations that bring them together' (1988: 13).

At the heart of this Western antinomy, Strathern suggests, lie the relations of *domination*. Class analysis for example, requires a 'holistic model' of society in which specific interests would be 'located in relation to one another':

> From this point of view, ideas such as property or person belong to the common ideology which these relations promote and of which they are part. The particular forms that internal conflict and contradiction take are determined by productive processes, and it is the interconnections between processes and relations that analysis lays open. (Strathern, 1988: 26)

The only relations that 'count' in this all-too familiar reification of society are those seen from the viewpoint of 'society'. Specific interests are located in a *perspectival* relation to one another: so that the 'subordination or exploitation of particular categories of person' – such as that of landowner over peasants, bourgeois over proletariat, and men over women – becomes viewed as 'a systemic consequence of relations of production' (1988: 26).[3]

The contrasting view of individuals 'shaping' society retains these relations of domination, albeit at a different scale. It is precisely Strathern's point that the perspective of holism merely transfers the reification from society onto the 'holistic' individual. At least for the Melanesians, the plural and the singular are 'the same':

> They are homologues of one another. That is, the bringing together of many persons is just like the bringing together of one. The unity of a number of persons conceptualised as a group or a set is achieved through eliminating what differentiates them, and this is exactly what happens when a person is also individualised. The causes of internal differentiation are suppressed or discarded. (1988: 13–14)

This 'bringing together' is something the Melanesians are quite at home with. Indeed, in Melanesia, 'the one holistic condition may elicit the other'.

The subtlety of the foregoing analysis should not be lost. Strathern's argument is not that the pendulum of analysis swings back and forth between what might be called 'simple wholes' – comparable to the way much talk about organization builds its theories upon the putative existence of *either* society *or* the individual. In their holistic form, the latter, as much as the former, becomes 'an ordering and classifying, and in this sense a unifying force'.[4] It is the *perspective* of holism that is at stake, not an ontological dispute over the relative completeness of its base 'figures'. As argued next, the figure of 'the individual' acts as much as a reification as that of 'society'.

The reification of relations

Strathern thinks in terms of *relations*. Relations for her are formed and reformed, even performed, first and foremost in the materialized groundings of time and space. What the perspective of 'society' has scaled down, Strathern is determined to 'scale up'. But if relations are not to be abstracted off into the realm of society by virtue of their 'function' (and few today would disagree about this), then neither should relations be re-allocated as the mere 'property' of individuals.

Strathern's ambition is thus to rethink relations as *forms* of connecting – but to avoid the reifications inherent within the Western antinomy between 'society' and 'the individual'. Thus to approach her general understanding of relations, and Melanesian relations in particular, we must first set aside the holism inherent in the concept of the Western 'individual':

In so far as 'society' constructed the set of relationships between its members, the individuality of the latter was taken to be logically prior. Individuals thus appeared as primary phenomena of life, relationships as secondary. (Strathern, 1996: 62)

For Strathern, we are not persons who are individuals first, 'individuals' who then subsequently enter into 'relationships'. Rather it is our entering into relations that helps create us as persons.

Many anthropologists would dispute the holism of there ever being such firm or finished entities as 'individuals' with which to divide up the world. Far from being regarded as 'unique entities' – wholes of a different order – Strathern (1988: 13) proposes that 'Melanesian persons are as dividually as they are individually conceived'. The term 'dividuals' here is borrowed from Marriott's (1976: 111) analysis:

> persons – single actors – are not thought in South Asia to be 'individual', that is indivisible, bounded units, as they are in much of Western social and psychological theory, as well as in common sense. Instead it appears that persons are generally thought by South Asians to be 'dividual' or divisible. (quoted by Strathern, 1988: 348n)

Within Melanesia, persons are 'frequently constructed as the plural and composite site of the relationships that produced them':

> Thus a group of men or a group of women will conceive of their individual members as replicating in singular form ('one man', 'one woman) what they have created in collective form ('one men's house', 'one matrilineage'). In other words, a plurality of individuals as individuals ('many') is equal to their unity ('one'). (1988: 14)

While collective events in Melanesia do, indeed, 'bring together disparate persons', Strathern (1988: 13) states that this is not to 'make' them into *social* beings.

In Strathern's view, the key transformations in Melanesian cultures are not concerned with this kind of relation of domination. Individuals are not pro-created, in the Western idiom, only then needing to be 'finished off' by being *made* social (Strathern, 1992). To the contrary, the kind of 'de-pluralized, collective events' she has studied 'have as much an amoral, antisocial character to them as do autonomous persons who go their own way' (1988: 13).

The idea of 'dividuals' should not therefore be interpreted too literally. Melanesians, as much as Euro-Americans, are also in the business of reification, especially in the making up of themselves as persons. Drawing on her earlier work (1988: 282) Strathern argues the person:

> emerges as an individual agent through the singularity of action. In the same way, a clan appears as a collective individual . . . when it is engaged on one enterprise, acts as a unit. It is the act which, through its temporality, individuates. (1999: 96)

Conditions permitting, Melanesians can 'cut' the figure of the individual as well as anyone. But, for Strathern, the 'individual' is not fixed but 'temporalized in the image of body-time' (1988: 282). This matter of *cuttings* is now discussed.

Cuttings

According to Strathern, the holism of Melanesian imagery never meant the Melanesians did not envision 'cutting':

> On the contrary, images of partition, extraction, severance were commonplace. But what was 'cut' were persons and relations themselves: person from person, relation from relation, not persons cut off from relations. (1994: 215)

Far from being fixed in time at the moment of birth, as had been presumed within models of kinship, a point returned to below, Strathern states, 'relations were the active life on which persons were for ever working' (1994: 215).

As Strathern claims, separations are intrinsic to the Melanesian ability to perceive ('personify') relations:

> The activities that Hageners, for instance, distinguish as production and transaction are themselves composed of distinctions. In the first case, the products of work are separable from those who produced them in order that they stand for the relationship between the producers. In the second case, the transactors are separable from each other in order to create a relationship between themselves. (1988: 180)

This analysis, in line with Wagner (1975: 52; 1977a: 624), suggests that the necessity to differentiate becomes an explicit burden of people's interactions with one another.

Cuttings are also gendered, but in particular ways rather than in general:

> I shall also make it apparent that the assumptions of natural difference that Westerners locate in the bodily constitution of men and women are no more useful a guide to understanding the Melanesian imagination than is the Western privileging of relations between individuals as the locus of society. (Strathern 1988: 35)

She would not deny that aspects of class or gender can be asymmetrical. But she hones in ethnographically on precisely what is being divided up locally and specifically, rather than seeing matters as predetermined.

Specifically, Hagen women, Strathern (1999) argues, take what advantage they could in pressing their 'particularistic claims'. Where for Hagen men 'it was a question of securing a home base from which to engage in the world', the compensation for blood spilt in a quarrel was 'generally satisfied if the husband paid her male relatives':

> Women were structurally 'in between' groups of men, their multiple loyalties showing in a constitutional multiplicity of mind. Men on the other hand were alleged to overcome their conflicting emotions and orientations much more easily, and display the 'one mind' that was the predicate for successful action. (Strathern, 1999: 91)

Strathern's argument is that Western questions about male dominance 'in society' subsume the problem of women as a universal one for the organization of relations. Without that problem, the character of men's prominence, she suggests, becomes interesting in its own right.

Strathern's interest is also with how the idea of division is made to operate more generally. The intricacies of continuous division in Melanesia contrast with the ready-made and taken for granted divisions of Western thought; for example the tri-partite division of organization into the levels of society, institutions and individuals as respectively representing of the macro, the meso and the micro. Her challenge to this rather restricted notion of a hierarchy in 'scales' is the idea of 'changing scales' and this is developed in the final section below. Ahead of this, we explore the way division in Melanesia escapes what she calls the 'mode of comparison'; the kind of divisive division favoured by Euro-Americans (see also Strathern, 1997), in which one side of the division is denigrated while the other is privileged because of an implicit and hidden 'aesthetic'.

II

A comparison of 'wholes'

In seeking to unlock analysis from the pendulum of 'society' and 'the individual', Strathern focuses on processes of *objectification*. By objectification, she understands the *manner* in which persons and things are construed as having value. This is to say they become 'objects of people's subjective regard' (1988: 176). In analysing the 'creative' aspect of these kinds of relations, she draws on an earlier use of the comparative method, an example that weakens it to a 'mode of thought that juxtaposes but does not classify' (1988: 175).

Objectification, according to Wagner (1975: 45), takes place in every cultural act and is a twin process in which invention makes its differentiations in an 'explicit and masking' role, while convention takes the 'implicit and masked' role of putting things together. By way of an illustrative example, one thinks of the 'convention' of publishing whereby academics put their own names to works; implicit in this practice is the idea of each work belonging to an individual (a matter that the 'invention' of intellectual property makes explicit) and what is masked is the extent to which the work is the product of a wider collectivity.

As Wagner (1975: 53) suggests, any act involves an interplay of invention and convention. For example, the 'invention' of the Research Assessment Exercise (RAE) picks up on and makes explicit what the above 'convention' has left implicit and masked: the idea of the intellectual environment of universities as a 'culture'. Yet by ascribing each work to an individual, the RAE makes explicit only the contribution of the individual's institution (in the context of elaborate allocation mechanisms to ensure this). What the RAE is 'masking' is the extent to which works are produced in what Strathern (1996: 173) calls 'the environment of a second collectivity', namely the 'collective environment of knowledge and ideas'.

Wagner argues this interplay between invention and convention encapsulates both Western and Melanesian proclivities. This is what sets up the 'similarity' from which comparison might proceed. As in mathematics where the same term, even if unknown, can be dropped from either side of the equation, so too, in making comparisons, the possible 'fictions' in understandings on either side also cancel out, leaving us to ponder the difference. If Westerners create the incidental world, as Wagner (1975: 87) says, by 'constantly trying to predict, rationalize, and order it', then 'tribal, religious and peasant people' create their universe of innate convention by 'constantly trying to change, readjust, and impinge upon it'.

Reification and personification

Reification and personification, for Strathern, are 'the symbolic mechanisms or techniques' by which objectification is done. She sums up Wagner's 'most elegant formulation' in the following way:

> the idea of a symbol as *both* a conventional, artificial expression of something already (invented) existing in itself, *and* as the inventive desire to draw out of relations and persons the innate (conventionalized) capacities that lie within them. (1988: 174)

As she explains, the terms reification and personification 'refer to nothing other that the relations between concepts'. Yet the replication that results from this interplay between invention and convention can produce very different effects.

Although commodity thinking creates 'an internal play on the analogy between things and persons' – the very kind of fiction Strathern wants to avoid[5] – the fiction is common to different visions of culture:

> If these concepts refer to anything it is to the forms in which persons make things appear and the things through which persons appear, and thus with the 'making' (-ification) of persons and things. (1988: 176)

This figuration back and forth between persons and things is specific in Melanesia and should not be attributed entirely to 'convention', as Euro-Americans think of it. This is made clear by the example of 'money'.

'Money', as Strathern (1999: 96) pithily remarks, 'has a lot of work to do'. In the past, as one of her informants Manga asserts, if it was a question of returning bridewealth at a divorce, one simply collected the shells and pigs and handed them over:

> There was not any other work for these things. Each item was entire. It was both a single thing and had a single purpose – no one thought about keeping back part of a shell. (1999: 96)

As Strathern interpolates, this is why money is so different: unlike a shell or a pig, money can be divided into small amounts. 'Too many thoughts', as Manga adds, contemplating the way a sum of money cannot stay 'entire', 'accompany its use' (1999: 96).

In this way, the introduction of modern forms of currency can be understood to alter how people see things. The division being enacted by Manga here between 'the past' and 'the future' arises not just because money itself is an 'invention'. What makes it a *technology* able to overthrow all 'convention' (and abandon the past as 'tradition') is that money arrives in a form in which it is entirely divisible. The effect, I would add, along the lines that Manga suggests, is to induce endless *inventions* about what to do with the money. *So that if no single purpose or connection can hold onto money, the use of money dissolves relations back into 'things'.* That in a commodity economy 'things and persons take the form of things' is encompassed in the proposition that objects (of whatever kind) are 'reified as things-in-themselves'. All 'prior' relations vested through the objects are nullified and all connections to persons are effaced.[6]

Concomitantly, in a gift economy, Strathern suggests 'objects act as persons in relation to one another'. First, there is the case of unmediated work:

> In the direct, unmediated activity of work, the object of relatedness may be taken for granted (as between kinsmen), but work makes the specific relations visible – kinsmen do things for one another as kinsmen should, as spouses also work with each other in mind as spouses should. (1988: 180)

In a gift economy, social relations are made the overt objects of people's activities. Yet, contrastingly, something different happens when transactions are involved:

> Transactions, however, appear to make relations afresh, for the instruments of mediation – the gifts – appear to be creating the relationship. Transactions are thus experienced as holding out the possibility of relationships ever newly invented, as though there could be an infinite expansion of social connections. (1988: 180)

Brought together, Strathern claims that these modes of exchange compose an explicit practice of personification. It is the *social relations* that are made visible. But, as already indicated, this potential for 'invention' does not mean that just any form of replication is possible. 'From the perspective of Western knowledge practices', the modes of exchange conceal their own conventions – 'the further mechanism of reification' (1988: 180). This tendency for the social to be 'recessive' (Munro, 1995) brings us to the matter of understanding performances not only as a display of 'relations' but also *as* evidence.

Performance and evidence

Gifts, according to Strathern, were 'generally handed over in a public context to critical and judgemental recipients before a critical and judgemental audience':

> The scrutiny of form drove home the fact that, ipso facto, a form can only appear with its appropriate properties – or else it has not appeared. A return gift is not a return gift if the items are too few or too poor; prestige does not emerge from a display if the display fails. (1999: 15)

These circumstances call up the reliance Robert Boyle had on the presence of 'gentlemen witnesses' for the veracity of his experiments. But this is not the analogy Strathern pursues.

Instead, Strathern draws her comparison in forms of reification with the status of Western 'art objects'. For the people of Hagen, it is 'the evidence that is visible':

> What transpires between persons becomes reified, graspable, 'on their skins', whether it is the skin of the land or the body or the clan with its universe of names. (1999: 253)

Whether or not an artefact is deemed art at all, she suggests, is 'a debate precisely about the appropriateness of form' (1999: 15).

But if the evidence is made visible, what creates the evidence is not. Modes of reification, Strathern claims, hide the principles of their own aesthetic:

> Their *conventional* nature is made covert in people's overt experience of these forms as *invented*, individuated performances, for all they perceive is their own activity, freshly instigated. (1988: 181, emphasis added)

The key point to absorb, I think, is that the establishing of attributes – the nature of things – is not the explicit focus of these symbolic operations. Rather these are present as 'an implicit technique of operation'.

In the terms developed above from Wagner's analysis, Strathern argues that 'the operation thus conceals its conventional base'.

> Indeed, there is a very small number of (conventional) forms that will do as evidence that relations have been thus activated. They must display certain attributes. (Strathern, 1988: 180)

The objectification of relations as persons simultaneously makes them into *things* in so far as the relations are only recognized *if they assume a particular form*.

> The Western relationship is 'between things', each with their own form (as in imagining the way an item, such as a shell valuable 'expresses' a child). Whereas Melanesians 'must instead *make the form appear*' when they personify relations (i.e. endow valuables with human attributes and human capabilities). (Strathern, 1988: 181)

Strathern's argument is that only 'certain specific forms of interaction', which she calls *performances*, will have the appropriate aesthetic that can make the relations that they objectify properly 'appear'. Performances, she states, must be recognizable by their attributes.

> Only certain specific forms of interaction will be taken as evidence of the successful activation or maintenance of relationships. In being conventionally prescribed these are reified: they-in-themselves hold evidence of the successful outcome. (1988: 181)

Without these, the relations being summoned, such as those of ancestral ghosts, do not appear. (And worse, I would add, *other* relations might appear!)

In making objectification a basis of comparison for Western and Melanesian 'economies', Strathern does recognize dangers in presuming similar processes. Yet it is the prospect of being able to cancel out the 'fictions' from either side of the equation that frees up a way to perceive their difference:

> The commodity logic of Westerners leads them to search for knowledge about things (and persons as things); the gift logic of Melanesians [is] to make known to themselves persons (and things as persons). (1988: 176–177)

As she adds, the one makes an explicit practice out of apprehending the nature or character (convention) of objects, the other their capabilities or animate powers (invention).

Visibility and knowledge

Strathern (1999) returns to a question she suppressed, although it troubled her at the time: what was the underlying motive for making relations visible? This was, for her, a 'blind spot':

> For it seemed a self-evident fact of social and cultural life that people make themselves explicit to themselves in various ways for which visibility is a powerful metaphor. This was the dazzle: they are anthropologists too! The dazzle of technical symmetry, that is, a symmetry in artistry and technique. (1999: 258)

Looking back, Strathern sees that it 'had the same grip as the notions of convention and norms had gripped earlier anthropologists in their perception of social order as the matter of rules'.

Strathern (1999: 258) goes on to confess that the idea that 'people must make themselves explicit to themselves' probably came from the 'kind of productionist view of culture and society' roundly criticized by Viveiros de Castro (1998) and others. She does not, however, entirely abandon her earlier position. Instead, she argues that 'All we need do is drop the Euro-American link between visibility and knowledge of the world'.

The emphasis in Melanesia, as Strathern goes on to argue, is on performance and presentation helping to preserve or create *what is to be seen*.

> What you see is there to be seen because the observer is in the appropriate social condition to register the effect. And the cause of the effect is ultimately another person. (Strathern, 1999: 259)

As Strathern suggests, visibility is very much the point for Hagen men. So that conversely, in the case of Hagen women being 'mostly not to "be seen" in the way men are', it follows that 'what you do not see is what is not to be seen'.

On reflection over her past fieldwork, what Strathern (1999: 258) thinks is 'mistaken', is the 'axiomatic assumption that visibility is somehow for the sake of knowledge, and that knowledge addresses, and thus gathers information about, the larger world in which one lives'. In failing to free itself from a doctrine of wholes, Western ideas of organization appear to have become enslaved to the idea of boundaries – subjects living in a skin of 'representations'.

The tendency in Euro-American thought is to imagine 'systems' of relations which are open to information, but otherwise 'organizationally closed – the information being drawn from signs from which, problematically, there is no escape. In contrast a Melanesian view 'keeps relations in view'. For Strathern's Melanesians, what you see is 'not a representation of the world' (ie, an abstract model). To the contrary, it is 'evidence of your point of being in it' (Strathern, 1999: 259; cf. Viveiros de Castro, 1996). This is a profoundly existential position.

III

Reification and relations

Anthropologists, as Strathern notes, 'route connections through persons' (1995: 11). This means they attend to the relations of logic, of cause and effect, of class and category, that people make between things. And it also means:

> They attend to the relations of social life, to the roles and behaviour, through which people connect themselves to one another. And habitually they bring these two domains of knowledge together, as when they talk about the relation between culture and society. (1995: 11)

At one level, under the influence of W. H. Rivers and his pupil A. R. Radcliffe-Brown, society could be perceived as working in terms of a 'system'. At the other, 'with their penchant for the concrete', these abstract descriptions were equated with the 'regulatory functions of the rules to which people adhered'.

'Routing relations through persons', Strathern suggests, 'had become the substance of anthropological empiricism'. What could be seen only in the abstract, social structure, was taken to be inhered in relationships relevant to people's acts and intentions, the concrete. Social order 'became simultaneously the description of society and the perceived means of its cohesion':

> There was a double emphasis then on [first] relations known to the observer as principles of social organization and [second] relations observed as interactions between persons. (Strathern, 1995: 12)

What Strathern calls British Social Anthropology remained 'closely tied to the conviction that at the heart of systems were persons' dealings with one another, the systems they created for themselves being second-order manifestations of their primary human ability to make relationships' (1995: 14).

The 'invention' of kinship had its primary impetus in making 'explicit' persons in the form of their being related through kinship models. Drawing on Wagner's formulation, outlined earlier, it is arguable then that these abstractions also had the effect of 'masking' the 'conventions' of the indigenous models. Mistaken as second-order terms, as well as having to be 'revealed' through the inventions of the ethnographer, the indigenous orders could amount to little more than ideology (similar to the way in which Marxists imagined the super-structure of culture as reflecting the economic mode of production).

Despite this cul-de-sac, the door had already been opened to observations of a different kind. With the invention of field notes, it is the *material* form which relations take that comes to be made explicit:

> Social relations may be abstractions, wrote Fortes, but "in order to be at the disposal of those who engage in them, [they] must be discernible, objectified . . . *bodied forth* in material objects and places, in words, acts, ideas [and] rules. (Strathern, 1995: 14, emphasis added)

The mid-century job of the anthropologist might well have been to codify social relations in the abstract. But, for Fortes, 'pre-literate people had to body forth such abstractions in material objects as well as in words and rules' (Strathern, 1995: 22).

The way in which relations are 'bodied forth' in terms of both words and materials had already begun to be documented.[7] And when the focus on kinship, with all its systems baggage of holism and logic, was eventually punctured, the material was there to evidence that 'distinctions between kinds of kin may thus distinguish different orderings of social life'. As Strathern (1995: 15) adds, by making the relations of kinship, both a 'concrete vehicle for conceiving of a social order' and 'an abstract articulation of the relational quality of all social existence', Fortes had transformed the scale of the earlier strategy.

Material extension

I have argued elsewhere that understanding Strathern requires a shift in focus from the Western preoccupation with the contents of consciousness – 'intentions' – to a stress on *extension* (Munro, 1996). Attending to the materials of culture, rather than the abstractions of its 'models', cannot of itself shift the locus of analysis.

Where the consciousness of individuals is regarded as primary (eg, Cohen, 1994; Rapport, 1998), the tendency is always to re-locate relations inside these 'wholes' – to the domain Kant called the 'universe within'. The result is to make relations appear as a kind of 'property' of individuals: stuff more or less like clothes, or other belongings which people can pick up at whim and even 'pick and mix'. What is expanded in this view, Strathern suggests, is the element of choice between 'what is given and what is open to choice'. Excepting the cases where the children or the spouse have specific legal rights, it becomes up to me to dispose of friendship or kinship whenever I want: 'I would hardly call them relatives!' (Strathern, 1995: 20).

256

As Marriott indicates, however, what goes on '*between* actors are the same connected processes of mixing and separation that go on *within* actors (1976: 109, emphasis in original, cited by Strathern, 1988: 349).

> To exist dividual persons absorb heterogeneous material influences. They must also give out from themselves particles of their own coded substances – essences, residues, or other active influences – that may then reproduce in others something of the nature of the persons in whom they have originated. (Marriott, 1976: 111)

That much happens 'between' actors has of course long been understood. The importance of the exchange of materials for understanding relations had been evident, for example, in the case of shells. As Strathern (1999: 255) claims, gift exchange between Hagen men 'takes the form of an exchange of substance'.

What is critical about 'gifts' for Strathern, I submit, is that they evidence how changes in *scale* are enacted before, it seems, our very eyes:

> wealth flowing between donor and recipient indicates the detachability of the donor's assets which go to swell the size of the recipient's body in turn. . . .
>
> With the substance of the gift goes the 'capacity' for enlargement: the 'enlarged body is made visible through decoration'. Conversely, and simultaneously for the donor, the depleted body is made visible through its absence. (Strathern, 1999: 255)

Scale, for Melanesians, is not something outside their ken. Nor, indeed, is it something that lies outside their capacities. Scale does not exist autonomously, as it does with the Western conception of levels of 'wholes', such as the tripartite set of society, institution and individual. To the contrary, it is arguable that changing scale – the effect of 'magnification' or 'diminishment' (see also Munro, 1996) – is precisely a demonstration of 'capacities'.

The eyes of anthropologists were opened up to the idea that people 'demarcate between the differences in scale through diverse distinctions'. And just as importantly, the *materials* which 'bodied forth' the very different abstractions were made 'explicit' by being documented. Relations could be seen to change depending on what was being 'attached' to persons; or, indeed, what was being 'detached'. Attachment, as I have stressed before (Munro, 1996; 1999), has a double meaning for Strathern, relating to the way affiliations also can move around with the prosethetics of material objects.

The idea of 'abstractions' having to be at the 'disposal' of 'those who engage with them', as expressed by Fortes, proved decisive. In turn, however, the 'materials' that bodied forth these abstractions also had to be re-imagined in order for them to act as the basis for re-thinking 'what the devil people were up to'. Materials, rather than intentions, had become the fulcrum on which the perspectives (including those of the native and the anthropologist) could be exchanged.

Exchanging perspectives

An emphasis on the exchange of materials for *understanding* relations would presage nothing new, especially given Marxist readings on the interdependence between culture, as superstructure, and the economy as structure. In elaborating her ideas, however, Strathern gives the idea of extension a further twist by seizing on the importance of materials for understanding the *exchange of relations*.

Rather than the exchange of materials merely 'expressing' known and fixed relations, much as Mary Douglas imagines consumption mirroring production, Strathern sees the potential for gifts (as well as other materials) to have the effect of *perspectives* being exchanged:

> When I write about exchange of perspectives, for instance, I have in mind the image of a Hagen man handing over an item (shells, pigs, money) with the expectation of a return gift and, thus, with the counterflow contained in the same gesture. (Strathern, 1999: 15)

What differentiated relations in Melanesia was the way material entered into the *exchange* of perspectives between persons.

For Strathern much more is being exchanged than the items being handed over: 'these gifts had a further compelling effect on this ethnographer for the reason that they seemed to compel responses from people who saw them' (1999: 15).

As Strathern (1988) puts the matter, the transfer of valuables guaranteed that a woman would bear her husband's child and not her father's. Or, again, if more cryptically, the work of a spouse in procreation, with this work having to be repeated before birth and supplemented by nature afterwards.

As discussed earlier in respect of Strathern's conception of 'performances': 'One simply has to make or create oneself in a form that can be consumed by others' (1999: 259).

> Perspectives may be overtly paired, and the positions may be reversible, but a person's gaze is not returned as such; the man does not see himself but himself, transformed, in another body. (1999: 255)

And what person is this? asks Strathern. It has to be, she says, the person engaged in the exchange. This implies therefore that it is 'the exchangeability of people's capacities that is at issue' (1999: 255).

Nothing of this then is to suggest that perspectives can be swapped at will, more or less as Euro-Americans imagine switching from one intention to another.

> For a body or mind to be in a position of eliciting an effect from another, to evince power or capability, it must manifest itself in a particular or concrete way. This then becomes the elicitory trigger. (Strathern, 1988: 181)

Elicitation is not, however, a foregone conclusion. For example, not all accrual brings with it 'magnification' or enlargement. Foster (1995a: 259, 20n) compares the Tangan who perversely hoards wealth with witches from elsewhere; the retention of wealth 'ultimately denies him the only culturally recognized means for attaching the qualities of those objects to his person, namely display' (at the point of giving it away) (Strathern, 1999: 259). In a hint of the emphasis on power and coercion she is developing, she adds that reciprocity, for Foster, is willingness to become an instrument of another person's self-definition. In Strathern's 'vocabulary', it is 'persons' who 'hold perspectives in one another':

> Relations between donor and recipient are predicated on the fact that at any single moment one is either in one position or the other in relation to one's counterpart (a donor to a recipient) . . . to be a donor is to have been a recipient, the anticipation of the reversal is ever present. (1999: 254)

This is not a matter of vision, but 'the kind of effect that people have on one another'. As Strathern adds (1999: 260), there 'would not be a visible world to see if the world was not making itself visible towards the viewer':

> Rendering oneself visible, just as the holder of wealth does, offers a sight which is then reduplicated when at the moment of handing it over men, and sometimes women, on the donor's side decorate themselves. They create a form as it is intended to appear from the perspective of the viewer (recipient). That form is put before the viewer, and thus forced on an audience, (the coercive metaphor is appropriate) for the audience to confront. (Strathern, 1999: 260)

At work here, Strathern suggests, is a type of knowledge that consists in 'seeing' relations.

Importantly, she suggests her aphorism of 'seeing relations' could do well for 20th century Europeans as well as for 20th-century Melanesians. But she is insistent also that an exchange of perspectives is 'not to be confused with the European gaze':

> A mutual gaze in the contemporary Euro-American mode is two perspectives each from an individual standpoint on the world. In my model of Melanesia, for which I have imagined a visual theory of sorts, any one perspective elicits another. (Strathern, 1999: 260)

As she emphasises, her 'Melanesian constructs' do not end up with relations – they *start* with relations. Relations, for her, are 'what make people "see" anything at all'.

Discussion

Organization theorists have been busy trying to de-totalize the concept of organization in ways that have led to a 'pluralism' of perspectives, if not an abandonment of the very idea of organization. Yet Strathern only goes part of the way with those like Clifford (1988: 11) in their readiness to celebrate 'fragments over wholes'. While she might agree with Clifford that one is always caught in telling one's story 'in pieces', she would never consent to the idea that we can just tell it *'as it is'* (quoted by Strathern, 1994: 215, emphasis in original). This is the mistake of pluralism, an approach that purports never to valorise one society's 'stories' over another. Just as there never were any 'wholes' in the first place, Strathern argues, so it is a mistake to continue to characterize 'parts' in terms of them being *fragments* of a whole.

Contemporary talk of individuals as 'hybrids' also freezes this idea of 'parts' *as* fragments. It returns the 'capacities' over which Strathern has laboured to Western conceptions of the volume of the body. Humans are still envisualized as 'wholes', even if this is being like a 'curate's egg' – good in parts – or like a 'cyborg' – part organs and part machine.

What Strathern's analysis accomplishes, however, is quite another notion of 'parts', one more akin to dramaturgical conceptions of a 'part' as a *performance*. Again, it would seem a mistake to envisage such 'parts' as a property of the social actor (however embodied certain 'repertoires' become). It is a change in the 'view' of the recipient that is being demanded. And sometimes this change in perspective is elicited, as Strathern indicates, through the process of enlargement. This is to say that the 'attachment' and 'detachment' of prosthetic devices to persons can accomplish a magnification or diminishment that amounts to changes in 'scale'.[8]

Although Strathern remains somewhat cryptic in her position over hybrids, my understanding of her work is that what is elicited is not an 'essence' of someone else – a ready-made 'half' of a hybrid – but a *perspective*. What counts is what is being made 'explicit' to an audience through a process of materialization. This is why I have given special emphasis to the 'exteriority' of the locus of material extension – what Strathern calls the 'explicit'. As noted earlier, 'for a body or a mind to be in a position of eliciting an effect from another' – to evince the power or capability – 'it must manifest itself in a particular concrete way'. Aspects of this analysis that can help us re-imagine the way power works are further developed, as acknowledged by Strathern, in Latimer's (2004) theme of 'commanding materials'.

My question is whether an emphasis on *motility* is perhaps more consistent with Strathern's ideas of persons 'changing scale' than her term 'merographic'[9] – which she coins to refer to a 'doubling', even 'endless' proliferation of perspective in which one thing is presupposed to differ from another 'insofar as it belongs to or is part of something else' (1992: 73). I do not doubt the acuity of this term to capture the double-jointed way in which the English handle kinship; nor, indeed, its applicability to the 'infinite capacity of western views to proliferate, to endlessly extend, to pluralise' (Strathern, 2005). But too great a reliance on this term merographic seems to me to repeat the mistake of conceiving of persons as 'hybrids' – except that it is now the perspective, rather than the person, that is decomposed into 'parts': namely, the thing we are to 'see' and the (implicit) context that frames the meaning.[10]

I shall not develop the trope of 'motility' here. Suffice to say I use the term to capture the way in which a change in view does more than change the 'part' we are to see; the 'dazzle' to which I have referred earlier. Such a shift in sight can be sufficiently 'totalizing' as to also carry with it a change in the very 'world' that we – as 'members' – find ourselves making up. Motility thus addresses the drama of the 'undecidability' of the 'lived' world as its enframing unfolds from moment to moment, even to the point of enveloping us as 'insiders'. Merographic, in contrast, seems to capture the exercise of an 'observer', shifting through the more abstract 'volumes' that perspectives on knowledge proliferate in order to demonstrate that terms, like that of 'persons', typically have no fixed abode. The difference seems to be the contrast between a pianist going through the scales to show how the same notes get caught up in technically different frames and the visceral *affect* of experiencing a shift from the major scale to a minor when listening to a late Beethoven quartet.[11]

I agree that sometimes 'culture belongs to the domain of human activity, and in that sense is universally part of it'; and that sometimes, 'as an idea it may also be claimed as the specific construct of a specific era and thus (to the contrary) also part of a particular culture at one point in time' (Strathern, 1992: 73). However, what the rather abstract and distanced analysis of merography elides is the existential affect of our being 'inside' the very worlds that are being moved about. Put bluntly, merography seems to say much about the resources that service the 'English' restraint. What Strathern calls 'the English view' that 'anything may be part of something else' might capture precisely, and ethnographically, the way in which English people resist their involvement from being 'totalized'. They *insist* on the 'partial' nature of the situation; so rather than consume entirely the magnification of what is being made present, they are adept in 'producing' another, alternative perspective, in which the 'same' part is diminished.

What matters to Strathern about merographic connections is not so much the 're-description' aspect as its 'displacement effect'. The effect is not to substitute one entity for another. Rather it is the 'network' that appears to alter: 'the substitution connects the entity to a whole, other (distinct and unique) domain of phenomena. A different order of knowledge is introduced' (1992: 73). Her example is of 'the ultrasound image of the unborn body brings the foetus into a social domain where individual persons have legal rights and the body of the mother is redescribed as a life-support system'.

Implicit in such examples is a new understanding of how power works. What interests me is precisely the way in which each of us can be moved about in and out of these different *worlds*: one moment to see 'maternity', one moment to see a 'life-support' system; one moment to see the legal rights, one moment to see the equivalent of a photographic plate. To the extent that persons can cue each other's *performances* into conforming with these switches in knowledge domains, and thus make visible different 'networks' as they command different materials, I call this 'motility'.

Conclusion

Strathern's contribution, especially prominent in her analysis of the gift, is to help show how a movement of materials that is ostensibly caught within the [micro] 'scale' of interaction can actually elicit a 'switch' in viewpoint that draws on a wholly other ('distinct and unique') domain of phenomena at the [macro] 'scale'. The repercussions of what I am calling motility for making 'networks' visible one moment – and invisible the next – go far beyond the quite different notion of 'mobilities' – a concept which relies heavily upon the fixtures of the very divisions it reifies. (There is, for example, more than a whiff of the distinction between the micro and the macro in Habermas's separation of 'system' and 'lifeworld').

Ethnographers, I suggest, do not need a 'chaos' theory to assert the fertile possibilities for Strathern's 'exchange of perspectives' here. They can easily demonstrate matters like the butterfly effect, and much much more, within the documentary method of social science. And Strathern's commitment is precisely to the ethnographic moment. She persistently challenges ways in which the theoretical foundations of her discipline *organize* the interpretation and arrangement of fieldwork. The twists and turns of her writing act as an Archimedean screw, in which the complexities of ethnographic realities are slowly but firmly pumped back into the explanatory bathwater of comparison. What makes her critique of structural-functionalism in social science so compelling, and original, is her ability to refocus her ethnographic attention from structure and process onto persons – without losing sight of their being, first and foremost, *social*.[12]

Unlike much contemporary social theory in sociology, Strathern's analysis does not, as explained earlier, entail a shift from the 'society' perspective to a focus on 'the individual'. The holism of the one, for Strathern, is as bad as the other, creating such disasters of contemporary theory as the 'hybrid' and the 'fluid'. The danger in thinking that one can move one's analysis from the larger scale (macro) to the smaller (micro) is just that of being caught in an antinomy like that between 'society' and 'the individual' (or, as indicated above, between the 'system' and the 'lifeworld').

Strathern's analysis of the way in which either Euro-Americans or Melanesians can 'change scale' in their performance of 'relations' has profound implications for understanding these complexities of 'division'. Too often organization theory proceeds by merely changing the ontological base of its premises. Structure is replaced by process, systems effects are deleted in favour of human agency, modernism is given over to postmodernism, but the essence of reductionism is maintained. There is always this macho insistence on there being some central motor to movement and change, some basic core from which everything swings and sings.

As a post-structural feminist – a position she has made definitively her own[13] – connections for Strathern are 'provisional' as well as 'partial'. The severity of her challenge here to the nature of relations (as either fixed or abstract) applies as much to contemporary ideas about 'hybrids' and 'cyborgs', as to conventional, ideas about the organization of division. The 'boundary' problem has long haunted attempts to define organization, due to a tendency to look for divisions that can be held to 'exist'. What should interest future researchers more is to pick up on those divisions or boundaries which are, often creatively, being *displayed*.

The vexed issue of display, especially with regard to its proliferation of 'meanings', deserves further comment. Strathern's gift is to stay within 'interpretation'; unlike Malinowski, she refuses to reduce interpretation to a 'functionalism'. But neither will she allow the blandness of that contemporary symbolism in which materials become *merely* 'expressive'. She keeps returning to the 'dazzle' – the 'totalizing' effect – of each ethnographic moment, questing after its power. So rather than just glory in particular and local effects, the celebration of an endless pluralism, she understands the potential both to bring theory to the surface – to see it 'on the skin' – and to question who, or what, it compels.

Notes

1 Within her own discipline, Strathern is largely accredited with having turned that centrepiece of anthropological thought, kinship, upside down, both at home and abroad. Other prescient contributions include rethinking gender, especially in her *Gender of the Gift*. More recent writings, however, also draw explicitly on the ideas of a number of organizational writers, including Power (1997), Tsoukas (1996), and Munro (1996a; 1996b; 1998; 2001[1992]). In addition, her work has also addressed several prominent organization themes including the nature of science (2003c), intellectual property (1998), virtual organization (2003a), audit (2000) and accountability (1997; 2003b).

2 Strathern's radical stance includes rethinking methodology. The idea of society as 'organization' not only permeated anthropology early, it also became enshrined in the very method of field studies:

> This tenet [the similarity of the organization of societies] yields the rubrics of cross-cultural comparison: to consider the ways in which societies are similarly organized and to comprehend the variety of organization as evidence of the complex systems people devise for themselves. (Strathern, 1988: 31)

This legacy (see 1995: 11) proved difficult to remove. At what appeared to be the 'scale' of society, Malinowski's functionalism merely came to replace one version of holism with another (cf Leach, 1957: 134) and at what was taken to be the 'scale' of individualism, transactional theory rendered society as an 'interactive marketplace' (Strathern, 1996: 63).

3 This point of 'perspective is at the heart of Strathern's critique of early feminist thinkers. For them: ' "The system" that puts women in a dependant position is regarded as an artifact of men's interests' (1988: 26).

4 Strathern has analysed the idea of self-constructing systems as being answerable only to their own closed orders (open to information and closed to organization). But she would treat these as the *effects* of analysis, not as its primary units.

5 The commodity axis is used by Strathern (1988) to typify what she sees to be certain clusters of 'organizing concepts'. In a personal communication, she also suggests that 'commodity thinking' is one of the organizing devices for *The Gender of the Gift*.

6 In passing it might be noted here that it is not simply the buyer and the seller who wash their hands after a transaction in modern markets (see Callon, 1999); it is the object itself that is decontaminated from all previous connection (a process that in turn facilitates the 'branding' beloved by advertisers).

7 As illustrated here, Strathern (1999: p. 274–275n) is ever alert to the intrusions of the ethnographer: the role of the outside observer in making practices explicit is obviously different according to what is already explicit. When divisions are only implicit, then conflict can be uncovered as concealed by social practices. When division and conflict is explicit, then we may look for the implicit connections such a division sustains. The former has a commonsense appeal to Euro-Americans who like to uncover the 'reality' of conflict from beneath a glossy surface of harmony; the latter produces the rather stiff functionalist arguments familiar, for instance, from Radcliffe-Brown's work on joking and avoidance relationships.

8 If my reading is right, Strathern's conception of 'changing scales' should not be confused with the kind of altering of scales that is the focus of Wagner's 'fractal person'. Strathern's analysis is certainly conducted in reference to the on-going debate in anthropology about the 'big man' but Wagner's (1991) discussion seems to be rooted in something more akin to movements between micro and macro forms of visibility (even though he problematises this division).

9 In defining 'merographic Strathern (1992: 73) refers to the 'English view that anything may be a part of something else, minimally part of a description in the act of describing of it. In this view, nothing is in fact ever simply part of a whole'. This is because another view, another perspective, another domain, may redescribe it as 'part of something else'. On this basis, it would seem hard to think of a single example of anything that is not merographic. This curious fact serves, I think, to draw attention to Strathern's analysis. Euro-Americans are perhaps so used to their everyday practice of merography, that it seems they have no idea of it!

10 In addressing the English handling of kinship, Strathern (1992) adopts the term 'conglomerate' rather than hybrid. The person 'as a relative', she suggests is also a conglomerate: 'Conglomerates constitute mixes of parts from different domains, such that one kind of relationship coexists in conjunction with another of a different kind. The connection between 'child' and 'mother' likened to 'an individual on a life-support system' captures the asymmetry' (Strathern, 1992: 83). What Strathern is seeking to capture is the person as a moveable feast in which, for the English, 'the person is more than the life he or she has enjoyed, and is more than simply the social relations and cultural values he or she manifests'.

11 In drawing out a possible contrast with these terms, Palli's (2004) study of a laboratory suggests that the visibility of 'portraits' changes depending on the perspective that jut out: at some moments, the head of the laboratory will be perceived as an entrepreneur, at others she will be again the scientist in charge of the group:

> The flickering 'between figures' does not resolve into one, there is no perspective more true than another, though each them leave imprints in this persona. If under a merographic perspective the head appears as a *mobile* figure (crossing boundaries in and out of science) we could now see her as a *motile* figure (Munro, 1999; 2003): suffering transformation without movement from one place to another . . . (Palli, 2004: 298 emphasis in original). This contrast is interesting, but it is not the fact that it is the other person's 'identities' which are being swapped (rather like someone merely changes 'hats' to think under). What matters to those who are seeking to retain their 'relations' with the 'head', including the ethnographer, is that their 'whole' view of the world is being changed as they go (see also Munro 2004).

12 The emphasis here can perhaps best be appreciated where we also insist on seeing 'selves' as social (see Munro, 1996; Skeggs, 2004).

13 Where Strathern is different from the first wave of social constructionists is that she able to focus critically on what 'the devil' it is that people are up to in a truly feminist manner. This is to say that she can do theory without banging any big drum and without 're-centring' the subject. Specifically, she appears to eschew conventional assumptions about the kind of illumination consciousness brings. Like Geertz (1970), she accepts there is mystery over what it is people think they are up to, but she would go on to insist on a much greater symmetry here between

observer and informants. Consciousness grants awareness, certainly, but this awareness is restricted. Knowledge of what it is we are up to, so often, is as mysterious to ourselves as it is to others.

References

Callon, M. and B. Latour (1981) 'Unscrewing the big Leviathan: How actors macrostructure reality and how sociologists help them do so' in K. D. Knorr-Cetina and A. Cicourel (eds.) *Advances in Social Theory and Methodology: Towards an Integration of Micro- and Macro-Sociologies*. London: Routledge & Kegan Paul.

Clifford, J. (1988) *The Predicament of Culture: Twentieth Century Ethnography, Literature, and Art*. Cambridge, MA: Harvard University Press.

Cohen, A. (1994) *Self-Consciousness: An Alternative Anthropology of Identity*. London: Routledge.

de Certeau, M. (1984) *The Practice of Everyday Life*, trans. S. F. Rendall. Berkeley, CA: University of California Press.

Derrida, J. (1982) *Margins of Philosophy*, trans. A. Bass. Hemel Hempstead: Harvester Wheatsheaf.

Heidegger, M. (1962) *Being and Time*, trans J. Macquarrie and E. Robinson. Oxford: Blackwell.

Kuhn, A. and A. M. Wolpe (1978) 'Feminism and materialism' in A. Kuhn and A. M. Wolpe (eds.) *Feminism and Materialism: Women and Modes of Production*. London: Routledge and Kegan Paul.

Latimer, J. (2004) 'Commanding materials: Re-legitimating authority in the context of multi-disciplinary work' *Sociology*, 38 (4): 757–775.

Leach, E. R. (1957) 'The epistemological background to Malinowski's empiricism' in R. Firth (ed.) *Man and Culture*. London: Routledge and Kegan Paul.

Marriott, M. (1976) 'Hindu transactions: diversity without dualism' in B. Kapferer (ed.) *Transaction and Meaning*. Philadelphia: ISHI Publications (ASA Essays in Anthropology).

Munro, R. (1996a) 'The consumption view of self: Extension, exchange, identity' in S. Edgell, K. Hetherington and A. Warde (eds.) *Consumption Matters: The Production and Experience of Consumption*. Oxford: Blackwell.

Munro, R. (1996b) 'Alignment and identity work: The study of accounts and accountability' In R. Munro and J. Mouritsen (eds.) *Accountability: Power, Ethos and the Technologies of Managing*. London: Thomson International Business Press.

Palli, C. (2004) *Entangled Laboratories: Liminal Practices in Science*. Unpublished Doctoral thesis, Universitat Autonoma de Barcelona.

Power, M. (1997) *The Audit Society: Rituals of Verification*. Oxford: Oxford University Press.

Skeggs, B. (2005) 'Self after Bourdieu' in B. Skeggs and L. Adkins (eds.) *Feminism After Bourdieu: International Perspectives*. Oxford: Blackwell.

Strathern, M. (1972) *Women in Between: Female Roles in a Male World*. London: Seminar (Academic) Press.

Strathern, M. (1985) 'Kinship and economy: Constitutive orders of a provisional kinds' *American Ethnologist* 12: 191–209.

Strathern, M. (1988) *Gender of the Gift*. Berkeley, CA: University of California Press.

Strathern, M. (1991) *Partial Connections*. Maryland: Rowman & Little.

Strathern, M. (1992) *After Nature: English Kinship in the Late Twentieth Century*. Cambridge: Cambridge University Press.

Strathern, M. (1994) 'Parts and wholes: Refiguring relationships' in R. Borofsky (ed.) *Assessing Cultural Anthropology*. New York: McGraw-Hill.

Strathern, M. (1995) *The Relation: Issues in Complexity and Scale*. Cambridge: Prickly Pear.

Strathern, M. (1996) 'The concept of society is theoretically obsolete: For the motion' in T. Ingold (ed.) *Key debates in Anthropology*. London: Routledge.

Strathern, M. (1997) 'Gender: Division or comparison' in K. Hetherington and R. Munro (eds.) *Ideas of Difference: Social Spaces and the Labour of Division*. Oxford: Blackwell.

Strathern, M. (1998) 'What is intellectual property after?' in J. Law and J. Hassard (eds.) *Actor Network Theory and After*. Sociological Review Monograph, Oxford: Blackwell.

Strathern, M. (1999) *Property, Substance and Effect: Anthropological Essays on Persons and Things*. London: Athlone.

Strathern, M. (2000) 'New accountabilities: Anthropological studies in accountability, ethics and the academy' in M. Strathern (ed.) *Audit Cultures: Anthropological Studies in Accountability, Ethics and the Academy* . London: Routledge.

Strathern, M. (2003a) 'Abstraction and decontextualisation: An anthropological comment' in S. Woolgar (ed.) *Virtual Society: Technology, Cyberbole, Reality*. Oxford: Oxford University Press.

Strathern, M. (2003b) 'Accountability across disciplines' Paper presented at CBA Workshop, Languages of Accountability. Girton College, Cambridge.

Strathern, M. (2003c) 'Living science', Paper presented at the ASA Decennial Conference Anthropology and Science, Manchester University, Manchester.

Tsoukas, H. (1996) 'The firm as a distributed knowledge system: A constructionist approach' *Strategic Management Journal*, 17: 11–25.

Viveiros de Castro, E. (1996) 'Cosmological deixis and Amerindian perspectivism: A view from Amazonia' *Journal of the Royal Anthropological Institute*, 4: 469–488.

Viveiros de Castro, E. (1998) 'Cosmological perspectivism in Amazonia and elsewhere', Lectures given to the Department of Social Anthropology, University of Cambridge.

Wagner, R. (1975) *The Invention of Culture*. Englewood Cliffs, NJ: Prentice-Hall.

Karl Weick: Concepts, style and reflection

Barbara Czarniawska

Introduction: The invention of organization

In 1961 Dwight Waldo, then a central figure in administration theory, wrote a review essay for *Public Administration Review*, at that time a leading journal in the field. The article was entitled: 'Organization Theory: An Elephantine Problem'. Waldo's review encompassed six books, most of which were edited volumes, and among the most frequent contributors were Herbert Simon, James G. March, Richard Cyert, Chris Argyris, Mason Haire, Anatol Rappaport, Jacob Marshak, Rensis Likert, Peter Blau, William Foote Whyte, James Thompson, and Kurt Lewin.[1] Waldo noted:

> nearly all the pieces printed or reprinted are the product of the past ten years; and . . . a high proportion of the authors are in their early professional years. In short . . . there is no doubt that organization theory and research are in a boom period. (1961: 212)

Waldo discussed the main trends in this boom as he saw them. One was a transition from administrative theory to organization theory. This shift resulted from an aspiration in social science methodology – behaviorism – initiated by following the lead of the natural sciences. Such an approach did not conform with the notion of administration, which was 'an applied science – if it is not indeed a profession, and art, or something less. "Administrative theory" suggests an engagement with the world, a striving after values' (Waldo, 1961: 217). Organization theory was, on the other hand, a theory not of action, but of a unit existing 'out there'.

This unit had to be created, and the motive for its creation was the growing fascination with systems theory. The mainstream conceptual apparatus of today's organization theory was created in the 1950s in an attempt to apply systems theory to what used to be the object of administrative theory. 'Organization' was formerly employed as a noun denoting a state of being organized and was rarely used in the plural. The application of systems theory required a creation of 'organizations', separate units divided by 'boundaries' from their 'environments' and related to them by 'adaptation'.

This conceptual move must have been attractive at the time of its construction, providing a kind of middle ground between mechanistic Taylorism and idealist administration theory, and permitting close bonds with what was then the most attractive branch of science – cybernetics. It must also have been a relatively easy kind of conceptual move, because it basically imitated a much earlier step made by Darwin. As Richard Lewontin (1995) pointed out, by introducing 'organism', 'environment', and 'adaptation', Darwin sought to mechanize biology, at his time still all too prone to mystification and idealism. Alas, 'what is a necessary step in the construction of knowledge at one moment becomes an impediment at another' (Lewontin, 1995: 131).

At present – that is, in the 2000s – this set of metaphors is not doing good work in either human biology or organization theory. The environment is not a pre-existing set of problems to which an organism, or an organization, must find solutions: the organisms or organizations created the problems in the first place. The environment of organisms consists to a great extent of other organisms, and the environment of organizations consists to an even greater extent of other organizations. By the same token, the notion of adaptation is misleading when applied to indicate a one-way relationship between an organism and its environment. Further, while it can be claimed that organisms have boundaries separating them from their environments, it is much more difficult to apply the notion of pre-existing boundaries to organizations: mergers, acquisitions, transnationals, and networks make such an idea appear highly tenuous. New concepts and metaphors are constantly being sought.

By saying this I do not imply that the presence of systems theory was a 50-year-long mistake, a hiatus in the development of the body of organizational knowledge. On the contrary, cybernetics in general, and systems theory in particular, has been and remains the main inspiration for organization theory. But if organization theory itself was shaped so as to fit systems theory 50 years ago, at present it is systems theory that is adapted and selectively used by organization theoreticians.

Among those, Karl E. Weick's work has a central role. Aged 25 at the time of Waldo's publication, he took in the new wave of thought and went beyond it later. Throughout the 1980s and the 1990s, he launched a new style in organizational theorizing by combining a sophisticated use of systems theory with insights from the world of music and literature, which steadily acquired a growing circle of followers. He coined several imaginative concepts that are widely used throughout organization theory; his works are exemplary of vivid, persuasive and attractive writing style; and his reflection over the state of discipline attracts, strangely enough in a grouping of egocentric authors, a lot of respectful (although not necessarily compliant) attention. Last but not least he is keenly interested in the concerns of organizational practice and in the world outside the academy.

In what follows I review the best known terms coined by Weick, attempt to characterize his style, and try to summarize the reflection he offered the discipline of organization studies.

Organizing

Among those works which in the 1960s attempted to draw a massive loan from systems theory, there was one which was especially prominent: Daniel Katz and Robert L. Kahn's *The Social Psychology of Organizations* (1966). The title of Weick's book – *The Social Psychology of Organizing* – published in 1969 but best known in its revised edition from 1979, clearly announced its intention to continue but also advance beyond their perspective. Such a move was needed because the concept of open systems became the mainstay of organizational analysis, but remained underdeveloped (Weick and Sandelands, 1990: 337). Weick undertook its development whilst simultaneously transcending it through the adoption of concepts related to autopoietic, ie, self-regulating and self-reproducing systems (Maruyama, 1974, Luhmann, 1990, see Nassehi, in this volume). It is this later innovation that permitted him successfully to relate biological metaphors to those coming from literature, poetry, and the arts: while organizations as systems depending on an energy input are obviously best treated as open systems, as information systems they are best described as autopoietic. Furthermore, it is Weick's understanding of how metaphors work which made him use biological concepts in organization theory so successfully.

He argued that the focus of organization theory must be set in the process of organizing, of assembling 'ongoing interdependent actions into sensible sequences i.e. generate sensible outcomes' (Weick, 1979: 3). The result of organizing is interlocked cycles which can be represented as causal loops rather than a linear chain of causes and effects. This idea, by the way, was one of the sources of inspiration for my notion of 'action nets' (Czarniawska, 2004).

Organizing runs through stages reminiscent of biological evolution and is triggered by a perceived change in environment that is followed by an enactment: organizational actors bracket out a certain segment of their environment for active treatment. This innovation stage corresponds to variation. The subsequent treatment consists of selection, ie, attempts to reduce the ambiguity of the ongoing events by applying accessible cognitive schemes to them, which makes it possible to (temporarily) assemble them. This step is followed by retention, ie, saving the successful results of such sensemaking that enlarges and renews the repertoire of cognitive schemes, but, paradoxically, also limits the possibility of noticing subsequent changes in the environment.

Organizing is thus an ongoing encounter with ambiguity, ambivalence, and equivocality; being part of a larger attempt to make sense of life and the world. It is this assumption that sets Weick's theorizing apart from the rest of the organization studies' field that evolved around the notion of 'uncertainty', understood as a negative state that must be eradicated for organizing to take place. Weick cherishes ambiguity and gives it a central place in evolutionary processes. Whereas organizing is an effort to deal with ambiguity, it never completely succeeds. Furthermore, the ordering it involves is a complex and inherently ambiguous process of sensemaking rather than that of imposing the rules of rationality on a disorderly world.

Social Psychology of Organizing as we know it from its 1979 edition was exceptionally rich in metaphors, anecdotes, and pictures borrowed from high and popular culture, jazz, business, politics, and sports. The anecdote that is best remembered concerns three baseball umpires who represent the three most common variations of the theory of knowledge. Asked how they call balls and strikes, the objectivist says 'I calls them as they is'; the subjectivist says 'I calls them as I sees them', while the constructivist says 'They ain't nothin' till I calls them'. This last stance, together with the set of concepts introduced in this early work, was to characterize Weick's work in the years to come.

Loosely coupled systems

Like its outcomes, organizing itself does not develop along a linear sequence. Different stages are loosely coupled in everyday organizational life. This loose coupling provides organizations with the flexibility and slack necessary for survival.

The idea of loosely coupled systems comes from Robert B. Glassman (1973) and was borrowed for organizational purposes by several organization scholars, for instance March and Olsen (1976), who used it in their notion of the garbage-can decision model. Weick originally applied the idea for understanding the erratic organizing typical of educational institutions (1976) and later for grasping the occurrence of disasters in high reliability organizations which tend toward tight coupling (Weick, 1990). As the attention of organization researchers turned away from hierarchies and toward networks, the idea was adopted by many researchers studying various organizational contexts. Its attraction lies in admitting the existence of both rationality and indeterminacy in the same system.

There is a tendency, however, to mistake loosely coupled systems for the opposite of tightly coupled systems, rather than a combination of tightly coupled and decoupled systems: 'If there is responsiveness without distinctiveness, the system is tightly coupled. If there is distinctiveness without responsiveness, the system is decoupled. If there is both distinctiveness and responsiveness, the system is loosely coupled' (Orton and Weick, 1990: 205). In other words, decoupled elements are no longer systems; 'loosely coupled systems' are the result of partial decoupling, or a coupling not quite tight. Orton and Weick (1990) quote examples of confusing interpretations of the concept. This confusion can be partly explained by the fact that some of Weick's followers mixed up loose couplings as a state with the operation of decoupling. Herein lies both the great attraction and a risk in borrowing Weick's concepts: they are complex, and therefore suitable for grasping the complexity of practice. Simplifying such notions results in forfeiting their power.

Enactment and high reliability organizations

Another concept which turned out to be seminal in organization theory was that of enactment, which is both the process of making ideas, structures, and visions real by acting upon them and the outcome of this process, 'an enacted environment' (Weick, 1988). It reverses the idea of implementation – which is the putting of a plan into operation – by showing that people are able to act as if their ideas were already implemented. It exchanges the idea of environment as given for the one as constructed. This is not to be confused with wishful thinking, as at best enactment is only partially successful, but the concept certainly allows a better understanding of the dynamics of collective undertakings.

The notion has been widely used, as it blends well with the increasing constructivist strand in organization theory. Weick used it most spectacularly in studies on high reliability (or high risk) organizations. While crises are the everyday happening of all organizations, they become especially acute and visible in this type of organization. The theory of crisis management, developed through the analysis of accidents, catastrophes, and disasters (Turner, 1978; Perrow, 1984; Shrivastava, 1987), conceptualized it in terms of reactions to the situation already existing. The perspective of enactment erases the division between crisis prevention and crisis management, revealing how enactment can produce a crisis-prone environment, but also how the understanding of it may help to avoid crises and to reduce danger (Weick, 1988, 1990). In his recent work with Kathleen M. Sutcliffe (2001), Karl Weick coined the concept of 'mindful management' in the context of organizing taking place on aircraft carriers and in nuclear power stations. Management is 'mindful' when it is aware of its own expectations, of the limited horizon of these expectations, and of the need for ongoing corrections.

Sensemaking

Organizational sensemaking, the term introduced in the work by the same title, is contrasted with interpretation, ie, sense-giving and sense-taking. In the latter cases, a frame of meaning is already in place, and it is enough to connect a new cue to an existing frame. Where there is no frame or at least no obvious connection presents itself, one has to be created – and this is sensemaking. This distinction was not present in Weick's first book, where organizing equalled sensemaking, which seemed at the time to encompass all three processes.

Seven properties of organizational sensemaking were explored: 'identity, retrospect, enactment, social contact, ongoing events, cues, and plausibility' (Weick, 1995: 3). Most of these were known from his earlier writings, but here they are all brought together. After discussing plausibility – which in organizational practice is much more important than accuracy, the fetish of perception studies – Weick concludes:

> If accuracy is nice but not necessary in sensemaking, then what is necessary? The answer is, something that preserves plausibility and coherence, something that is reasonable and memorable, something that embodies past experience and expectations, something which resonates with other people, something that can be constructed retrospectively but also can be used prospectively, something that captures both feeling and thought, something that allows for embellishment to fit current oddities, something that is fun to contrast. In short, what is necessary in sensemaking is a good story. (Weick, 1995: 60–61)

This, in his opinion, is what is most needed 'in an equivocal, postmodern world, infused with the politics of interpretation and conflicting interests' (Weick, 1995: 61). Such a postulate is consistent with another, also known from his earlier work: that of requisite variety, which suggests that complex situations must be met by complex models. Although stories simplify the world and are therefore useful as guides for action, they simplify it less than the kind of formal models which we learned to revere as true science.

Scientists may not always make sense, but practitioners constantly try. Even though sensemaking is an ongoing activity, it is not always equally intensive. After all, there are routines, stereotypes, 'received ideas' and inherited truths. The activity of sensemaking increases with ruptures and discontinuities, shocks and interruptions.

What does sensemaking consist of? A frame of meaning, which is relatively large and lasting (Goffman, 1974), a cue, and a connection. The frames can be usefully conceived as inherited vocabularies of society, organization, work, individual life projects, and tradition.

Sensemaking, in Weick's view, can be driven by beliefs or by actions. Beliefs shape what people see, and give form to the actions they take. This idea resembles Gabriel Tarde's 'belief and desire' (Tarde, 1893/1999), where desire would be that which prompts action, while belief gives it its form. This connection may not be incidental: Weick, as a social psychologist, is closer to Tarde than to Durkheim in his reasoning. Disparity of beliefs in any social context leads to argument, which is one form of sensemaking. Further, beliefs can be projected onto the future, thus forming expectations. In discussing this last point, Weick retrieves Merton's notion of the self-fulfilling prophecy (Merton, 1948) as a 'fundamental act of sensemaking' (Weick, 1995: 148).

Action-driven sensemaking in organizational practice generally assumes two forms: creating commitment and manipulating the world. Weick points out that organized anarchies (such as universities) are the ones which excel at creating commitment as in them there is a continuous need for sensemaking, unrelieved by routines, standard operating procedures or organizational memories.

Style

As I claimed in a recent work on styles in organization theory (Czarniawska, 2003), organization theory has many impressive stylists, probably as the result of its much bemoaned lack of clear standards. I have also dedicated some attention to the definition of style; in order to avoid repetition, I will use here the one suggested by Northrop Frye, as it is probably best known and accepted, summarizing as it does many debates:

> In all literary structures we are aware of a quality that we might call the quality of a verbal personality or a speaking voice . . . When this quality is felt to be the voice of the author himself, we call it style: *le style c'est homme* is a generally accepted axiom. The conception of style is based on the fact that every writer has his own rhythm, as distinctive as his handwriting, and his own imagery, ranging from a preference for certain vowels and consonants to a preoccupation with two or three archetypes. Style exists in all literature, of course, but may be seen at its purest in thematic prose: in fact it is the chief literary term applied to works of prose generally classified as non-literary. (1957: 268)

A half century later, readers may object to the masculine pronouns and point out that it is the Model Author (Eco, 1989), a narrative character, not a real person, to whom the style is attributed. Still, the unpretentious idea of style as 'an interesting verbal pattern' (Frye, 1957: 75) and the observation that the style is especially visible in non-fiction, is very convincing. Also, the topic of style, and the critique of what Case (2003: 166) calls the 'style of nonstyle' in scientific writing, has only recently become relevant in the methodological reflections over organization theory.

What are the characteristics of Weick's 'verbal pattern'? John Van Maanen (1995) called this style 'allegoric breaching'. Allegory, in his opinion, consists of conveying an abstract message through the narration of a concrete set of events, whereas breaching concerns conventional textual practices of the field. This style favours an essay form, ambiguity of reasoning, dialectic reconstruction, and a rhetorical strategy of presence (Van Maanen, 1995). As much as these traits break against the recommended style of academic writing, says Van Maanen, the success of Weick's style speaks most eloquently for itself.

I would like to spend some more time commenting on the allegoric aspect of Weick's writing. Allegory is usually understood as an extension of a metaphor, although its literary meaning is much wider than the rhetorical one (Lantham, 1991). Although the metaphor is also understood more widely in literary critique than in rhetorical analysis (often it stands for all the tropes), it is interesting to notice the pragmatic difference between a metaphor and an allegory.

A metaphor is a figure of speech that creates a connection between terms and consequently a similarity between concepts, a connection that did not exist before. Such a connection is usually created between a concept that is well known and one that is not, in order to explicate the latter. Now, in an allegory, both concepts might be relatively unknown, but exploring one of them is 'safer' – in political but also in psychological sense – than exploring the other. Thus Aesop (if he ever existed) and Jean de La Fontaine (1625–1695) did not populate their fables with animals because they believed that their listeners and readers were especially familiar with zoology. They did it on the assumption that the readers will more easily learn some unpleasant truths about themselves if they are explored on another example. La Fontaine had to be wary of the King and the Church in the way Karl Weick needs not be concerned about the Academy of Management, but all these institutions were, and are, fully aware of the slight touch of satire – never indignation – contained in the allegory. '1. Leaders are spineless. 2. Being spineless is a good thing', ends the chapter on 'The Spines of Leaders' (Weick, 1978: 60) in an amazingly good but little known anthology of writings on leadership, *Ambiguity of Leadership*.

The chapter begins with a serious exploration of three types of spines: steel spines, plastic spines, and bony spines. The fascinated reader learns first about a tool called a contour gauge that consists of 180 steel spines (observe that you must really trust the author to become involved in what might seem like a completely irrelevant pursuit), then about a plastic spine, ascribed to Marcello Mastroianni (in *Dolce Vita*, I imagine), and finally about bony spines, found, for example, in a fish called Mexican sierra. The points – one about leadership, one about research methodology – are that leaders with plastic spines are to be cherished, and that counting spines is not the best way to understand Mexican sierra. A similar double allegory can be found in his writings on firefighters: 'drop your tools!' is a cry that applies to people in danger of fire but also to researchers inseparable from their traditional tools (Weick, 1996).

Whatever his trope of choice, all Weick's writings are filled with images. He said himself of the *Social Psychology of Organizing* that it is 'more concerned with metaphors and images than it is with findings' (1979: 234). Indeed, the images remain with the reader: the three baseball umpires, the Hungarian soldiers lost in a snowstorm in the Alps equipped with the map of the Pyrenees, the firefighter climbing a chair believing it was a stairway. After all, '[i]f any old map will do to help you find your way out of the Alps, then surely any old story will do to help you find your way out of puzzles in the human condition' (1998: 1). He paints with words, but also enacts his paintings: they are moving images indeed.

A virtuous cycle is in place: Weick's reputation as a stylist permits him to experiment with 'interesting verbal patterns', and the reader gladly suspends disbelief in a certainty to be rewarded with a way out of some puzzle. Van Maanen is surely right when he says that this is not a recommended style of scientific writing, but the question is whether any style can be a matter of following a recommendation. Paradoxical as it might seem, the imitation of good writing may be a safer way to finding one's own voice than is the application of abstract recommendations.

Reflection

Karl Weick has played a central role in shaping the discipline of organization theory in the 1980s and 1990s. This role is highly unusual in that he was never a part of the so-called mainstream (but cf Brewis, in this volume), and yet his influence was not exerted from the margins of the discipline. He is neither a school builder nor the critical deviant, but more a constructive deviant, in the sense that his deviation from standard concerns and perspectives at any given time gives shape to the concerns and perspectives to come. For this reason, many other organization theoreticians tried to assess and understand his influence upon the field.

Weick himself was of the opinion that 'theorists often write trivial theories because their process of theory construction is hemmed in by methodological strictures that favour validation rather than usefulness' (Weick, 1989: 516). Might 'validation' be another allegory, this time for 'publication'? Favouring usefulness, he suggests that theory making is an organizing process, a sense-making process which consists of 'disciplined imagination'. A desired result brings out 'a plausible theory, and a theory is judged to be more plausible and of higher quality if it is interesting rather than obvious, irrelevant or absurd, obvious in novel ways, a source of unexpected connections, high in narrative rationality, aesthetically pleasing, or correspondent with presumed realities' (Weick, 1989: 517).

Beginning with his 'Tactics for thinking about organizing' chapter in *Social Psychology of Organizing*, Karl Weick was at the forefront of the authors who made 'the tacit craft of theorizing more explicit' (Weick, 1999: 797). Here, I would like to attract the attention of the reader to one specific trait of his own crafting of theory. In the current parlance, there exist 'theoretical' and 'empirical' works. This new-fangled dichotomy has replaced two previous ones: theory-oriented versus practice-oriented works, and theory based on empirical data versus theory based on speculation. As a result, literature reviews, often atheoretical, claim the status of 'theory', whereas all interviewing has acquired a status of a 'data collection'. Weick's works ignore such dichotomies. His theorizing is always attentive to the needs of the field of practice of management, and is based on whatever material he judges adequate for his reasoning. It would be difficult to claim that any student of management is doing 'empirical studies', in the proper sense of registering the sense-data as they appear. If, however, the definition of empirical needs to be extended to collecting stories from the field, it is hard to understand what kind of an insurmountable epistemological divide separates reading a story in a newspaper from hearing it retold by a manager and then reading it again from one's transcript. Within the same strange logic, a fragment of a corporate newsletter classifies as 'empirical data', while a similar quote from a newspaper is 'an anecdote'. The material that Weick collects to develop, corroborate, and illustrate his theories is amazingly wide; he is a master of collage, and his criteria of selection are relevance, accessibility, and theoretical satiation.

Why, in an epoch of an extraordinary 'reflexivity' of the field, do such issues tend to be neglected? One answer can be found in the concepts launched by Weick in his discussion of 'the reflective turn' (1999; 2003b). He calls a 'real-time reflexivity' 'an observational moment when something unexpected occurs [permitting one] to get a quick glimpse of a presupposition or tendency that may affect observing and interpretation' (2003b). It is similar to seeing ourselves in a mirror without recognizing ourselves, and for a split second we see ourselves as other people see us – a frightening moment indeed. In contrast, a reflection in the 'present-at-hand' (Heidegger's expression), retrospective mode, is detached, general and abstract, no matter how skilfully and richly we depict the objects of such reflection.

I would like to continue this thought, claiming that the 'present-at-hand' reflection is decoupled from an actual experience and is guided by the 'reflection rules' dictated by the fashion of the moment. All of a sudden, for example, organization scholars took over all the worries and self-critiques of anthropologists, as it was the latter who were the fashion-leaders of reflexivity. By saying this, I intend no critique of fashion following (I believe, like Blumer, 1969, that fashion is the central mechanism of collective choice) and neither would I like to diminish the importance of learning by imitating. I am suggesting that when reflecting only in a present-to-hand mode, we are reflecting on topics already given, and might be neglecting issues that are specific to our peculiar mode of ready-to-hand engagement with the field of management practice. Thus Weick's postulate of making use of the 'unready-to-hand' mode, that is, when still engaged but momentarily at loss – not knowing what to do, and too disconcerted to lean back and reflect properly – trying to capture what it was that disconcerted us. Tricky, uncomfortable, and sometimes painful, but promising. The present 'armchair reflecting' tends to leave big blind spots that might be discovered by such a reflection 'on your feet'.

Organization theory in times of transition

Karl Weick's influence on both form and context of present theorizing in organization studies is profound. He turned the attention of organization scholars from structures to processes, from the relevance of academia to the relevance of the field, from mystification to imaginative interpretation. His exceptionally sophisticated use of biological metaphors permitted their combination with cultural metaphors in a seamless way. His works remain a source of wisdom – of consolation as well as of gentle chiding. What is truly amazing is the continuous relevance of his insights in the face of changing reality – and academic fashions. This is, perhaps, where the secret lies: perhaps unlike anybody else in organization theory, he is unwaveringly attentive to all the new events, incorporating them into his theory, and adapting his theories accordingly – an inveterate sensemaker. His special sensitivity concerns all situations of change and transition, thus making him uniquely suitable to comment on the times of transition, such as these we are currently experiencing. Thus,

> the byword for educating in times of transition is 'hope in place of knowledge.' But in the context of seemingly incompatible truths, hope now gets expressed in the form of accepting the necessity for paradox, oscillation, ambivalence, and hypocrisy if one

wishes to map shifting ground. To hold incompatible truths in tension is to adopt an attitude of wisdom and appreciate the sense in which knowledge and ignorance co-vary. It is also to treat ambivalence as the optimal compromise, to equate hypocrisy with adaptability, and to equate paradox with effectiveness. Ambivalence, hypocrisy, inconsistency, and equivocality may be pejorative labels in times of stability, but they are markers of heightened awareness in times of transition. In times of transition people are especially sensitive to the fact that they talk reality into existence and need plausible stories to retain their successes in doing so. We all want stories that work, which is all that the managers are asking for. (Weick, 2003a: 381).

And, all along, Karl Weick has been trying to make helpful suggestions as to how such stories might be constructed.

Notes

1 The books reviewed were: *Human Organization Research: Field Relations and Techniques*, edited by Richard N. Adams and Jack J. Preiss, 1960; *Understanding Organizational Behavior*, by Chris Argyris, 1960; *Modern Organization Theory*, edited by Mason Haire, 1959; *General Systems: Yearbook of the Society for General Systems Research*, vol. IV part II, *Contributions to Organization Theory*, edited by Ludwig von Bertalanffy and Anatol Rappaport, 1960; *Comparative Studies in Administration*, edited by the staff of the Administrative Science Center, University of Pittsburgh, 1959; and *Some Theories of Organization*, edited by Albert H. Rubenstein and Chadwick J. Haberstroh, 1960.

References

Blumer, H. (1969) 'Fashion: From class differentiation to collective selection' *Sociological Quarterly*, 10: 275–291.

Case, P. (2003) 'From objectivity to subjectivity: Pursuing *subjective authenticity* in organizational research' in R. Westwood and S. Clegg (eds.) *Debating Organization: Point-Counterpoint in Organization Studies*. Oxford: Blackwell.

Czarniawska, B. (2003) 'The styles and the stylists of organization theory' in H. Tsoukas and C. Knudsen (eds.) *The Oxford Handbook of Organization Theory*. Oxford: Oxford University Press.

Czarniawska, B. (2004) 'On time, space, and action nets' *Organization*, 11(6): 773–791.

Eco, U. (1989) *The Open Work*, trans. A. Cancogni. Cambridge, MA: Harvard University Press.

Frye, N. (1957) *Anatomy of Criticism*. London: Penguin.

Glassman, R. B. (1973) 'Persistence and loose coupling in living systems' *Behavioral Science*, 18: 83–98.

Goffman, E. (1974) *Frame Analysis: An Essay on the Organization of Experience*. Boston: Northern University Press.

Katz, D. and R. L. Kahn (1966) *The Social Psychology of Organizations*. New York: Wiley.

Lantham, R. A. (1991) *A Handlist of Rhetorical Terms*. Berkeley: University of California Press.

Lewontin, R. C. (1995) 'Genes, environments and organizms' in R. B. Silvers (ed.) *Hidden Histories of Science*. New York: New York Review of Books.

Luhmann, N. (1990) *Essays on Self-Reference*. New York: Columbia University Press.

March, J. G. and J. P. Olsen (1976) *Ambiguity and Choice in Organizations*. Bergen: Universitetsforlag.

Maruyama, M. (1974) 'Paradigms and communication' *Technological Forecasting and Social Change*, 6: 3–32.

Merton, R. K. (1948) 'The self-fulfilling prophecy' *Antioch Review*, 8: 193–210.

Orton, J. D. and K. E. Weick (1990) 'Loosely coupled systems: A reconceptualization' *Academy of Management Review*, 15 (2): 203–223.

Perrow, C. (1984) *Normal Accidents*. New York: Basic Books.

Shrivastava, P. (1987) *Bhopal: Anatomy of a Crisis*. Cambridge, MA: Ballinger.

Tarde, G. (1893/1999) *Monadologie et sociologie*. Paris: Institut Synthélabo.

Turner, B. A. (1978) *Man-Made Disasters*. Oxford: Butterworth/Heinemann.

Van Maanen, J. (1995) 'Style as theory' *Organization Science*, 6(1): 133–143.

Waldo, D. (1961) 'Organization theory: An elephantine problem' *Public Administration Review*, 21: 210–225.

Weick, K. E. (1976) 'Educational organizations as loosely coupled systems' *Administrative Science Quarterly*, 21: 1–19.

Weick, K. E. (1978) 'The spines of leaders' in M. W. McCall and M. M. Lombardo (eds.) *Leadership: Where Else Can We Go?* Durham, NC: Duke University Press.

Weick, K. E. (1979) *The Social Psychology of Organizing* (second edition). New York: Addison-Wesley.

Weick, K. E. (1988) 'Enacted sensemaking in crisis situations' *Journal of Management Studies*, 25(4): 305–317. Reprinted in *Making Sense of the Organization* (2000). Oxford: Blackwell.

Weick, K. E. (1989) 'Theory construction as disciplined imagination' *Academy of Management Review*, 14(4): 516–531.

Weick, K. E. (1990) 'The vulnerable system: An analysis of the Tenerife air disaster' *Journal of Management*, 16(3): 571–93. Reprinted in *Making Sense of the Organization* (2000). Oxford: Blackwell.

Weick, K. E. (1995) *Sensemaking in Organizations*. Thousands Oaks, CA: Sage.

Weick, K. E. (1996) 'Drop your tools: An allegory for organization studies' *Administrative Science Quarterly* 41(2): 301–313.

Weick, K. E. (1998) 'Sensemaking as a vocabulary for innovation management' Distinguished address to Technology and Innovation Management Division, Academy of Management, 11 August.

Weick, K. E. (1999) 'Theory construction as disciplined reflexivity: Tradeoffs in the 90s' *Academy of Management Review*, 24(1): 797–806.

Weick, K. E. (2003a) 'Commentary on Czarniawska' *Management Learning*, 34(3): 379–382.

Weick, K. E. (2003b) 'Real-time reflexivity: Prods to reflection' *Organization Studies*, 23(6): .

Weick, K. E. and L. E. Sandelands (1990) 'Social behavior in organizational studies' *Journal for the Theory of Social Behaviour*, 20(4): 323–346.

Weick, K. E. and K. M. Sutcliffe (2001) *Managing the Unexpected: Assuring High-Performance in an Age of Complexity*. San Francisco: Jossey-Bass.

Everything you wanted to know about organization theory ... but were afraid to ask Slavoj Žižek

Steffen Böhm and Christian De Cock

Introduction: An encounter, not a dialogue

Slavoj Žižek has produced a plethora of books over the past 15 years (at the rate of over one a year), many of which are all curiously alike, as he recycles compulsively a limited number of key themes. Yet, one never feels any sense of sterile repetition. In revisiting a topic, he often sheds new light on it, and so continues the conversation he seems to be having with himself. Žižek is not much interested in establishing a rational, sensible dialogue with his readers. Instead, he is a firm believer in clear-cut positions. His writing is invariably crisp, provocative, and devoid of any coyness. One of Žižek's favourite one-liners is (paraphrasing Freud): 'Why are you saying that you're only giving a modest opinion when what you are giving is only a modest opinion'. Žižek doesn't 'do' modesty.

Žižek is also unconventional with the choice of philosophies he reads. Although all of his work goes through Lacanian concepts, he is not simply someone who fetishizes post-war French thought (as so many organization theorists do today). Instead, he uncompromisingly connects Lacanian categories to German idealist philosophy – the latter hardly being overly popular in organization theory. But the real uniqueness in Žižek's writing lies in the fact that he effortlessly blends together 'the 'highest' theory (Hegel, Lacan) and unrestrained enjoyment in the 'lowest' popular culture' (Žižek, 2002a: 3), whilst casually (some would argue naively) moving from the psychoanalytic to the political and back again. Some might say: he's all over the place.

At first glance he seems to write for the browser: 'They came up with the idea to do a CD-ROM, because I write in the same manner: click here, go there, use this fragment, that story or scene' (Žižek, 2002b: 43). And indeed, the typical Žižekian unit of discourse is a wittily titled (eg, 'the non-analysable Slovene'; 'let the emperor have his clothes') passage of between 5 and 15 pages, containing a dazzling cataract of demonstrations and examples from popular culture, for which a particular idea often seems a mere pretext. Wave upon wave of interpretation leaves the reader at somewhat of a loss as to how these brilliant but seemingly arbitrary sequences fit together.

If anything, Žižek's prime purpose seems to be to shake the foundations of his readers' commonsensical assumptions. One of his stock phrases is 'I am tempted to turn the standard formula around by . . .'. Joan Copjec, in a back-cover-commentary on a recent book (Žižek, 2004), has therefore called him justifiably 'the master of the 180 degree turn'. Žižek tries to turn the table. He calls himself 'ruthlessly radical': someone who turns the taken-for-granted assumptions of society upside down. Today's typical anti-terrorist rhetoric of Western democratic leaders often emphasizes the need to defend 'our way of life'. Žižek is someone who aims hard at turning the ideologies of democracy and the assumptions of the Western way of life upside down. In this sense, he is inextricably involved with the 'war on terror' (Žižek, 2002d).

In this chapter we aim to broadly outline Žižek's radical project and explore possible connections to, and subversions of, lines of thought in organization theory – an academic field which, despite the popularity of Žižek's work in the wider social sciences, seems to have largely ignored his writings, with a few recent exceptions (Fleming and Spicer, 2003, 2005; and Jones and Spicer, 2005). Perhaps this ignorance is not all that surprising since Žižek likes to profile himself firmly *against* a background which more or less overlaps with the currently fashionable 'critical' agenda in organization theory:

> This background is formed by the set of (often more implicit than explicit) theoretical, ideological, and ethico-political prohibitions and injunctions. For the last two decades, multitude has been in, unity out; contingency in, necessity out; subjectivation in, subject out; multiculturalism in, the European legacy out; difference in, universality out; antinomy in, contradiction out; resistance in, revolution out; up to much more refined injunctions concerning style. (Žižek, 2003a: 499)

Having said that – and hopefully having lured the reader into this chapter – our encounter with Žižek is not so much a matter of carefully analysing every detail of his philosophical project and applying it to organization theory. It is more like the occurrence of some kind of short-circuit as a result of which 'the reader should not simply have learned something new: the point is, rather, to make him or her aware of another – disturbing – side of something he or she knew all the time' (Žižek, 2003b: preface). Ultimately, Žižek is not really interested in 'careful' theoretical analyses of texts. He cares mainly about events: events that shock; events that reveal the dirty underbelly of taken-for-granted social reality. And this is how one should approach Žižek's work: rather than subjecting it to careful textual scrutiny and debate, one should see the mountain of texts he has produced over the past 15 years or so as an event. The task of this chapter is to give the reader a glimpse of this event and begin to evaluate its significance for organization theory. Whilst his work clearly provides strong connections with important organizational themes – power, subjectivity, ideology, and the philosophy of organization – Žižek would probably balk at being described as an 'organization theorist'. Indeed, a Žižekian approach to 'doing organization theory' would probably result in the destruction of the very idea of organization theory, as the field would have to confront its own impossibility. Perhaps we should see Žižek therefore not so much as an organizational theorist, but rather as the *objet petit a* of organization theory; 'that 'bone in the throat' which gives a pathological twist to every symbolization' (Žižek, 2003b: 67).

Lacan and Hegel: Žižek's theoretical matrix

Žižek's work is characterized by a unique blending of Lacanian psychoanalysis, Hegelian dialectics and the philosophies of a range of mainly German thinkers (particularly Marx, Kant, and Schelling). Due to space restrictions we will concentrate our discussion on Žižek's interpretation of Lacan and Hegel, as they provide the backbone for his theoretical project. Much of Žižek's writing turns around the Lacanian *RSI* triad, tracing the relationship between the Real, the Symbolic, and the Imaginary (see eg, Lacan, 1977, 1998). Žižek's Lacan is very much the Lacan who, at the end of the 1950s, began to move away from the relation between the Symbolic and the Imaginary in favour of a sustained interrogation of the interplay between the Symbolic and the Real (Nicol, 2001). Žižek understands the Symbolic as the arbitrary system of meanings into which we divide our world, an entity which pre-exists us, and into which we are born, learning and abiding by its rules. Its anonymity and vaguely sinister air is conveyed by its alternative name, 'the big Other'. One of the most fundamental insights Žižek borrows from Lacan is the idea that the Symbolic or the 'big Other' is always incomplete and both constituted and subverted by the Real. One could also say that the Real is the lack of the 'big Other'; it is the surplus of reality that cannot be symbolized. For Žižek, reality is not just 'out there', fully constituted and given, unconcerned by our painful progress. Our stumbling search for knowledge, our confusions and failures; precisely that which seems to *separate* us from the way reality 'really' is 'out there', is the innermost constituent of reality itself.

> You symbolize nature, but in order to symbolize nature, in this very symbolization, you produce an excess or a lack symmetrically and that's the Real . . . the very gesture of symbolization introduces a gap in reality. It is this gap which is the Real and every positive form of this gap is constituted through fantasy. (Žižek and Daly, 2004: 78)

The other main theoretical source Žižek draws upon is Hegel and his philosophy of dialectical negativity. Now, it is probably an understatement to say that dialectics has not been particularly popular within the realms of organization theory in recent years (for a discussion, see, for example, Carr, 2000; Hancock and Tyler, 2001; Reed, 1996; and Willmott, 1990). A typical interpretation of the dialectical process is delivered by Burrell and Morgan when they state that 'the dialectic stresses that there is a basic antagonism and conflict within both the natural and the social world which, when resolved, leads to a higher stage of development. This dialectical process is seen as a universal principle, which generates progress towards the state of 'absolute knowledge' (1979: 280–281). Within such a view, the dialectical process is seen as the bringing together of antagonistic categories – thesis and antithesis – in order to produce a new, progressive synthesis. Žižek, however, reads Hegel very differently. In his view, the synthesis does not heal any wound cut open by an antithesis; it is not necessarily progressive and it does not return to a positive identity (1989: 176). Instead, the synthesis is characterized by antagonisms as much as the 'original' thesis is. This brings us back to the Lacanian Real. If reality can be seen as a kind of social synthesis, Žižek maintains that this synthesis can never be a finality or totality. Instead, social reality – the synthesis – is always subverted by the Real: a plethora of antitheses that constitute the failure of the closure of society or any form of organization.

Žižek's popularity partly hinges on the fact that he does not simply reproduce 'dry' theoretical constructs, but constantly seeks to illustrate them by making reference to popular culture and other examples. Lévi-Strauss' famous anthropological study of the spatial disposition of buildings of the Winnebago is one such example Žižek uses to illustrate his theoretical position. The tribe Lévi-Strauss studied is divided into two subgroups. When an individual from each subgroup is asked to draw on sand the ground-plan of his or her village we obtain two quite different answers depending on his or her belonging to one subgroup or the other. Both perceive the village as a circle; but for one subgroup there is another circle of central houses within this circle, so that we have two concentric circles; while for the other subgroup the circle is split in two by a clear dividing line. The two drawings of the ground-plan are two mutually exclusive endeavours with the function of inventing imaginary representations of social contradictions. The Real here is not the actual spatial arrangement of houses, but the traumatic core of the social antagonism that distorts the tribe members' view:

> The site of truth is not the way "things really are in themselves", beyond their perspectival distortions, but the very gap, passage, that separates one perspective from another, the gap (in this case social antagonism) that makes the two perspectives radically incommensurable. The 'Real as impossible' is the cause of the impossibility of ever attaining the 'neutral' nonperspectival view of the object. There is a truth; everything is not relative – but this truth is the truth of the perspectival distortion as such, not the truth distorted by the partial view from a one-sided perspective. (Žižek, 2003b: 79)

Such a conceptualization provides a formidable challenge to so-called 'Critical Realist' voices within organization theory (eg. Ackroyd and Fleetwood, 2000; Mingers, 1995; Morgan and Sturdy, 2000; and Reed, 1997 – for a short overview of 'critical realist' writings within organization theory see Burrell, 2003). Contrary to Žižek's understanding of the 'Real as impossible', Critical Realists – whose work is influenced by writers such as Bhaskar (1989) and Archer (1995) – maintain that the Real has an inner constitution and is made up of essences which are not amenable to human observation. Yet, the position that the truth of social reality lies exactly in its *impossibility* clearly resonates well with the theoretical project of Laclau and Mouffe (1985), which conceptualizes social organization as a 'structural undecidability', as Laclau (1996) calls it (Laclau being an important 'father figure' who introduced Žižek to the Anglo-Saxon publishing world).

Žižek's theoretical matrix has a range of implications that should be of interest to organization theorists. In what follows we concentrate our discussion on his conceptualization of self and society, his understanding of the workings of ideology, and his critique of capitalism.

Subjectivity, ideology, capitalism

For Žižek, the Real penetrates both society and the individual, which means that both are always thrown out of kilter. Thus, what we take for substantive entities (eg, self and society), are actually hollow. The only substance is the Real of *jouissance*, which is excluded from both, but which subtends the sense of everyday 'reality'.[1] The core of subjectivity is a void filled in by fantasy, and the fact that we can only ever plug our lack with fantasy after fantasy is what keeps us up and running (Eagleton, 2003). Žižek's (1997) point is that this fantasy is also characteristic of what we call 'society' or 'organization'. That is, the social – the political and economic relations that make up society or organization – are fantastic in the sense of being both illusionary and real fillings of the fundamental gap that describes them.

Precisely because *jouissance* restlessly invests across the boundaries of self and society, the libidinal cannot be confined to subjectivity or psychology. It provides the tissue of fantasies that make up the social/organizational whilst the narrowly libidinal itself is a web of social and political representations. In this breaking down of the barriers between concepts of desire and libido (the 'subjective') and the social, political and economic (the 'objective'), Žižek's project has clear resonances with that of Deleuze (see Žižek, 2004, see also Sørensen, in this volume), although they seek to achieve their ends by different means and in different forms.

Žižek is probably best known for his interventions in the theory of ideology, as it was the core topic of his breakthrough work, *The Sublime Object of Ideology* (1989). For Žižek, the important hold ideology has over us lays in its capacity to yield *jouissance*; ideological power finally rests on the libidinal rather than the conceptual, 'on the way we hug our chains rather than the way we entertain beliefs' (Eagleton, 2003: 198). Because ideology is an illusion which structures our social practices, for Žižek the 'falsity' lies on the side of what we *do*, not necessarily of what we *say* or *know*. His standard line of argument goes something like this: 'we' (eg, the 'ethical' consumer, the 'left-leaning' Western academic, or the 'democratic' politician) know exactly how things are – that 'the West' exploits 'the South' and that the Western way of life is utterly unsustainable. However, although we might *know* all sorts of things about how capitalist society works – and although we might create a certain cynical distance to these things – Žižek argues that we are still *doing* them; we are still engaging in the reproduction of capitalist relations precisely because these relations are objectively 'false' and act as systematic fantasy (1989: 32).

Žižek thus performs his trademark '180-degree turn' on traditional forms of ideology critique, which assume that social practices are real but that the beliefs used to justify them are false or illusory. Such arguments are practised, for example, by some labour process theorists within the realms of organization theory (eg, Ackroyd and Thompson, 1999; Rowlinson and Hassard, 2001; Thompson and Ackroyd, 1995; and Thompson and Smith, 2001). Žižek's key point is that the central ideological ingredient is to be located in the mode of enjoyment it makes possible, which is indifferent to so-called 'social realities'. The aim of Žižek's version of ideology critique is to create the conditions in which we can experience that there is nothing behind ideology. We can resist ideological power most effectively not by repudiating it but by fully accepting its dictates, and doing so in an overly literal way that brings them to the point of their inherent contradiction. Keeping a 'critical distance' points to ideological delusion at its worst: precisely by not identifying with the web of power one is truly caught in it.

Arguably, such conceptualizations of subjectivity and ideology pose a formidable challenge to some corners of organization theory. For example, Foucauldian labour process theory (eg, Knights and Willmott, 1989; Knights, 1997, 2001; and Willmott, 1990, 1997, see O'Doherty, in this volume), which has been one of the most popular and influential theoretical developments over the past two decades, conceives the subject as the *effect* of discourses that are produced by 'micro-political' relations of power and knowledge. Knights and Willmott's concern – and that of other Foucauldians in organization theory – is to show that social reality is the constitutive product of a plurality of disciplinary techniques of power and knowledge (1989: 549). They argue that 'forms of power are exercised through subjecting individuals to their own identity or subjectivity, and are not therefore mechanisms directly derived from the forces of production, class struggle or ideological structures' (1989: 553). What is thus important for Knights and Willmott is the emphasis on *individual* subjectivities and the way people become tied to themselves by self-discipline and self-knowledge (1989: 550). Such readings of Foucault's work maintain that subjectivity is a 'performative' process of continually reshaping and choosing alternative 'subject positions'.

For Žižek, Foucauldian 'micro-political' subject positions designate a form of subjectivity that corresponds to 'late capitalism', which brings us back to his conception of the workings of capitalist ideology. His line of argument is that today we are 'allowed', for example, to be gay, radical feminist and even cynical critics of capitalism. All these different subject positions and identities are possible within contemporary capitalist relations – as long as we still engage in the labour process and capitalist forms of accumulation and reproduction. 'Late capitalism' enables a whole host of differences without necessarily challenging the fundamental logic of capitalist relations – this argument can also be connected to Hardt and Negri's (2000) conceptions of 'Empire' as a fundamentally open regime that enables a multitude of differences to exist (see also Mandarini, in this volume). Žižek's point is that rather than forming all sorts of different subject positions that aim to escape the core of capitalist fantasy, one should engage the fundamental fantasy of capitalist relations in a direct, uncompromising fashion. The way forward is therefore to 'traverse the fantasy' – a phrase which he borrows from the outcome of Lacanian therapy (Kay, 2003).

Žižek's radical politics

Žižek has been politically active in his home country Slovenia. He finished fifth in the 1990 elections – narrowly missing becoming one of the four-person rotating presidential team – and fully supported the liberal-democratic party. Whilst such a move fitted in with his early writings against totalitarianism from a position that was, at least in outline, liberal; in his most recent writings he has become an increasingly virulent critic of liberal democracy which he sees as utterly intertwined with capitalism: 'It is only in this way, by problematizing democracy – by making it clear that liberal democracy *a priori*, in its very notion (as Hegel would have put it), cannot survive without capitalist private property – that we can become truly anti-capitalist' (Žižek, 2002c: 273). Whilst Žižek refuses to look to communism as a solution to capitalism – 'I don't have any fundamental hopes in a socialist revolution or whatever' (Žižek, 2002b: 40) – and even describes communism as 'a fantasy inherent to capitalism itself' (2000a 18), he nevertheless likes to portray himself as 'an old-fashioned left winger' (2002b: 39).

Žižek's radical politics is founded, not in the notion of a difference that must be contained or embraced, but in the notion of the universal. He sees the political problem as one of struggle against the current of dominant, differentiating, particularist interests. He particularly takes issue with the ontologization of 'Democracy' into a depoliticized universal frame which cannot be (re)negotiated.

> The radicalization of politics into open warfare of us-against-them discernible in different fundamentalisms *is the form in which the foreclosed political returns in the postpolitical universe of pluralist negotiation and consensual regulation.* For that reason, the way to counteract this reemerging ultrapolitics is not more tolerance, more compassion and multicultural understanding, but *the return of the political proper . . .* True universalists are not those who preach global tolerance of differences and all-encompassing unity but those who engage in a passionate fight for the assertion of the truth that engages them. (Žižek, 1998: 1002)

Žižek thus does not feel that society would be improved by a greater commitment to order and democratic institutions or a more urgent call to civic duty – a position which stands in clear contrast to some liberalist voices expressed within the realms of organization theory (eg, Armbrüster and Gebert, 2002; du

Gay, 2000). Furthermore, he is also pessimistic about the possibility of a gradual production of alternative organizational regimes and sees a kind of conversion between the dynamic of capitalist power and the dynamic of resistance (Žižek, 2004). It is not that Žižek is against political activity (his own concrete political actions prove otherwise, and indeed demonstrate the necessity of such actions), but he believes that traditional political activity simply does not have the capacity for radical change: 'alternative social formations . . . are, in their innermost core, mediated by Capital as their concrete universality, as the particular formation that colours the entire scope of alternatives' (*ibid*: 186). His point is that alternative approaches typically intervene at a superficial, symptomal level. They amount to 'doing things not in order to achieve something, but to prevent something from really happening, really changing' (Žižek, 2002c: 225).

But does Žižek thereby condone a pessimist vision of social life caught in a repetitious deadlock, without any prospect for resolution, and thus opening the way to the 'celebration of failure', or even 'utter passivity' as critics (eg, Kay, 2003; Robinson and Tormey, 2004) have suggested? His answer is a dismissive 'No!', as he grasps back to a 'proper' universalism in his most recent works (eg, 2000a, 2002c). For Žižek, politics proper always involves a kind of short circuit between the universal and the particular; it involves the paradox of a singular that appears as a stand-in for the universal, destabilizing the 'natural' functional order of relations in the social body. Thus, we should not see the universal (eg, 'the non-exploitative', 'the egalitarian') in terms of an acontextual absolute, but rather as a culturally specific absolute (manifested as exception, the bone-in-the-throat, to the dominant form of the day). One way to effect change therefore is to seize on this exception, or on the random, contingent factor in the current scheme of things, and force its universal implications so as to produce a new order (Žižek, 2001a). Here his point of reference is what Badiou (2002) designates as *Event*: the art of seizing the right moment, of aggravating a conflict *before* the System can accommodate itself to the demand.

> The undecidability of the Event thus means that an Event does not possess any ontological guarantee: it cannot be reduced to (or deduced, generated from) a (previous) Situation: it emerges 'out of nothing'. (Žižek, 1999: 136)

The cause immediately triggering it 'is, by definition, trifling, a pseudo cause signalling that what is at stake is the relationship to the Other' (Žižek, 2004: 205). For Žižek, all social and organizational attempts which try to establish a plural, egalitarian and 'just' order through a regime of social dialogue and bureaucratic rules, only hide the taken-for-granted (and misconceived) universalism of Western 'Democracy'.

Žižek's critics and his 'style'

Many of the features of Žižek's thought that I tried to identify – rapidity, passion, high philosophical and political seriousness, a certain will to excess, and pure intellectual power – are in evidence here [in Žižek's reply], and the stakes of his work are spelled out with admirable precision. On a personal level, too, I am grateful to Žižek for providing the bracing, once-in-a-lifetime experience of having a man I had just praised as the most formidable philosophical mind of his generation immediately denounce me as a lunatic (Harpham, 2003: 504).

Žižek usually does not respond well to criticism. In his replies he tends to be disdainful of his critics (viz. Žižek, 2000b, 2003a), spending a handful of sentences composing a response to their critique and then proceeding to write about something entirely else that pre-occupies him. This can be seen as somewhat symptomatic for his general writing 'style', which often relies on engagements with other authors' work that are far from 'careful'. His writing often utilizes 'isms', particularly 'postmodernism' and 'deconstructionism', without engaging with the work of individual authors in great detail. For example, he has been accused of making outlandish claims about Derrida's work and 'deconstructionism' without citing a single source of Derrida's or other deconstructionist writings (Gilbert, 2001).[2] Žižek's project can be further qualified by an extreme reliance on the philosophies of Lacan and Hegel, which he utilizes to explain almost everything. Critics, such as Laclau and Butler (Butler *et al.*, 2000, see also Borgerson, in this volume), maintain that his psychoanalytic insights are not historicized enough and therefore act as almost essentialist concepts that stand in for a rigorous historical analysis of the social contingencies of capitalism and left politics. A related, and milder criticism concerns the fact that at certain stages in his books Žižek feels the need to rev up the metaphysical engine to such an extent (for example, in his explorations of Hegel and Schelling) that even eminent critics admit they cannot always follow his line of thought (eg, Eagleton, 2001; Harpham, 2003a; Kay, 2003). Žižek's writings also have been criticized for overly relying on a multiplicity of analogies from popular culture (such as cinema references or popular jokes) which do not always make sense; indeed these can be seen as almost arbitrary. In an all-too-scarce instance of self-criticism, Žižek himself expresses some reservations about the 'succession of anecdotes and cinema references in the *Sublime Object*' (Žižek, 2002a: xi). Furthermore, Kay (2003) points out that the interpretive zeal with which Žižek tackles his examples is very much at odds with Lacan's wariness of interpretation and precipitate understanding. Finally, it is not all that clear from Žižek's writings what it is we can legitimately engage with. His uncompromising language often seems to preclude productive engagement in empirical and normative debates and offers only a stark 'all or nothing' choice (Robinson and Tormey, 2004).

However (and it is a very big 'however'), one has to tread carefully when critiquing Žižek's work: it is precisely because he is a man who doesn't watch his back that it is extremely easy to find fault with the details of his work. Žižek's way of proceeding, in terms of style and content, poses a fundamental challenge to conventional academic methods and practices. When Fleming (2004: 41), in his review of the four-volume *Critical Perspectives on Business and Management* behemoth, points out that 'It is in the ominous spirit of an anti-modernist, anti-enlightenment, anti-progress and anti-emancipatory stance that the editors proceed to define what they mean by 'critical',' this only serves as a reminder of how awkwardly Žižek's project sits within a 'critical' organization studies.[3] Very often the target of his vitriolic critique of 'postmodernists' and 'deconstructionists' are precisely these scholars who cherry pick concepts and frameworks for intellectual comfort, so that they can 'relieve us of the duty to think, or even actively *prevent* us from thinking' (Žižek, 2001b: 3). For Žižek, the hope of finding theoretical foundations that can unambiguously shore up an academic field is necessarily illusory. His own thought relies on perpetual movement, fuelled by the constant switches of perspective on his eclectic assembly of materials. He, in effect, follows Lacan in proceeding in a 'mildly maniacal manner' (Eagleton, 2001: 50), placing a continuous positive valuation upon ambiguity and bringing theory to the brink of its own impossibility. For Žižek, theoretical concepts are both necessary and impossible.

> What sets in motion the dialectical progress in Hegel's *Logic* is the inherent tension in the status of every determinate/limited category: each concept is simultaneously necessary (ie, indispensable if we are to conceive reality, its underlying ontological structure) and impossible (ie, self-refuting, inconsistent: the moment we fully and consequently 'apply' it to reality, it disintegrates and/or turns into its opposite). (Žižek, 1999: 99)

Žižek uses examples from popular culture not in order to 'apply' his theory – as if there could exist a ready-made conceptual apparatus. On the contrary, his theory is developed precisely through, or in-between, these examples. The point is not to neatly place them within a theoretical framework but to see them as a gesture of the *jouissance* of the Real. The dissatisfying obliqueness of Žižek's approach is precisely meant to enable the reader to see that the Real cannot be signified directly, but is always stumbled upon in a way that is at once contingent and unavoidable. He strives, perhaps impossibly, 'to include within thought that which is heterogeneous to it' (Eagleton, 1991: 126). Thought is always hollowed out by the inassimilable Real.

> The apparent misfit between the theoretical context and the illustrative instance provokes Žižek's readers to work out the reason for it . . . this working out leads us to the problematic at the core of his writing: that of our relation to the real. By the same token, for the reader, a relation to the real, both as something lost to conscious thought and as a fearsome threat, is conjured in the very effort of trying to understand his text. (Kay, 2003: 11)

There is a fundamental problem in the fact that Žižek tries to conceptualize something which cannot really be conceptualized. Since what is awry is the whole cast and frame of our consciousness, conditioned as it is by material constraints, no amount of intelligence or ingenuity will serve to get us further forward. Yet, the premise is a simple one, and in following it he is utterly logical in his radical politics: if a transformation would be intelligible, if we can talk about it, it could not possibly be radical enough; if it is full-blooded enough, it threatens to fall outside our comprehension. We simply 'cannot get rid of our subjection through a merely intellectual reflection' (Žižek, 2002c: 253). Thus Žižek's 'style' should not merely be critiqued, but seen as part of the aporia of radical political writing as such.

Notes

1 *Jouissance*, or enjoyment, is not simply pleasure. For Lacan, pleasure is produced by the symbolic order, the Other. *Jouissance*, in contrast, is beyond socially sanctioned pleasure (1998: 184); it is located in the Real, that which is not symbolizable. *Jouissance* is therefore never fully attainable; it can never be subsumed or incorporated into the Other.

2 In defence of Žižek, it has to be said that in some places in his work he provides very thoughtful readings of Derrida (eg Žižek, 2002a: 31–38).

3 Perhaps, one of the only recent examples in organizational writing that remains true to both Žižek's style and his exhortation to 'fully identify with the symptom' (without referring to him at all) is O'Doherty's (2004) excessively literal (and hence deeply subversive) reading of the *Financial Times Handbook of Management*.

References

Ackroyd, S. and S. Fleetwood (2000) *Realist Perspectives on Management and Organization*. London: Routledge.

Ackroyd, S. and P. Thompson (1999) *Organizational* Mis*behaviour*. London: Sage.

Archer, M. S. (1995) *Realist Social Theory*. Cambridge: Cambridge University Press.

Armbrüster, T. and D. Gebert (2002) 'Uncharted territories of organizational research: The case of Karl Popper's *Open Society and Its Enemies*' *Organization Studies*, 23(2): 169–188.

Badiou, A. (2002) *Ethics: An Essay on the Understanding of Evil*, trans. P. Hallward. London: Verso.

Bhaskar, R. (1989) *Reclaiming Reality*. London: Verso.

Burrell, G. (2003) 'The future of organization theory: Prospects and limitations' in H. Tsoukas and C. Knudsen (eds.) *The Oxford Handbook of Organization Theory*. Oxford: Oxford University Press.

Burrell, G. and G. Morgan (1979) *Sociological Paradigms and Organizational Analysis*. London: Heinemann.

Butler, J., E. Laclau and S. Žižek (2000) *Contingency, Hegemony, Universality: Contemporary Dialogues on the Left*. London: Verso.

Carr, A. (2000) 'Critical theory and the management of change in organizations' *Journal of Organizational Change Management*, 13(3): 208–220.

du Gay, P. (2000) *In Praise of Bureaucracy: Weber, Organization, Ethics*. London: Sage.

Eagleton, T. (1991) *Ideology: An Introduction*. London: Verso.

Eagleton, T. (2001) 'Enjoy' *Paragraph*, 24(2): 40–51.

Eagleton, T. (2003) *Figures of Dissent*. London: Verso.

Fleming, P. (2004) 'Progress, pessimism, critique' *ephemera: theory and politics in organization*, 4(1): 40–49.

Fleming, P. and A. Spicer (2003) 'Working at a cynical distance: Implications for power, subjectivity and resistance' *Organization*, 10(1): 157–179.

Fleming, P. and A. Spicer (2005) 'How objects believe for us: Applications in organizational analysis', *Culture and Organization*, 11(3): 181–193.

Gilbert, J. (2001) 'Contingency, hegemony, universality' (book review) *New Formations*, 48.

Hancock, P. and M. Tyler (2001) 'Managing subjectivity and the dialectic of self-consciousness: Hegel and organization theory' *Organization*, 8(4): 565–585.

Hardt, M. and A. Negri (2000) *Empire*. Cambridge, MA: Harvard University Press.

Harpham, G. H. (2003a) 'Doing the impossible: Slavoj Žižek and the end of knowledge' *Critical Inquiry*, 29(3): 453–485.

Harpham, G. G. (2003b) 'Response to Slavoj Žižek' *Critical Inquiry*, 29(3): 504–507.

Hegel, G. W. F. (1977) *The Phenomenology of Spirit*, trans. A.V. Miller. Oxford: Oxford University Press.

Jones, C. and A. Spicer (2005) 'The sublime object of entrepreneurship' *Organization*, 12(2): 223–246.

Kay, S. (2003) *Žižek: A Critical Introduction*. Cambridge: Polity.

Knights, D. (1997) 'Organization theory in the age of deconstruction: Dualism, gender and postmodernism revisited' *Organization Studies*, 18(1): 1–19.

Knights, D. (2001) 'Hanging out the dirty washing: Labour process theory and its dualistic legacies' *International Studies of Management and Organization*, 30(4): 68–84.

Knights, D. and H. Willmott (1989) 'Power and subjectivity at work: From degradation to subjugation in social relations' *Sociology*, 23(4): 535–558.

Knights, D. and H. Willmott (eds.) (1990) *Labor Process Theory*. London: Macmillan.

Lacan, J. (1977) *Ecrits: A Selection*, trans. Alan Sheridan. London: Tavistock.

Lacan, J. (1998) *The Four Fundamental Concepts of Psychoanalysis*, trans. Alan Sheridan. London: Vintage.

Laclau, E. (1996) 'Deconstruction, pragmatism, hegemony' in Chantal Mouffe (ed.) *Deconstruction and Pragmatism*. London: Routledge.

Laclau, E. and C. Mouffe (1985) *Hegemony and Socialist Strategy*. London: Verso.

Mingers, J. C. (1995) 'Information and meaning: Foundations for an intersubjective account' *Information Systems Journal*, 5: 285–306.

Morgan, G. and A. Sturdy (2000) *Beyond Organizational Change*. London: Macmillan.

Nicol, B. (2001) 'As if: Traversing the fantasy in Žižek' *Paragraph*, 24(2): 140–155.

O'Doherty, D. (2004) 'Management? . . . whatever' *ephemera: theory and politics in organization*, 4(1): 76–93.

Reed, M. (1996) 'Rediscovering Hegel: The "new historicism" in organization and management studies' *Journal of Management Studies*, 33(2): 139–158.

Reed, M. (1997) 'In praise of duality and dualism: Rethinking agency and structure in organizational analysis' *Organization Studies*, 18(1): 21–42.

Robinson, A and S. Tormey (2004) 'Žižek is not a radical' *Thesis Eleven*, 78.

Thompson, P. and C. Smith (2001) 'Follow the redbrick road: Reflections on pathways in and out of the labor process debate' *International Studies on Management and Organization*, 30(4): 40–67.

Thompson, P. and S. Ackroyd (1995) 'All quiet on the workplace front? A critique of recent trends in British Industrial Sociology' *Sociology*, 29(4): 615–633.

Willmott, H. (1990) 'Subjectivity and the dialectics of praxis: Opening up the core of labour process analysis' in D. Knights and H. Willmott (eds.) *Labour Process Theory*. London: Macmillan.

Willmott, H. (1997) 'Rethinking management and managerial work: Capitalism, control, and subjectivity' *Human Relations*, 50(11): 1329–1358.

Žižek, S. (1989) *The Sublime Object of Ideology*. London: Verso:.

Žižek, S. (1997) *The Plague of Fantasies*. London: Verso.

Žižek, S. (1998) 'A leftist plea for Eurocentrism' *Critical Inquiry*, 24(4).

Žižek, S. (1999) *The Ticklish Subject: The Absent Centre of Political Ontology*. London: Verso.

Žižek, S. (2000a) *The Fragile Absolute or Why is the Christian Legacy Worth Fighting For?* London: Verso.

Žižek, S. (2000b) 'From proto-reality to the act: A reply to Peter Dews' *Angelaki*, 5(3): 141–148.

Žižek, S. (2001a) *On Belief*. London: Routledge.

Žižek, S. (2001b) *Did Somebody Say Totalitarianism? Five Interventions in the (Mis) Use of a Notion*. London: Verso.

Žižek, S. (2002a) *For They Know Not What They Do: Enjoyment as a Political Factor* (second edn.). London: Verso.

Žižek, S. (2002b) 'Civil society, fanaticism, and digital reality' in G. Lovink (ed.) *Uncanny Networks: Dialogues with the Virtual Intelligentsia*. Cambridge, MA: MIT Press.
Žižek, S. (2002c) *Revolution at the Gates: Selected Writings of Lenin from 1917*. London: Verso:.
Žižek, S. (2002d) 'Are we in a war? Do we have an enemy?' *London Review of Books*, 24(10).
Žižek, S. (2003a) 'Critical response: I a symptom – of what?' *Critical Inquiry*, 29(3): 486–503.
Žižek, S. (2003b) *The Puppet and the Dwarf: The Perverse Core of Christianity*. Cambridge, MA: MIT Press.
Žižek, S. (2004) *Organs Without Bodies: Deleuze and Consequences*. London: Routledge.
Žižek, S. and G. Daly (2004) *Conversations with Žižek*. Cambridge: Polity.

Notes on contributors

Steffen Böhm is Lecturer in Management in the Department of Accounting, Finance and Management at the University of Essex. He is a member of the editorial collective of the journal *ephemera: theory and politics in organization* and has two books forthcoming: *Repositioning Organization Theory* (Palgrave) and *Against Automobility* (Blackwell, edited with Campbell Jones, Chris Land and Matthew Paterson). His main research focus is on political philosophies of organization. Part of this is his keen interest in the organization and politics of the social forum movement, which has challenged the politico-economic hegemony of capitalist organization in various ways. He has been involved with organizing a number of research activism events; among them the Radical Theory Forum.

Janet Borgerson is Lecturer in the University of Exeter School of Business and Economics. She received her BA in philosophy from the University of Michigan and her MA and PhD in philosophy from the University of Wisconsin, Madison, and completed postdoctoral work in existential phenomenology at Brown University. She has taught philosophy and management at the University of Rhode Island, Stockholm University, and the Royal Institute of Technology, Stockholm. Her research has appeared in the *European Journal of Marketing*; *Advances in Consumer Research*; *Consumption, Markets & Culture*; *Culture and Organization*; the *Journal of Knowledge Management*; *Organization Studies*; *Gender Work & Organization*; *Feminist Theory*; *Radical Philosophy Review* and the *Journal of Philosophical Research*.

Finn Bowring is Lecturer in the School of Social Sciences, Cardiff University. He is the author of *André Gorz and the Sartrean Legacy* (Palgrave, 2000), and *Science, Seeds and Cyborgs: Biotechnology and the Appropriation of Life* (Verso, 2003).

Joanna Brewis is Reader in Management at the University of Leicester. She has previously worked at UMIST, Portsmouth and Essex, so appears to be making her way round the country in order to end up back where she started some 35 years ago, in Newcastle upon Tyne. Apart from watching ER and CSI avidly and buying ridiculous quantities of shoes and bath products, Jo has written on various aspects of identity, sexuality, the body and processes of organizing using a framework derived from the later Foucault, and the three volumes of the *History of Sexuality* in particular.

Steven D. Brown is Senior Lecturer in Psychology at Loughborough University and Visiting Professor of Psychology and Critical Theory at Universiteit voor Humanistiek, the Netherlands. His research interests are around organizational communication, collective remembering and critical psychology. A co-authored text *The Social Psychology of Experience: Studies in Remembering and Forgetting* (with Dave Middleton) was published by Sage in 2005, and *Psychology without Foundations* (Sage, with Paul Stenner) will appear in 2006.

Barbara Czarniawska holds a Science Research Council/Malmsten Foundation Chair in Management Studies at Gothenburg Research Institute, School of Economics and Commercial Law, Göteborg University, Sweden. She is also a Titular Professor at the European Institute for Advanced Studies in Management, Brussels; Visiting Professor in the Management Centre, University of Leicester; Faculty Associate at Center for Cultural Sociology, Yale University, New Haven, CT. She has published in the area of business and public administration in Polish, her native language, as well as in Swedish, Italian and English, the recent English positions being *A Tale of Three Cities* (Oxford University Press, 2002) and *Narratives in Social Science Research* (Sage, 2004).

Christian De Cock is Senior Lecturer in Organization Studies at the University of Exeter. He was awarded his PhD degree by the University of Manchester. Christian conducts research on organizational creativity, organizational discourse, and the interface of literary theory and organization theory. He is becoming increasingly interested in the notion of materiality.

Peter Fleming is Lecturer in Organization Studies at the Judge Institute of Management Studies, University of Cambridge. He has held academic posts at the University of Melbourne (Australia) and University of Otago (New Zealand). He has published papers on power and resistance in a number of peer reviewed journals, including *Sociology, Human Relations; Organization; Work, Employment and Society; Business and Society* and the *Journal of Management Studies*. Peter is currently interested in space and organization, workplace radicalism and organizational democracy.

Philip Hancock is Lecturer in Organization Studies at the Warwick Business School, University of Warwick. He worked previously at University College, Scarborough (RIP) and Glasgow Caledonian University where he taught sociology and the philosophy of the social sciences. His current research interest is in the management and organization of aesthetics and the relationship between art and business. He is a co-author of *Work, Postmodernism and Organization* and *The Body, Culture and Society*, and a co-editor of *Art and Aesthetics at Work*. He has also published work in a number of internationally recognized journals.

Jan Harris is a researcher at the Institute of Social, Cultural and Political Research at the University of Salford. His main area of focus is the intersection between culture, technology and philosophy, and recent publications include *Digital Matters*, co-authored with Paul Taylor (Routledge, 2005).

Campbell Jones is Director of the Centre for Philosophy and Political Economy and Senior Lecturer in Critical Theory and Business Ethics at the University of Leicester Management Centre. With Steffen Böhm and Chris Land he co-founded the electronic journal *ephemera: theory and politics in organization*, and for several years was involved with editing that journal. He has published in organization theory journals such as *Organization* and *Culture and Organization*, and his books include *For Business Ethics* (with Martin Parker and René ten Bos) and *Philosophy and Organization* (edited with René ten Bos). He has also written on women actors, entrepreneurship, violence, automobility and vampires.

Ruud Kaulingfreks works as a free-lance consultant and is Lecturer at the University for Humanistics in Utrecht. He is also a member of the Centre for Philosophy and Political Economy at the University of Leicester. His first passion was aesthetics before converting to organization studies. Luckily he hasn't forgotten his love for art and tries to integrate aesthetics into his organization research. He has published on, among others, Magritte, Cortazar, Heidegger, Chillida, Duchamp, Nietzsche, Bergson, strategic management, hygiene, cowboys and evil.

Matteo Mandarini is an independent researcher working between London and Rome. His PhD, at the University of Warwick, concerned politics, time and ontology in Marx, Deleuze and Guattari, and Antonio Negri and he has since translated books and articles by Negri, Sandro Mezzadra, and Giacomo Marramao. His translation of Negri's *The Political Descartes* will be published by Verso in 2006. His current research projects include a book studying Negri's work for Pluto Books and a study of political ontologies of immanence for Duke University Press.

Rolland Munro is Professor of Organization Theory and Director of the Centre for Culture, Social Theory and Technology at Keele University. He has published in a wide range of journals on topics such as accountability, identity, organization and culture and co-edited the books *Ideas of Difference* and *The Consumption of Mass*.

Armin Nassehi is Professor of Sociology at the University of Munich. Born in 1960 in Tübingen, Germany, between 1979 and 1985 he studied Philosophy, Sociology, Pedagogy and Psychology. In 1992 he received his PhD in Sociology and in 1994 his Habilitation in Sociology at the University of Münster. Fields of research and teaching include social theory, sociology of culture, political sociology, sociology of organizations and qualitative methodology. Recent books include *Differenzierungsfolgen* (1999); *Klassische Gesellschaftsbegriffe der*

Soziologie (2001, ed. with G. Kneer and M. Schroer); *Der Begriff des Politischen* (2003, ed. with M. Schroer); *Geschlossenheit und Offenheit* (2003) and *Bourdieu und Luhmann* (2004, ed. with Nollmann).

Damian O'Doherty is Lecturer in Organization Analysis at the Manchester Business School in the University of Manchester. His research interests include labour process analysis, developments in organization theory, and the philosophy of social sciences. He has published work in *Sociology, Culture and Organization, ephemera* and *International Studies in Management and Organization.* Damian is a board member of the journal *ephemera: theory and politics in organization* and sits on the executive committee for the Standing Conference on Organizational Symbolism. He holds an ESRC research grant under the Evolution of Business Knowledge programme in which he is looking at the development of Enterprise Resource Planning and Customer Relations Management information systems. Damian is writing an interlinked series of four papers that seeks to advance theory-in-organization. He is currently reading the works of Mechtild of Magdeburg and is listening to Avril Lavigne, the punk princess.

Bent Meier Sørensen is Assistant Professor in Management Philosophy at Copenhagen Business School. He has worked with technology, art as critique, and entrepreneurship, albeit in a 'bio-political' version. Currently, he is developing further the Master in Business Administration and Philosophy which CBS features, and which attracts a wide range of engaged students. He is engaged in the editorial collective of the journal *ephemera: theory and politics in organization.* Dr Sørensen (the title adding some Strangelove-aura to his very common Scandinavian name) is – together with Martin Fuglsang – pulling together the edited volume *Deleuze and the Social* for Edinburgh University Press. He also believes in the virtues of Japanese karate and Tango Argentino. And in the writings of St Paul.

André Spicer is Lecturer in Organization Studies at the University of Warwick, UK. He holds degrees from the University of Otago (New Zealand) and the University of Melbourne (Australia). He is interested in developing a political theory of Organization. He is currently working on a monograph with Peter Fleming examining the theory of power, resistance and struggle.

Sverre Spoelstra is a PhD candidate at the Centre for Philosophy and Political Economy, Management Centre, University of Leicester. He received Master's degrees in Philosophy and in Organization Studies at the University of Nijmegen, The Netherlands. His current research interests include critique, Spinoza, wonder, the multitude and marketing. He is a member of the editorial collective of *ephemera: theory and politics in organization* and an editor of the Dutch journal *Filosofie in Bedrijf.*

René ten Bos is Professor of Philosophy and Organizational Theory at Nijmegen School of Management, Radboud University Nijmegen. He also works as a management teacher for Schouten & Nelissen. He is the (co-)author of *Fashion*

295

and Utopia in Management Thinking (2000), *For Business Ethics* (2005, with Campbell Jones and Martin Parker), and *Philosophy and Organization* (2006, with Campbell Jones) and a number of other titles that he rather prefers to forget about (no kidding). His work has been published in *Organization Studies, Organization, Journal of Management Studies, Scandinavian Journal of Management, Employee Relations, ephemera, Culture & Organization, Theory Culture & Society, Sociological Review*, and also in numerous Dutch journals. His research interests include management melancholia, organizational hygiene, strategic management, animal voice (especially rats and monsters) as well as the pervasive role of water in philosophy.

Melissa Tyler is Lecturer in Organization Studies at Loughborough University. Her work on gender, sexuality, feminist theory, subjectivity and the body has been published in various journals and in a number of edited collections. She is the co-author of *The Body, Culture and Society* (Open University Press), of *Work, Postmodernism and Organization* (Sage) and of *An Introduction to Sociology: Feminist Perspectives* (Routledge). She is currently working on a critical, visual ethnography of gender and abjection, funded by the British Academy.

Subject index

event 5, 113, 115, 120, 125–8, 131, 149,
181–2, 188, 221, 248, 286
existentialism 41, 135, 139, 143, 154
exploitation 1, 36, 74, 137, 140–3, 192–5,
198–9, 201–4, 207, 210, 233, 245, 247,
283, 286; capitalist 141–3, 192–5,
198–9, 201–4, 207, 210, 283; super 233;
non 286

face, losing 127
Farewell to the Working Class (Gorz)
136, 139
farming 238–9
fear of freedom 151
feminine, the 5, 63, 65, 70–1, 82–5, 87,
90, 92, 228–30, 233–4, 262, 284;
feminism in management 85;
femininity 63, 65, 70; feminist
organization theory 82–4; feminist
organizations 5, 85; feminist theory
63, 71, 82–4, 87, 90, 92, 228–30, 233–4,
262, 284
figurational sociology 155, 251
Fordism 136–8, 142, 144, 196, 206;
post-Fordism 137–8, 142, 144
foreclosure 64, 68, 71, 76, 81, 92, 285
Frameworks of Power (Clegg) 99, 101–2
functionalism 50, 92, 262–3
Functions of the Executive, The (Barnard)
82
Futur Antérieur 142

gender 63–5, 68–71, 76, 80, 83, 84,
86–92, 124, 128, 150, 174–5, 233–5,
238, 245, 249; common notions of 76;
obsession with 87; and cuttings 249;
as performance 65, 69–70; roles 68–9;
studies 63, 65, 70–1, 124 (see also
feminine, the and masculine, the)
Gender Trouble (Butler) 65
genealogy 68, 83, 160, 170, 208, 224
geometry 215, 218–26
geophilosophy 121–2, 128
gifts 137, 252–3, 257–9, 262
globalisation 22–3, 84–5, 136–7, 215,
217, 235, 238
Gnomon 220–6
Grundrisse (Marx) 140
Guantanamo Bay 17–8

happiness 1, 18, 26, 28, 34
hegemony 19, 27, 51, 65–6, 98–9, 197, 201
hell 56
'Heathrow organization theory' 54
Hermes (Serres) 217
Hidden Order of Art, The (Ehrenzweig)
116
hierarchy 37, 55, 84, 92, 123, 135, 139,
173, 180, 183, 250
Holocaust, The 17, 19, 36–9, 57
Homo Sacer (Agamben) 18–9
Human Condition, The (Arendt) 136, 138
Human Resource Management 4, 123
Human Side of Enterprise, The
(McGregor) 82
hygiene 9

Idea of Prose (Agamben) 25
ideal speech situation 52
identity 5, 16, 18, 20–3, 27–8, 63, 68,
70–2, 76, 101, 108, 113, 135, 141,
148–57, 160, 241, 271, 282, 284
ideology 46, 50, 246, 256, 280, 283–4
Imaginary, the 281
immaterial labour 137, 140–5, 209 (see
also labour)
imperceptibility 113, 131
imperialism 206–11, 236, 238
impossibility 38, 65, 158, 281–3, 288
indeterminacy 51, 220, 270
Information and Communication
Technologies (ICTs) 216–7
international business 235, 8
International Monetary Fund (IMF) 208
In Praise of Bureaucracy (du Gay) 40
In Search of Excellence (Peters and
Waterman) 82
institutionalisation 115
iteration 64, 68–71, 76

jouissance 283, 288
justice 18, 38, 40, 104, 148, 184, 189,
133–4, 237, 240–1

kinship 72, 245, 249, 255–6, 260
knowledge society 138–40, 143

L'etranger (Camus) 41
L'immatériel (Gorz) 137, 140, 145

Author index

Abbas, N. 216
Ackroyd, S. 5, 50, 151, 282, 284
Adam, B. 5
Adorno, T. 46, 59
Agamben, G. 6, 8–9, 16–28, 110
Akrich, M. 163
Albertsen, N. 129
Ali, T. 18, 20
Althusser, L. 67, 199
Alvesson, M. 5, 231–2
Amaral, P. 5
Anscombe, G. E. M. 24
Archer, M. S. 155, 282
Arendt, H. 136, 138
Argyris, C. 267
Aristotle, 24, 109–110
Armbrüster, T. 285
Ashby, W. R. 180
Assad, M. 216
Atlan, H. 222
Austin, J. L. 7, 69

Bachelard, G. 217–8
Bachrach, P. 96, 99
Badiou, A. 286
Baecker, D. 181
Bakhtin, M. 55
Balakrishnan, G. 211
Bannerjee, S. B. 238
Baratz, M. S. 96, 99
Barnard, C. I. 82
Bartlett, C. A. 142
Bateson, G. 158
Baudrillard, J. 21
Bauman, Z. 8, 30, 33–44, 100
Bayou, M. E. 124
Beardsworth, R. 232

Benjamin, W. 25, 42–3, 59
Bennington, G. 232–3
Berger, P. L. 49, 155
Bergmann, F. 139
Bergson, H. 126, 163, 171
Bertalanffy, L. V. 180
Bertens, H. 46
Bhaskar, R. 50, 282
Bittner, E. 4
Blanchot, M. 35, 149
Blau, P. 267
Bloor, D. 164, 173
Blumer, H. 276
Bogard, W. 129
Böhm, S. 5–6, 63, 107, 165, 231
Boje, D. 5
Boreham, P. 95, 98
Borgerson, J. 6–7, 70–2
Bosquet, M. 134–5
Bourdieu, P. 71
Bowker, G. 215
Bowring, F. 4, 141, 143
Bowring, M. 63
Boyle, R. 253
Braidotti, R. 124
Brannigan, J. 228
Braverman, H. 112
Brewis, J. 4–5, 20, 55, 63, 238, 274
Bricmont, J. 174
Brown, B. 169
Brown, S. D. 6, 163, 165, 216, 221
Buchanan, D. 150
Buchanan, I. 121, 124, 126
Bunting, M. 141
Burrell, G. 2, 5–6, 8, 20, 46–60, 106, 115,
    150, 156, 238, 281–2
Butler, J. 6, 8, 63–76, 287